Downcan

———

Downcanyon

A Naturalist Explores the Colorado River

through the Grand Canyon

Ann Haymond Zwinger
with drawings by the author

The University of Arizona Press   Tucson

The University of Arizona Press
Copyright © 1995
Ann Haymond Zwinger
All Rights Reserved

oo 99 98 97 96 95   6 5 4 3 2 1

Library of Congress Cataloging-in-Publication Data
Zwinger, Ann.
    Downcanyon : a naturalist explores the Colorado River
through the Grand Canyon / Ann Haymond Zwinger.
        p.   cm.
    Includes bibliographical references (p.   ) and index.
    ISBN 0-8165-1163-2 (cloth). — ISBN 0-8165-1556-5 (paper)
    1. Natural history—Arizona—Grand Canyon.   2. Natural
history—River (Colo.-Mexico)   3. Grand Canyon (Ariz.)
4. Colorado River (Colo.-Mexico)   5. Zwinger, Ann.   I. Title.
QH105.A65Z95   1995   95-7005
508.7913—dc20   CIP

British Library Cataloguing-in-Publication Data
A catalogue record for this book is available from the
British Library.

Frontispiece: near Mile 24 Rapid

For Sally Ann Roberts

Contents

Autumn

Reference Material

Preface

This book focuses on the Colorado River as it flows through the Grand Canyon from Mile 0, at Lees Ferry, to Mile 278.5, at the Grand Wash Fault. My approach has been that of observer at the river's brim, writing about and drawing what catches my eye and piques my interest, the delightful details of a rich river world, what one can see if one takes time to look, and the joys thereof.

To be honest, I would have postponed this book's completion as much as possible—who, my dear reader, in his or her right mind would willingly give up the chance to run this extraordinary, magnificent river several times a year and in every season, meet delightful people who have Colorado River water in their veins, and engage in fascinating research? I would have been ecstatic could I have written a book the size of *Webster's International III* for, like the river, words about it could flow on forever. In the end, perhaps, I write not only about a great river but about what flows in the veins of the earth and the channels of the mind.

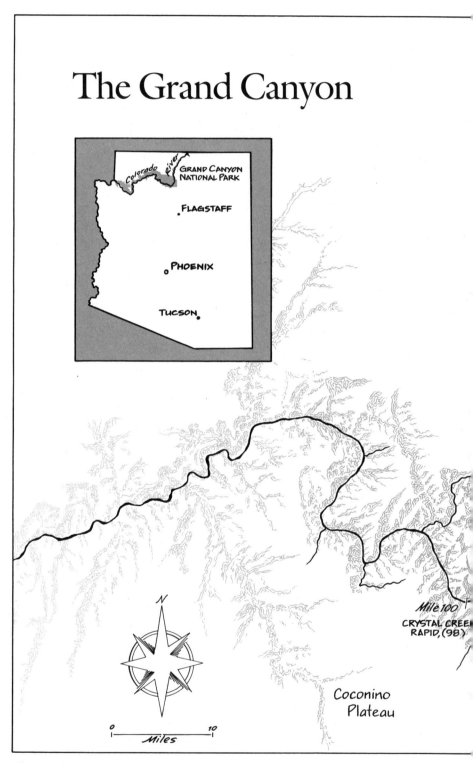

The Grand Canyon

GRAND CANYON
NATIONAL PARK

Colorado River

FLAGSTAFF

PHOENIX

TUCSON

Mile 100
CRYSTAL CREE
RAPID, (98)

Coconino
Plateau

N

0   10
Miles

The Grand Canyon from Mile 0 at Lees Ferry to Mile 100.

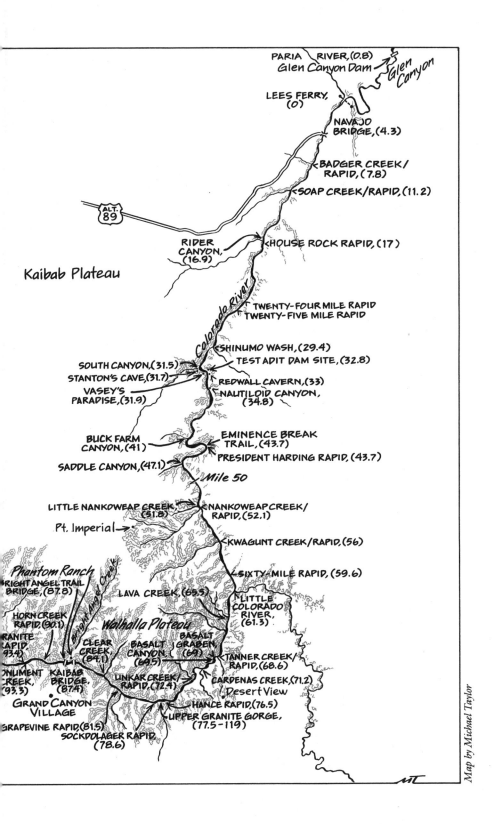

PARIA RIVER, (0.8)
Glen Canyon Dam
Glen Canyon

LEES FERRY, (0)

NAVAJO BRIDGE, (4.3)

BADGER CREEK/ RAPID, (7.8)

SOAP CREEK/RAPID, (11.2)

ALT. 89

RIDER CANYON, (16.9)

HOUSE ROCK RAPID, (17)

Kaibab Plateau

Colorado River

TWENTY-FOUR MILE RAPID
TWENTY-FIVE MILE RAPID

SHINUMO WASH, (29.4)

SOUTH CANYON, (31.5)
STANTON'S CAVE, (31.7)
VASEY'S PARADISE, (31.9)

TEST ADIT DAM SITE, (32.8)
REDWALL CAVERN, (33)
NAUTILOID CANYON, (34.8)

BUCK FARM CANYON, (41)

EMINENCE BREAK TRAIL, (43.7)
PRESIDENT HARDING RAPID, (43.7)

SADDLE CANYON, (47.1)

Mile 50

LITTLE NANKOWEAP CREEK, (51.8)

NANKOWEAP CREEK/ RAPID, (52.1)

Pt. Imperial →

KWAGUNT CREEK/RAPID, (56)

SIXTY-MILE RAPID, (59.6)

Phantom Ranch

RIGHT ANGEL TRAIL BRIDGE, (87.8)

LAVA CREEK, (65.5)

LITTLE COLORADO RIVER, (61.3)

HORN CREEK RAPID, (90.1)

Walhalla Plateau

BASALT GRABEN (69)

RANITE RAPID, (93.4)

CLEAR CREEK, (84.1)

BASALT CANYON, (69.5)

TANNER CREEK/ RAPID, (68.6)

ONUMENT CREEK, (93.3)

KAIBAB BRIDGE, (87.4)

UNKAR CREEK/ RAPID, (72.4)

CARDENAS CREEK, (71.2)

Desert View

GRAND CANYON VILLAGE

HANCE RAPID, (76.5)

GRAPEVINE RAPID, (81.5)

UPPER GRANITE GORGE, (77.5 – 119)

SOCKDOLAGER RAPID, (78.6)

Map by Michael Taylor

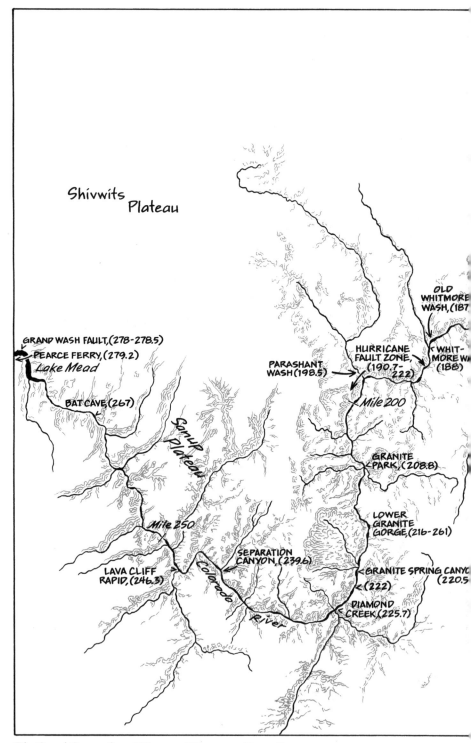

Shivwits Plateau

OLD WHITMORE WASH, (187

GRAND WASH FAULT, (278-278.5)

PEARCE FERRY, (279.2)

Lake Mead

HURRICANE FAULT ZONE, (190.7-222)

WHIT-MORE W (188)

PARASHANT WASH (198.5)

BAT CAVE (267)

Mile 200

Sanup Plateau

GRANITE PARK, (208.8)

LOWER GRANITE GORGE (216-261)

Mile 250

SEPARATION CANYON, (239.6)

Colorado

GRANITE SPRING CANY (220.5

LAVA CLIFF RAPID, (246.3)

(222)

DIAMOND CREEK (225.7)

River

The Grand Canyon from Mile 100 to Mile 279.2 at Pearce Ferry.

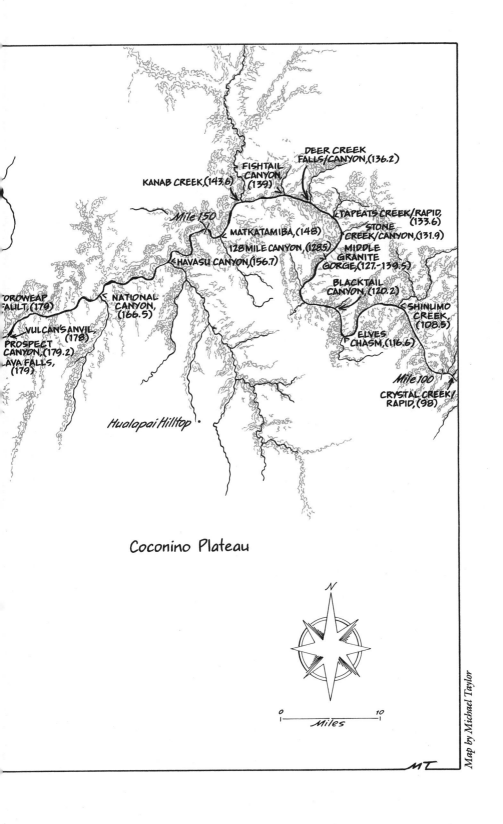

DEER CREEK
FALLS/CANYON, (136.2)

FISHTAIL
CANYON
(139)

KANAB CREEK, (143.6)

Mile 150

TAPEATS CREEK/RAPID,
(133.6)

STONE
CREEK/CANYON, (131.9)

MATKATAMIBA, (148)

128 MILE CANYON, (128.5)

MIDDLE
GRANITE
GORGE, (127.-139.5)

HAVASU CANYON, (156.7)

BLACKTAIL
CANYON, (120.2)

TOROWEAP
FAULT, (179)

NATIONAL
CANYON,
(166.5)

SHINUMO
CREEK,
(108.5)

VULCAN'S ANVIL,
(178)

ELVES
CHASM, (116.6)

PROSPECT
CANYON, (179.2)

LAVA FALLS,
(179)

Mile 100

CRYSTAL CREEK/
RAPID, (98)

Hualapai Hilltop

Coconino Plateau

N

0   10
Miles

Map by Michael Taylor

MT

Winter

just above Tapeats

1

In winter some of the characteristics of the Grand Canyon are emphasized. The black gneiss below, the variegated quartzite, and the green or alcove sandstone form the foundation for the mighty red wall. The banded sandstone entablature is crowned by the tower limestone. In winter this is covered with snow. Seen from below, these changing elements seem to graduate into the heavens, and no plane of demarcation between wall and blue firmament can be seen. The heavens constitute a portion of the façade and mount into a vast dome from wall to wall, spanning the Grand Canyon with empyrean blue. So the earth and the heavens are blended in one vast structure.

John Wesley Powell, 1875, *The Exploration of the Colorado River and Its Canyons*

Prelude: Lees Ferry

On the third day of January at Mile O, Lees Ferry, cold curls off the river as if off a glacier. The massive New Year's Day storm that swirled through Arizona yesterday still hangs in the canyon today, draping it with curtains of clouds. Sun shines on the plateau above but not down here. Here, in the inner canyon, there are only infinite shades of gray and white: plump swags of snow along the shore, reflecting white in black water, a delicate fretwork of frost on the bushes, rocks marbled with traceries of ice. What a glorious way to begin a year. On a river. On the Colorado River.

Not needed for the moment, I stand at the edge of the river and watch the infinitesimal lappings of little waves. In the course of writing this book there will be many launches but, of course, none so memorable as this first. I am curious as to what's ahead, and a little uneasy. I suspect that downcanyon there *may* be dragons.

Savoring these embarkations every month of the year will color the way I come to feel about the river. The only way to travel the Colorado River in the Grand Canyon is by boat, and my perspective too will be affected by, as a practical matter, riding in almost every kind of craft that goes down the waves: thirty-seven-foot S-rigs and J-rigs and eighteen-foot Green River rafts, motored and rowed and, in the ultimate, intimate river trip, dories. I will join many kinds of trips: large study groups, commercial, working research trips, small private rowing trips, trips that stay in one place for two weeks or roll through 280 miles in eight days.

When I use the amorphous, undefined "we" I do so because it is impossible to identify so many different and delightful companions by name, and this is a book not about fascinating people but about a fascinating river. By the same token, the first person singular gives homage to the fact that even on a crowded commercial trip it is possible to get off by oneself and soak up the landscape in solitude.

The year-round picture will, in the end, grant me a different perspective on the river than that of the summertime visitor with only a week to shoot the rapids. The river is not folded up like a neoprene raft and stored away between summers, but is an ever-flowing, energetic, whooping and hollering, galloping presence, whether there's ice along the edge or a flotilla of yellow willow leaves floating in a back-eddy or summer sunshine glinting off a cross chop. Against the seeming immutability of the canyon walls pass a parade of seasonal delights: bald eagles fishing in Nankoweap Creek in February, redbuds blossoming in April in Saddle Canyon, the summer's hatch of cicada shells dangling from bushes beside Crystal Creek in July, magenta windmills blooming in a rich slice of autumn at Tanner Creek, snowflakes inhaled by the river in December, adding up to this observer's four-dimensional snapshot of "what's down there."

Toes at water's lap line, I wonder how long it takes molecules of Colorado River water and silt to hone the river pebbles at my feet to such perfect, gleaming ovals. If a man is known by the company he keeps, surely a river is known by the stones it smoothes, and some of these are beauties. A smooth, bright white quartz pebble is the size of a black-chinned hummingbird's egg, laid next to a charcoal gray pebble lined with salmon silt trapped in its surface scratches, a mythical raven's egg. Under this inch of water abide all the colors of the canyon: rosy red, cool gray, warm beige, charcoal, olive, eggplant, persimmon. Gray blue, tangerine, rust, Indian red dotted with coral. Pink quartz. Ocher. Veins, lines, smudges, bands, speckles and spots, intricacies and simplicities, nestled together in patterns the river devises. Tiny white rectangular crystals speckle an oval of forest green, the distinctive San Juan porphyry, a rock molded from slowly cooling magma in the San Juan Mountains of Colorado and found only in the Colorado River drainage system. The crystalline water glosses the stones and renders them as shining as if tumbled and polished, intensifies their colors, turns them into gleaming perfection. Tiny pieces of foam on the river surface float cloud shadows on the pebble landscape beneath.

Lees Ferry, at Mile 0, is the dividing point between the Upper and the Lower Colorado River Basins as established in 1922 by the Colorado

River Compact. In 1923, the Birdseye Expedition, looking for potential dam sites, started the business of mile markers. Like the roadside mileposts of colonial New England, the canyon has been calibrated to human dimensions, some sort of reference in this fast flowing, hang-loose world: we need to know where we think we are.

This ferry, which Mormon missionary Jacob Hamblin established in 1858, took many miles off long, hard journeys. Commercial traffic used it as well as young Mormon couples going north on the Honeymoon Trail to get married in the Church in Utah. While waiting for the ferry, they inscribed their names, still visible, on a boulder on river left, near the old dugway (the conventions of "river left" and "river right" are from the viewpoint of facing downstream). Travelers paid three dollars per wagon and seventy-five cents per horse, in produce or freight, never mind cash. The ferry became redundant in 1929, when Navajo Bridge was finished a few miles downstream.

Almost every river party from day one has either begun or paused or ended here at Lees Ferry, including that of Fray Francisco Atanasio Domínguez and Silvestre Veléz de Escalante, the Spanish missionaries who completed their epic reconnaissance in 1776. John Wesley Powell sojourned at Lees ferry several times, including New Year's Day 1871. Engineer Robert Brewster Stanton, back to continue an ill-fated survey for a railroad in the canyon, had a Christmas dinner to end all Christmas dinners—complete with cigars and port—at the ferry in 1889. Trapper George Flavell delivered his famous ultimatum in 1897 to his helper, Ramón Montéz, on only the third passage down the river: "You can come along with me or you can float down dead." The same winter Nathaniel Galloway ran the length of the canyon and introduced a style of rowing still in use today.

In 1903 Hum Woolley made a brief appearance in river history when he put his boat together here and ran the Colorado, accompanied by two unsuspecting cousins who had no idea of what they were in for. Julius Stone, on the sixth trip but the first "sportsman's trip" down the canyon in 1909, camped here on October 27. Stone gave advice to Ellsworth and Emory Kolb, who in 1911 made the first movies of the canyon and stopped here to pick up their mail. Emory Kolb was head boatman of the Birdseye Expedition in 1923, the first group to carry a radio and a typewriter. While the expedition readied to survey the canyon in the steamy months of July and August, his daughter, young Edith Kolb, had the time of her life splashing in the water and writing in her diary about "the most wonderful ride" through the Paria Riffle. Two honeymooners, Clyde and Bessie Hyde, paused at Lees Ferry on their 1928 trip, were advised to abandon the trip but went anyway, without life jackets. They disappeared below somewhere below Lava Falls; their bodies were never found. Bus Hatch began the trip from Lees Ferry in 1934 that would discover Stanton's Cave, and Norm Nevills, on the canyon's first botanical trip four years later with botanists Elzada Clover and Lois Jotter, reprovisioned here. Three French kayakers paddled their collapsible kayaks all the way down from Green River, Wyoming, intending to run the Grand Canyon all the way, but had to take out here on November 9, 1938, because of cold weather.

The restless, impatient chirr of a ruby-crowned kinglet sounds in the tamarisk and follows me as I walk upstream to the well-cut sandstone buildings that once housed the business of Lees Ferry, named for John Doyle Lee, who lived here and ran the ferry from 1873 until 1877 (the Board on Geographic Names eschews the grammatical apostrophe because of potential confusion on maps). The buildings sit in front of rugged cliffs of Wingate Sandstone and multicolored Chinle Formation (a formation is a basic rock unit of one rock type), striped with lavenders, ghostly jade greens, and roses; beneath them, the somber sandstones of the Moenkopi Formation create a platform reaching to river's edge. Lees Ferry allows the last such roadway access to the river until Diamond Creek at Mile 225.7, or Pearce Ferry on Lake Mead at Mile 279.2.

I walk upstream to get a feel for where journalist and fellow Hoosier John H. Beadle crossed the river and blundered into history. Beadle started out for the West from Evansville, Indiana, in June 1868 to better a bronchial condition that "had in a year of army life developed to a confirmed asthma," and wrote a book that purported to be "a Complete History of that vast region between the Mississippi and the Pacific," published in Philadelphia in 1873.

Accompanied by Navajo Indian guides, Beadle approached Lees Ferry from the south. They reached a cliff whence they could see a house and garden across the river, set on "a rich flat, shut in above and below by precipitous cliffs." While Beadle was shouting and waving his arms, trying to get the attention of someone at the ferry, his Indian guides found a boat half-buried in sand and brush. When they dug it out, on the stern Beadle read *Emma Dean*, the name of one of Powell's boats, rowed on both his 1869 and 1871 explorations of the Colorado River. Actually, Beadle was guilty of historical inaccuracy: the *Emma Dean* lay at Kanab Creek 143 miles downstream, and what Beadle saw was the *Nellie Powell*, which Powell left at Lees Ferry and which served as the first ferry boat until Lee built his own.

The Navajos cheerfully carved oars, which left Beadle with the unwanted responsibility of rowing across this restless, silty river, so unlike the quiet Midwestern waters of his childhood. On arrival, Beadle faced Emma Batchelder Lee, who told them that her husband, "Major Doyle," would soon be back and suffered them to wait. When the major returned, Beadle discovered that he had a third name: Lee (Beadle had no room to cavil, for as a correspondent for a Cincinnati newspaper he too was using an assumed name). Beadle immediately recognized the Mormon widely thought to be the leader of the infamous Mountain Meadows Massacre of 1857. Briefly, immigrants from Missouri and Kansas, states in which the Mormons had been persecuted, encamped near present-day St. George, Utah, to rest stock and replenish food before crossing the desert. Some of them taunted and ridiculed the Mormon settlers. Already under pressure from attacks on their way of life, the Mormons took the immigrants' presence as an affront. By prevalent accounts, Mormons warned the immigrants that Indians were about to attack but insisted they would help the immigrants to safety if each adult male would drop his gun and accompany an armed Mormon. After each immigrant separated from the group, his escort shot him, and Indians murdered the wives and older children.

After trying to gloss over the tragedy for fourteen years, church elders shunted Lee down to the Colorado River in the winter of 1871 to get him out of the limelight. Six years later they recalled him to trial. An all-Mormon jury delivered a split verdict. He was tried again. Witnesses such as Jacob Hamblin who had testified for him now testified against him, and this time he was convicted. Twenty years after the tragedy, he was executed, having kept his Mormon vow of silence.

Mixed flocks of ducks float in a back-eddy. Lesser scaups here from the Canadian prairies, tiny buffleheads small enough to nest in trees, common redheads, American widgeons grazing algae out of the river, and chunky little goldeneyes, trailing neat thin wakes, all find winter quarters in the quiet waters around Lees Ferry.

Heavy hissing signals the inflating of the two outer pontoons of the raft, huge silver sausages that flank an amorphous oval doughnut. As air courses into them, each segment rises slowly out of its primeval warehouse sleep. Metal frames bang into place, straps tighten, chains clinch, fastenings snap, sounds that reverberate sharply in the cold. The first two weeks in January are scarcely the height of the river season, nor did any of us come just to get a suntan and run some white water. Scientists organized and staff this trip. The rest of us are volunteers in a Glen

Canyon Environmental Studies project to count bald eagles at Nanko-weap Creek at Mile 52, the largest concentration of wintering eagles in the Southwest, and to monitor their food base, the trout that come up the creek to spawn in January.

Glen Canyon Environmental Studies projects are ongoing investigations into the changes wrought by Glen Canyon Dam on the Colorado River and cover the river's 280 miles between Lees and Pearce Ferries. The bald eagle study is but one facet of Glen Canyon Environmental Studies, a broad research program being carried out under the sponsorship of the Bureau of Reclamation and other government agencies, funded by the Western Area Power Administration, the federal agency responsible for marketing the hydroelectric power generated at Glen Canyon Dam by the Bureau of Reclamation. The secretary of the interior authorized the first Glen Canyon Environmental Studies projects in 1982, when the Bureau of Reclamation's plan to increase capacity by rewinding the eight generators at Glen Canyon Dam triggered an Environmental Impact Statement. The studies were designed to answer two questions: "Are current operations of the dam, through control of the flows in the Colorado River, adversely affecting the *existing* river-related environmental and recreational resources of Glen Canyon and Grand Canyon?" and, "Are there ways to operate the dam, consistent with the Colorado River Storage Project water delivery requirements, that would protect or enhance the environmental and recreational resources?"

The arbitrarily imposed two-year length of the first Glen Canyon Environmental Studies study period may strike even a nonscientist as too short for gathering the amount and kind of data needed. Add to that a river far more complex, far more intricate, far more variable than any other river in the United States, one that requires at least quadruple the research time to compile comparable data, and finally add to *that* a near total absence of baseline data for comparison. When Glen Canyon Dam was under construction researchers conducted well-coordinated salvage studies of Glen Canyon itself, which would be inundated, but inexplicably no studies were made of the potential impact on the river *downstream* from the dam. Invaluable and irreplaceable data about the river are forever missing.

Then, in 1983 and 1984, an aberrant and quixotic act of nature jolted the Glen Canyon Environmental Studies: snowpack three times higher than normal in the Rockies, combined with heavy rains during runoff time. The Bureau of Reclamation policy of maintaining Lake Powell close to full pool, resulted in disastrous flood-level flows—admittedly, bureau staff would have had to be clairvoyant to foresee the volume of inflow months before it occurred, but there were warnings. When the bureau released water early in July 1983, it was already ten weeks too late. The pound of huge, uncontrolled volumes of water through the discharge tubes in the porous Navajo Sandstone flanking the dam caused cavitation so great that the tubes regurgitated their cement linings into the river. Lake Powell came within eight feet of overtopping the dam, saved only by some quickly rigged plywood panels that momentarily raised the height of the dam.

The original two-year Glen Canyon Environmental Studies projects, disrupted as they were, verified what anyone with half an eye already knew: a big dam causes big changes on a big river. Recognizing that the first Glen Canyon Environmental Studies research period was not long enough to establish a reliable body of data or to address research problems properly, the National Academy of Sciences, the oversight group for Glen Canyon Environmental Studies, recommended a second group of studies to begin in 1989, which would form the basis for an Environmental Impact Statement and would establish a program of ongoing, long-term monitoring.

Anyone who, for the moment, isn't rigging does a little stiff-legged polka. In down jackets and caps and pants, we look like dancing bears, each stepping to our own interior music, keeping muffled time by clapping mittened hands, huffing and blowing, anything to keep moving, to keep warm. Mercifully, considering how January-cold it is, on shore there is little wind but, then, neither is there circulation to drive the mists away and open the canyon to sunshine.

Gradually everything is cleared off the ground. A bucket brigade passes the last river bags to the raft where they are lashed or clipped in, along with white plastic buckets, orange plastic water jugs, lines, rocket boxes (those army-surplus waterproof metal boxes that hold all the river trip necessities, from utensils to spices to first aid supplies to research forms to the trip's library), tarpaulins, propane tanks, folding chairs and, last, fish biologist Bill Leibfried's sheepherder stove, which requires three men to lift it onto the prow of the raft and will prove to be a lifesaver for us all. The tempo is endemic to all river leavings: the cadence of rigging and loading, whether hurried or leisurely, always takes about two hours.

As loading finishes, clouds continue to hover above us like a luffing gray silk tent. Fog hangs in columns that rise and sink like wavering wraiths, lost spirits of the river. Downstream a white shroud blanks out any vistas, draping water's edge and flanking wall in an all-encompassing whiteness into which we will disappear and, I could easily be persuaded, from which we will never return—perhaps in a sense those once captivated by this extraordinary river and its canyon never do revert completely to the rim-world.

At last we struggle into dry suits, pull on the second mitten with our teeth and, rendered clumsy by our swaddling, jump, haul, and clamber onto the raft. The warmth generated by the exertion lasts but a moment. Almost as soon as we reach midchannel, gravel terraces mark the entrance of the Paria River at Mile 0.8. Shortly after the Paria the pale, hard ledges of the Kaibab Limestone Formation appear at river level—Kaibab Limestone is what visitors walk on and fall off of on the South Rim. Strongly cemented, the limestone narrows and cloisters and initiates a canyon that closes out the world. As the river begins its work of carving into flat-lying sedimentary beds, formation after formation, that make up the Colorado Plateau, going down in time, yesteryears and yestereons and yesterforevers: the alternation of water-laid deposits with land-laid deposits. As an ancient sea advanced, sandstone gave way to shale, which gave way to limestone; as the sea retreated, limestone gave way to shale, which gave way to sandstone, repeated again and again.

We plow through a riffle and spray hits like bullets of ice. Every hand grasps a line. In January there is no show of insouciance. With river temperature just above 40°F, survival time is measured in minutes if you fall in and are not pulled out immediately. And even then, hypothermia—that fatal cooling of the body that brings about lethargy, loss of alertness, and uncontrollable shivering—remains a major danger. A sudden gust of wind assails every inch of bare skin. Out come extra mittens and balaclavas and scarves that turn us into a raftful of bundled, unrecognizable creatures, only eyes suggesting an anima.

While I wrap on an extra scarf, the dazzling Coconino Sandstone rises out of the river, Coconino being the Hopi word for the Havasupai Indians. Art Nouveau curves of crossbedding uncoil across the wall, layers of ancient sand dunes indurated into beige rock flushed with hints of peach and gold, ancient winds trapped in the grain, sinuous crossbeds up to sixty feet thick and seventy long. The dunes piled up on the northwest edge of a huge, single, massive supercontinent named Pangaea when, 250–280 million years ago, chance shoved all the land masses then floating separately into a single mass, a time also of one of the five great waves of plant and animal extinctions in the geologic record. Winds out of the north picked up sand and piled it into dunes, over the vast area of Pangaea's western coast, sliding the grains up the slope and dropping them down the lee side, just as dunes arise today.

Wind sorts the sand it blows, and dune sands are usually even-sized, rounded and frosted from abrasion. The dunes were preserved by being covered with other sediments and saturated by mineral-bearing groundwater, which "froze" them in place to form beautiful pale walls now whittled by the river.

Serpentines of bright green algae, *Cladophora glomerata*, waft and waver in the current, some attached to boulders, some blowing downstream in the underwater winds, preternaturally vivid in the clear, cold winter river. After closure of Glen Canyon Dam, these algae increased exponentially between Lees Ferry and Glen Canyon Dam, seventeen miles upriver, and became the dominant attached alga in the river.

When Glen Canyon Dam closed in 1964, the changes in the river below were instant and dramatic. Instead of a silt-laden, seasonally fluctuating river with varying seasonal temperatures, water now came from two hundred feet below the surface of Lake Powell at a constant, very cold, average 46°F all year long, essentially sediment-free. The big yearly shifts in flow—rising, often flooding in the spring, falling in late summer—were replaced by daily fluctuations, sometimes rapid, tied to the flow of water through the generators in response to demands for electric power in the Western Area Power Administration grid.

An average of 380,000 tons of silt a year used to grind past the gaging station at Bright Angel Creek ninety miles downstream. Lieutenant Joseph Christmas Ives, chugging up the Colorado River from the Gulf of California in 1858, complained that the fine sand in suspension was "sharp as emery" and ruined his engines. Now upper tributary streams enter Lake Powell and so almost no silt enters the river from upstream; only the Paria and Little Colorado contribute appreciable amounts. Before the dam, the river was fed by the chemically pure water of snowmelt (70 percent of the Colorado's flow comes from melting snow in the Rockies) plus the calcium and bicarbonate that used to be flushed through during upper tributary floods. Now the chemical composition of the river changes little during the year. The dam also holds back the phosphorus that enhances plant productivity, and what does filter through is usurped by the masses of *Cladophora* just below the dam.

Cladophora is well adapted to withstand the fluctuating flows that result from short-term pulses of power generation rather than the predam roaring spring floods. Its long outer strands collapse on themselves when exposed, trapping water and protecting the innermost filaments from desiccation. The intricate branching of *Cladophora* also provides a huge attachment area in relatively little space for the myriad Lilliputian flora and fauna. Clustered on the plant stems minute midge larvae may reach 100,000 per square meter, joined by astronomical numbers of diatoms, small aquatic insects, and crustacea.

Over half of the minute plants clinging to the *Cladophora* are the microscopic algae called diatoms. They increased 1,600-fold after the closure of the dam, also responding to the new stability of water temperature and chemistry. Diatoms are unicellular algae that encase their photosynthetic cells in delicate transparent boxes of silica, which under a microscope reveal exquisite packets shaped like boomerangs, spindles, rods, and cat's-eyes, precisely scribed with lines and hyphens and dots that tell their species. Although they exist by the trillions here, only four species dominate, a typical lack of variety that characterizes river ecosystems below dams.

Quarter-inch amphipods, little wiggly shrimplike creatures, also cling to branches of algae and munch on the diatoms. These amphipods, *Gammarus lacustris*, originally from Asia, were dumped into some of the clear-flowing tributaries in the 1930s to provide food for yet another exotic species, rainbow trout. Trout were first stocked in tributaries of the Colorado River perhaps as early as 1919, then repeatedly between 1922 and 1931, with absolutely no thought of what introducing a new species might do to native fish. The accounts of rangers who backpacked the fry in carry a tone of self-congratulation, symptomatic of a time when bringing in exotic species and overseeing their establishment was a human triumph over the things nature forgot, a kind of Manifest Destiny for the natural world. After the dam closed, the river and some tributaries were heavily stocked, and trout began to spawn up Bright Angel, Tapeats, and Clear Creeks. Now they are the most prevalent fish in the river, their large population a detriment to endemic fish like humpback chub already under pressure from the drastic habitat changes engendered by the dam.

The ultimate irony is that the combination of habitat alteration and the accompanying shift in flora and fauna the dam brought, plus the introduction of exotic species, has brought world fame to the Colorado River between Glen Canyon Dam and Lees Ferry: it is one of the five premier "trophy trout streams" in the world.

As the raft passes, a steely gray great blue heron takes off against the light, a resident river spirit carrying good omens on its wings. Fishermen stand knee-deep in the river, looking like herons themselves. Shadows still cloak the river ahead except for a single stripe of brilliant turquoise green limned by a brief slot of sunlight. Currents from the rising river flick up little swirls of silt that well to the surface in ovals and circles, as if there were underwater spotlights casually placed here and there.

I find the green river's clarity unnatural, its pellucid emerald color hard, adamantine. I am used to the soft, silt-laden, café-au-lait color of Southwestern desert rivers, made up of all the colors of the walls that flank them, a summary that is a comfort to the eye, a balm to the psyche. That's just the way I prefer my rivers, thank you. For the first sixty-odd miles the Colorado remains clear unless the Paria flushes in swirls of opaque putty-colored silts, when it becomes what one of Powell's colleagues, geologist Clarence Dutton, called pistachio green, or farther down, when the Little Colorado River tinges it red with silts and clays from the plateaus above.

Water swishes and swirls around the raft, chatters and gargles, suddenly garrulous. Hypnotizing trains of bubbles skitter back and forth, link together, pop apart. Buttons of foam mix and swirl with the bubbles, appearing and disappearing, like a thimblerig: now you see it, now you don't. The river charges against rock ledges, having already cleaned the snow off a couple of feet above the water. The wall is a register of floods past. The most recent mark, about a yard above present river level, records the floods of 1983–84, when the river measured at Lees Ferry ran up to 97,300 cubic feet per second (cfs). The flood of 1884 ran 300,000 cfs, one in 1921 ran at 200,000 cfs, and the monster flood of 1862 peaked at 500,000 cfs and left the highest stripe.

This morning the river runs a placid 10,000 to 11,000 cfs and travels at around four miles per hour. The measurement cubic feet per second is easy to define but hard to visualize: one cubic foot of water, about seven and a half gallons, traveling past a point in one second. Fundamentally, "cfs" measures how much water flows in the river. To conceptualize cubic feet per second, think of standing at the edge of a creek one foot wide and one foot deep, with a cube of water a foot on each side flowing past your big toe every second. Double or triple it, and there runs a rill. Multiply it ten times for a good flowing creek. Increase it one hundred times for a good stream. Multiply it five hundred times, and 5,000 cubic feet per second require a wider, deeper channel. At 10,000 cfs, if you haven't moved, the water likely runs well over your head.

Someone calls, "Big bird, upper left!" Half a dozen binoculars bang half a dozen noses too cold to feel the insult. Everyone is so keyed to seeing bald eagles that the identification of a golden eagle elicits a communal groan. From a distance a golden eagle's head is just a bump, its tail is longer, its legs feathered to the toes, and its underwings show white. A bald eagle's neck and head are sizable, more than half the length of the tail.

A park naturalist recorded a single bald eagle in the canyon in 1929. In 1985 an observant boatman on a winter rowing trip sighted bald eagles fishing in numbers at Nankoweap Creek. Primarily fish eaters, likely an overflying eagle or two chanced to find spawning trout here and remembered when coming through the next winter, for eagles have good long-term memory, and their tremendous long-distance vision enables them to see at least fourteen miles. One eagle hunting attracts others, usually within half an hour or less.

Trout began entering Nankoweap Creek to spawn in the mid-1970s. Before the dam, trout stocked in side streams (which did not include Nankoweap) remained confined to those tributaries with their clear, well-oxygenated water—trout do not spawn in the mainstream, which is too silty. But all tributaries run in narrow defiles with walls too close for eagles to maneuver well, hence they seldom visited the canyon for fish. At Nankoweap Creek the landscape opens and attracts the only known concentrated population of fishing eagles in the canyon.

Adult identification is *not* the problem. The challenge is recognizing the distinctive preadult stages to record and assess the value of the river as a winter resource to young birds. When bald eagle young fledge, their bodies and eyes are completely dark, the head disproportionately large, wings and tail mottled with white. In silhouette young eagles have longer tails and wings than adults, providing them with greater lift in flying. In flight they flap more slowly than adults, whose wings are better adapted to the long-distance soaring needed for migration. As an eagle matures to a subadult, white on the body begins to disappear, and the head lightens, retaining a black eye stripe. Between three-and-a-half and five years of age, the bill turns yellow and the unmistakable white plumage appears on its head, the brown eye phases into the bright, fierce yellow of an adult. At five years a bald eagle is a complete adult with an eight-foot wingspan and striking clear-cut plumage of white head and tail, dark body, yellow legs and beak.

"Big bird!" This time two birds soar, an immature and a mature bald eagle. With its fresh, unbattered yellow beak and a few white feathers still remaining on the breast, it is a handsome, spanking new adult.

Ten Mile Rock is an anvil-sized boulder of Toroweap Sandstone plopped in midstream. Just a mile beyond, the dark red beds of Hermit Shale appear, easy to miss because they rise near the first attention-getting major rapid on the river, Badger Creek. All of a sudden, the unmistakable cocoa red rock looms above our head, zebra-striping the slanted talus slopes. Although officially named shale, many of the layers are sandstones or siltstones, the grains of which are coated with hematite, a highly oxidized form of iron of a deep rusty red that endows the canyon with its characteristic ambiance and glow as it dissolves and slathers the gray limestones below, transforming a gray wall into Redwall.

Corrugated, hollowed, wrinkled, Redwall Limestone emerges some fifteen miles farther, jutting fins and flanges into the river. At water's edge the river has scooped and polished elegant feathery flutes. Vertical joints and cracks between beds hatch the cliff face, pitting and netting it with fine shadows that transmute it into a historiated Greek-figured frieze, a history of river gods, its original Parnassian elegance worn to roughness—marble is, after all, just a fancy limestone, and it was this semblance that prompted Powell to name the eastern part of the canyon Marble Canyon.

Redwall Limestone is a pure calcium carbonate limestone, recording three separate transgressions and retreats of a Mississippian sea. The early geologists Jules Marcou and John Newberry, who traveled with Ives when he pushed up the Colorado River, estimated the age of the Redwall by correlating its fossils with those of the Mississippian "mountain limestones" of England, laid down 320 to 360 million years ago. Redwall limestones were deposited under quite constant environmental conditions, built up out of the remains of countless creatures that roamed, crept, slept, siphoned and scraped away their lives, leaving behind their equally countless shells—whorled, spiraled, turreted, and paired. Of all the formations along the river, the Redwall most strongly gives the inner canyon its character and massive presence and, once visible, it remains in sight most of the length of the canyon.

Downstream, frigid, gauzy vapors pour over the cliff tops and obfuscate their outlines, swirl between the walls, sucked downstream to the place where good mists go to die. Like nubilous elevators, the mists slide up and down the cliffs, floor to floor, stratum to stratum. When they descend, only the snow-fretted terraces are visible. As they lift they reveal a rock lightening to salmon, crevices and ledges glyphed with snow. Fog snuggles itself around this turning or that, lavishes itself against the river, shinnies up a slope, wreathes, wraps, ravels, a ne'er-do-well, irresponsible weather, negligent, careless, and chilling. A silvery line, thin as a platinum cloison, separates green enamel river from gray enamel sky. For a brief moment the clouds shred. A slice of sunlight illuminates a pale apricot rock facade that shimmers coldly peach in the river. The river syrups on, dragging its frigid reflections with it.

*between Sockdolager
and Grapevine*

2

_____

It becomes very dark, but now and then through a cloudrift we can see the snow falling on the rim, though the precipitation reaches us mostly as a chilly rain. Intermittently we hear the distant or nearby crash of rock masses falling in the side gorges around us. Fortunately, our camp is in the open and we are wholly out of harm's way. Still, these reports, like the sound of distant guns, the whistle of the wind, and the swish of the driven rain and sleet make us appreciate the security of our position very keenly. The rolling storm with its gathering gloom about and above us, composes and completes an elemental panorama in as grand a setting as few have ever had the privilege of beholding. I am glad this glory has fallen to our lot once, but once is just enough.

Julius F. Stone, 1909, *Canyon Country: The Romance of a Drop of Water and a Grain of Sand*

Fishing Eagles
and Spawning Trout

―――――――

A day later, the bow of the boat grates ashore at Nankoweap Beach at Mile 52.1. Powell named Nankoweap using a Paiute name of rather confused etymology but never mind: it's a euphonious name and a beautiful place. Behind the tamarisk- and arrowweed-stalked beach, the terrain steps upward to the old high-water line, which in turn rises into a talus slope footing a high cliff that catches the first morning sun and houses a pair of peregrine falcons.

I pitch my tent in the tamarisk thicket, annoyed at the minute, prickly twigs that stick to everything and, in general, at this pushy intruder that spring floods once cleaned off and, with spring spates gone, has now taken over the river banks. Introduced from the Middle East at the end of the nineteenth century as an ornamental shrub, tamarisk probably entered the canyon sometime after 1925 but did not proliferate until the 1950s. With its long taproot and ability to loose astronomical amounts of tufted, airborne seeds, it has spread throughout Western watercourses. An efficient, greedy colonizer, it can withstand inundation for up to six weeks or low water for several years. At Nankoweap, a well-used beach, only the continual trampling of campers maintains paths and niches for camp spots.

In the midst of my carping, Bryan Brown, head ornithologist of this project, reminds me not only that Lake Powell inundated thousands of acres of riparian habitat upstream, but that throughout the Southwest 90 to 95 percent of lowland riparian habitat has disappeared. The postdam Grand Canyon, with its tamarisk thickets, has become a major new refuge for birds, ironically created by a dam that destroyed much of their original habitat. Displaced riparian birds moved downstream in an "instant mitigation." Of the three hundred bird species listed along the Colorado River, forty-one breed here, and 90 percent of those nest in tamarisk. In the summertime tamarisk houses huge populations of leafhoppers and all manner of minute gnats and tiny bees, which make a munificent insect buffet for breeding and migratory birds.

In the tamarisk sheltering my tent, an avian architect engineered a teacup-sized nest in the fork of a branch, about five feet off the ground. Fashioned of tamarisk bits and scraps of paper, with strips of plastic woven in, it was constructed by a frugal bird that believed in recycling.

Each of us is responsible for one shift a day at the observation post, with one day off a week. The morning team leaves camp early enough to be on post by first light at 7:00 a.m. The second shift sits from noon until dark at 5:30 or 6:00 p.m. At least four people staff each watch, three as constant observers, one or more as recorder. The main spotting scope is always focused on the creek mouth where the greatest activity occurs. An observer, binoculars affixed to face, stays glued to the bird he or she picks up, delineating the bird's actions to the recorder, who writes it down and marks activity time by the second. The forms record each foraging eagle and the age group to which it belongs, its success at taking a trout or lack thereof. We do not record what eagles do best of all, which is stand around.

Anticipating the chill that lack of movement brings in this twenty-five-degree weather, I layer on one of everything I own, ending with a down jacket, which now for obvious reasons will not zip closed. Like an overstuffed penguin, I waddle up to the observation point along a circuitous path that meanders through willows and arrowweed, then through mesquites that trace the bottom edge of a terrace at the old high-water line. Some trees burned in an accidental fire in the summer of 1967, and now younger sprouts proliferate from the old roots, although the grove is far from recovered.

As the path rises, mesquite trees give way to desert scrub. The path breaks out into the open and begins a sharp climb up an ancient debris flow that rises almost two hundred feet above the river. The gravels in the lower part of the hill are detritus from far upstream, studded with rocks brought in by the river when its channel ran farther west. The gravels in the uppermost part of the hill are local and match those in the Nankoweap Basin to the west. Over time the ridge has been considerably eroded by the Colorado River, which borders it on the east, and Nankoweap Creek, which borders it on the north. If the river once flowed atop this ridge, it would solve the mystery of a pile of driftwood found in Stanton's Cave twenty miles upstream at Mile 31.7, a cave that opens one hundred and fifty feet above present river level.

From the top of the ridge the path hangs a left and goes straight up, paved with slippery, loose limestone scree, fraught with unstable handholds, one of those slopes vastly easier to negotiate going up than mincing down. The observation post nestles under a minuscule overhang three hundred feet above and half a mile from the mouth of Nankoweap Creek, opening to a magnificent view of the river upstream and downstream and facing a grand thousand-foot wall immediately across the river. To expedite locating eagles, we memorize the wall formations against which the eagles fly: Kaibab, Toroweap, Coconino, Hermit, Supai, Redwall, Muav, Bright Angel. The impact of this wall vastly exceeds the sum of its parts, and for all the hours I spend here, I never tire of looking at it, this record wall where animals snorkeled in the silt and cycad fronds trembled in the rain, seas ebbed and flowed, continents melded and rafted apart, dunes sifted in, ancient rivers blew out of their banks, strange fish swam, fossils formed, species developed and expired, moons rose, suns froze, and whatever else that could happen, did.

As watch begins, the landscape lies so far beneath us it resembles a dish garden scribed with a tiny pewter stream, a carved jade river, gray-green velour terrain, miniature wire trees, tiny sponge bushes, hovered over by pink cotton candy clouds. The river runs low, "Sunday's water" (from the day when dam releases are minimal) reaching here on Tuesday. From the adults we saw on the way downriver, we can assume that bald eagles have moved into the canyon but are still dispersed because trout are not yet spawning and the peak of eagle presence correlates with the peak of spawning. Although trout cluster in the shallows in the river at the mouth of the creek and about a sandbar downstream, and although the river is high enough that fish can enter, only a very few have done so. We end the day with no bald eagle sightings but several soaring golden eagles noted, more interested in small rodents on the rim than in fish in the river.

As late afternoon sunlight slants into the gorge downstream, the view is elegant, classic Colorado River. The bays and walls of limestone wedge the river into zigzags of turquoise green that angle out of sight in the floating light, dappling the water with alternating malachite and lapis lazuli shadows. The cliffs glow smoky rose, gathering in the afternoon shadows.

After dinner, we hike upstream to Nankoweap Creek, working in the dark to avoid disrupting the eagles' diurnal feeding patterns and the fishes' equanimity since they seem calmer at night. My headlamp beam narrows vision to a surreal world, a dinner-plate-sized light moving just ahead of my feet, popping over boulders and sliding across a row of stones outlining the path. Depth perception gone, I founder into rocks and bang into bushes. The rest of the world is a morass of darkness— height of cliff, width of stream, distance from river I know not.

We traipse all the way to the mouth of the creek, then work back upstream to census the number of trout that have actually entered. A jagged white rim of ice traces the banks. Headlamp beams flash on the streambed boulders, bounce off the water, bury in the pools, but spot-light only six fish along the way, small and not in good breeding con-dition. Grand Canyon trout cannot be aged in the normal way, which is to count growth rings in their scales. Ring formation depends upon seasonally alternating warm and cold water, and here, where water is consistently cold, rings are largely lacking. Tonight the creek water runs at 33°F, too cold for any sensible trout. The dip net freezes stiff on the instant, supercooled when it hits the 20°F air.

Researchers expected to find trout eating the tiny freshwater *Gram-marus* along with other invertebrates commonly eaten by rainbows. In-stead the fish were ingesting massive amounts of *Cladophora*, the com-mon green algae in the river, gobbling up with the algae all the minute diatoms clinging to them. Diatoms differ from green algae in that they store fats from photosynthesis not as carbohydrates, as most plants do, but as rich-in-fat lipids, a tremendous source of nourishment. The trout thrive upon these minutiae, growing to fifteen inches and more, gener-ally with a healthy layer of fat.

Trout spawn varies week by week and seems to be, at Nankoweap anyway, a function of temperature and water volume. Last year at this time trout spawn was well underway. There were so many that they jammed every pool in the creek, so thick, last year's researchers swear, that you could walk across the creek on their backs and never get your feet wet. At times trout spawning was so intense that eggs colored the beach orange at the mouth of the creek. But even this prolific egg pro-duction may not be sufficient to maintain the population naturally. The reproductive success of trout here probably runs 10 percent or less, but for this population to maintain itself requires 60 to 80 percent survival. Trout reproduce poorly in Nankoweap Creek probably because of a too-small waterway, too many fish, wrong-sized gravels and insufficient room for redds (the nests trout construct), fluctuating creek flows that expose eggs or spring spates that ream out a season's production, too few quiet pools in which larvae can develop, and shallow water that heats up too quickly in the spring. Since trout require eight weeks from egg to larva, any of these disturbances bring heavy mortality.

Back in camp, I huddle as close as I can get to the sheepherder stove without singeing. In the darkness I sense the quality of this place along with its cold and overwhelming presence, river and sky held apart by monumental walls. The river converses only with itself, a one-on-one conversation, no beginning, no ending, no yesterday, no tomorrow. Tonight the river's presence is so commanding that it steps between me and my life, separates me from all that I hold dear, entraps me in an endless winter.

Not until almost nine o'clock the next morning does a reluctant sun tinge the rim line downstream. Last night the North Rim was so cold that a flock of pinyon jays came down into the canyon to get warm and filled camp with their grievances. Rockfalls punctuated the night with a racket that kept me awake, waiting for the other shoe to drop.

Ruby-crowned kinglets, some already red-capped, phasing into breeding plumage, scold with quick raspy notes. Oregon juncos, mountain chickadees, and bushtits are common here, although none are summer nesters. The kinglets often appear singly, each in its own feeding territory. The juncos flicker through the tamarisk in twos and threes. The mountain chickadees arrive in singles or pairs. Bushtits are rare but when they flock in they turn the bushes into twittering trees. A Bewick's wren sings a sweet broken song, not all the way formed, only snatches of what will be a full melody at breeding time, like a composer picking out tentative phrases on the piano. The waste management patrol, the ubiquitous ravens, check the beach as they do every day. The supply boat readies to leave. Until the next one arrives two weeks hence, the beach will be boatless, and the clean view adds a lot to my day.

On afternoon watch, cold weighs on us like a ten-ton block of ice. We huddle under a sleeping bag for surcease from wind and galloping hypothermia. During the five days we have been here, the sun has come to the beach two minutes earlier each day, and those precious minutes becomes as sixty when ice skims the cup of water outside my tent every morning and the sand is so frozen that it crunches underfoot. But the sun is of little use at this moment, and time scarcely moves as we survey the sky and spot only golden eagles and ravens.

Suddenly out of nowhere two golden eagles appear and strike each other in midair, lock talons and tumble twenty feet—aggressive, not courting, behavior. One breaks away and flies off. The other lands clumsily, holding its left wing as if injured. After forty-five minutes it waddles into the creek, pulls a big trout out and stands on it—but not firmly enough. The fish wiggles away. The golden chases it with wings akimbo like a cleaning lady after a cockroach. It locks the fish in its talons, takes off with it, labors across the river, and lands about fifty feet up from shore and feeds. Primarily mountain and desert birds dependent on a diet of small rodents, they are seldom seen fishing.

The sound of Nankoweap Rapid pushes up through the clear gelid air. High clouds net the sky with wefts of frozen crystals. Time must be frozen too, it goes so slowly. By this point we are no longer waiting for eagles but simply trying to survive until 5:30, when it gets dark enough for us honorably to go down to camp and get warm. Still, congealed as we are, we scan incessantly up and across, down and over, and see nothing but sandstone and limestone and shale and clouds sidling in.

Teresa Yates, a researcher whose eyes are so attuned to eagles that she can sense one crossing the Mexican border, whispers, "Bird." A speck streaks across the middle of the Redwall, flying right to left, a good greeting from the gods. It is an immature bald eagle, quickly tallied before it wheels up the river and out of sight. Speech changes cadence. A moment of excitement, even for that brief flyby, engenders a shift of metabolism that miraculously warms and revitalizes.

The next year's eagle count (the second of three counts) is scheduled for six weeks, with volunteers coming in for two-week segments. I choose the middle two, the last week of February and the first week of March, some six weeks later than the first year's count. As last year, six hours of our day are devoted to formal watch, other assorted hours to fish counting, record keeping, and rotational dinner duty, and one whole day off to count stars, explore ledges, wander creeks, and watch the river go by. These two weeks turn out to be so different from January's count a year ago that I could be stationed on another planet.

Our arrival causes a "disturbance day" and eagle watching is abandoned for the rest of the day. The only obvious evidence of disturbance is when a bird leaves and does not return even at a time when eagles ordinarily fish. Past experience has shown that when the eagles flush at a boat's arrival, they do not return that day (although they seem used to regular crew changes at noon). Disturbance is very difficult to measure, for there's no way to quantify, no way to get eagles to check off "satisfactory" or "unacceptable" on a multiple-choice list for habitat evaluation and fill in reasons why.

As there is a great deal of work to be done along the creek, disturbance days and nighttime afford the only times to do it. Mercy, what a difference six weeks makes! The full creek rushes three to four feet wide, gabbling over basketball-sized boulders, foaming and frothing, with the current flicking back and forth from bank to bank. The first ten feet are awash with trout four layers thick. Crowded into a pool blocked by knee-high falls, they fan the water and turn it dark with their bodies. Sometimes dozens of fins and tails stick up out of the water like little black signal flags, so deeply stacked are fish. When the water is very shallow, whole backs are out. Those in the fast water face upstream, those in slower face into shore, big healthy-looking fish between fourteen and sixteen inches long. When they try to jump the falls, frothing water obscures them and they tumble and flop as if sloshed in a washing machine. One attempts to barge its way up the step, flails, fails, falls. Another leaps, clears the step, and spurts to the next riser.

We count and record the tag color and number as well. The first netted has a U.S. Fish and Wildlife green tag 027588, the color denoting that this fish was caught in the river, not in the creek. Sometimes a fish slides into the net easily, but other times its frantic splashing startles the whole pool into a frenzy, and sixty thrashing fish create a cascade of free water that drenches anything within five feet. We tally forty-five recaptures, wearing tags of all colors.

The higher pools are sparsely populated, usually with only two or three fish, some engaged in desultory courting. In one quiet pool a male and a female swim about a foot apart but evidence no mating behavior even though they hang over a bed of clean gravel. In another pool a pair pass over each other, the female often swimming on her side. A third fish, a much smaller male, lurks in close attendance. Termed a "precocious parr," it is kept at a distance by darting attacks from the larger male. When eggs drop the parr whisks in and releases milt over the eggs in a hit-and-run tactic. At the end of the count we tally nearly eight hundred trout in the first five hundred meters of creek, about half of peak spawn, when there may be over fifteen hundred trout packed into this tiny rill.

Later that afternoon I sit on the beach writing out forage forms because eagle activity has been unusually high and we are running out of printed ones. Of everything else we have ample, labeled and canned, stacked and full. Of forage forms we do not. The logistics of mounting a scientific trip on the Colorado River are Herculean, and what one does not have, one improvises or does without. Hand-copying forage forms makes one appreciate a copy machine.

Only a week later, as I traipse up the first hundred yards of Nanko-weap Creek, I am astounded at what has happened to the fish. Of the nearly two hundred in the first hundred meters, most are battered, several straw yellow, many missing skin in patches, with tails whitened and fins shredded, eyes gone, in extremis or already dead. Almost none attempt to jump between pools, and there are many fewer fish within the pools. The count ends with a total of some three hundred trout and one bluehead sucker.

That night, as the river rises, late light washes the Bright Angel Shale, picks out the fine layers of cool tan, sage green, grape. Above, the ruddy Redwall rises to heaven. Over my shoulder scalelike green shoots sprig out of new alizarin tamarisk twigs. For once I am not moved to rancor at their presence. New green is everywhere and still unfurling. Everything I need is within reach.

While I wait for six o'clock for my watch of counting fish entering or exiting the river to begin, I observe a researcher cast and pull trout out of the river. She grapples the flapping, frantic fish onto a calibrated board to measure it and presses its abdomen to see if it extrudes eggs or milt, followed by a final indignity: setting a tag between the embedded spines of the dorsal fin, just beneath where the fin structure exits the body, a task requiring accuracy and finesse. Finally she carries the gasping fish gently to the river and cradles it until it has gained enough equilibrium to swim away. Then the whole slapping, smacking, slippery, slithery process begins all over again.

My watch begins as daylight dims. The behavior of exiting and entering trout strikes me as indecisive at best, and watching fish not make up their minds is about as exciting as watching paint dry. The number of fish coming into the creek usually burgeons as soon as the sun goes down, rising water plus nightfall engendering the largest runs up into Nankoweap Creek. No one knows if fish may sense themselves less exposed to predators, or to what other factors they react.

As darkness comes I hear rather than see fish beating downstream. I turn on my headlamp and focus on the sounds. Toward the end of the watch, a huge fish skates downstream, misses the turn, and beaches itself on a gravel slot barely skimmed with water. It lies stranded, fruitlessly slapping its tail, gills flaring with effort. It is still stranded when I turn the watch over. I am unreasonably concerned, reluctant to let a creature die when I could prevent it, trapped in the human hubris of wanting to play Mother Nature instead of respecting a perfectly good natural law: Don't zig when you should have zagged.

As I hike back to camp, the splashing of fish follows me, a pulsing sound that keeps time to the beat of stars traveling down their nightly rivers. The next morning I find out that the water came up and my stranded fish slid safely out into the river. I am moved to sentimentality: Nature took care of her own.

On early morning watch, when it becomes light enough to see, the river slowly recedes. Sunlight seeps down the Redwall, turning it deep salmon, then a blatant red orange. Upstream the Kaibab has a peculiar luminosity as sunlight glazes it pink. Five Canada geese skid onto the river with five splashes. Across the river willows and arrowweed band the edge in gray green and rust, replicating the colors of the Muav and the Redwall, all doubled in a river that looks like warp-dyed silk.

Suddenly someone gasps, "Will you look at *that!*" Five pairs of binoculars slide across the Redwall and we count: six . . . eight . . . nine! *Ten*! The eagles roost upstream, nobody knows where, but probably at a communal roost in a protected site where the concentration of birds in close quarters preserves body heat. But last night they roosted in niches in the Redwall across the river, basalt statues in marble niches.

Below, a raven materializes, struts about, pecking in desultory fashion at carrion left from yesterday. Another glides in and lands on a mesquite branch. A third, then a fourth and fifth, arrive, and then suddenly there are over a dozen. Generally early morning action follows a daily pattern: after the ravens land, the eagles arrive and wait some distance away before coming in themselves, and may well watch the ravens for any sign of disturbance. So far, no eagles have been observed preceding the ravens. The first eagle usually alights just before seven, followed by a few more. Some sneak in, some materialize out of a solid rock wall, others swoop in with the panache of a Parisian model on the runway. When one arrives, others generally follow. Typically, after they arrive, nothing happens for up to an hour or more, a period scientists interpret as "staging time."

But this morning, because it is windy, the eagles stay high after they lift off from the Redwall, and fourteen bald eagles float across the sky in lazy helices, catching the early thermals, adjusting their primaries individually, like the spoilers on a jet plane's wing, increasing their stability and ability to maneuver, reducing turbulence. Their alternate soaring and gliding takes about a twentieth of the energy that flapping does, which they generally do only on take off or to insert themselves into a thermal.

The wind lessens and the eagles zoom in like kamikazes. This morning they begin moderately high, wings spread, spiraling downward. Once over the creek, they drop. They don't stoop to gain velocity like falcons, they don't close their wings so that they are bullet-shaped like swallows, they don't glide like pelicans. They chose a spot, angle in, and plummet. Like a stone. The medieval chronicler who depicted them as "coming down like a thunderbolt" had not watched Nankoweap eagles.

One eagle stalks to the creek edge. Over 75 percent of their foraging takes place within the first forty feet of the creek mouth, so any trout entering or leaving runs the gauntlet. The eagle waddles into the creek, nails a fish, and hops to shore with its catch in its talons—whomp, whomp, whomp—battering the poor fish with every hop. A focused, fierce eater, it strips the fish with its beak. One fish weighing a pound or a pound and a half is adequate for a bald eagle's daily diet, since eagles need consume only 6 to 11 percent of their body weight each day. The eagles take more trout than they can consume, but in the end all the leftover fish are consumed by somebody, most commonly golden eagles and ravens. During highest forage times, birds take anywhere from fifty to seventy-five trout a day. With up to a thousand trout in the stream some days, the food supply is essentially unlimited. Rather than by food availability, the eagle population here is determined by social tolerance, human disturbance, and other habitat limitations. Eagles present on these days of high trout concentration total twenty or more, paralleling the concentration of trout. And always in close attendance, like lugubrious, sharp-eyed, nineteenth-century undertakers, are the ravens.

Another young eagle stands in the water at the mouth of the creek when a trout wiggles past. The eagle takes two steps toward it, pounces on it, and has it on shore but a minute when it is pirated by another sub-adult. Pirating another eagle's catch is simply a way of life with eagles, and there is less display of animosity than one might expect (at this time of year eagles are not territorial). Evidently there's a quick assessment of the other eagle's size, the most important factor in releasing prey or defending it. Pirating is opportunistic, and eagles do it only when it takes less energy than getting food other ways, which may explain why more pirating usually occurs when a very large fish is involved. Here, where there is ample food and hunger is not a factor, pirating takes on a rather perfunctory, ho-hum aspect and would confirm Benjamin Franklin's suspicion that eagles are of bad moral character.

Usually five to ten seconds elapse before a fish is pirated. One fish, taken by a young eagle, is pirated first by another immature one, second by a subadult, and third, by yet another youngster. Generally, immature eagles will pirate from an eagle of any age, whereas adults predominantly pirate from other adults. Adult males often challenge each other but seldom challenge females, thus female pirating attempts have the highest success rate. Pirating occurs with ravens as well. Two ravens can work an eagle like a confidence man and his shill. A pair of ravens land beside a feeding eagle, one bobs and weaves at the eagle's head while the other tweaks its tail. When the eagle drops its fish to confront its tormentor in the rear, the front raven pirates the fish. Honest: Teresa saw it.

At 10:20 an adult golden eagle sails into the mouth of the creek. It trots four feet along the bank, pounces on a fish in the water, hops to shore with it, mantles over it, and devours it on the spot. Its whole aspect is dark, a Dracula-like specter, wings raised like a great, dark cloak. Goldens dominate bald eagles, who immediately abandon their fish without challenging the goldens. Even the ravens do not hassle them. When this golden flies off without finishing its kill, the ravens swarm in like jackals.

Two adult bald eagles stand downstream where pockets of trout blacken the water. After what seems an eternity of standing on one foot and then the other in what looks like eagle body language of reluctance and indecision, one eagle finally walks into the water and impales a fish. Curious about the amount of time an eagle stands around, we later clock an eagle that remained for an hour before making a forage, and this is the rule, not the exception: eagles can spend a *lot* of their time, sometimes over 90 percent, just standing around.

Finally, as the day wanes, only one immature eagle remains. It grabs a foot-long fish and takes it up on the bank but abandons it to the ravens. The bird may be full but it keeps on catching fish anyway. In most bald eagle populations the ratio of young to adult is 1:1. Here the ratio is consistently 2:1 or higher, and it goes up even further when the adults migrate out first. Adult bald eagles range widely in winter, remaining in one place as long as the food supply lasts, but young move around more and also need more food sources than adults because they forage less efficiently. At Nankoweap immature eagles, not yet skillful hunters, have a very high success rate, perhaps up to 95 percent, and the number of young eagles here surpasses that for the river as a whole. They remain here because foraging is so easy, and their proficiency enables them to build up more fat and strength to help in migration. Already dressed for success, a new adult pounces on a fish and drags it up on shore immediately, a trick younger birds usually do not practice, often losing their fish as a result.

Since midmorning a minimum of four to five eagles have been in view all the time, but within the hour all exit and there comes a sudden quiet. Only three ravens remain. An inventory of the common perching sites shows none on the Bright Angel ridge below; across the river, none; in the mesquite trees, none; on the big rocks at the entrance to the river, none. Only one eagle soars. A day's-end emptiness comes at noon.

just above Kanab Creek

3

Plants which survive here are, in general, those especially adapted to conditions of extreme heat and drought . . . The vegetation owes its heterogeneity to a diversity of habitats which depend upon climatic and edaphic factors. Conditions within canyon walls furnish interesting opportunities for micro-climatic studies. Within a small area several separate influences may act as association determiners. Extreme exposure to sun, topographic peculiarities, soil structure, and conditions of moisture may cause variations in a plant habitat.

> Elzada Clover and Lois Jotter, 1944, "Floristic Studies
> in the Canyon of the Colorado and Tributaries,"
> *American Midland Naturalist*

River Marshes
and Familiar Faults

———————

Early one March morning at Nankoweap the scream of one of the resident peregrine falcons awakens me. The chill morning air rustles with
busy bird sounds: Whissp. Tee-whit. Chr-r-r-r. Tee-hee tee-*hee*. Whit?
Whit. Did you? I did. Will you? I won't.

Sunlight ravishes the horizon. Upstream, back and above, slopes and
walls extend to a skyline of definitive sandstones curving into a huge
apse ending in a fin of rock that looks thin as a knife, notched with one
large V—an architectural place, begun in stone, designed by river, inlaid
with sky.

Today is my day off. No eagle counting, no helping with meals, no
washing willows, no waxing beaches. I leave the responsible eagle-
counter suit behind, hoist on my daypack, stuff in a thermos, a peanut-
butter-and-euphoria sandwich, a notebook, a down vest, a geology
guidebook, a jar of anticipation, and an extra pair of dry socks.

From a boat on the river the footpath between Nankoweap Creek
at Mile 52.1 and Kwagunt Creek at Mile 56 doesn't look like much of
a challenge. It strings along the open slopes on river right, up hillock
and down gully, over rounded, stylized hills like those in a thirteenth-
century Tuscan painting. But walking the trail becomes a repetitious
trek of up, across and down, then repeat from "up," tediously crossing every drainage crease in the Bright Angel Shale that cuts the slope
every hundred feet or so. Rome had seven hills, Nankoweap down to
Kwagunt has seventy plus (by honest count), but Kwagunt back up to
Nankoweap has seven thousand, give or take a couple.

Chips of maroon and celadon Bright Angel Shale pave the bare slippery slopes above the path, speckled like a breeding trout's back. I've been reading John Van Dyke's *The Grand Canyon of the Colorado*, which sensitizes one to the richness of color in the canyon. He describes the Bright Angel Shale as "Nile-green" and sprinkles his descriptions of strata with words like raspberry red, heliotrope, mauve, and purple. Van Dyke was an Easterner, a professor of art history at Rutgers, who came west for his health at the turn of the century. Enchanted with the clear air and brilliant light, he wrote vibrantly about what he saw in *The Grand Canyon of the Colorado*, published in 1920. His plush prose borders on the florid, but his ornate vocabulary often matches perfectly the canyon's opulence.

The sound of quacking ducks rises from a small marsh at Mile 55. Common mergansers float peaceably beyond a narrow screen of reed grass. Mallards and American widgeons spin and beat the water, their noise alone sufficient to alert every peregrine within miles. Ducks are being counted for the first time in an attempt to quantify the large wintering population and to find out whether they also breed here.

This marsh is part of a new zone that appeared after Glen Canyon Dam closed, forming at river flows between 10,000 and 20,000 cfs. When banks were no longer scoured by floods, quiet shallows and backwaters and eddy-return channels formed where water slowed and, if there were a good supply of sand and silt, sedges, rushes, and cattails rooted. In the 1983–84 floods these marshes were harder hit than any other habitat on the river. High flows ripped out more than 95 percent and flushed them downstream, reducing them to around two and a half acres from an estimated preflood sixty acres. But marsh plants, with their air- and water-borne seeds, recolonized rapidly.

Across the river, travertine encrusts the talus slopes, obscuring the neat Muav Limestone layers beneath, witness to wetter times. Here, between Kwagunt and the Little Colorado River, springs flowed only on the left bank, seeping out of the basal strata of the Muav. Travertine is a form of limestone, created when calcium carbonate precipitates out of heavily mineral-saturated water, and has a characteristic globby, porous texture. Enough water to cement these huge amounts of talus was available after the last full glacial period 15,000 to 21,000 years ago. One can still watch it forming today downstream in Havasu Creek.

Just below Kwagunt Creek's entrance into the river at Mile 56, Kwagunt Rapid boils into turquoise-green and white waves, as curling and stylized as those of a Chinese brush painting. Under the pulses of wind the trumpets of river gods blast, riding to battle. I hunker down in the dry creek bed to get below the wind and discover the first forecast of spring: greening rosettes of inflated-stem buckwheat, a tiny milkvetch with a few lavender flowers, a miniature fiddleneck, all nestling close to the sand.

"Winter annuals" like fiddlenecks typically germinate after good rains the previous fall. This tiny plant sprouted months ago, produced a rosette of leaves close to the ground, and wintered over as such. When spring rains and warming temperatures arrived, it did not have to wait for the precise conditions it required for germination but could rely on a root system already in place to take up water and nourishment immediately. Winter annuals register some of the highest photosynthetic rates ever measured. In years of massive bloom (which occur every five to ten years along the river), the biomass production of these plants can easily equal that of larger shrubs and woody perennials. The mystery is how these tiny fiddlenecks manage to allocate their resources in the unpredictable growing season down here. How long should they produce leaves and stems to build up reserves before they bloom and how soon should they bloom and set seed? The multitudes of these little plants year after year show they do "know" when to switch from vegetative to reproductive growth and how to combine the two, adjusting their timing efficiently.

A solitary bumblebee cruises low over the ground, sampling as it goes. Often the earliest bees out foraging, bumblebees wear a thick insulating pile and, by vibrating their flight muscles, can warm up enough for flight at low temperatures. They also regulate their body temperature while in flight and while incubating their brood, or while foraging and, incredibly, adjust head, abdomen, and thorax temperatures individually. Typically, insects out earliest are the largest and darkest, and fly early in the day in full sunshine, taking advantage of the warmth.

Along the river there are many more solitary bees than colonial ones. A solitary bee builds its own nest and collects pollen and nectar from flowers, activities that social bees share; a solitary bumblebee queen incubates her own brood, which will die in the fall, leaving only a single overwintering queen. The larvae of many Hymenoptera—bees, ants, and wasps—depend upon constant care by workers to protect and nourish them, and can winter over. Solitary bees and wasps deposit eggs, never to see their offspring. The young develop with no further care on the mother's part and usually do not emerge from the pupa until the following year. Although broadly genetically programmed, each generation must learn their food plants anew.

A few feet away, a miniature turpentine bush opens inky purple bells.

Its heavily glandular yellow-green leaves deposit a pungent oil on my fingers (it belongs to the same family as orange and grapefruit). It appears on the first inventory of plants along the Colorado River, compiled by Elzada Clover and Lois Jotter in 1938, not only the first botanists to survey the canyon but also the first women to run the whole length of the river in the canyon (in 1928 Bessie Hyde ran an undetermined length before she died or disappeared, still a matter of speculation).

A botanist specializing in cacti at the University of Michigan, Clover went collecting in southern Utah and stayed at a lodge in Mexican Hat fortuitously owned by Norman Nevills. In asking Nevills about places to collect, she discovered someone crazy about boats and about doing a big project with a major university. Nevills suggested that if they could find more paying passengers or some funding, they could run the San Juan River from Mexican Hat to the Colorado River, through Glen Canyon to Lees Ferry, and down the Grand Canyon.

Clover rounded up two passengers, her laboratory assistant, Lois Jotter, and a member of the Zoology Department at the University of Michigan. The university and an anonymous "collector from Colorado Springs" bankrolled the expedition. It was not an expedition made in paradise. A split developed between the younger and older members of the party, food was meager and dull, the small wooden "cataract" boats lacked sufficient space for plant presses or means to keep pressed specimens dry, and passengers wearied of Nevills's fuddy-duddy scouting of rapids. The zoologist and another passenger left the party at Lees Ferry. Despite snags, the trip continued to Lake Mead, picking up famous Grand Canyon photographer Emory Kolb on the way.

Clover, captivated by the canyon, stayed on in the Southwest until deep into the fall and returned again the next year. She well understood the dynamics of the river canyon, and her and Jotter's excellent text includes a discussion of plant communities well thought through and still valid; they noted, for example, that the flora along the river includes plants of the three major deserts through which it flows—the Great Basin, Sonoran, and Mojave. Their observations provide a historical comparison with the last, more complete, plant inventory of the Grand Canyon, made in 1975 by Barbara Phillips, Arthur Phillips, and Marilyn Ann Bernzott. This trio recorded slightly over eight hundred species in ninety-two families along the river corridor. Eighteen years later in a 1993 Glen Canyon Environmental Studies survey, Larry Stevens and Tina Ayres added over two dozen previously unrecorded species and listed almost a dozen of these as endemic. Among them are *Euphorbia aaron-rossii*, a small spurge named for Dr. Aaron Ross, who collected it near Navajo Bridge, and *Flaveria mcdougallii*, a shrubby sunflower rare in the canyon, named for a canyon botanist.

I idle up Kwagunt Creek, past the alignments of rocks laid by prehistoric Indians sometime between A.D. 1050 and 1200, crossing over sandy bars, sidling along Muav Limestone ledges in a futile attempt to maintain a straight path up a corkscrew canyon. I scuffle along the creek for a while, with damp gravels scrunching deliciously underfoot. Behind me the river pounds, all percussion and brass, fortissimo; here play piccolos and magic flutes and silver bells. A side-blotched lizard, darker than usual, patters under a buckwheat. Two head-high cottonwoods unwrinkle pale green leaves. On the snag of one tree a Say's phoebe perches, dives and swoops after insects, flies back to its same perch, calling a plaintive "tee-you."

Water surfaces and feathers through the dark sand. I hop back and forth across a rivulet never more than two inches deep, feeling like the Colossus of Rhodes straddling the harbor. Above me, a small terrace walled with vibrant Bright Angel Shale fills the inside of the meander, rising a dozen feet above the stream, chock full of Mormon tea and boulders. On it pose three deer, looking as if made of porcelain, glazed and fired, eternally motionless, eternally alert.

None of the mostly limestone cobbles littering the ground are worked smooth. Typical of the rocks in small side canyons, not enough water has flowed here to round off their edges. The jointing and surface cracking of the Muav shales and limestones cosset a series of salad-plate-sized gardens, all Lilliputians in a Brobdingnagian world: thumb-high grass sprigs, an agave rosette five inches in diameter, a three-inch cactus with one tiny magenta red fruit, a brief daisy, an aggressively pungent start of deerweed, a minute spurge with alizarin stems and leaves, and an asterisk of moss sending up pinhead capsules that proclaim "spring" even though ice floated in my cup this morning.

At a fork I stand between two rills. There is good flow in the creek today, and the wet margin shows it has been higher quite recently but nothing like the huge flows of yesteryear that tumbled in the boulders I must now edge around. In 1928 the first park naturalist, Glen Sturdevant, found seven beaver dams with slides and a beaver house up Kwagunt Creek. Sturdevant established *Grand Canyon Nature Notes* in 1926, "a series of bulletins to be issued from time to time for the information of those interested in the natural history, scenic grandeur, and scientific features of Grand Canyon National Park." He wrote with an earnest, innocent humor and an obvious joy in learning and teaching about the canyon, delighting the many park visitors who took his nature walks. In

February 1929 he drowned when his light boat capsized in Horn Creek Rapid at Mile 90.1.

Ahead, the cliffs open out to a wedge of North Rim, some seven miles away as the crow flies. Behind me, the orderly cliffs of the South Rim rise only half a mile from the river. Because of the southward tilt of the sedimentary strata, drainage from the North Rim flows into the canyon, and that of the South Rim, away. Hence the south wall sits closer to the river while the north wall has been cut farther back.

In contrast to those orderly walls, where I stand is a mishmash of rock and slope, outcroppings distorted and twisted, shuffled, disturbed, jumbled, boiled and simmered, and thrown out to cool: the Butte Fault, so named because it trends alongside several buttes. A fault is the surface along which one block of rock moves relative to surrounding rock. When rock breaks but the two sides of the break remain stationary, it is termed a joint. When there is movement on either side of the break, in any direction or any distance, it becomes a fault. "Kindly earthquakes," as John Muir would have it, occasionally jolt the canyon, giving notice that some of these fault systems are still active. The Butte Fault is a normal fault that dropped seventeen hundred feet on the downstream (west) side around 825 million years ago and was reactivated in the opposite direction some 60 million years ago during Laramide times (when the Rocky Mountains formed), raising the eastern side and leaving a present displacement of around eleven hundred feet.

The Butte Fault forms the eastern boundary of the East Kaibab Monocline, one of the gently sloping humps superimposed on the Colorado Plateau, a huge land mass of 130,000 square miles that dominates a large part of Utah, Colorado, New Mexico, and Arizona, and through which the river cuts. North-trending fault systems—Butte, Bright Angel, Toroweap, Hurricane, and Grand Wash—stripe this plateau fifteen to twenty miles apart and separate the plateau's principle blocks, accompanied by clusters of lesser faults. The Grand Wash Fault, farthest west, terminates the Grand Canyon at the entrance to Lake Mead at Mile 278. The Butte Fault parallels the river, then crosses it just below Tanner Creek at Mile 68.6. In cutting down, the river reveals these hitches and jerks, these offsets and nudges, these unmistakable earthly glitches. As Clarence Dutton, one of the first geologists to study the Grand Canyon, wrote with appreciation in 1882, "In the Plateau Country Nature has, in some respects, been more communicative than in other regions, and has answered many questions far more fully and graciously."

The ravaged rock here looks scraped and beaten by a Herculean sculptor who hurled formations against the wall in a thundering rage. Sheets of rock on edge thrust out of the slope, listing like knocked-over gravestones. Black volcanic rock, heaved up from below, twists like taffy and a slab of Muav Limestone curves like bent cardboard. One side of the wall goes up and beyond a ridge of shattered rock, the other side goes down. An apron of fine cindery talus at a steep angle of repose makes the whole expanse look as if some gigantic mining machine had scooped up a basketful of world and let it fall where it may.

The sun shatters over the edge of the ridge and its sudden warmth overwhelms me. The sandstone boulder on which I perch to take notes sparkles when its small facets of quartz catch the sun. I slip off my pack and feel the heat penetrate my backbone. Too many frigid mornings at the observation post must have congealed my marrow. Washed in the full-spectrum white light, my pineal gland rejoiceth.

On the way back to camp, before I turn upstream, I settle on a boulder close by the river, intending to begin a drawing, unconsciously acknowledging all the trade-offs involved, accepting that, in the end, all that can be done is an impression of imperfect knowledge, the record of incomplete data, filtered through a prejudiced eye and a disciplined hand. And that may be what this river canyon is anyway, for each of us: a series of melodic impressions strung together with a continuo of river beneath, a fugue that continuously changes key, and all that any of us ever know of it is the coda that our own psyches choose.

I open my sketchpad to a clean sheet and settle down to drawing, lost in concentration. Suddenly a massive *kavoom-oom*-oom-*oom*-ommmm!!!* blasts off across the river, an unwieldy penetrating cannonade whose edges blur and rumble, accompanied by an immense reverberating thunk I feel right through my seat. Totally astounded, I look up to see a cliff face downriver fuming with a cloud of tan dust. I drop everything and race down the beach while dust still blurs the air. It smokes across a slightly paler patch of cliff face and rises behind a couple of huge slabs balancing on a few yards of slope between cliff and river. But I cannot differentiate between what just fell and what has lain there for centuries. The air still vibrates like a bass drum before it is damped. I feel like a witness without a crime: a gunshot heard, a murder committed, but no corpse. I see the circumstantial evidence hanging in the air, but standing here with only my own astonished senses to rely upon, I missed the deed.

Small rockfalls, most frequent during the winter rainy season, are fairly common. They usually release along a joint system, the network of natural fractures that develop when a coherent body of rock, like a cliff, is freed from pressure. Because the weakening process has gone on over a long period, these rocks may give way at any time, needing just a degree more heat or a crystal more ice to trigger them. As a consequence blocks as big as refrigerators or garbage trucks or garages litter these slopes. Many rotated backward and snuggled solidly into the slope; sand filtered between them, plants grew around and on them. Still, many look as if they hang by a thread and will, at any moment, tumble into the river. Most don't, because they rest on talus pedestals solidified by travertine.

The layer cake of alternating hard and soft rock produces the steplike profile of the canyon. Sandstones and limestones are strongly cemented while shales, lacking that cohesion, break away easily. As the friable rock crumbles, it removes support from the strata above, and slabs sheer off in massive chunks that thunder and pummel the ground when they fall. Two processes, rockfalls and downcutting, create this splendid river-scape. Much of the widening of the gorge to its average 200–250 feet has come about by rockfalls of various sorts—avalanches, talus slides, landslides. Rather than a few instances of massive faces falling away all at once, broadening seems to be a series of small-scale events such as the one I almost witnessed, knapping the walls bit by bit, nibbling away at the eons, an average of one inch per two thousand years. The other force of canyon widening is downcutting, the work of the river. Using its silts like a sandpaper slurry to grind down its bed, the river is incessant and effective, albeit slow.

When I get back to camp, misled by the relative warmth of afternoon, I take what will have to pass for a bath. Even in the sunshine there is only so much frigidity a body can withstand. Not only do I not know where my feet are in the roiled water close to shore, but I don't know even *if* they are, numbed by water my thermometer registers as 48°F. I stand ankle deep near a broad stone big enough to hold soap without having it slide off into the river, and I wash a square inch at a time, drying and slathering on thick lotion as I go.

My fingers are raw and cracked open, miserably sore. Painters have always used hands as the purveyors of inner meaning: the portent of Giotto's annunciate angel's hands; the aristocratic, imperious elegance of Velásquez's duke with his hands resting on his sword; the piety of Dürer's praying hands. I look at mine and see the raw misery Van Gogh painted into a peasant's hands, symbols of wintertime on the river.

While helping at dinner I discover the perfect job available tomorrow: gauge watch, sitting a quarter-mile upriver from camp to read the U.S. Geological Survey gauge every fifteen minutes, ideal for me as I covet the solitude and, typical housewife and mother, am already practiced in a life predicated on interruption. The gauge, a white rod calibrated in tenths of meters, is mounted against a rock across the river and continuously registers temperature, chemical composition, pH, salinity, conductivity, and orthophosphate content. The horizontal vector is so variable that the vertical rise and fall cannot be assessed without a gauge; the frequent readings give a picture of the ramping rate, the speed at which the river rises and falls.

The next afternoon when I arrive, I find that the river shore here is not noticeably more attractive than the shore of a drawdown reservoir. The river edge is a fluctuating zone, submerged and bared on a quotidian basis from dam releases, leaving a band of treacherously slick, ripple-marked silt. Horsetails, usually a thick luxuriant dark green fringe along the river, sustain bleached and browned shafts, with joints askew, slovenly and disheveled. Silt webs the soft squirrel-tail-like heads of rabbitfoot grass, still damp from recent inundation. Mud slathers every rock. Cobbles are rough, broken, fist-sized lumps except for pebbles of Hermit Shale reduced to the size and color of kidney beans. A little amphipod stranded on a dry rock pulses feebly while it desiccates in the sun. I scoop it back into the river, where it slithers into the darkness between two rocks. This dank transition band is a tidal zone without the cleansing of the tides.

Waves pulse onto the shore, tug at the sand, quicken and fall back, furl and flutter, curl and billow—little slippery tan waves that keep the fine shore silt in suspension as they ruffle between rocks like crimped chiffon. They spread out in lobes and crescents and make quick, liquid smackings, so delicate that they are difficult to hear over the gossip of the main current. They leave mysterious swash lines like lace curtains on the beach, lobes and swags of silt two grains high, signatures of their brief existence. Every once in a while a small plash accompanies a chunk of bank that yields to undermining, a microcosm of what has happened to many sandbar beaches since the dam.

Beach erosion occurs most frequently from seepage. As the river rises, so does the water table in a sandbar. The water remains stored there until the river goes down, at which time it begins to seep back into the river. If the ramping rate is too fast and the river goes down faster than water can drain out, the face of the bank gives way, and large chunks of sand slump into the river. Many sandbars good for camping have lost immense amounts of sand, often in a few minutes, sand that is generally not replaced because the dam now holds back sediments.

Only a foot out from shore the main current spins purposefully downstream, punctuated with tiny quarter-sized whirlpools all spinning clockwise. Farther out, the water runs molasses taffy, glossy and smooth. Reflections quiver on the shadowed river, emphasizing the swift, scintillating sheen of its flowing. Upstream pale gold sparkles on dark green like a sheet of gold mail. Downstream the surface looks like hammered copper. But it is the little waves that draw my eye back to shore, the constant susurration, the obbligato to the river's continuum, the delicious swishy taffeta sound, the quiet ever-changing repetitions of sibilant molecules softly shifting succulent sand and sending it downstream.

As I prepare to leave I stand, as I so often do, watching the river go by, thinking no deep thoughts, just watching. The river. The endless, shifting fascination of the water surface is as hypnotic as watching flames in a fire. Sometimes the surface is glass-smooth, then suddenly it burbles with big swirly boils that pick up lines of moving light. A tributary somewhere upstream flushed in some silt yesterday, and the river color encompasses all the hues of all the walls in their proper proportions—beige sandstones, ruddy brick and olive-colored shales, gray and beige and lavender limestones—pigments left on a palette, mixed together to beget a lovely, warm putty color. The river. Go by.

Relieved of watch, I drift back to camp, unwilling to give up this peaceful, solitary afternoon. Walking my reluctance, I unconsciously deviate from the straight route back and muddle into a grove of mesquite trees at the old high-water line, as gnarled and twisted as an Arthur Rackham drawing come to life. Predam spring floods that habitually ran around 90,000 cfs cleaned off the river banks here to around twenty feet above present river level, high enough for mesquite roots to escape being torn out but low enough for them to tap deep moisture. Little reproduction takes place in this zone now that yearly inundations are gone, and sprouting occurs nearer the river, where seedlings must compete with grabby exotic invaders like Bermuda grass and tamarisk.

The mesquites remind me of trees in an old olive grove in Greece, arthritic survivors of better times, left to live out their lives without pruning or care, frazzled wild men of the river, chanting gibberish at night into a restless wind, shouting imprecations at the whippersnapper bats, muttering in their twigs, rheumy-eyed, cantankerous, lonely, abandoned.

One old patriarch's canopy stretches at least twenty feet, branches and twigs fretting an intricate, complex silhouette. Its roots grow out of and over and through each other, embracing boulders, anchoring into the hillside, claiming a corner of the world for their own. Its bark is as shaggy as an inky cap mushroom, and the new limbs are more quirk than curve, more angle than arc, cells dividing just so, buds swelling just so, leaves unfolding just so, decade after decade, just so. Its multiple interlocking branches, knees and elbows and bony shoulders, bend and beckon and bless.

In one of the convolutions of its roots nestle three derelict planks, once neatly incised with letters, now weathered the same color as the tree: the old boundary sign between national park and national monument, rendered obsolete when the lower segment of the river also became park. Stuffed between a fragment of sign and a curve of trunk is a fine wood rat nest, richly roofed and nicely situated. Wood rat nests, because they are solidified with crystallized urine, last for hundreds, often thousands of years and, because they are organic, can be radiocarbon dated, giving a reliable picture of local vegetation of times past, since wood rats generally foraged within a hundred yards of their nests.

A canyon wren carols, the only descending notes I know that sound so heartening and cheerful. A canyon wren's song is one that once heard, is never forgotten: clear, lucid, poignant, and distinctive. It's what I request for my requiem—no cantatas, no fugues, just a canyon wren doing what it's doing right now, what it was genetically programmed to do, without sentience or aesthetic, but producing a song that is joyful, sprightly, and melodic, a threnody as appropriate as a river flowing downstream.

Crossing Nankoweap Creek I muse that technically this has not been a "wilderness experience." Other people are here. In exchange for solitude, we work with each other under easy conditions, have plenty of water and food, and focus on the research project at hand. It is a momentary utopia where everyone cooperates, has a chance to contribute, perhaps held together by the knowledge that it won't last forever.

I, for one, shall miss being here. When I first came the sound of the winter river and the rockfalls kept me awake and I dreamed odd dreams. Now they are a part of my sleeping and if I dream, I do not remember. I shall miss the cold, the miserable climb to the observation post at 5:30 in the morning, the eagles and crazy ravens. I shall miss the doing, the helping, the sound of peanut butter lids being unscrewed, the crinkling of bread wrappers, the fish counting and gauge watching, the familiar cliffs across the river that have become a wall of my mind. I shall miss the total satisfaction of each day.

A toast to this day: there may be better days (and many a lot worse) but to *this* one, with its joys and irritations, its sightings of eagles, its songs of canyon wrens, its washing of dishes and exchanges of information, its gossips about the day's sightings, its bulging half moon, its notations of spring in milkvetch and turpentine bush.

When I get back to camp, the supply raft that will take us out has arrived. The vernal equinox approaches, when day and night weigh even, the equilibrium that lasts but a split second before the earth tumbles into the next season. In the darkness I listen to the river hurtle downstream toward spring.

Spring

———

near Shinumo Creek

4

―――――

Within twenty miles of the river the walls of [Kanab] cañon gradually close in, until, in many places, they reach within fifty feet of each other. They also gain altitude, until, at the junction of the Colorado, they tower three thousand feet in air. The sun is seen only three hours during the day. Words are inadequate to describe the sensations of one entering the tomb-like vastness. The upper strata of the cliffs is composed of tinted sandstone, beautifully veined with purple. A few miles farther this changes to limestone, of a bluish gray, filled with slate-flint and chalcedony.

> E. O. Beaman, 1874, *The Cañon of the Colorado, and the Moqui Pueblos: A Wild Boat-ride through the Cañon and Rapids, a Visit to the Seven Cities of the Desert, Glimpses of Mormon Life*

Springtime Bloom
and Buzzing Bees

Springtime ties together disparate parts of the canyon, brings them similarities of beginnings and unfoldings that they do not have the rest of the year. Spring along the river is a potpourri of hatchings and bloomings, surprise packages ribboned by a flowing river. Nearly every sandbar or side canyon hosts its own ruffle and flourish of spectacular spring bloom: giant helleborine orchids in dazzling profusion at Matkatamiba, Mojave asters and purple sage perfuming the air in Stone Canyon, delicate pink mariposa lilies nodding above Crystal Rapid, saturated blue larkspur along Tapeats Creek, Whipple yucca at Granite Park with a stalk like a giant asparagus that bends under its own richness. And at Saddle Canyon, just about everything.

In Saddle Canyon at Mile 47.1, the spirits of springtime tie origami buds to empty branches, unfold them into flaring flowers and gild their stamens with pollen, pulse leaf veins with streaming green sap, breathe verdure into every silken stalk and blade, nudge the bee larvae and the spiderlings awake, shake out a dust mop of midges to quiver in the air, polish the canyon walls, and orchestrate odes to joy.

In this cloistered canyon, nighttime's soothing drafts twine downslope, and daytime's hot upslope winds are damped by the high walls that give shade most of the day. Hushed and verdant, the deeper greener greens of barberry and box elder and maidenhair fern mark the foliage, brightened by the feathery leaflets of mesquite and the round pale green leaves of redbud. A merry flickering light filters through ovals and oblongs of green, constantly shifting. Thousands of leaves tatter the sunshine into dancing circles and cast quadrilles of moving light on the ground beneath. Knee-high grasses hang exposed stamens like tiny golden clappers from jade bells, waiting for a breeze to swirl incredible quantities of pollen into the air. A tiger moth with crisply patterned black and white wings hangs on a pink rockcress, taller than in the desert outside, rich with four-petaled lavender pink flowers and fruits of long, thin, dangling pods.

Sunlight backlights and intensifies the bright lavender blossoms of redbud trees so that the flowers glow like amethysts displayed against the jeweler's dark gray velvet walls. A huge carpenter bee shuttles between blossoms, flying swiftly to force cooling air over its flattened head. It also avoids overheating from flying by shunting heat from its thorax, where its flight muscles are, into its large abdomen. Now that the days are warming, it flies at cooler times of the day. Since its tongue is not long enough to reach the nectar in the redbud flowers, it often copes by nipping a hole in the blossom and siphoning out the nectar, bypassing its pollination duties. The carpenter bees, along with smaller honeybee-sized and tiny iridescent ones, endow the whole tree with an aura of celebratory buzzing, a springtime delirium of transferring pollen on furred bodies and basketed legs and bristled heads.

We tend to think of insects, with their advantage of mobility, as capable of controlling plants, but in truth plants clearly manipulate their pollinators, for to survive both plants and pollinators must profit from the relationship. A plant needs to set the largest number of viable seeds possible, which requires efficient pollination. Pollinators, in their turn, need to be "cost-effective," to harvest as much energy as possible after subtracting the cost of flight and metabolism, so they frequent only those plants that reward them sufficiently. Plants program their pollinators by producing nectar at different hours of the day, at different locations on the plant, and at different stages of flowering, and bees adjust their behavior to mesh with the nectar's availability. In a springtime bloom like this one, bees tap every available bloom, and myriads of little black flower beetles wriggle ecstatically among pollen-powdered stamens.

Beneath the redbud, buttercup petals shine like butter and a bee fly, loud and buzzy and fast, zips between open-faced flowers, catching a meal on the wing, so small it needs no heat regulation in flight. Bee flies are the teddy bears of the insect world, the sun lovers, round furry little creatures that maneuver close to the ground. So named for their fuzzy bodies, they give themselves away as flies by spreading open their single pair of wings when they alight and following a quick, direct, no-nonsense flight pattern. A bee fly's formidable stylet serves only for supping nectar from flowers, not for stinging. When laying eggs, bee flies hover over the ground, scouting for a place to drop an egg near the burrow of a solitary bee. The egg hatches into an active larva that vigorously ferrets out the bee's nest. Once there it molts into a sluggish vampire, snacking off morsels of live larva, feeding at such a slow rate that its prey remains alive as long as possible, thus avoiding the complications of putrefaction. When the bee larva is consumed, the bee fly larva pupates, cuts open its pupa with scissorlike mandibles, and flits off to the sun-polished buttercups.

Horsetail stalks as big as my little finger rustle like taffeta. On a boulder, lichens shine with moisture and push out fruiting bodies, black and gold and chocolate brown. On the bank, liverworts imbricate the soil in scalloped fronds as slippery as wet leather. Golden brown capsules stalk plump emerald green mosses. On top of a rock, a tree frog tucks in its feet and smiles its secretive, smug smile, a handsome prince awaiting a gullible princess.

A foot-wide stream twinkles through the canyon's green thatch in tiny tinseled brightness. Mushrooms spring up in damp, grassy places beside it; small spindly ones with chocolate-colored caps sift spores with thick walls that protect them from desiccation. "Desert mushroom" is not an oxymoron. Some even turn up as dried crusts in the sand at river edge, tough and scaly, many of them species of puffballs, sometimes growing in a damp nook. They seldom have common names but bear fragrant, fungal genus names like *Schizostoma, Phellorina, Podaxis,* and *Tulostoma*, which sound as if they might be the names of the fairy courtiers in *A Midsummer Night's Dream*.

Instead of the one or two narrow layers of plants in the hard-bitten desert vegetation, in Saddle Canyon there are many layers, ranging from mosses and liverworts no larger than a fraction of an inch, all the way up to trees. Plants crowd together, their long-petioled, thin leaves pivoting quietly in any breath of air. Without special adaptations of leaves and stems to cope with or reduce water loss, these riparian plants must have abundant water when growing season arrives. Seeps, springs, side streams, and the river itself irrigate this limited but very important percentage of the canyon.

The diversity of plants and the biological richness of these riparian areas far outweigh their limited acreage in habitats provided for a variety of insects and mammals. Throughout the Southwest the array of plant species is remarkably similar in similar situations—usually some combination of crimson monkey flowers, maidenhair ferns, golden columbines, and giant helleborine orchids. Larger springs like Saddle Canyon support bigger trees such as cottonwood and birchleaf buckthorn.

But even paradise has its nemeses. White dots speckle the box elder leaves, and their edges curl and dry. Many leaves are chewed and mined in patches, leaving little casement windows near the veins. One curled leaf houses a small green caterpillar growing fat on plant cells. Multitudes of tiny whiteflies, chalky from their covering of waxy powder, dust the undersides of canyon grape leaves and waft off them in clouds. In their midst a small, rotund tan spider relishes whitefly pâté.

Galls plague the leaves of a hackberry, little protrusions and excrescences, bumps and turrets. Most every hackberry along the river is infested with blister, nipple, and bud galls, all caused by species of psyllids, the nymphs of tiny insects around whom plant tissue grows in a characteristic shape. Psyllid mating and egg laying coincide with the unfurling of the new springtime leaves. Eggs hatch in seven to ten days, and the feeding nymph instigates the formation of the gall. They summer inside the gall's protection and emerge as adults in the fall, less than an eighth-inch long, resembling tiny cicadas endowed with long back legs for jumping. They winter in cracks in the tree's bark, ready for the cycle to begin anew the next spring. The galls seem not to damage the trees severely, considering the plethora of them—I tally six dozen on one small leaf. Their population is controlled by chalcid wasps, which parasitize them, sometimes destroying half the crop, and by tiny weevils that gobble both larvae and nymphs.

At the upper end of Saddle Canyon water frizzles into a long narrow pool, and threads of cool water nudge at my ankles like small fish. In a sunlit spot spiders stretch silk threads from side to side a foot off the water surface, a glittering golden ceiling in which the innocents snag. At the far end of the pool a rock chute leads to a grotto with a waterfall that Respighi would have added to his tribute to fountains. The sound of water falling here has a special timbre, a consummate clarity. The plash of this waterfall, especially on a warm spring day, is the reason behind fountains, the aural manifestation of water's silvery enchantment. Water slithers thirty feet down the back wall and swirls clear and transparent over the floor, a delicious 54°F. The walls that frame the grotto rise twenty feet or more and almost meet at the top, seeming to filter light not only through the slotted opening but through the rock itself. Small reflections, like aqueous northern lights, flicker on the underneath of the overhangs, bright cross-hatchings of sideling light, all the elegant variations of what can be done with a limestone wall and an imaginative stream of water with enough time on its hands.

That evening down by the river, as I collate the day, dusk fades gently to dark; the air is considerate and clement, warm for April. Moonlight tats the edges of roiled clouds and sends a shaft to blanket my knees. A small, narrow beetle flies into my headlamp and I shoo it away, intent on writing. I find it on its back in a fold of my ground cloth, where it responds by doing a prodigious pole vault, a click beetle practicing its acrobatics. A tiny moth flutters onto my notebook, orange eyes gleaming. A soldier beetle bustles onto the page, a quarter-inch-long creature with short, wide-set antennae and a translucent shield that partially covers its black head. Its filmy wings extend beyond its body like a chiffon cape. A breeze flutters around my head and a cricket sings a roundelay. Tonight, for a cricket, life sounds seventy-eight degrees good. For me too.

At dawn, sun cracks the rim and changes everything.

The beach at Shinumo Wash at Mile 29.4 provides another sampler of the river canyon's springtime wares (there is also a Shinumo Creek downstream at Mile 108.5). Where Shinumo Wash enters the river at Mile 29.4, a boulder apron denuded of its sand forms a rough, rocky jetty. Algae cling to surfaces kept washed by the river's fast water, rowdy as it sluices through the rocks. Plump pads of wet dark green moss insinuate themselves into damp crannies. The eighth-inch sprigs pack together in a tight mat, black green where dry, emerald where damp, sprouting in even the tiniest cavities. They look the way evergreen forests do from ten thousand feet above—small dark trees clustered close, outliers pioneering into the empty meadows and casting their spiky shadows across the land. Minute midges bounce on and off the moss like water drops off a hot skillet. In contrast to the serenity of Saddle Canyon, springtime charges Shinumo beach with life on the run and on the wing, frenetic feedings and multiple matings, harried hatchings of frittery flies and skittery spiders, all programmed to get after it between the last cold snap and the first heavy heat.

Wolf spiders flicker across the rocks, swift day hunters on the prowl. This time of year females carry white silken sacs of eggs on their backs so at times all that's visible are white dots going every which way. A female piggybacks her young until they are strong enough to shift for themselves (the poor dear will carry other objects substituted by devious researchers). She also opens the cocoon for them since the spiderlings cannot do it themselves. Freed, they climb up on her back where they remain until their first molt, when they go sprinting off on their own. Such wonderful caregivers—how can anyone not like spiders?

Adults look long and narrow, not only because of their slender bodies but also because their long legs, straight forward and straight aft, emphasize the elongation. That characteristic shape, plus their quick dashes, easily identify them, as do their eight eyes set in two straight rows, four large eyes above, four smaller ones below. Many wolf spiders have a brush of hairs under each leg's last segment, which permits traction on slippery surfaces and enables them to skitter over the slick river-edge rocks. Not web builders, wolf spiders form almost 90 percent of spider species in the desert and are everywhere along the river.

Big plants of datura snuggle against the cliff wall that backs the beach. There they are protected and garner extra water off the cliff face when it rains. Nearly every leaf is blotched with irregular bleached spots and cut with a lacework of holes. A member of the potato family, the whole plant datura is toxic. Despite that, the tomato hornworm caterpillar dotes on it. After the hornworm metamorphoses, it emerges as a large, easily identifiable gray-winged moth with a four-inch wingspan and orange-yellow spots along its abdomen. Older caterpillars hang hidden underneath the large leaves, holding onto the petioles with their back claspers and crawling outward with their front legs, thus bowing the leaf over themselves; under its protection they chew backward toward the petiole, consuming the whole leaf. Their smaller siblings, not strong enough to manage this balancing act, eat holes instead, avoiding the leaf veins with their toxic sap. Insects that feed on datura handle the toxins in various ways, something that humans have been unable to do, as hungry Revolutionary soldiers discovered when they ate fresh datura leaves as pot greens and got thrown in jail for disorderly conduct in Jamestown, Virginia, endowing datura with its other name, jimsonweed.

Although the smoke of the plant has bronchio-dilating properties that relieve asthma, it can also be fatal because the concentrations of alkaloids are so unpredictable. Younger plants contain mostly scopolamine, but older plants contain hyoscyamine, which is a nerve toxin— rub an eye after handling datura and it may affect your vision for a day or so. Ingesting any part of datura causes a series of symptoms that include increased blood pressure and body heat, failing muscle coordination, confusion, and hallucination. A partaker, if quickly treated, usually recovers. In worst cases, datura is fatal. Eerily visible in the dark, it glows like some mysterious *fleur du mal*, deceptively virginal, with moon-goddess flowers serviced at night by sphinx moths, whose long proboscises reach the nectar lodged deep in the flower's throat.

Beneath the datura shelters a small waterleaf with deep lavender flowers and oak-shaped leaves furred with white glandular hairs, Ives phacelia, named for Lieutenant Joseph Christmas Ives. In 1858 Ives steamed *up* the Colorado River as far as Diamond Creek and wrote the immortal observation: "Ours has been the first, and will doubtless be the last party of whites to visit this profitless locality. It seems intended by nature that the Colorado River, along the greater portion of its lonely and majestic way, shall be forever unvisited and undisturbed." As John Van Dyke remarked, Ives didn't take into account the American tourist.

59
—
*Spring-
time
Bloom
and
Buzzing
Bees*

A whirligig swarm of midges spins above my head, too diaphanous to make a shadow. They likely emerged from their pupae early this morning, and then those that weren't breakfast for something bigger lifted off into this midge version of a single's bar, a dangling swarm of lavishly feather-antennaed males through which females cruise and mate. Although they more often appear on warm summer evenings, it may not yet be warm enough late in the day so they swarm earlier, to take advantage of the higher temperatures and the convection currents rising from heating ground to give them some lift. They are such small motes of existence that it takes more than half a million to weigh an ounce, yet they are among the tiny, irreplaceable necessities of a natural world that could not run without them.

The fleeting, flickering shadows of violet-green swallows crosshatch the walls. The swallows themselves scythe the sky, this year's fledgling feeding on these most momentary midges, which wouldn't have lived the day through anyway. Making whirlpools in the air, the swallows never seem to rest, chittering as they go. Their swirling flight is like some wild trapeze act without net or trapeze. Their flashing white tail spots make them look like flying dominoes. Sometimes they skim low over the water, ticking it with their beaks. Sometimes they hang unbelievably still for a breathtaking instant. As they bullet into their nests in holes in the Redwall, they look as if they will smash their heads against the stone, but at the very last minute they tuck in their wings and disappear into impossibly small openings like magic.

Spring is really here when white-throated swifts fast-flutter, hang, sideslip, swoop, stall and roll, sailing like paper airplanes while they scoop up flies and midges. Swifts are parasitized by tiny wingless flies whose emergence from the larval state coincides with the bird's return in the spring. They flock into the canyon for the summer and spend all their time in the air, because their legs are too weak for lengthy perching or walking. Although there have been no population counts made in recent years, as their food base of minute insects that swarm above the river may have enlarged, so too the number of swifts and swallows may have increased. But cliff swallows are gone from the river corridor: the absence of mud along the shore since the dam was built has left them without material for nest construction. Only abandoned nests plaster the walls, baseball-sized globes set under overhangs above the river, their openings like hundreds of eyes, as if the cliffs were watching.

Down the beach a narrow windrow of debris scallops the sand a few feet back from present water's edge. Sundry small flies explore the flotsam of the canyon while several wasps putter in the debris and a ponderous carpenter bee drones overhead. In the windrow lie juniper seeds the size of small peas, bleached to tan; an exquisite violet-green swallow feather, white tipped, with iridescent green on one side and olive gray on the other; a raft of white insect eggs; bristly snippets of tamarisk; tumbleweed twigs; and weathered white millipede segments.

Linked together, millipede segments usually carry two pairs of legs each. Newly hatched millipedes have but three pairs altogether, adding more, up to thirty-some, with each molt. Since the backstroke of the legs (in sand) takes much longer than the forward thrust (against air), such a gait requires the presence of many legs, and many legs need numerous body segments for attachment. Although millipedes generally live in moist organic soils, some, like this desert millipede common in the canyon, *Orthoporus ornatus*, are adapted to arid regions and have been for millennia, as fossil millipede tracks in the Coconino Sandstone document. Today they survive by remaining underground for eight or nine months of the year.

Tarrying along the windrow, I reflect that while these bits and pieces of leftover life at my feet are found along beaches almost everywhere just for the scuffling, here they are common folk in an uncommon place and take on the grandeur of a nowhere-else combination of sheer vertical and notched horizontal and a violet-green swallow's feather woven into a magnificent river's purling.

Only in springtime can one venture up certain small side canyons with any comfort, for when summer comes these narrow passageways develop into reflector ovens. One of these is 128 Mile Canyon in the Middle Granite Gorge, which cuts through a monadnock, an island of harder rock remaining above the surrounding countryside before being covered with sediments. The gorge is a short three miles long, the width of the monadnock.

The little canyon resembles a Japanese garden embroidered with a narrow thread of water. The walls are shiny black schist, veined with white lines or brown bands, brush strokes of orange, thumbprints of white, wispy traces of gray. Boulders judiciously rounded and exquisitely placed cause the water to whisper and gossip over a foot-high waterfall. A small change of foam, pennies and dimes of bubbles cluster in whirlpools and elongate into scarves before the current spins them out of sight. Sound transforms to moving light, concentric circles echo off a wall like musical chimes, a gentle little stream playing with its reflections.

In the rivulet, tiny stone fly larvae with two long cerci, their wing pads already developed, wait out hatch time, and caddis fly larvae drag cases made of minute pebbles across the floor. Adult caddis flies are dun-colored, like many moths, but caddis fly wings are haired, not scaled as moth wings are, and at rest they hold their wings tentlike over their bodies. They have short lives as adults, probably thirty days or less, these unremarkable creatures who could rob a bank without anyone remembering their faces.

The adults may be ordinary, but ah, the lovely little cases the larvae fashion! They are something to search out in a springtime stream, some with tiny stones neatly laid and cemented into exquisite little tubes, others with slightly larger cases with tufts of plant debris on top, which their occupants drag briskly across the floor, crocheting quirky lines in the bottom silt as they feed. Others cement their cases to a rock and wait for food to waft to them.

Case construction is distinctive to genus and begins shortly after hatching. The larva picks up its preferred material with its front legs—bits of leaves, pieces of twigs, sand grains or tiny stones, even minute snail shells. Large glands produce a sticky substance that glues the chosen particles to each other, or the larva may spin silk to bind them together. As the larva grows, it simply adds more pieces to the front end of its case. Most case-dwelling larvae have "spacing humps" on the first abdominal segment, to keep the body away from the walls of its case so that freshly oxygenated water can flow over as much of the body surface as possible.

This modest, caddis fly–laden, gently trickling stream has ladled out a million tons of rock and portioned it into the river grain by grain. It wedged a rosy pebble into a black slot, left pink sand in a hollow shaped like a map of Italy, wrote of other worlds, other times, and the persistence of chance.

Powell gave Kanab Creek at Mile 143.6, one of the longest tributaries to the Colorado River, the Paiute name for willow. Kanab Creek's Muav Limestone walls create a narrow, pale-layered, steep-walled canyon less than a third of a mile wide, enclosed by walls more than sixteen hundred

61
—

Spring-
time
Bloom
and
Buzzing
Bees

feet high. Ellsworth Kolb, who rowed and took the first movies of the river with his brother in 1911, called it a "narrow, gloomy gorge." The river now runs at the base of the Muav Limestone and just begins to eat into the underlying layers of Bright Angel Shale. As the river exposes the shales, the weaker layers will ultimately fail, removing support from the limestone above. Just upstream sections of Bright Angel Shale between Deer Creek and Fishtail Canyons (between Mile 136.2 and 139) did just that, and massive landslides slid into the river on the right, such as will also happen here in time.

Powell decided to end his second trip down the Grand Canyon at Kanab Creek on September 7, 1871. His announcement was a surprise to his men. He gave as his reasons the dangerously low water at Separation Rapid and reports that Shivwits Indians were ready to attack. Jack Hillers, the trip photographer, recorded, "Everybody felt like praising God," while the young romantic Frederick Dellenbaugh wrote with characteristic nostalgia, "We unpacked the good old boats rather reluctantly. They had come to possess a personality as such inanimate objects will, having been our faithful companions and our reliance for many a hundred difficult miles, and it seemed like a desertion to abandon them so carelessly to destruction. We ought to have had a funeral pyre." When Dellenbaugh came back three years later, all that was left was a hatch and the major's chair.

The water of Kanab Creek is nicely warm, unlike the toe-numbing river, and in the springtime it is as pleasant to walk in the water as beside it. A reddish-tan fuzz coats the stones in the creek, calcium deposits that armor the bottom cobbles and cement them together, and silt fumes up at every footstep. The shallow stream heats quickly so the photosynthetic potential is high and, rarely disturbed by flooding, it provides a warm nursery for juvenile fish.

I misstep in a depression between cobbles and it explodes with quicksilver flashes. When underwater life returns to normal, I make out a dozen three-inch speckled dace, tan like the bottom, flecked with dark spots, and marked with their characteristic black mask. They school, all facing upstream, in a little scooped-out grotto upstream from a boulder, where the bottom gravel is finer. Some tug and pull algae off the bottom cobbles, their bodies jerking with the effort.

Since closure of the dam, speckled dace have adapted to the less turbid waters of the Colorado River and now swim throughout, although they cannot reproduce in the cold mainstream water and depend upon warmer tributaries like Kanab Creek for egg laying and larval development. Speckled dace live in every kind of running water habitat, from desert springs to mountain streams, from southern Arizona to Canada, the most wide-ranging freshwater fish west of the Rocky Mountains. In the Grand Canyon young fish appear in late May and June and remain with the adults in the lower parts of Kanab Creek until they filter back into the main river for the winter.

63
—

Spring-
time
Bloom
and
Buzzing
Bees

A dead speckled dace bumps gently against a rock. Attached to its belly is a parasitic anchor worm, *Lernaea cyprinacea*, introduced from the Mississippi River system. It is not a worm but a copepod, one of a group of small invertebrates that includes many parasites. Its head has space-age star-shaped jaws with which it hooks into its host's tissue. From each side dangles an egg sack from which nauplii, copepods in their immature stage, release and seek out other hosts. (Many copepods have a parasitic adult stage and a free-living planktonic larval stage whose first function is dispersal, a not uncommon arrangement among the Crustacea.) Although not necessarily fatal, an anchor worm is at best an added stress on fish. They are exotic to this area, and still thrive best in fish hatcheries and ponds. They probably entered the Colorado River system in the late 1800s or early 1900s. Now they are increasing in the tributaries and should a strain resistant to cold water develop, they could enter the river and become a threat to endangered native fish.

Four dark ovals outlined in light swirl upstream, shadows on the bottom tracking the dimples made by the feet of a big water strider. As it sculls, a strider holds its two front legs up like a begging dog, hence only four legs touch the elastic membrane of the water surface. With some impunity from attack themselves because of unpleasant scent-gland secretions, they are busy predators on a wide variety of prey, including their own ilk. They overwinter as adults in protected crannies near the creek's edge, and springtime has brought them out today en masse.

Attached to one of the cobbles where the dace swim is something I've never seen before: the net of a caddis fly, which lives in deeper water and spins a trumpet-shaped net out of a tough, sticky thread that hardens when it hits the water. The wafty cornucopia fastens to a boulder, oriented so that the current balloons it open. The larva, cloistered inside, nibbles edibles swept into it by the current.

Farther upstream a graceful apse of Muav Limestone rises high overhead, limned with thin bands of salmon beige, blue gray, tan, warm beige. Big slabs have tumbled into lecterns and benches, and their drip lines leave dotted strings of indentations in the sand. Narrow ledges of limestone shelve into the stream above a long quiet pool, fed at its upper end by tiny businesslike waterfalls, segueing into a channel that pours by a cobble bar, catching the sheen of pink sand and gray rock before it perks out of sight.

Suddenly five forms materialize out of the pool's murky water, foot-long, full-bodied gray fish: bluehead suckers. I glimpse bodies rounded above and flattened beneath, shaped to rest on the bottom when they rasp insect larvae and algae off rocks with broad disk-shaped mouths. They have thick skins with small embedded scales and tiny eyes, traits common to other native fish in the Colorado River system. They do a grand nose-to-tail circle once at my feet, unwind, and repeat with the precisely spaced fidelity of circus elephants, before they fade back into the murk.

Spawning runs of blueheads are familiar in Havasu, Kanab, and Shinumo Creeks in spring and early summer. Male blueheads appear here in February with tubercled heads, a sign of breeding readiness. From late April to June the somewhat larger females enter tributaries and scoop out depressions in a sandy bottom. Awaiting males respond to the movement and as many as ten may surround one female, compressing her between their bodies until all the sticky eggs are extruded and the water clouds with milt. The eggs hatch in about five days, and the fry grow rapidly until they reach sexual maturity at around ten inches.

I dawdle back to the river along the edge of the creek. Minute empty midge pupal cases speckle the stems of foot-high rushes at water's edge. The stiff rushes, both leaves and especially flowering stems, gave support for these tiny insects to cling, wiggle out of a confining case, leg by filament leg, to pump blood into wrinkled wings, harden an integument, and fly free. No softer-stemmed plant holds a case: how *do* these midges choose? how *do* they know?

A small triangle of color, a butterfly wing figured with black and white and burnt orange, floats slowly in the current, a mere bagatelle, a lovely scrap of what was. It eddies around a boulder and rotates out of sight.

below Separation Canyon

5

_____

Marble walls polished by the waves. Walls 2000–2200 ft. high. 3 portages before dinner. This afternoon I had a walk of a mile on a marble pavement, polished smooth in many places, in others embossed in a thousand fantastic patterns. Highly colored marble. Sun shining through cleft in the wall and the marble sending back the light in iridescence. At noon a cleft or cañon on left, quite narrow with a succession of pools one above another, going back and connected by a little stream of clear water . . . After dinner we found a spring gushing from an orifice in the marble, as silvery foam glad to see the light released from prison. A bank of brilliant verdure (ferns chiefly) on the talus below.

Many little springs this afternoon with patches of verdure below. A huge cañon ½ mile below spring. Vast number of caves and domed alcoves in this region. Walls about 2500 ft. high. At 3 p.m. just below spring the high water mark comes down to 10 or 12 ft., and the first mesquite seen. Camp in Mesquite Grove. No. 28.

John Wesley Powell, August 9, 1869, _Journal_

Anasazi Ways
and Stanton's Surveys

Where South Canyon enters the river at Mile 31.5 is the first good foot access from the North Rim after Lees Ferry. The river runs twenty-seven hundred feet below the rim here, a lot of room for a lot of cliffs and a lot of slopes, but along the river it's Redwall, Redwall, Redwall, often sheer to the river's edge on both sides. The calcite crystals of Redwall Limestone dissolve easily, leaving perforations and apertures, giant owl eyes, handholds, hyphens and dots in Morse code, oval windows framed with hieroglyphics, holes behind holes, small grottoes dripping with maidenhair ferns and cardinal flowers. Redwall Limestone is an evocative rock, full of theatrical architraves and friezes and pediments, half-stored in the wall like old stage sets.

About thirty feet above the beach at South Canyon a blocky ledge runs parallel to the river. Here dozens of prickly pears languish across the ground like rolls of greenish barbed wire. Prickly pear cacti often accompany prehistoric sites because they quickly colonize disturbed soil. This year's pads bear short, thick, curved, furtive leaves that will drop as soon as summer's dry heat hits.

The woolly tufts of cochineal bugs dot many of the pads. When I scrape off a tuft, a rich carmine red stains my fingertips. "Cochineal" means scarlet-colored, but only the female bug is red, the male, drab gray. A mature female lays a single egg under her body, which can hatch into a pinpoint red larva in as quickly as fifteen minutes. A female larva, as soon as she finds a place to settle permanently, begins producing a protective, white waxy covering, under which she metamorphoses to adulthood. Coccids belong to the same insect family as leafhoppers and cicadas, all plant-feeders with sucking mouthparts. Immobile as adults, their plugged-in siphoning eventually kills the cactus pad upon which they live.

Cochineal insects have been used as dye for textiles and body paint for thousands of years (cochineal was replaced by aniline dyes in the late 1800s). Spaniards found the Aztecs using the dye and took both plant and insect back to Spain. A wildly labor-intensive industry, it requires a full day of labor to produce only two ounces of dried cochineal and 70,000 insects to provide a pound of dye. Cochineal insects are an anomaly in this desert world with its difficult environment, which gives generalists a better survival chance than specialists. These particular coccids put their faith in and their feet on only prickly pear cacti, a case of biochemical coevolution: plants develop chemicals to deter insects, insects develop defenses to keep on feeding. At the moment, the coccids look to be one up.

Fifty feet or so wide, the terrace drops off sharply to the river. On this shelf the Anasazi built a typical Kayenta Anasazi site of one or two habitation rooms with a storage or food-processing room, occupied sometime between A.D. 950 and 1150. A small site like this may have housed a nuclear family, subsisting on its own, of probably twenty-five to fifty people. Nuclear families tended to use a large number of sites over a decade or more, with an average occupancy length of thirty-four years per site.

The Grand Canyon lies on the western edge of the Kayenta Anasazi homeland. The Kayenta Anasazi occupied some ten thousand square miles, including the major portion of the Colorado Plateau across northern Arizona and southern Utah and into a corner of southeastern Nevada. Despite the size of this theatrically divided landscape—riven by canyons and rivers, and stacked with mesas—the Kayenta Anasazi remained remarkably consistent in the way they laid walls and made stone tools and painted bold black designs on a white slip to decorate their pottery. The widespread and similar pottery styles tell of constant communication through a healthy trade system. This keeping-in-touch contributed to the egalitarian nature of the Anasazi world, in which there was little personal property for a people always on the move. By the standards of those who have admired places like Mesa Verde and Chaco Canyon, this site is meager—while the simple architecture along the Colorado River was being built, Chaco Canyon already had the glorious Pueblo Bonito.

Judging from the stone tools left behind, toolmakers spent little time or energy on fashioning finished implements. Instead, they expeditiously took advantage of what was available, such as the chunky chert in plentiful supply in the Redwall. Visible in the limestone as glossy nodules and narrow lenses, chert chunks range from the size of an egg to that of a hotdog bun. Chert forms when hard and glassy silicates replace the carbonates on the seafloor, often in an area where fresh- and seawater intermingle, and has the same chemical composition as quartz. Because of its hardness and characteristic crisp conchoidal fracturing, chert was preferred for pressure flaking to make points and cutters. Often tools made along the river were used when only partially worked, then tossed away, the original "disposables." Few finely finished tools turn up in the inner canyon and those that do were likely made elsewhere.

Although this site has never been excavated, nothing here indicates permanent residence—no burials or ceremonial kivas, no signs of agriculture. More than 3,000 Anasazi sites exist within the Grand Canyon, and a recent survey found nearly 500 below the rim and along the river, perhaps 60 to 70 percent of them as yet unexplored. Sites within the canyon, except for the Palisades Creek–Unkar Delta area forty miles downstream, were not large settlement centers, or even villages, but the temporary living spaces of a few hunters and gatherers here on a sporadic basis, taking advantage of the seasonal availability of the canyon's plants and animals. This one would have been one of several residences occupied at different harvest times—when prickly pear fruit ripened, when ricegrass heads filled, when mallow and Mormon tea and the dozens of other plants the Anasazi utilized were at their best.

For early hunter-gatherers, the Southwest was a high-risk environment then as now. Along the river, even in good times, it is difficult to find and gather enough wild plant foods. Opulent stands of a single plant species seldom occur, nor are they reliably there year after year—for example, pinyons bear prolifically, on the average, only once every seven years. Only during years of good rainfall can a sufficient amount of edible plants be found within short distances. To gather enough seeds and plants, to find enough game, demanded great mobility, sometimes to the point of replicating the nomadic character of the prey they hunted, always governed by the "law of minimum effort": the energy expended in obtaining and preparing food cannot be greater than the energy derived from eating it. Anthropologists suggest that any round trip much over six miles to obtain food cost more than it was worth.

In their incessant travels, gatherers (usually women) developed a

thorough and sophisticated knowledge of plants, what parts were poisonous and how to use them so that they were not, how to communicate
this knowledge to others and pass on customs, ceremonies, and lore
relating to plants. Fifty to 80 percent of their food came from plants,
a more reliable source of nutrition than animals. Gathering is a social
activity in which everyone shares the bounty. Only humans share on a
regular basis, and without that sharing, human society could never have
evolved or persisted. Sharing meant the survival of young children who
could not hunt or gather, and of elders who could pass on their wealth
of knowledge of plants and animals.

About a quarter of modern pharmaceuticals were originally derived
from wild plants well known to prehistoric peoples. Willows, abundant
on the canyon beaches, contain the compound salicin, chemically close
to acetylsalicylic acid (aspirin), whose analgesic effects were appreciated
by the ancient Greeks and Romans as well as by prehistoric Indians.
Scanning this dry pantry shelf at South Canyon, I cannot imagine how
anyone could have survived in this stringent landscape. Yet the plants the
Anasazi utilized grow all around me—many grasses, yucca, prickly pear,
mesquite, goosefoot, and amaranth. Grasses formed a significant part of
their diet, especially dropseed, which has easy-to-harvest, hull-less, long-
lived seeds, and ricegrass with its tiny, nourishing black seeds. More
seeds came from lamb's-quarters, amaranth bee plant, bunchgrasses, and
sunflowers. They recognized plants that could wake you up or make you
drowsy, plants with sap that healed, plants that gave you dreams, plants
that made soap, and plants that belonged in a prayer bundle.

They ate the young stems of saltbush, fruits from prickly pear, cholla,
and yucca, which also provided fibers for cordage and soap for washing—the leaves and roots contain saponin, a soaplike steroid. Ample
yucca still grows here today. Chewing softened the leaves so they could
be stripped for the fiber, producing quids that could be resoaked for
later use in weaving sandals and baskets. The fruit is edible, and the inner
core at the base of the leaves is said to taste somewhat like an artichoke.

Hunters, like gatherers, observed their environment with perceptive
eyes and canny minds sharpened by hunger. They unconsciously and
continually collated evidence of animal presence from weather signs and
retained memories of past hunts, dreams and visions, and proper ceremonies. The Anasazi harvested the numerous rock squirrels and ground
squirrels, various mice, undoubtedly bats and birds, insects, and perhaps small fish. Interestingly enough, no fish bones have been found in
Grand Canyon sites, although fishhook cactus grows here and a good
population of native fish swam the river. In the Southwest carnivores

tend to be solitary and fairly small, seldom abundant, and consequently never represented more than a minor part of the prehistoric diet. More reliable were the canyon's omnipresent rodents and the big ungulates, deer and bighorn sheep and, higher on the plateau, elk.

Sparse years meant that prehistoric people often lived close to starvation. The Anasazi's table was never a laden one, their searches were arduous, and seasonal stress was a part of existence; hunter-gatherers often lived at the edge of survival. For good health, diet must supply the forty-five nutrients that the human body needs to function well, including the amino acids that make up protein, plus carbohydrates, fats, and various minerals and vitamins. Age, activity, and gender affect caloric needs, but the average minimum necessary is probably around twenty-four hundred calories. Prehistoric people, with their arduous outdoor activities, probably needed more. Yet today's researchers find that their diet, with less fat, more vitamins, and more variety, was in many ways healthier than some modern ones.

A table-top boulder displays an assortment of shards, picked up and placed there by well-meaning visitors, who unknowingly remove them from their archaeological context. Many shards are Tusayan Corrugated, a comely utilitarian pottery made by coiling, pinching, and scraping, manufactured between A.D. 950 and 1150. A simple, useful ware common throughout the area, it shows only minor variations in style. At first glance it all looks alike: coils about a quarter-inch in diameter, surface repeatedly pinched like the crimped edge of a piecrust. Even given limited means and material, the human hand must delight in diversity, for sometimes indentations create a checkerboard effect, other times, diagonals. The crimping varies in size and rhythm through the use of larger or smaller coils, sometimes slightly flattened, sometimes not. The minimal curve of this shard says it came from a large jar, probably used for carrying water or storing grain—pots where access needed to be quick and easy had generous handwide openings and were usually finished with a plain flared rim. Corrugated cooking vessels could be relatively large; their textured surface made them easier to hold on to and spread cooking heat more evenly.

Tempers for corrugated and decorated wares differed according to their use, and Anasazi potters added a coarser temper of sand or crushed rock to the clay for cooking vessels because it provided greater porosity and thus higher resistance to thermal shock. Porosity relates to the size of particles and inversely relates to vessel size, suggesting that potters selected raw materials with particular physical properties for different types of vessels. Because pottery was widely traded, the distribution of a particular style gives insight to prehistoric settlement patterns and trade. An expert can often date a piece of pottery to within twenty-five years and sometimes even identify the style of an individual potter. Pottery, along with tree rings, is a mainstay of establishing chronology in the desert Southwest.

Pottery production implies a trend toward a more settled lifestyle. While baskets are light and unbreakable, pots are fragile and difficult to carry about. Their forming and firing took time and care. Despite the chance of breakage, pottery's advantage is that it is sturdier over time than baskets and infinitely more versatile for cooking. You can shake seeds with hot rocks in a basket to toast them, but such hard use quickly destroys basket fibers. Dropping heated stones in a well-tempered pot can be done again and again without damaging the vessel. Cooking creates chemical reactions that make some foods easier to digest and, in the case of meat, greatly reduces the risk of salmonella and botulinus.

I find another triangle of sun-warmed pottery, one side smoothed with a pale gray slip, the other painted with thin, crisp black lines, witness of creative decisions and aesthetic judgments made, thoughts in clay expressed with skill and sophistication in handsome wares. These shards are tantalizing fragments with presence far out of proportion to their size. They speak eloquently for the hand that made them: I create, therefore I am.

Shortly downstream at Mile 31.7, 155 feet above the river in the Redwall Limestone, an almost perfect Gothic arch opens into Stanton's Cave, named after Robert Brewster Stanton, who in 1889 and 1890 surveyed the Grand Canyon for a railroad. Frank M. Brown, original leader of the survey, proposed that the Denver, Colorado Canyon, and Pacific Railroad Company finance, construct, and operate a railway through the middle and lower canyons of the Colorado River. Following an even gradient that his chief engineer, Stanton, thought would never exceed one-half of one percent (or 26.4 feet) per mile, Brown proposed that the river route would be more efficient than those in use over mountain passes that were frequently snowed in: "The line as proposed is neither impossible nor impracticable, and as compared with some other transcontinental railroads, could be built for a reasonable cost."

To run and survey the river Brown considered everything but safety. He insisted, out of hubris or ignorance or both, that life preservers were superfluous and provided none. His thin boats were suitable for a calm day of punting on the Thames. With inexperienced boatmen, Brown launched an enterprise primed for disaster.

The group left Lees Ferry on July 9, 1889. They portaged the first two rapids at Badger and Soap Creeks. According to Stanton, Brown dreamed darkly of rapids that night. The next day they decided they could safely run the tail waves below Soap Creek, manageable at most water levels. Brown took the lead with Harry McDonald, a prospector and trapper he picked up at Lees Ferry after two of his original boatmen quit. Rowed backward into the waves, the round-bottomed, unstable boat flipped. Brown drowned in a whirlpool that was not that dangerous unless you weren't wearing a life jacket. McDonald survived. Peter Hansbrough, who himself would live only a few more days, chiseled "July 29, 1889/opposite this point" into the wall on river left.

Committed to the expedition, Stanton took command. The party endured another three days, and then two more members, Hansbrough and Henry Richards, drowned. Good swimmers and in good condition, both men would have survived in calmer waters. Stanton wrote that he "then realized fully what it meant to be without life preservers, in such work on such a River." That night a terrible storm in Marble Canyon proved the decision maker: Stanton cached their equipment in the cave and the party climbed out South Canyon.

Stanton, determined to return, took his high-flown enthusiasms back to New York and crusaded for money. He was not above using "great quantities of fine gold dust" to entice investors with the prospect of a railroad that would bring access to those "very rich and valuable" deposits and, according to his plan of damming the tributaries, would provide sufficient hydropower to run the railway. He raised enough money to return, added $12,500 of his own funds (a not inconsiderable amount in those days), and prepared to complete the survey.

For the second expedition he and McDonald designed three heavy, flat-bottomed boats. After a magnificent Christmas feast at Lees Ferry they embarked on December 28, 1889, with everyone wearing life vests. This time photographer Franklin A. Nims began the trip badly. On New Year's Day he stepped too near the edge of a cliff not far from Rider Canyon at Mile 16.9, tumbled twenty-two feet, and broke a leg and his jaw. Stanton climbed out Rider Canyon and hiked thirty-five wintery miles to bring help from Lees Ferry. Somehow Nims survived, cradled in a litter fashioned of two oars and a piece of canvas, roped and jimmied and jerked up dangerous, loose talus slopes. He remained at Lees Ferry for a week, unconscious, until some Mormons passed through and took him to Winslow, where the doctor discovered two dislocated ankles plus a slight skull fracture. Stanton stopped Nims's pay from January 1, 1890, the day of the accident, because he judged him no longer on "active duty," and paid none of Nims's onerous medical expenses, an injustice to which Nims gave smoldering notice.

Stanton took over the photography as well as the survey, aided by the newly invented roll film that did not have to be developed on the spot and was not as fragile as glass plates. He kept an almost continuous record of the walls of the Grand Canyon the length of the river, a Herculean accomplishment. The over 2,200 negatives are almost the only baseline data extant of how the canyon looked then compared to how the canyon looks now.

The party exited the river near the Grand Wash Cliffs on April 26, 1890, minus Harry McDonald, who had had enough and climbed out at Crystal Creek at Mile 98. Railroad backers were not convinced by Stanton's figures, and the Denver, Colorado Canyon, and Pacific Railroad Company never laid a foot of rail. Stanton did raise money to prospect in Glen Canyon by estimating an annual return of $1.2 million, but this venture too failed, losing money for his investors, one of whom was Julius F. Stone, an industrialist from Columbus, Ohio, who visited Stanton's digs and caught river fever, and would soon run the length of the Colorado River himself.

On July 19, 1934, Bus Hatch, one of the pioneer boatmen on the river, launched his first trip (and only the eleventh through the canyon) onto a river flowing at a meager 1,600 cfs, one of the lowest flows recorded. Poking around South Canyon, he entered Stanton's Cave and made a provocative discovery: small split-twig figurines of deer and bighorn sheep. Radiocarbon dating places their manufacture around four thousand years ago, the earliest evidence of human presence in the canyon.

The sprightly figurines, deft creations of hand and mind, were made by splitting a long slender willow twig almost to the end and, with ingenious bending and winding, creating a four-legged figure, often surprisingly vivacious in the tilt of head or slant of leg. Sometimes a small pointed stick pierces the animal figure. Robert Euler, park archaeologist in charge of excavations at Stanton's Cave, refers to this as "ritual deposition," a ceremonial use of caves by a nomadic, preagricultural, and prepottery civilization. In Stanton's Cave all figurines lie on the surface or, if buried, covered by no more than a few inches of silt. No evidence of occupation—no pottery shards, no middens, no fire-blackened rocks, no remnants of foodstuffs—appear in any of the caves in which the figurines remain.

Caves and arches are fairly common in the Redwall, still actively forming in association with joint systems. The 36 Mile joint system crosses the river several times in this area, revealed as stuttering breaks in the smooth bedding sequences of the limestone. Carbonic acid, formed by groundwater and carbon dioxide, dissolves limestone along fissures in the joint system. Caves develop when the top of the water table is above their ceiling; as streams cut deeper and lower the water table, water drains out of the cavern, and further enlargement ceases. They remain hidden until the river or a tributary stream opens them, many so high in the Redwall that they are as yet unexplored.

When Euler and a cadre of scientists walked into Stanton's Cave through the thirty-foot-high doorway in 1969, they found a cave two hundred feet deep with ceilings up to fifty feet high. Inside, besides the split-twig figurines, were entombed the bones of an extinct camel and those of many birds (including one similar to a condor) and of an extinct mountain goat, as well as a puzzling pile of driftwood.

Many of the bird bones scientists identified belong to species that still ply the river today, especially mallards, which make up almost one-third of the duck bones recovered. The nearly seventy species of birds represented include avocets, phalaropes, the same phoebes that still nest here, and the same swallows, ravens, and scrub jays. Owls probably roosted in the cave and could have brought in many of the perching-bird and songbird bones. Also here were birds now absent from the canyon, like sage grouse and clay-colored robins, which currently nest farther south on the gulf slopes of southern Mexico. Since passerine birds often have restricted ecological requirements, they are useful in establishing the paleoecology and paleoclimate of the habitat in which they were found.

The largest bones were those of a giant teratorn, *Teratornis merriami*, a monstrous bird with a twelve-foot wingspan, ancestor of the California condor. Its bones lay sealed in a wood rat midden, enabling them to be carbon dated to around 15,000 years ago. Sand also entombed the bones of a condor *Gymnogyps amplus* (larger than the present day *Gymnogyps californianus*), birds so huge that it took almost a year to incubate and fledge a single young. They nearly survived the climate and habitat changes since the last Ice Age and nested along this river corridor, but prospectors shot the last one seen in the Grand Canyon in 1881.

Most of the mammal bones interred in the cave are those of animals in the vicinity today, wood rats and small mice who denned in the cave, along with two species of bats, a ringtail cat, and rock and ground squirrels. Intermixed with the extant species are bones of two animals that are no longer here, muskrat and river otter, although otters were present when Julius Stone came down the river in 1909 and wrote that "at nearly every camp and at our noon stop to-day we have seen otter sign, usually quite fresh, but we catch no glimpse of even one. Here, as we land, are seen the tracks of two from the water to the rocks that must have been made but a few moments ago, because the sand is still wet with the drippings from their fur."

In winters with heavy snowfalls that made food scarce along the rims, larger animals migrated into the Inner Gorge to forage. Living in the canyon at the same time was the now extinct Harrington's mountain goat, here until just a geologic yesteryear of 10,800 years ago. Its fecal pellets intermix with those of prehistoric desert bighorn sheep in the cave. Smaller than bighorns, Harrington's goats ate herbs and shrubs (desert bighorn eat more grasses) and survived here for at least 7,200 years.

Plant remains contained in fecal pellets and wood rat middens from Stanton's Cave cover 35,000 years. They tally the change from a moister to a drier climate that occurred between 12,000 and 8,000 years ago, when some Pleistocene species, tailored to a cooler, damper climate, disappeared. Until plants adapted to a warming, drying environment arrived, there were fewer plant species available for food and cover. Fifteen thousand years ago the plant cover at the high-water line consisted of plants that now grow only in the cooler, upper part of Marble Canyon: redbud, scrub oak, netleaf hackberry, and Apache plume. Today's woody vegetation around Stanton's Cave, as in most of the Inner Gorge, is a spare scrubby cover dominated mostly by Mormon tea and Utah agave, plants characteristic of the southernmost Great Basin.

The enigmatic pile of driftwood cluttering the cave contained primarily coniferous wood and rested either on a layer of fine unconsolidated silt or on bedrock. The silt showed no stratification as it would have had the driftwood washed into the cave one or two pieces at a time and this suggests that both the silts and driftwood rode in during a single episode of flooding. Logs floating into a cave 150 feet above the present river presuppose a river flowing high enough that a single flood pulse could loft driftwood into the cave, an impressive thought when you stand at river level and look up.

From Stanton's Cave, water surging out of the right wall a scant tenth of a mile downstream looks like an Italian baroque fountain in a set for a Cecil B. deMille epic. Huge jets of water, 125 feet above the river, leap out of two openings: Vasey's Paradise. Powell named it after the U.S. Department of Agriculture botanist and authority on grasses who accompanied him on his trip to Colorado in 1868 but who was unable to join the later trips down the Colorado River. Part of one of the cave-and-channel systems in the Redwall and Muav Limestones, it is the only place on the Colorado River where one of these solution channels carrying water opens directly onto the river itself.

A garden of plants gentles the pound of the falls onto a slanting apron of rock. A variety of water currents burble and bounce over travertine chutes and corrugations. Freshets tatter over the limestone steps and nourish lush and verdant plant life. On the left water rushes down the slope, shouldering masses of watercress, fanning out. Where it races across the limestone pavement, dark quarter-inch caddis fly cases, evenly spaced, adhere to the rock, and Kanab amber snails, an endangered species, rasp their dinners. Buffalo gnat larvae attach themselves to rock surfaces where the water is highly aerated, little black threads quivering in the push of the current. In the willows above, a yellow warbler, darting after insects, flashes gold. A brilliant red-orange dragonfly clatters a few inches above the water. Although water flow visibly varies according to season, the water temperature remains much the same. The cascades create their own breeze, which riffles through drifts of red and yellow monkey flowers, frets the horsetails and canes, flickers the willows and milkvetch, worries the bee plants, the paintbrush, the milkweed—and the poison ivy. Jets of water create a visual, aural, aromatic flash and sparkle, gleaming against a tapestry almost half the height of the cliff, hooked of bright, fresh, water-greened pile.

Downstream, Hermit Shale from above drizzles down and slathers the gray limestone walls with cinnamon red. The walls reach the water on both sides and extend a mysterious forever below, walls that may reach from the top of the sky to the center of the earth.

On this quiet Saturday afternoon my sandbar veranda looks across the river to elegant Redwall facades and Muav cloisters. The view downriver is one of those juxtapositions of cliff and contour and color and light that makes it one of at least a couple hundred "quintessential" views of the canyon. Upstream ripples reflect a sky animated with violet-green swallows falling in and out of the glow, lacing the limestone walls together like cat's cradles. Downstream the walls glow garnet in the afternoon light.

On the wall opposite is an old river channel cut in the Muav Limestone, filled in by a wandering Devonian stream before it too was planed off and the sediments of Redwall limestones flowed in on top. The top of the Devonian channels marks the shift from Muav to Redwall. After the Muav limestones formed, rock formations of three succeeding periods encompassing 130 million years—Ordovician, Silurian, and part of the Devonian—either were never deposited here or were all planed off by erosion down to the Muav limestones beneath. On the newly bared limestone surface, running water gouged out dendritic channels.

Into those Muav channels trickled sediments of early Devonian seas that would harden into limestones and mudstones, named the Temple Butte Formation after a Grand Canyon landmark near the confluence of the Little Colorado and Colorado Rivers. Fossils of the first ocean-swimming fish lie entrapped in its layers, brackish-water species that probably lived in saltwater lagoons occasionally sloshed with freshwater. In late Devonian times the seas withdrew, leaving a land surface again above sea level. During this period some fish, faced with losing their habitat, made tentative, finny excursions onto the alien world of dry land. Erosion then ground both Temple Butte and Muav limestones down to a common peneplain. In the eastern end of Grand Canyon the Temple Butte survives only in the old Muav channels; at the western end of the canyon it forms cliffs more than a thousand feet high. Nearly 180 million more years ticked away before new seas hauled in the sediments that would indurate into Redwall Limestone.

The half-moon cross sections of Temple Butte are easy to see after your eyes attune to the subtle change in color and surface—slightly more lavender, a little rougher in texture. Elsewhere the river has cut through other Devonian channels, leaving a streambed on either side, now connected only by air. Across the river, this small channel is a gray smile across the eons.

I sit with a handful of willow withes across my knees and, anchored open by two river cobbles, the diagram of how split-twig figurines are made. With a knife I slit the first willow branch to within a few inches of the end and try fashioning a figure according to the diagram. When I bend it to a near right angle to form the back legs and back, the twig snaps. I start over. This time the proportions are better and I wrap one of the split ends around the unsplit section to form the body. The other thin split end bends down and up for the front legs, then continues up to form the head, reversing to wrap around and construct the neck. Like the original weavers, I find that smaller twigs make neater figures. But the proportions are tricky—funny how such a simple thing can be so difficult. The seventh twig has the right size and pliability and I the right fingers, and the figure of a deer emerges with a hint of the verve that many of the ancient ones have—an animal observed and translated in an economy of form that is all the more potent for its stringency, a bit of magic that is as mystical as a word, a complex thought woven of willow withes, sunshine, and belief.

As I work, the afternoon fades gently. Muted light floats across the walls, red softens to rose, shadows lose their edge. Idling air scarcely moves the leaf-embroidered arrowweed curtains. The repeated verticals of arrowweed shadows gently stripe the beach, fret the hollows of footprints, this day's comings and goings. This afternoon there comes a gentleness I do not often feel on this big river because there is so much to learn, so many puzzles that gnaw, so many complex layerings, so many angles and turnings, so many thickets and so many thorns, and always, always the pressure of time, schedules to be maintained, miles to be made, promises to keep. Never enough time. No centuries to wander around in, no millennia to cross, no epochs to explore.

This afternoon is the sum total of years of quiet afternoons, at times and places completely different, but for some peculiar, stumbling glitch of time, today sums them all up in a new way, with words that ring like anthems: Kaibab, Muav, Redwall; Coconino, Hermit, Bright Angel, and always, the flowing color—Colorado.

Redwall near South Canyon

6

Colorado River waters not needed to maintain a steady stream for scenic purposes in the park could be diverted through a tunnel 44.8 miles long to a power plant near the mouth of Kanab Creek. With an installed capacity of 1,250,000 kilowatts this Kanab Creek power plant operating under an average head of about 1,100 feet could produce 6.5 billion kilowatt hours of firm energy annually. A 300-foot dam constructed at the Marble Canyon site would divert water to the tunnel and form a reservoir of 500,000 acre-feet capacity extending upstream to the potential Glen Canyon Dam. Water released from the dam in Marble Canyon for scenic purposes in the park would pass through a 22,000-kilowatt power plant at the dam under an average head of 275 feet. This plant would be capable of producing 164,000,000 kilowatt-hours of firm energy annually. . . . The deep canyons cut by the Colorado River as it falls over 10,000 feet in its wild dash to the ocean provide some of the best power sites in the world. With full development the river channel could become a great stairway of reservoirs—quiet mill ponds—extending upstream from Parker Dam on the boundary between Arizona and California, through Arizona, Nevada, and Utah, into Wyoming and Colorado. In most cases each dam would back reservoir water to the toe of the dam next upstream.

U.S. Department of the Interior, 1946, foreword to *The Colorado River: A Comprehensive Report on the Development of the Water Resources of the Colorado River Basin for Irrigation, Power Production, and Other Beneficial Uses in Arizona, California, Colorado, Nevada, New Mexico, Utah, and Wyoming*

Redwall Cavern and Dam Sites

At the back of Redwall Cavern, a huge clamshell of a solution cavern worn into the Redwall Limestone at Mile 33, the soft warm sands of springtime caress my ankles. The river elbows to the right here so that the current beats against the left wall and undercuts it, at one point causing a rockfall that unsealed the cavern and opened it to wind, blowing sand, and ballooning spiders. Despite its spacious protection, Redwall Cavern was unused by prehistoric people because access is possible only by river.

An apron of boulders from the rockfall ballasts the front lip of the cave like a collapsed portcullis, and scattered through the limestone are the fossilized stems of crinoids that occur in this strata of Redwall, a sea that covered a large area from here into Canada. Crinoids are often called "sea lilies" for their resemblance to a lily, but only if you can't count— the lily family of plants has parts in multiples of three, while crinoids are animals belonging to the echinoderms, the phylum that contains sea urchins and starfish, with parts based on fives. With delicate and easily broken stems, sea lilies could live only in quiet, fairly shallow waters with a felicitous combination of enough current to waft minute particles of food by the head but not enough to snap the flexible stems made up of stacked disks with a hole in the center. The stem housed the connection between holdfast, anchored in the silt, and a five-part cup above that bore mouthparts. Bits of stem are the most commonly preserved segments of a crinoid, replaced by crystalline chert that colors them deep salmon. Embedded in the rock, sometimes scribed with radiating lines, they look like tiny Life Savers.

A filigree of mice tracks runs along every meeting of rock and sand. The drag line of a tiny tail accompanies one set of dainty mouse prints— rock pocket, canyon, or cactus mouse—no one has done a survey in the cavern. All three are seed eaters although only a few scattered tamarisks survive here. Low light intensity within the cavern plus the trudging of thousands of visitors through the sand, keeps the vegetation minimal, which adds up to slim pickings for mice.

Other tracks, quirky and looping, follow the base of the cave's curving wall. Made by the way an ant lion larva spurts sand while it travels from one trap excavated in the loose sand to the next, the tracks connect hundreds of pits. The sand pits are "thermal devices" in which the larva can use the warmer side when outside temperatures are low, or retreat deeper into cooler sand when temperatures warm. The rapacious larva lurks at the bottom of the inverted cones, detecting prey by the drizzle of sand grains an ant or wasp makes when it finds its footing disappearing and tries to scramble out. The ant lion pounces, impales its prey on lethal, sickle-shaped jaws, and sucks out the juices. Ant lions in turn are preyed upon by the female of a tiny parasitic chalcid wasp, which locates the burrow of an ant lion and provokes it into emerging. When it does, she seizes its front legs, inserts her ovipositor into the membrane between head and thorax, and deposits her deadly little egg.

So seldom are ant lion larvae seen that it was easy for a literal-minded twelfth-century scribe to fantasize them with a lion's face and foreparts and an ant's hinder parts: "Its father eats flesh, but its mother grains. If then they engender the ant-lion, they engender a thing of two natures, such that it cannot eat flesh because of the nature of its mother, nor grains because of the nature of its father. It perishes, therefore, because it has no nutriment." Judging from the plethora of ant lion pits, there must have been a lot of randy lions and a plentitude of willing ants.

Poking around the back of the cave I come to a narrow ledge about seven feet off the ground. On it sits a nest the size of half a tennis ball, woven of twigs and lined with downy white feathers and soft spiderweb shreds. (When I revisit the cavern six weeks later, in mid-June, there are young there.) The phoebe, still nest-building, flits across the cave, a small windup toy, a charming artifact in a fanciful stage set, here for only one day a year.

From the back of the cave I look out through the operatic proscenium arch over a grandiose stage on which could be mounted the triumphal procession from *Aïda*, complete with giraffes, horses, and elephants.

Across the river rises an immense sheer face of monolithic limestone. Hazed with desert varnish, scrubbed with white salts, wavering stripes further band the wall caused by lenses of chert that weather darker than the lighter stripes of limestone and dolomite. The layers of steel and pearl gray alternate in the subtle striping of a Navajo Two Grey Hills rug.

Circles in the sand materialize at my toe: a minute red-winged wasp struggles, one leg encumbered by a piece of spiderweb fluff so that it winds round and round trying to escape. Overhead, gossamer spiderwebs swathe the entire ceiling of the cavern, multilayered scrims filming the limestone with an iridescent sheen. Gossamer as they are, the webs are still strong enough to ensnare tiny feathers, dead gnats, insect legs and heads, and sometimes chips of limestone. They are not the neat and orderly webs of orb-weaver spiders but look like gauzy swaddlings, with more holes than Swiss cheese, multiple openings from one layer to the next, the work of millions of desert recluse spiders.

Where sand catches on the sticky web filaments, they appear the same color as the rock so that the rock looks intricately carved into threadlike bridges. In all the dimples of the limestone cluster caper-sized, pale tan egg cases, a ceiling nursery. When a section of web becomes overladen with trash and frass and body parts, it shreds away from the wall and hangs like one of Miss Havisham's curtains before it drops onto the sand. Little sticky, wispy packets litter the ground, and it is in one of these that the small wasp became enmeshed.

I would love to be here at night with a lantern catching the gleam of glistening eyes—they must jewel the ceiling, thousands of facets glittering like minikin sparklers in the heat of the hunt, minute constellations, a ceiling of dippers and necklaces and winged horses all on the move. In the cavernous silence, surely if one listened carefully, one could hear the motherly clicking of knitting needles and the exchange of recipes on how to prepare wasp ragout.

Three river parties unload into the cave, unlimber their frisbees for a fifteen-minute workout, and depart, having never left water's edge, having never seen an ant lion metropolis or a spider megalopolis, what six and eight legs can create, and what worlds lie between grains of sand.

Nautiloid Canyon is a narrow cleft that enters from the east on river left at Mile 34.8—close-walled, paved and paneled in cool, pale limestone, puddled with peach-colored sand, lit by a thin slot of sky. Here the Redwall shows its elegant gray essence, undecorated by red oxides, with a smooth hard surface polish as luscious as that of an Elgin Marble. A

Sierra Club trip in May 1966, looking for a warm lunch stop, shinnied up into this small slot and discovered fossils of orthocone nautiloids embedded in the floor, the first found in the Grand Canyon. "Ortho-" refers to their straightness, in contrast to the more familiar coil of the chambered nautilus.

At the canyon's entrance a redbud tree's newly unfurled leaves have been neatly scalloped by leaf-cutting bees, one of the nonsocial bees who do most of the pollinating in Southwestern deserts. Leaf-cutting bees are sturdy, medium-sized bees, half an inch or so in length, with large heads, clear wings, and pale tan hairs covering the black thorax and abdomen in faint bands. Females who collect pollen carry it not on their hind legs like honeybees but beneath their abdomens on pale red brushes. Leaf-cutting bees cut precise disks out of leaves to line their nest cells. Some bore tunnels in the soil or in wood, but all find some sort of a cavity in which they fashion a cylindrical case that looks like nothing so much as a tiny, flat-ended, neatly wrapped cigar, sometimes placing several end to end. Before sealing the nest, the female bee provisions it with pollen and nectar and lays an egg inside. To ensure the health of the larva, many solitary bees also deposit an antibiotic in the nest cells at the time of laying.

Finally the female seals the cylinder with a circular piece of leaf that fits snugly because she has cut it a fraction larger than the diameter of the cell. The bee's antennae are elbowed, and the tips diverge so that they automatically calibrate openings and measure width. Henri Fabre, an amateur entomologist whose patient observations and devotion to insects in his dry corner of France provide such charming reading a century later, makes much of the leaf-cutting bee's precision in cutting just the right size disk with which to close her nest. He compares it to a human's challenge in going to the store to buy a lid by memory alone that will fit precisely on a saucepan at home. Fabre calculated that each cell required around 42 pieces of leaves plus the two smaller round ones that are the lids. In one nest cavity he counted 1,064 leaf pieces trimmed by "one dauntless creature and one alone, one solitary, inveterate worker." Often males occupy the quick-exit-end cells and emerge first, drugstore cowboys who hang around awaiting the appearance of nubile females on the town looking for their first drink of nectar. Solitary bees hatch as their favored flowers come into bloom and may, in fact, respond to identical stimuli such as temperature and moisture.

An unnaturally quiet leaf-cutting bee clings to a brittlebush flower, and I take advantage of its stillness to look at it through a hand lens only to discover that it is quiet because a small crab spider, the precise yellow of the flower, clasps it by the head. Crab spiders sidle sideways when they run, hence their name. Perfectly color-matched, they lurk in flower petals, waiting to seize an incautious visitor in their powerful outstretched front legs. Firmly anchored to their plant platform, they have the leverage to capture and feast on insects much larger than they. After capturing its prey, a crab spider pulls its own front legs back out of danger of a sting or bite and buries its jaws in the meaty head or thorax. Since duplicating a flower's hue is imperative for hunting, they can achieve a match in a few days after they move to a differently colored flower.

Behind it mud dauber wasps have glued their cells in the crease of an overhang. Made of soft mud carried grain by grain, they have hardened into crisp firm cases. Although it looks like one large nest, the outer shell covers half a dozen individual cells, each of which contains a larva. The female mud dauber provisions her nest with sundry small spiders of a quantity sufficient to nourish a larva to maturity, then lays an egg in the tangled legs of her immobilized victims, seals the nest, and never returns. The larva works on nonvital body parts first, saving the vital organs for last. With luck the stunned spiders will not die and mold but remain alive until the wasp larva is ready to pupate.

The painted "B" on the wall on river right is for "base"; "C" equals "center," and "A" designates the downstream end of a dam proposed by the U.S. Department of the Interior in 1946. In 1923, on only the sixth trip through the canyon, Claude Birdseye, chief topographic engineer of the U.S. Geological Survey, was charged with mapping the canyon for potential dam sites. He located twenty-one, including this one, and produced the first topographic maps of the canyon bottom. He also measured the fall in the rapids and discovered that previous estimates were, as might be expected, uniformly too generous.

In 1941 the bureau proposed dams that would turn the Grand Canyon into a series of continuous reservoirs. The reservoir created by a dam built here would have, at full pool, reached to Navajo Bridge and consumed Redwall Cavern, Vasey's Paradise, and Stanton's Cave. The permeability of the Redwall, which creates its caves, would have allowed considerable leakage. In addition, proposals were based on faulty figures: in 1916 E. C. LaRue, a USGS geologist conducting an extensive survey for dams on the Colorado River in the Grand Canyon, calculated that the evaporative loss from a Lake Powell–sized reservoir would be a mere 5 acre-feet per year. As measured today, Lake Powell's evaporation rate runs around 750,000 acre-feet per year.

A test tunnel entrance opens just downstream, and its tailings slide down to the river beneath it, after all these years still gray and raw. The tunnel entrance is the size of a reefer door, now half-blocked by a wooden barrier. Standing in front of it is like standing at an open grave site. Inside, heavy dead air muffles footsteps on the wooden planks. The tunnel goes back, back, into an endless darkness. When the tunnel becomes totally dark, I walk hand-to-wall. Total darkness is a peculiar sensation, mind-blotting and soul-blanking, inanimate: no sounds or scents of river, no ruffling breeze, no sparkling light. The inside of the earth holds an appalling blackness, four forks to the four corners of hell. It takes a different mind-set than mine to walk in total blackness under untold burdens of rock. Without being given conscious direction my feet turn back. I lack the courage of Demeter. Persephone will have to manage on her own. Enough. The dam dreamers' tunnel remains, witness to a belief that men could control the Colorado River by putting a dam wherever they wished and to their eternal urge to build, which sometimes borders on the single-mindedness of the beaver.

When I emerge from the tunnel, the view has a different cast, as if a lifetime's journey were completed, of going through and coming out the other side, of plans lost but not forgotten, of ideas unsorted, as if everything out here were normal and in that tunnel was some mental Minotaur against whom one needs a ball of sunshine to unwind for the way out.

Back on the river the boat weaves in and out of the sunlight. Sharp chill drafts snake off the water: warm air, cold air, currents inexplicable and quixotic. Sometimes a draft huffs like an overheated hair drier, other times chill air bursts in your face as from opening an ice chest, and with it comes the fresh, enticing river scent of damp clay. Water flashes and sparkles in dots and dashes, and light hyphenates the ripples, translating the aural language of the river into the visual, dah-dit-ditting of its own Morse code.

At the beginning of May the beach at Buck Farm Canyon, Mile 41, mysteriously erupts with fine, erratic spurts of sand. I watch until I finally make out a small winged insect emerging, then another and another whose lightly striped narrow bodies identify them as western sand wasps. The wasps swiftly appear, disappear, emerge, fly quick short loops, cooling themselves through these rapid flights, and return to the same angled hole in the blink of an eye.

Solitary sand wasps, like solitary bees, are far more prevalent in the canyon than social ones. Although sand wasps frequently nest in the same area, this grouping may be due more to available compatible terrain than to sociability, for they nest singly in the ground and provision the nest alone. The female digs numerous tunnels with a single brood chamber at the end, eight to ten inches deep, in sand that has enough residual dampness within to keep the tunnel from collapsing. In it she places a single paralyzed fly on its back which serves as a tripod for the egg and is not eaten. "My beloved wasps," as Fabre called the sand wasps, will resupply the larva every few days and will not "leave the cell for good until the larva, distended by a purply paste, refuses its food and lies down, stuffed to repletion, on the jumble of legs and wings of the game which it has devoured." Since the entrance to the nest fills in every time she leaves, each return requires reopening the burrow. A new spate of digging brings a moment of high danger, for it reveals the nest's location to a patrolling parasite like a velvet ant. Despite its name and cute fuzzy appearance, a velvet ant is a virulent ground-dwelling wasp.

A few weeks later I check this segment of beach again. The wasps are gone. The sand is too hot to walk on barefoot. Perhaps a few inches beneath my feet the temperature is kinder and a whole congregation of gourmand pupae await emergence, enduring the unfriendly season underground like the seeds of desert annuals awaiting the spring rains.

In the shade of a big boulder, a short way up Buck Farm Canyon, winding pencil-sized mounds made out of sand and silt crisscross a patch of ground, the architecture of Southwestern desert termites. As they identify new food sources, these termites extend their galleries outward, cementing soil particles together with saliva into a papier-mâché-like substance called carton, small modest tunnels that cover their peregrinations and protect them from desiccation and the predation of ground-feeding birds, lizards, and their severest predators, ants. Termites' soft cuticle allows them to excavate and maneuver in constricted spaces but also condemns them to a sequestered life. Unlike ants and bees, they have no sting for defense since a sting, to be effective, must be mounted on a firm abdominal segment.

Termites communicate via a rich vocabulary of chemical cues contained in pheromones, volatile chemicals emitted and diffused instantly into the air in all kinds of animal communication: when a female moth calls to a feather-antennaed male, when ants and termites identify members of their own colony, when aphids signal danger. It takes two to tango and the production and dissemination of pheromones is an elegantly coupled procedure. For every whiff of chemical vapor discharged, there has to be a nervous system to receive and separate those specific molecules from hundreds of thousands of others, decode the signal, and respond in proper manner. The ability to release, receive, and process quickly information encoded in pheromones makes possible, and indeed is one of the trademarks of, social and semisocial insects, which, because of their social organization, dominate and outcompete solitary insects. Pheromones are so universal that biologist E. O. Wilson writes that 99 percent of animals orient by chemical trails, "puffs of odor released into the air or water, and scents diffused out of little hidden glands and into the air downwind." Termite pheromones signal danger, instigate grooming, alert to nest damage and initiate repair activities, and foster the efficient exchange of nutrients and essential secretions that need to travel as quickly as possible throughout the colony. Each colony develops its own individual, distinctive odor, which every member can identify.

Termites lack the true worker caste that characterizes ant colonies, where it is once a worker, always a worker. Instead, termites have pseudergates, which develop in a single molt from larvae. They continue to grow and molt but retain the same form until, in response to some trigger, they metamorphose into alates (a winged and mating form) or into replacements for soldiers, which have huge heads and extra large mandibles. The colony slowly grows in size and population (termite colonies along the river are likely in the hundreds) until it contains all the castes characteristic of the species. As in all social insect societies, the number of castes is economically limited. Each separate caste needs a minimum number of individuals to carry out its particular tasks. Too many castes would require too many individuals to complete an "operative set," so each individual nest establishes its own cost-benefit ratio in which each termite contributes most efficiently to its caste and to its colony.

Termites feed mainly on cellulose, amply available in wood, dung, and leaf litter, something that most animals cannot digest. Indeed, most herbivores prefer plant food in direct proportion to its absence. Termites can break down and utilize cellulose because of flagellate protozoa that live in their gut, transferred from generation to generation. The ability to digest cellulose opens resources unavailable to most other insects and may be a major reason termites are so successful in Southwestern deserts.

Since dead wood decays so slowly in the river corridor, termites play an extraordinarily important role in recycling wood and nutrients into riverside soils, enhancing their fertility. When abandoned and collapsed, nest particles mixing with the soil better its physical and chemical properties. Termites are by far the most important invertebrate decomposers in arid places, yet little is known about termites along the Colorado

River other than that they have colonized sections of the new high-water zone in numbers.

One of many unmaintained trails into the canyon, the Eminence Break Trail, reaches the river at President Harding Rapid at Mile 43.7. Camped on the beach here, I join some hikers on the trip to walk the trail at first light. Pads of moss luxuriate along the trail, and plants brighten the dry streambed. As usual I lag behind to take notes, a fatal error with a destination-oriented group. I take the path less traveled and it *does* make all the difference. Now I sit a hundred feet above the rest of the group, happily dangling my legs over a parapet. Below me a phoebe flits and dips, snatching up this morning's insect hatch. Tiny bats lace the sky until 5:30, then disappear.

From my vantage point, President Harding Rapid silently flays the big boulder in its center. The Birdseye Expedition heard of President Warren G. Harding's death on their radio farther upriver. They reached Boulder Rapid on August 10, the day set for the funeral. Birdseye re-named the rapid after Harding and declared a day of rest devoutly needed by the men: those who were passengers rode the boats lying flat on the decks, drenched and soaked and battered, seeing towering waves from the underside up, while they hung on to lifelines for dear life.

I sight across the river to the top of Hansbrough Point, a mono-lithic wall when seen from below. Stanton, the railroad survey engineer, named it after Peter Hansbrough, who drowned upstream in 1889. He found the body of his foreman here the year following the drowning, beached on a rock, and identified the skeleton by Hansbrough's odd shoes still laced to the bones. Stanton buried him "with a shaft of pure marble for his headstone, seven hundred feet high with his name cut upon the base, and in honor of his memory we named a magnificent point opposite—*Point Hansbrough*."

It may just be the chill of an early spring morning breeze but the landscape up here, with its numerous stiff-twigged blackbrush bushes, reminds me of the Great Basin Desert, although nowhere are there enough plants to categorize the vegetation of that desert. Already com-plex with its altitudinal ups and downs, the Grand Canyon lies in a transition zone at the meeting of three deserts: the Great Basin Desert to the north, a high-elevation and high-latitude steppe-desert where freez-ing is common; the Sonoran Desert to the south, relatively luxuriant, at low latitude, and the most diverse both in species and variety of growth forms; and the Mojave Desert to the southwest, somewhat transitional between the two and with its own distinctive plant assemblage.

Great Basin plants filter down into the eastern end of the canyon. Mojave and Sonoran Desert species migrate upward along the river, and some Mojave Desert plants reach their easternmost extension around the Little Colorado River at Mile 61.3, where their upslope range is limited by cold winter temperatures. Mojave species are limited to areas where it seldom freezes, generally below four thousand feet. This vegetational mishmash of high- and low-desert plants results in a distinctive patchwork that to a botanist must look stitched together by a mad quilter, a landscape in which prickly pear and hedgehog cactus, brittlebush, barrel cactus, ocotillo, and creosote bush from the south blend with Mormon tea, blackbrush, rabbitbrush, and Utah agave from the north. By the Grand Wash Cliffs where the canyon ends, the 8°F gained for the almost two-thousand-foot elevation drop, plus the change in rainfall patterns, produces a much more homogenous flora closer to that of the Mojave Desert.

Blackbrush may well mark the lowermost limit of the Great Basin and the uppermost limit of the Mojave Desert. Perennial desert shrubs like blackbrush and Mormon tea are well adapted to severe environmental conditions all year long. The tiny leaves of blackbrush have a resinous, waterproof coating and can withstand temperatures of over 150°F. It holds its leaves all year long unless conditions are especially severe, when it sheds them all. Mormon tea blooms profusely and tiny conelike "flowers" poke out of most leaf scales. Mormon tea also has multiple, broomlike branches and reduced leaves, one of the unmistakable desert plants along the river.

In fact, all the perennial plants on this slope index the adaptations for desert living. Agave and yucca leaves are succulent, with protective waxy coatings. Many, like brittlebush, have leaves and stems covered with hairs or mealy particles that reduce water loss. Others, such as blackbrush and cacti, have extensive, shallow root systems that can absorb moisture from even the sparsest rains. Some plants endure as underground bulbs during the winter or drought, a case in point being the delicate funnel lily that blooms beside me with starlike lavender flowers and narrow leaves that arch up and over like croquet wickets.

As the sun rises, the breeze freshens and all the short, stiff branches become metronomes beating to a jiggly ragtime. The dry, eight-foot flowering stalk on a sentinel agave ticks to its own beat above a pedestal of its dried leaves, the main stalk easily six inches in diameter at the base, with dried flower stems still feathering the top. New rosettes, sprouting from the old rootstock, splay out around it. Another agave begins to bloom and complete its life span, its stalk only four or so feet high, buds just developing, a huge asparagus stalk on its way to heaven.

Padding the ground are the delicate crusts of lichens, mosses, microfungi, and algae that in the desert have an importance out of proportion to their insignificant appearance. These "cryptobiotic crusts" grow along river as well as most desert ecosystems. The algae that actually bind the soil together are a very primitive cyanobacteria, a type of blue-green bacterial algae, capable of reproducing by spores. Dormant when dry, they proliferate across or just under the soil surface when wet, secreting new material in front as they move, gluing soil particles together into a mucilaginous mat of sticky fibers. When dry the fibers draw up, giving the soil its puffy, wrinkled appearance. The crusts absorb the sun's heat in their dark colors, recycle dead organic material back into the soil, and add phosphorous, nitrogen, potassium, and calcium. As one botanist puts it, a cryptobiotic crust "protects itself, nourishes itself, warms itself, waters itself and has its own funeral parlor/garbage recycling system." Footsteps compress the soil and break the infinitesimal physical bonds that web the whole community together; they do the most damage when soils are dry and sand blows out between areas of crust. Now undercut, the whole community disintegrates. To reestablish such a protective crust in such a climate may take a considerable time.

A butterfly with strongly mottled green-and-white underwings hangs on a peppergrass stem, a small annual mustard with tiny four-petaled white flowers, masses of which perfume the path. Basking, wings tilted to receive the most sun, the butterfly remains long enough for me to sketch it into my notes for identification before it opens its wings to show a white upper surface geometrically patterned with soft black like an Anasazi pot: a checkered white, fresh and unblemished. The intensity of its underwing color may be due to the still chill season, a darkness that allows the wings to absorb more warming sunlight, a genetically controlled color difference linked to day length and temperature.

The white of Pieridae wings comes not from the incorporation of air into the cells, as with many white butterflies, but from uric acid wastes. Male checkered whites identify females by ultraviolet reflection: the wing pigments of females reflect ultraviolet rays whereas those of males absorb them. A female usually lays her pale yellow eggs on a mustard, which the larvae identify as their proper food plant. Members of the mustard family contain glucosinolates, the chemicals that give mustard and horseradish their familiar bite, but are toxic to most other insect species.

The butterfly flexes its wings, then lofts off over the river, transitory, fluttery, beginning its one-week life span.

Back down on the beach, packing up, I pick up my mattress, and an immense Teutonic blond female tarantula stalks out from beneath, on her way back to the silk-plugged darkness of her den. Since tarantulas do not travel more than a few yards for a night of hunting, her den is likely close by. In the cool of the morning she is fairly lethargic, raising first one leg, then another, with massive Wagnerian dignity. Having recently invited a handsome male in full tuxedo to cruise up my arm and shoulder, I am less put off by tarantulas than I used to be—it's just a matter of being introduced properly. The nonbiting arm trekker walked with a quiet deliberate gait, docile and dignified, a mild sort, having spent up to a decade in bachelorhood, now mature and on the town. But females are not so well mannered and do bite. Also, this Valkyrie's dense covering of hairs contains a venom that irritates the skin when she brushes them off onto a new acquaintance. I wait until she stalks off the ground cloth before shaking it. Vigorously.

As we leave, a huge, pompous raven—bill open, chest out—struts the sand. He has plenty of beach to pontificate from, as well as a pulpit in a large rock pile that fell twenty years ago at the lower end of the beach. With his sermonizing mien he is a William Jennings Bryant lookalike, swaying us by bombast and striving to convince us that the silver standard will truly serve us best.

On the river, the water swirls, chortles, muses as the boat travels from one sound focus to another. Passing through contiguous canyon wren territories, their songs wax, grow distinct, wane, overlap with the next, each song a little different from the one before it, each young learning the distinctive notes of its parent.

At Fifty Mile Canyon, the Eminence Break Fault crosses at river level. Like many of the faults in the Grand Canyon, this one moved first one way, took a deep breath for a few millennia, then moved in the opposite direction. The present displacement is around a hundred feet with the downstream side up, looking like a layer cake with a piece out, considerably rearranged in the cutting, one side offset lower than the other. When the river cut through the fault, it bared a crumbled and crumpled gateway into the Muav and Redwall limestones, revealed a Romanesque cathedral fallen and burned and left where it fell, charred timbers of Redwall evidence of arson and pillage. Extending across the river, the torn chancels and collapsed aisles and shattered transepts persist up Fifty

Mile Canyon. The great wrenching and tearing that transformed colors and swapped shapes, rotated order into chaos, is here spread out on the table and labeled for evidence.

The complexity of the fault, the clarity of its revelation, the concentration of trying to ink it on paper, has kept me sitting here so long and so unmoving that a fat desert spiny lizard has taken noontime respite in my shadow, disinclined to move until I do, a quiet, undemanding companion. We exchange unlisted phone numbers and promise to meet for breakfast.

the Great Unconformity

7

How distinctly it looked like a new day in creation where the horizontal, yellowish-gray beds of the Cambrian were laid down upon the dark, amorphous, and twisted older granite! How carefully the level strata had been fitted to the shapeless mass beneath it! It all looked like the work of a master mason; apparently you could put the point of your knife where one formation ended and the other began. The older rock suggested chaos and turmoil, the other suggested order and plan, as if the builder had said, "Now upon this foundation we will build our house."

John Burroughs, 1910, "The Grand Cañon of the Colorado," *Century Magazine*

Toads and Frogs
and Unconformities

One late spring evening in Blacktail Canyon at Mile 120.2, red-spotted toads and tree frogs deafen the air with trills and burrs and bleats, the vocalizing of all the newly risen frogs and toads who left wake-up calls with the rain. The marvelous acoustics of Blacktail Canyon magnify their ancient anuran love songs, gather and ricochet them between the walls, curl and pulse them up and down the canyon—warbling tremolos of hope, toad trumpets and frog fancies, slippery invitations to be translated into strings of black pearls that hatch into hapless little black commas that unfold into popping and hopping creatures, transferring genes down through time on arpeggios of song.

Canyon tree frogs sound like Civil War Gatling guns, a prolonged "brrr-rrr-up," or sometimes the "ba-a-a-a" of a lost lamb, a surprisingly assertive sound from such little bodies. Red-spotted toads trill like an old police whistle, overblown and shrill, coming in sustained bursts and at wider intervals than the tree frogs' shivarees. Neither have a specific breeding time, and both respond to rainfall and warm temperature. In this narrow canyon they rise to rock-concert decibels on warm springs nights. To use the temporary water as quickly as possible demands an intense call-forwarding communication system, one of the ways desert amphibians cope with this uncertain environment. Call individuality in males and call discrimination in females become acutely developed. If someone took the time to record and analyze individual calls, the researcher would probably find that each toad has a distinctive call to designate a pool as "home."

Adult toads and frogs have a good survival rate here but tadpoles don't, and red-spotted toads have developed a specific life strategy for this situation. Of all known toads, they spend the shortest time both in the egg and as tadpoles and can withstand the highest heat. Most are vegetarians, tugging away at algae so vigorously their little bodies quiver with the effort, but a few have carnivorous mouthparts and consume both animal and vegetable matter. As the pools dry, these few may cannibalize their less fortunate brethren, enabling them to mature more quickly and for some, at least, to survive and pass on their genes.

In the canyon suitable pools and puddles of water are likely to be separated by long distances. Generations of toads may spend their entire lives in the same pool and undertake the hazards of migration only when their population builds beyond the capacity of the pool to support them. The more complete the islandlike isolation of populations, the less chance there is of emigration and interbreeding, and the more chance for both the rates of speciation and extinction to accelerate. The river may serve as a migration path, but for animals who raft downstream on debris it's a one-way trip.

Between the pulses of the trilling, crickets chirp doggedly, woefully outsung. For them it must be like being in a room filled with a thousand cash registers all going off at once and no way to shut them off.

The next morning, after last night's cacophony, I again walk up Blacktail, rather thankful for the quiet. A big beetle the size of a pecan, head and thorax tinted burnt orange, sways across the sand, holding its wing covers up as it walks. Size and color identify it as an Arizona blister beetle, which as an adult feeds on desert shrubs. The larvae seek out grasshopper eggs buried in the soil to feed on, but otherwise its life cycle as a whole is incompletely known, another one of those unanswered Colorado River natural history questions waiting to be explored.

I came for my favorite hands-on close-up of the Great Unconformity. In Blacktail Canyon the Great Unconformity is at head height, 1.2 billion missing years right at eye level, a change between rock types so unmistakable and spectacular, so conceptually overwhelming, that once it engages your attention, you watch it weave throughout the canyon, a reminder of the human ability to conjecture about what has gone before, the briefness of life on earth compared to the eons recorded in this rock, and the need to stretch the little gray cells into new dimensions. The Great Unconformity first appears high on the walls of the Upper Granite Gorge at Mile 77.5, marked by what Stanton saw as a "black beaded fringe" of horizontal Tapeats Sandstone dramatically truncating the vertical and diagonal fins of schist beneath it. At Blacktail Canyon the ending of the Upper Granite Gorge drops the Great Unconformity to river level.

John Wesley Powell knew only a modest amount of geology when he made the first of two trips down this river in 1869, but he had enough experience to know what formations *ought* to be present to recognize where something was missing. Beset by hunger, wet moldy supplies, and an exhausted crew worn by the apprehension of not knowing what lay ahead, Powell stepped back, read a landscape, and speculated about the periods of erosion that left lacunae in the geologic record—indeed, most of geologic time in the Grand Canyon is invisible because the times of erosion have lasted far longer than the times of laying down. Powell gave the blanks in the Grand Canyon's geologic record a name: unconformities. He identified four major gaps in the main rock sequences in the Grand Canyon and, in 1876, named this one the Great Unconformity.

Where I stand, two thick, off-white granitic intrusions of Zoroaster Granite, as big as my arm, veined and marbled with cinnamon, raspberry, and gray, angle up through the 1.7 billion-year-old Vishnu Schist, the oldest rock of the Grand Canyon and one of the oldest on the North American continent. Both stop suddenly in a horizontal layer a few inches thick of rough conglomerate, a hodgepodge of cemented pebbles and cobbles. Above, gritty ledges of Tapeats Sandstone cantilever outward, big-grained and salt-streaked, edges rounded into pillowed shapes, laid by a Cambrian sea that reached here over 500 million years ago. That missing 1.2 billion years you can encompass between two hands.

The names of the formations, Vishnu Schist and Zoroaster Granite, were coined by Dr. Charles Doolittle Walcott, who succeeded Powell as director of the U.S. Geological Survey in 1894. He named Vishnu Schist the same year, taking his cue from a landmark butte, Vishnu Temple, designated in 1880 by geologist Clarence E. Dutton, who was fascinated with Oriental religions.

Some two billion years ago, right here where I stand, ocean lapped the edge of a proto–North American continent. The Granite Gorges record the addition of huge areas of new crust to a continent whose shore then lay in present-day southern Wyoming. The additions came as small ocean floor plates and volcanic islands butted against the landmass and stuck. Sediments off the eroding land interfingered with the volcanics as they welded together. The particular mineral combination of Vishnu Schist suggests that it was partly formed of volcanic rock,

103
—

*Toads
and
Frogs
and
Uncon-
formities*

and ghosts of old sediments still linger in shadow lines on its dark rock faces.

By around 1.7 billion years ago new rock fabrics stopped forming. Rocks originally at the surface were buried deeply enough that they were heated, squeezed, and metamorphosed. A second more intense period of metamorphism largely obliterated the first and formed the greenish black micaceous and quartzose schist and gneiss here now, in places up to fourteen thousand feet thick.

The somber schists are often shot through with brighter swaths of color that cross and loop, creating plaids and chevrons and arcane heraldic symbols: intrusions of Zoroaster Granite, named after the sixth-century B.C. Persian prophet. In color ranging from pink to ruddy rose to the intense salmon, and from cream to pewter white, ribbons of once-molten rock truss up the canyon walls, sometimes studded with sugar cubes of white quartz, often aglitter with the facets of tiny gemstones. Later folding and faulting raised these rocks into a chain of mountains, perhaps more than once. The temperature and torque of continent-margin compression contorted the beds even further. What the Colorado River now cuts are the roots of an ancient mountain system that once may have been as high as the Rockies.

Erosion removed at least fifteen thousand feet of Precambrian rock. Then, around 545 million years ago, Cambrian seas advanced eastward and began to wash the flattened Precambrian peneplain, crumbling outcrops of schists, loosening pebbles of quartz from the granites, tumbling and rounding and dropping them to form a layer of conglomerate, "the shingle of an ancient beach," one of the marks of an unconformity. Or, as Walcott described it, "sea breaking off and burying with drifting sand, fragments of rock islands." This rock debris, torn from the underlying formation, became incorporated into the oncoming sands and sediments of the Tapeats sea and hardened into these conglomerates.

I stand, one hand on Vishnu, one on Tapeats, fascinated by something I can intellectualize but only partway perceive the immensity of, a glimpse of time out of mind, a great galloping gap I can relate to only by touching the grit in the sandstone and the smoothness in the schist, spanning in the few inches between my hands a missing quarter of the earth's known history. I feel awed and silly all at once. I don't know what the proper cosmic incantation is, but a very reverent "Wow!" does it for me.

At Blacktail a month later I contemplate the results of unbridled passion beneath a desert moon. The pools perk with tadpoles, many with legs well begun. There are little ones and big ones, waiting to lose tails, add legs, take on a new job. In one bathtub-sized pool quarter-inch black snails vacuum trails across the bottom. These pulmonate snails have no operculum with which to seal themselves against desiccation and need access to both water and atmosphere. Caddis fly larvae prowl the silt, their cases scraping squiggly trails. A small diving beetle skims the water, black decorated with dashing yellow dots, false eye spots that protect against an inexperienced predator.

105
—

Toads
and
Frogs
and
Uncon-
formities

A tan dragonfly naiad, disturbed, jets an inch away, leaving a little fume of silt in the water. It operates on the principal of a jet engine, taking in air and ejecting it in a quick spurt from its anus, swift enough to elude almost any predator. The naiad follows any moving object within its line of vision but loses interest if it isn't proper food. If it is, the lethal labium, which normally covers the dragonfly's face like a divided mask, shoots forward, its tips meeting like a pair of tongs exactly where the nymph's eyes focus. Since few aquatic insects live in the big river itself, these side canyons are the markets that feed the canyon's birds and lizards, providing fresh meat delivery on a regular basis. Without them the canyon would lose much of its richness.

Floating just under the water surface is an exquisite, transparent six-legged creature, tail a fringed triangle, head with deadly looking sickle-shaped mandibles designed for piercing and sucking: the larva of a water beetle. I watch the larva's heart beating, its digestive tract pulsing, so transparent is it. Often called water tigers for their insatiable appetites and their penchant for attacking prey larger than they (up to and including tadpoles and small fish), water beetles predigest their food by injecting a fluid that turns the body of prey into a semiliquid state, which can then be siphoned up.

The adults are the familiar, shirt-button-sized diving beetles that zip back and forth in nearly every pool in the canyon, swift swimmers with long, flattened hind legs that they use like oars, popping to the surface every few minutes to place their spiracles—the "portholes" along an insect's body through which air passes—in touch with air and renew the air supply in their tracheal system. As a whole, insects have not been particularly successful in colonizing the vast underwater world. Of the huge number of insect species known, less than 4 percent utilize water during their life histories. True bugs, the Hemiptera, and beetles, the Coleoptera, are the only orders in which there are aquatic adults.

These little water beetles carry an air bubble under their elytra, an air store directly in contact with some spiracles. Over time the bubble gets smaller and smaller, so the insect must come to the surface anywhere from every few minutes to once in several hours to renew it. Prevalent as they are, water beetles are seldom preyed upon: in their necks they have glands that carry large amounts of steroids, toxic to frogs and toads as well as fish, their most likely predators.

Stone Creek and Canyon downstream at Mile 132 commemorate Julius Stone, a manufacturer of fire-fighting equipment in Columbus, Ohio, and sponsor of the first "sportsman's trip" down the canyon. One evening at Stone Creek, as I try to extract some wine from a recalcitrant container, something bats against my arm. Given the plethora of evening primroses in bloom this evening, I think perhaps it is spring's first sphinx moth and make a grab for it. It turns out to be a dobsonfly with a body as big as my index finger, flexing long, beautifully veined wings. Dobsonflies are the parents of hellgrammites, large larvae with impressive mandibles, often found under waterlogged wood at water's edge. Alerted, I find some under a slab of wood the next morning, in the wet sand near the high-water mark.

Spittlebugs foam the twig ends of ten-foot seep willows. Seep willow leaves, barely toothed toward the upper edge, have a slight sandpaper feel and a lovely witch hazel odor. Although they resemble true willows, they belong to the ubiquitous daisy family. Their flower clusters, stigmas sticking out like miniature pincushions, attract over a hundred species of insects, worked this morning by flies, small bees, and yellow jackets all assailing a veritable banquet table. The bees dive-bomb each other and roll across a flower head like two dogs fighting, take flight again, and resume their ill-tempered tussling on another flower.

Pendant dollops of spittlebug foam drip off branch tips, the top two-thirds sudsy but the bottom third clear. Hidden inside the froth, spittlebug nymphs safely siphon sap, cloistered from dry air and hungry predators. A ladybug beetle slowly works toward a foam-covered leaf. Thinking to help it nearer to a potential source of food, I pick it off and place it next to the spittle, where it backs off with alacrity and vigorously cleans its antennae, reacting to the repellant quality of the foam.

On my way to hike up Stone Canyon, I surprise a brightly colored zebra-tailed lizard, which streaks into a rock crevice. Uncommon in the Grand Canyon, this gorgeous small lizard is distinctively patterned and when it runs, it curls its tail high like a husky. Stone Canyon must also be chuckwalla heaven, for I always see more here than anywhere else on the river. The young have broad rugby stripes on their tails, chunkier than most lizards except the desert spiny lizards. Extra loose skin makes it possible for chuckwallas to slip into crevices and, once there, inflate themselves and wedge in tightly enough to thwart any would-be predator.

I splash up Stone Creek a short way until it dead-ends in a pool beneath a twenty-foot waterfall. Water spreads finely over the rim like a Battenburg lace curtain. The falls spray drops of water that catch the sunshine, throwing diamonds at the creek's rippled feet. On one side, shade canopies the wall and moisture drizzles over tiers of luxuriant maidenhair ferns. Cardinal flowers in a pebble window box flutter in the breeze from the falls. Every waterfall in the canyon has its own personality: the long, straight bridal veil of Deer Creek and the full-bore showers beneath the old cottonwood just up the creek; the fire-hose gushers of Shinumo Creek; the plash of Elves Chasm; the falls at Clear Creek at perfect shoulder height. But for sheer, delightful human scale in this immense river canyon, Stone Creek is everything charming; it even has a ledge behind the falls to stand on and look out through a crystalline screen of shredding, beading, scintillating water. The falls thrum like a guitar, pulsing with a half-remembered melody heard once in a departed dream. I hope Julius Stone was delighted to have this charming place named after him.

Across the creek an upper path traverses a steep, dark talus of pebbles from the diabase sill of altered lavas that here intrudes at various times into the Bass Limestone ramparts at river's edge. The dark rocks present a wood-block landscape in three colors: gray, gray, and gray, one of the four formations making up the 12,000-foot-thick Precambrian Grand Canyon Supergroup laid down between 570 and 1,200 million years ago. Faulting raised these formations into block mountains 10,000 feet high, much like those in today's Basin and Range Province of Utah and Nevada. Erosion planed the mountains down, and no new sediments arrived until early Cambrian seas lapped across the rock and began depositing the coarse sands that became Tapeats Sandstone. Bass Limestone was named for William Bass, who came west for his health in 1883 and went exploring using a map that Powell had drawn. After four days of walking he ran out of water and barely survived because "the drainage system as shown on his [Powell's] map was a delusion and a snare and nearly resulted in my disaster." Later, when Bass worked for Powell, proximity did not temper his opinion one whit. As a guide he set up a camp and cable car at Mile 107.5, which he sold in 1925 for $20,500, which meant that Mrs. Bass no longer had to make her weekly three-day trip from the South Rim down to the river and across to Shinumo Creek on the other side to wash her clothes.

As I ascend, color brightens the path: red firecracker penstemons,

107
—

*Toads
and
Frogs
and
Uncon-
formities*

yellow daisies as big as ten-dollar gold pieces, lavender Mojave asters, enamel blue damselflies. A purple sage flourishes blooms, its leaves even more pungent than those of mint. Showy magenta bracts clasp the deep lavender flowers, shaped so that a bee collecting pollen will transfer it from the stigma of one flower to the stamen of the next, assuring cross-pollination. Little else grows close to it—one botanist suggests that its pungent volatile oils inhibit other seeds from sprouting. In a rock crevice, where sun must never reach, a small tough lip fern grows, the back of its leaves woolly with tangled hairs.

On a bank, a few feet away from my plant perusals, two pebbles move. In a moment a small whiptail lizard surfaces between them, swings around, sticks its head in the hole and digs with the industry of a badger working its burrow. It disappears inside, emerges with more dirt, pushes it aside, turns, and begins digging again, repeating the work pattern like clockwork. Inches away red ants flicker in and out of their nest, oblivious to the fact that their peaceful neighborhood has gone to hell in a handbasket and that they will be hors d'oeuvres at the first whiptail housewarming.

That night a warm wind hustles down the canyon and over the beach, carrying a foretaste of summer's heat. Preceded by an intake of breath that forecasts its coming, it sashays past with a hollow whoosh that ruffles the leaves of the willows like a gambler riffling a deck of cards. In the darkness the restless spirits of the old silt-laden river come back to haunt their canyon and those who sleep here tonight, restless spirits that thump in the attics of the Redwall and rattle the doorknobs of the Tapeats, demanding attention. And in the morning the seep willows say, "Last night—did you hear . . . ?" And the answer is shushed away by the brisk no-nonsense breeze that ladles in the morning sunshine.

In a year with ample spring moisture, when both the river and Lake Mead are at the right height and flow—the lake low enough to provide an interim camp yet high enough to allow passage through the shallows to the take-out at Pearce Ferry—the ideal way to end a river trip becomes possible, and this three-week dory trip will do just this. The next to last night on the river falls at Mile 239.6, Separation Canyon, where the river current has almost entirely disappeared in the backwaters of Lake Mead. Separation Canyon takes its name from the exodus at noon on August 29, 1869, of three of Powell's men, Oramel G. Howland, his brother Seneca, and William H. Dunn. Powell had reprimanded Dunn and ordered him to leave days earlier, but this canyon was the first place that Dunn could climb out and he took it. Psychologist Frank Tikalsky, who has examined the situation as a professional and seasoned observer, suggests that disagreements and ruffled feelings are to be expected in a trip of such length, arduousness, and uncertainty. Powell was often abrupt and inconsiderate and, if not outright arrogant, at least kept aloof, and his single-minded sense of mission was not shared by his men. Ironically, these qualities may also have been the very ones necessary to hold a group together under such trying and difficult circumstances.

For whatever reason, the Howlands joined Dunn and the trio's decision was more fateful than anyone would wish. They walked north out of the canyon, reached Mount Dellenbaugh, where Dunn inscribed his name, then probably hooked up with an old Indian trail out of Toroweap Valley that led to the Mormon town of Toquerville, just across the Utah border, then suddenly disappeared. Powell's account of the incident was published in 1875 in *The Exploration of the Colorado River and Its Canyons*. In this report he treats events of both the 1869 and 1871 trips as one and overemphasizes the dangers of Separation Rapid, perhaps as a rationale for the trio's leaving. Robert Brewster Stanton, who spent a great deal of time and effort researching the affair, did not believe that the severity of the rapid was enough to cause the men to defect, although he did not cavil about its difficulty. Stanton criticized Powell's book, as scholars have since, as "beautifully done—as a piece of narrative writing. As *history*, however, it is sadly deficient, even misleading."

At the time the story was bruited that Indians had killed the three men, but even then many suspected that Indians were not to blame. When Powell heard the news, it came through his Mormon interpreter, Jacob Hamblin, who was in a position to pass on only the information he wanted Powell to have.

The truth may have reflected a far greater tragedy. In a letter written on February 17, 1883, and unpublished for over one hundred years, William Leamy, a Mormon elder, penned a troubled letter to an old friend, implying that he witnessed the execution of Powell's men in the Toquerville ward house in 1869. When young and on a mission in Tennessee, Leamy was helped by Dr. R. S. Aiden, whose son was among the company encamped at Mountain Meadows in 1857. The church had forbidden Mormons to help any of the trains coming through, so when young Aiden turned to Leamy for help and received it, Leamy's brotherly act was in defiance of the church. Unknown members of the priesthood struck him with a picket, fractured his skull, and left him for dead. Instead, he survived.

As in the case of the Mountain Meadows Massacre, the men of Toquerville undoubtedly took a "covenant of silence," for nothing has ever turned up in local literature, diaries, letters, or records, although strong circumstantial evidence, besides Leamy's letter, includes an odd telegram sent from Toquerville on September 7, 1869, ten days after Powell's men left the river, reporting that Indians had killed "Powell's three men," raising the question of how the operator knew who they were. Powell's men were skilled, wary mountain men, not apt to be ambushed, but three armed men appearing out of nowhere, saying they had run the Colorado River, would have struck anyone who knew the river as wildly implausible or an outright lie, and they might well have been thought federal agents, of whom Mormon settlers were extremely distrustful. Twelve years later, the paranoia that led to the Mountain Meadows Massacre of 1857 still tainted.

Two weeks later, on September 15, 1869, a short article in a Salt Lake City paper read, "Major Powell, of the Powell Expedition, who has been lost, drowned, and resurrected a dozen times (on paper), arrived here last night from the south, in the best of health and spirits, a plain unpretentious gentleman. B." "B" stood for Beadle, John H.

A newly minted sandbar shortly below Bat Cave at Mile 267 serves as last camp. Bat Cave was mined for guano from the late 1940s to the early 1950s; the guano was taken by tram across the river to Quartermaster Point, twenty-six hundred feet above, and trucked out. Like most of the commercial mining adventures along the river, it petered out, leaving a trace of failure in the air and debris on the canyon wall.

Mud and muck, silt and sand, band the acres of tonight's flat beach, each with its own texture and hue. Close to the water, little circles, puffy with salt, dimple the sand. Despite the obvious salinity of the soil, small weedy buttercups, rabbitfoot grass, speedwell in flower and seed, woolly daisies, and plantains grow here. Millions of coyote willow and tamarisk sprigs beard the next band of sand. Deep cracks reticulate the next drier strip. Twenty feet back from the water, it looks solid but is as jiggly as walking on a water bed.

The rise of Lake Mead created two distinctive vegetation zones. The upper one contains the typical lower desert scrub already in place for millennia, dominated by creosote bush, ocotillo, cactus, and brittlebush. The lower zone forms a new zone, created when Glen Canyon Dam closed and Lake Mead could not be kept full. Lake Mead was last at full pool in 1983–85; now it is difficult to fill Mead to its 30 million acre-foot capacity because of water held back by the upstream dam. The level of Lake Mead is controlled at Glen Canyon Dam and may vary as much as fifteen to twenty feet here, resulting in water-covered flats at high water and the exposure of acres of silty, often gooey, flats at low water, dominated by tamarisk that establishes a forest of sprouts on the instant, plus coyote willow, arrowweed, and seep willow.

For me, last nights are Januslike, as I look back to time on the river and ahead to life off the river. Everything winds down, as it should. To the west, sky and cliff fade together. To the east, colors gentle, blend into an opalescent sunset. The river barely moves, slips and gathers rather than flows. On last nights something is already gone: anticipation of a place never seen before, perhaps never to be seen again, a certain intensity fueled by apprehension and expectation.

I leave the group's last-evening reminiscences. Last nights are not for me. I walk back to find my sleeping bag drenched with dew, my pillow soggy and soaked, something that never happens on the real river. Red-spotted toads percolate all night. Occasionally a Woodhouse's toad bleats an elongated "wa-aaah wa-aaah." In the dark an owl calls, three short precise "hoos" followed by three to five, quickly repeated, tremulous, syncopated "hoos": a western screech owl, uncommon in the canyon. The call spirals through the chill stillness all night long, seems to reach miles, to come from far away and close by, a haunting wistfulness tunneling through space, a small tufted creature calling across time and ancient memory, that soft, sad refrain that reverberates from skull to skull, the hunter hunting, the sleeper waking.

At a cold, damp, five-o'clock in the morning we drift the river in total silence, floating in the dark under a half-moon pasted on the sky, the river as flat and serene as a George Caleb Bingham painting of the Missouri. As each dory drifts past, beavers completing their night's work smack their tails. A mourning dove's lonely call hangs in the air, as evocative as the shepherd's song at dawn in *Tosca*. Free of the overwhelming visual presence of the canyon, other senses sharpen. The most furtive sounds register: a drop of water plummeting off an oar tip, a carp's fin shattering the river's glassy surface, a beaver yawning, a pebble sighing, a grain of pollen tumbling, an eon passing.

Fleeting scents weave through the air, cool silt, wet bird feather, damp wool, cold wood. A Bell's vireo asks a question, answers it. As the stage lights come up, a black-crowned night heron stands in a screen of reeds at river's edge. Five egrets wing over, their reflections flying upside down in the water. In the crepuscular light creamy white flowers of rock nettle, big as demitasse cups, wedge in the granite crannies alongside the channel. Here Julius Stone saw five wolves and several bobcats.

Despite a stillness antithetical to the river's constant bustle, this terminus of the canyon is handsome and well proportioned, opening to walls reminiscent of the cliffs upstream—same characters, different script. The western end of the Grand Canyon is visually less complex, framed by the low, rolling, more stable slopes, which have a deeper soil and more vegetation with a richer variety of plants. Often travertine ices the walls, laid by the springs of yesteryears. The fine-lined Redwall cliffs, now set back from the river, look transposed from a gentle illustration by William Henry Holmes, whose delicately tiered portrayals of the Grand Canyon gave so many people an idea of its complex beauty. The air blooms with moisture that softens the brilliance of light, mellows the ending.

A red-winged blackbird, a bird not resident upstream in the canyon, sings as Thoreau heard it 140 years ago to the month when he noted that its "conqueree" was best heard while boating on a river. On an ending morning there is something appropriate about the softening, the grace of birdsong, the balance hanging before it begins to tilt toward summer.

We breakfast on the Grand Wash Fault, named in 1875 by Southern Continental Railroad surveyors. Its bold escarpment, through which the river cuts, is at its maximum four thousand feet high. The fault abruptly and neatly ends the Grand Canyon, perhaps the only thing that is simple and neat about the Colorado River in the Grand Canyon. The cutting of the canyon, when and where and how quickly, the river's course across both uplift and sink, and the fact that different parts of the canyon have different histories, make it a geologist's conundrum. USGS geologist Ivo Lucchitta, whose papers are the most cogent and accepted works on the origin of the river, points out that "erosion—or at least nondeposition—may have been typical of this river system through most of its life. This characteristic creates great difficulties for the geologist intent on reconstructing the history of the river because such a history can only be pieced together from evidence left behind by the river."

One point seems fairly certain: the Grand Canyon was cut in a relatively brief period of time. Lucchitta brackets the formation of the canyon as occurring between 1.7 and 4.5 million years ago, a mere sneeze of geologic time, a brevity he regards as "truly remarkable." For this to happen, the river had to cut down 1.2 to 3.2 feet per thousand years and cart off some 3.2 million cubic yards of rock per year down to the Gulf of California.

Far ahead a white string road on the hillside descends to Pearce Ferry, a replacement for the original, now under water, that Hamblin established in 1862. The water markedly shallows. In these lackadaisical waters breed the non-native fish species for which Lake Mead acts as a dispersal center, voracious striped bass, green sunfish, carp, and a variety of minnows now invading the canyon proper to the detriment of native fish species.

The dory drifts into the bay at the ferry and idles between tussocks of reeds and rushes. Shallow waves sparkle and crinkle. Small islands rose, dried, entertained seeds, now block passageways. The current, when it exists at all, is quixotic. The boat idles through a movie set for the *African Queen*, screened and bound by tamarisk and willow and arrowweed that seem to go on to infinity.

The reflections of people who have traveled the length of the canyon have a similarity of spirit, a recognition of the canyon's consistent magnificence and what the passage has required of, taken from, and given back to them, in psychological as well as physical terms. George Bradley, a member of Powell's 1869 expedition, wrote with unadorned, heartfelt relief that "all our trials were over." Powell's last field journal entry on August 28, the day they ran Separation Rapid, is as terse: "Boys left us. Ran rapid. Bradley boat. Make camp on left bank. Camp. 44." But the literary side of Powell understood that endings call forth summations and reflections. By 1875 he had upholstered that brief entry into a dramatic apotheosis: "Now the danger is over, now the toil has ceased, now the gloom has disappeared, now the firmament is bounded only by the horizon, and what a vast expanse of constellations can be seen!"

Stanton stood "spellbound in wonder and admiration, as firmly as I was fixed in the first few miles in surprise and astonishment." Flavell, dealing in capital letters, celebrated that "Wonderful, Fearful, Desolate Canyon." Buzz Holmstrom, on the first solo run of the river in 1937, kept a river journal that is a combination of good humor, appreciation, and a lovely sense of irony that remains one of the gems of river writing. For him, the gift was in the doing: "I had thought: once past there [Lava Cliff Rapid] my reward will begin. But now everything ahead seems kind of empty and I find I have already had my reward, in the doing of the thing." But it is the November words of Julius Stone that touch my heart. Stone was in his early fifties when he ran the river, fretting because boatman Nathaniel Galloway, protective of his crafts, wouldn't let Stone run all the rapids. On November 15, the day they left the canyon, Stone reflected that

> "the strenuous effort, the chance of failure, and the eager stimulation a difficult task inspires—all are ended. And yet, strange to say, I feel no sense of elation. Possibly it is because the hurrying years are leaving more and more of my life behind, and *this*, to which I have eagerly looked forward so long, has now passed into the shadows that fall and lengthen toward the east."

113
—
*Toads
and
Frogs
and
Uncon-
formities*

Summer

near Mile 211

8

It is difficult to describe the rapids with the foot-rule stan-dard, and give an idea of their power. One unfamiliar with "white water" usually associates a twelve-foot descent or a ten-foot wave with a similar wave on the ocean. There is no comparison. The waters of the ocean rise and fall, the waves travel, the water itself, except in breakers, is comparatively still. In bad rapids the water is whirled through at the rate of ten or twelve miles an hour, in some cases much swifter; the surface is broken by streams shooting up from every sub-merged rock; the weight of the river is behind it, and the waves, instead of tumbling forward, quite as often break up-stream. Such waves, less than six feet high, are often dangers to be shunned. After being overturned in them we learned their tremendous power, a power we would never have asso-ciated with any water, before such an experience, short of a waterfall.

Ellsworth Kolb, 1914, *Through the Grand Canyon
from Wyoming to Mexico*

Badger Creek
and Running Rapids

———

Summer is irrevocably connected in my mind with running rapids. Every river trip must negotiate around sixty of them between Lees Ferry and Diamond Creek. I do not particularly enjoy running rapids in 45°F water and 20°F air. Ideally rapids should be not a matter of survival on the cusp but a welcome wetting down on a hundred-degree day. Rapids should be a glorious orgy of splash and spray, splinters of shattered sunlight, brilliant turquoise shadows, screens of white lacy foam edged with rainbows, an entrance into a glittering, sparkling world, tilted off the horizontal and incandescent with light.

The rapids begin at Badger Creek. Once upon a time, at Mile 7.8, slabs peeled off the deep beige of the weathered Coconino Sandstone cliff like a paint scraper skins off paint, leaving an ivory scar pointing to one of the joys of summer and the unwary river passenger's first baptism, Badger Creek Rapid. Ellsworth Kolb's description of a rapid says it all. A youngster from Pennsylvania, he came west and discovered the Grand Canyon, decided to make a profession of running and photographing the Colorado River, and persuaded his younger brother, Emery, to join him. The brothers left Green River, Wyoming, on September 8, 1911, and reached Needles, California, on January 18 the following year, having made the first moving pictures of the Colorado River in the Grand Canyon.

It may be small comfort to the first-time passenger that Badger, named because Jacob Hamblin shot a badger there, has confounded as well as terrified many passengers. Claude Birdseye, the U.S. Geological

Survey engineer who led the 1923 expedition, wrote on seeing Badger that "the water looked forbiddingly rough," and their first boat knocked a hole in its bottom from striking one of Badger's boulders. On a trip in 1934 with outfitter Bus Hatch, Clyde Eddy, who didn't like rapids much at all, was "so frightened he got down in the bottom [of the boat] just like a wet hound." But in 1937 Buzz Holmstrom figured out how to run it beautifully, despite feeling "kind of blue this morning when I got up, but after breakfast felt much better. I kept looking at the rapid and thought I saw a way to run it." The classic run is still Holmstrom's, to "drop over the top on the right side of the main channel, which runs square into the rock below, and the suction below the rock sort of pulls the boat to the right so as to miss the rock. It worked fine."

When approaching Badger, one sees only a smooth, innocent line of river surface behind which an occasional gobbet of white water flies up and falls back, inexplicable handfuls of spray, flung as provocatively as the lacy garments ladies of the theater used to toss out from behind dressing room screens. The momentary calm in the pool above Badger, a quiet current running between 1 and 3 miles per hour, is deceptive, especially compared to the 4 to 6 mph the river generally runs in straight reaches. Not until the current accelerates and plunges the boat into the tongue is the roar and bombast of the rapid manifest.

In a configuration common throughout the canyon, the V-shaped tongue, a slick rolling chute, constricted and shaped by strong lateral waves, points to a path of no return. An unexpectedly crisp breeze smacks you in the face and then the rapid breaks loose—there is little to compare with that first frightening look into the maw of chaos and the river's careless and hypnotic power. Even at low-flow velocities, the speed of the current can increase more than ten times and may jump to as much as 20 mph in the rapid itself, creating turbulence that charges the water with so much air that it froths like beaten egg whites, a meringue gone wild.

The drop of fifteen feet at Badger takes place in a sixth of a mile, making it one of the steeper rapids in the canyon. Grand Canyon rapids have their own rating system from one to ten, and every good river guidebook also notes each rapid's difficulty at various levels of water. Larry Stevens's excellent river guide, *The Colorado River in Grand Canyon*, rates Badger's fifteen-foot drop as 8-7-6-5, the four numbers denoting difficulty at water levels of very low, low, medium, and high, warning that at lower water levels it becomes much more difficult.

From being a well-behaved, sensibly horizontal vehicle, the boat bounds and bucks and plunges into an incoherent mass of splashing, fuming chaos, where it's every wave for itself. The flow does not increase linearly but bunches in "hydraulic jumps," manifested in big haystack waves—standing waves that remain perpendicular to the current, spewing foam off their crests. Then the haystacks lessen to undulating rolling waves that finally peter out from the twin frictions of air and river bottom. The river returns to its usual swirling flow as if nothing had ever happened.

At the foot of the rapid the wrinkled ridge of an eddy line, interrupted by boils and small whirlpools, divides the upstream flow of the eddy from the downstream flow of the river. Where the bore of fast water from the rapid emerges and encounters the slower water along the edge of the river, a sheer line forms that sets the slower water spinning in the opposite direction: eddy flow is firmly upstream, and the only way to exit it is to row vigorously in that direction. Eddies usually form at the foot of rapids, but they may also form wherever the channel bends or obstacles interrupt or deflect the current. When a motor raft crosses an eddy line, the propeller's sound changes as different underwater currents give it different messages. Water within an eddy generally flows slowly, around a foot per second, not fast enough to hold sand and silt in suspension so they settle out and form sandbar beaches.

The boat rotates around into the eddy to wait for following boats. I look back at waves galloping upstream, peaking into great larruping pyramids of water, mantling menacing holes into which they break. Wind carries the roar away and without the rapid's fist-shaking fury, following boats seem to hover tranquilly, removed from the slam-and-spray reality, a slow-motion silent movie of a river ballet, graceful and lyrical.

To someone who has not run a rapid before and questions the need to do so at all, the lure of this charging volume of water pointing toward your very own vulnerable, frangible body is difficult to explain. For some it is the challenge to "beat the river." Those who row have the intellectual and physical challenge of coordinating head and hand and doing something difficult well, *very* well, even with grace and precision. For others rapids give an edge to living, a baptism that blesses with a reminder of mortality. Still others need the willingness to risk, to push the limits one more time, to cherish the sense of monumental natural power into which one must fit in order to survive. Once is enough for many, and forever not enough for some.

Rapids on the Colorado River account for a scant tenth of the river's length but for half its drop in elevation. Through its total fall of some nineteen hundred feet within the Grand Canyon, it drops an average eight feet per mile, about twenty-five times that of the Mississippi. Half that drop occurs in 160 rapids spaced an average 1.6 miles apart.

The influx of debris brought in by Badger Creek and washed slightly downstream of its mouth formed Badger Rapid, a process characteristic of all but a couple Grand Canyon rapids. Debris flows, shooting down steep side canyons, are responsible for 54 of the 57 major rapids in the Grand Canyon. The ability of small side canyons to contribute to the river anything from gravel fans and cobbles to tool-shed-sized boulders derives from the steepness of their gradients, which follow fault lines and fracture zones in the cliffs. The side canyons affect the river out of all proportion to their size through debris flows that combine high density with high velocity. The size of rock a flow can move is directly proportional to the square of the velocity of the water—that is, if the stream's velocity quadruples as debris flows have been known to do, the size of the rock it can carry multiplies a whopping sixteen-fold.

Badger initially formed in a relatively open channel. A debris flow cascaded down the side canyon and may have completely dammed the river or, more likely, shoved the river against the opposite bank. The river usually overtops or breaches an obstruction fairly quickly, leaving a narrow channel through which the river surges. Over time a rapid usually achieves some stability in the relationship of its width to that of the normal river channel, expressed as the "constriction ratio." The Colorado River has molded its rapids with remarkable constancy, to a surprisingly uniform ratio of 2:1, indicating that the regular channel has twice the width of the constrained channel in a rapid.

John Wesley Powell ran cumbersome, round-bottomed wooden boats with two rowers facing upstream, a man on the tiller, and the fourth man shouting instructions, hardly a comforting arrangement for oarsmen rowing as hard as they could into a disaster they could not see. Brown and Stanton used oarsmen in the same manner on the railroad survey. Both made laborious portages and suffered unnerving upsets.

The change in the way rapids were run and the kind of boats used came in late summer of 1896, when a trapper from California named George Flavell, inspired by an article Stanton wrote for *Scribner's* in 1890, decided to run the river from Green River, Wyoming, to Yuma, Arizona. Arriving in Green River with Rámon Montéz, a shadowy figure about whom little is known, in eight days Flavell built himself a flat-bottomed boat, fifteen and a half feet long, with a square stern, a narrow prow, and a double-thick planked bottom, which he christened *Panthon*. They started down the river on August 17, "First, for the adventure; second, to see what so few people have seen; third, to hunt and trap; fourth, to examine the perpendicular walls of rock for gold."

123
—
*Badger
Creek
and
Running
Rapids*

Flavell's technique was to face the bow, which he pointed downstream, and to stand up so he could see better, pushing through with his oars. By the time he and Montéz reached Lees Ferry in early October, Montéz, tired of sitting behind Flavell and getting soaked, announced he was leaving. Flavell's often-quoted and perhaps apocryphal reaction was, "You can come along with me or you can float down dead." At any rate, Montéz went. They portaged Soap Creek Rapid, which turned out to be "a little more exercise than we were used to," but otherwise ran every rapid in the Grand Canyon proper, without upsets or irrevocable damage, a remarkable accomplishment in a single boat.

That same winter of 1896–97 Nathaniel Galloway with another trapper from Utah ran the Colorado River from Green River, Wyoming, through the Grand Canyon to Needles, California, the common take-out for early river trips. With more than a dozen white-water trips under his oars before this run, Galloway also realized the futility of handling a large boat with a single oarsman or trying to build a boat strong enough to endure battering. He too designed a slender boat for speed and lightness, shallow and narrow with a definite rake at bow and stern, about the size of the modern dory, with watertight compartments bracketing an open cockpit. In rowing rapids, Galloway swiveled the boat to make the stern face forward into the white water as rowers do today, giving him not only better vision but also the ability to pull back from danger, since control in a rapid depends on going either faster or slower than the current.

Reportedly, Flavell met Galloway when he arrived at Needles in February 1897. Both had gone down the Green and Colorado Rivers ostensibly to trap furs. Galloway netted $600, which he did not consider worth his time, perhaps the last serious fur-trapping trip in the canyon. Flavell's name does not appear again on the river (he died four years later), but Galloway's does. In January 1898 he was working at Robert Stanton's placer mines in Glen Canyon. Stanton's gold-dredging operations were partially bank-rolled by industrialist Julius Stone. Stone, checking out his investment, met Galloway, judged him ingenious at fixing anything, "so dexterous that one would not be surprised to see him run a boat on a heavy dew." In 1909 they launched a trip together, only the sixth trip of the canyon's whole length, and Galloway became the first man to make two trips the whole length of the canyon—Powell's second trip ended at Kanab Creek.

At Soap Creek, where Mr. Hamblin's raccoon turned to soap when he tried to soak it overnight, and the only rapid that Flavell and Montéz did not run, the brothers Kolb looked long and hard at the rapid with the practical and jaundiced eyes of someone about to run it in a chilly October, in wooden boats without support. They knew that their predecessors, Stone and Galloway, in October two years earlier, had chosen to line Soap Creek Rapid, that is, to let the boat down by standing on the bank and jockeying it through the rapid, holding onto painter and stern lines. Nevertheless, the Kolbs ran Soap Creek, without mishap.

Hum Woolley chose to line Soap Creek in 1903 on the fifth trip of the river. Next to the trip of Bessie and Clyde Hyde, historian David Lavender finds Woolley's trip one of the most enigmatic. A certain Madame Schell, a widow living in Los Angeles, hired Woolley to do the legally required improvements to maintain mining claims she owned near the Grand Canyon. Rather than sensibly setting out overland, Woolley built a boat in Mrs. Schell's back yard, disassembled it, shipped it to Flagstaff, and reassembled it at Lees Ferry in August 1903. As helpers, he hired his two cousins, who obviously didn't know what they were getting into and spent most of the trip clinging to the decks in abject terror as they sluiced through rapids. On September 4 cousin Arthur Sanger wrote with desperate gratitude, "Thank God we are still alive, it is impossible to describe what we went through today."

Woolley made it through the canyon and got around to visiting Mrs. Schell's claims, then vanished into the nowhere whence he came, leaving the question of who on earth such a skilled boat designer and oarsman really was.

House Rock Rapid at Mile 17 takes its name from House Rock Valley. Father Escalante, approaching the river from the northwest on his reconnaissance of the Southwest in 1776, noted "the gorges and large rocks of the river basin which, seen from the western side, seem like a long chain of houses." Recently bighorn sheep have been brought into the valley, and one June morning, sixteen sheep, two lambs in a flock of females and young males, came down to water as the raft wallowed past.

House Rock is a ten-foot drop, caused by rocks brought down Rider Canyon. The river sweeps into a V, picks up speed, lathers into a white froth—except that "froth" is too dainty a word for the thick foaming maelstroms that churn off the left wall. Water in the huge hole in the middle of the rapid glints emerald green in the sunshine, icy teal blue in the shadows. In big rafts you can be as much as five feet above the water and the splash often depends upon the boatman's fancy. Not so in a dory. When you sit in a dory, the waves in House Rock are eye-level, in-your-face affrontive. Sitting high on the back hatch of a dory, I look down into a hole that transmogrifies into a huge obese wave and buries my present, my past, and my future being. I come up sputtering and drenched to the ribs. Water fills the dory up to the gunwales.

"Bail!" I never realized the urgency of that clarion call until I calculated the weight of the amount of water I heaved out in a calibrated five-gallon bailing bucket. A pint being a pound the world around, I figure I threw at least three hundred pounds over the side. Add roughly the same amount in the other bilge, and you're rowing a baby hippopotamus. On the plus side, the effort of bailing significantly warms up a body recently immersed in 46°F water.

Running rapids in a dory or a small oar-driven raft (both are sixteen to eighteen feet long) fosters a very intimate association with the river. In the 1920s the Norwegian Torkel Kaahus modified the Mississippi River "sweep scow," then used to barge up and down the Salmon River. He canted bow and stern upward, leaving less hull surface to interface with the water so it was easier to rotate, elongated the square stern into a point to cut through waves better, and used it on the McKenzie River in Oregon. Martin Litton and P. T. Reilly saw in the McKenzie boats the potential for Colorado River navigation and worked with boat builders to design and construct a boat sixteen feet long, with airtight compartments and oarlocks set at the widest part of the boat to get maximum leverage on the nine-foot oars, essentially today's dory.

At Mile 75, less than two miles above Hance Rapid, shale cliffs backing the beach radiate back the afternoon heat. Shade is virtually nonexistent on this June afternoon rapidly approaching the far edge of insufferable.

The guides huddle: to stay or not to stay, that is the question. The river runs just under 5,000 cfs and is falling, uncomfortably low to run Hance in the big thirty-seven-foot rafts of this trip. If we get there and cannot run, the campground at Hance has less shade than here and, according to the boatmen, is two hundred degrees hotter.

I believe them. If I don't believe them I don't believe anything. Experienced Grand Canyon boatmen and boatwomen are the best in the world, bar none. They deal with a fluctuating river whose fickle flow alters how rapids are run from hour to hour. They know how each rapid runs at each flow, and what river mile they've reached at any given moment. They explain the complexity and use of "the unit" with such panache that even the most prudish of Victorian ladies would not take umbrage. They are born performers, shills for the preservation of the canyon, talented teachers intriguing even the geologically impaired with complex ideas and practical identifications. They are responsible for the lives of those in their boats, bonded by necessity to people they have never seen before and may not see again. Many are fabulous cooks— for ten, twenty, thirty, forty people. Every morning. Every night. From scratch.

They inflate and rig boats, lug massive amounts of gear, load and lash, unlash and unload, de-rig (one boatman compares manhandling a deflated raft to hauling a dead elephant), pack up, and drive back to Lees Ferry to do it all over again next week. They are a sister- and brother-hood who greet each other lavishly, loan each other a pound of coffee, share a six-pack, trade recipes, describe hair-raising rides through rapids with extravagant gestures, commiserate over each other's hangovers, flaunt senses of humor that ought to be bottled and sold. Inveterate gossips, they know where everyone else is and with whom, this happy few, this band of brothers (and sisters) whose Saint Crispin's Eve is just above Crystal or Lava Falls. As boatman-historian Scott Thybony writes, on dry land Colorado River boatmen wake up at night "listening for a sound that isn't there."

And they very patiently answer questions like, "Does the moon affect the tides in the Grand Canyon?"

After an hour of debate, looking at the river, looking at the sun, looking at the sand, the guides decide to stay here and run Hance on the rising water of morning. I dump my gear and go wandering.

Across a sandstone ledge mysteriously inscribed perfect circles the size of small manhole covers appear, outlined as precisely as if scribed by a compass. The crossbedded sandstone here at river's edge belongs to the uppermost member of the Hakatai Shale Formation, one of the four sedimentary formations of the Grand Canyon Supergroup. The Super-group remains exposed until the Upper Granite Gorge some three miles downstream, outcropping elsewhere only as faulting wrenches it to the surface.

In the middle of a sandy path through the tamarisk, a tiny Grand Canyon rattlesnake has wound itself into a serene resting coil just four inches across. A resting coil is a flat spiral like a cinnamon roll, with the head at rest on the outer edge, very different from an aggressive striking coil, with the tail spread to serve as a stable base from which to launch a strike. Wavering dark gray lozenges pattern a back webbed with white, markings not yet clearly defined. The markings of an adult Grand Canyon rattlesnake are distinctive: discrete oval rings crosswise on a rosy pink ground, a background color that blends into the sandy soil eked out of reddish sandstones and shales. The little sleeper awakens and flicks out a threadlike forked tongue, two conjoined cylinders that diverge into a pair of distinct, delicate, and sensitive tips that sample the air and pick up odor particles. Slowly it unwinds itself to its full thirteen inches, its body not as big in diameter as my index finger. Its first retained rattle, only a button, gives a brave bumblebee buzz. The quiver probably developed to lure an enemy to focus on its tail rather than its head; the rattle developed later, a heart-stopper that several non-venomous snakes and burrowing owls are able to imitate with stunning effect.

127
—

*Badger
Creek
and
Running
Rapids*

Although rattlesnakes are usually thought of as inhabitants of dry, rocky places, the canyon rattler, *Crotalus viridis abyssus*, often occurs in riparian habitats within feet of water and dens in tamarisk thickets. Two rattlesnakes commonly prowl the canyon, speckled and Grand Canyon; the latter, endemic and more abundant, developed in the riverside "island habitat."

The population of both snakes appears to have increased since construction of the dam, as their food base of small rodents and lizards has burgeoned. Although night hunters, every one I've seen has been out during the day, albeit resting in the shade and not actively hunting. The rattler's success in the desert depends upon the two common adaptations to heat and desiccation: avoid or tolerate. Tracking prey by heat sensing, ground vibration, and smell enables them to be active at night, to avoid high temperatures, and to conserve body water. When prey is sparse they can fast for long periods, sustained by a low metabolic rate. Within the hour I meet a second rattler, two more than I usually see on a trip. It also snoozes, its broken diamond-shaped spots matching it to the webbed shadows of a silt-coated slab at river's edge. It unloops to a couple of feet in length and glides beneath a damp rock.

The next morning, Hance's ill-tempered grumble precedes it upstream. White streaks and a big burnt orange patch of Hakatai Shale color the left slope above the rapid at Mile 76.5. Some layers of the Hakatai (the Havasupai name for the Colorado River) contain brilliant purples and reds and startling patches of brilliant orange hornfels from the oxidation of iron-bearing minerals. When molten volcanic rock pushed into the shale, heat and pressure metamorphosed it to this vibrant color, which, where it outcrops, lights a canyon wall with hot coals. When polished by the rain it gleams like the elegant black and cinnabar red of Japanese lacquerware.

Hance was not always a rocky road to disaster. Once Red Canyon debouched into a narrow lake backed up behind a lava dam over a hundred miles downstream. Today the lake is long gone and debris flows now shoot down Red Canyon on the left and freight boulders of resistant diabase and Shinumo Quartzite directly into the water where their adamant hardness gives little away to the river. Hance has a thirty-foot drop in half a mile, the biggest drop in the Grand Canyon, and the black boulders make Hance look like the field where Cadmus sowed the dragon's teeth.

Across the river a wall of Hakatai displays the classic geology book illustration of a dike and a sill. Intrusions of molten rock create "dikes" when they wedge in along fractures and crosscut other rocks, and "sills" when they intrude along preexisting bedding planes. The dike traces a small diagonal fault up through the fine-grained sandstone layers of the Hakatai, then thins into a sill as it insinuates between the Hakatai and the overlying Shinumo Quartzite. Whereas the shale crumbles and the river handily carries it away, the lava intrusion has kept its integrity and stands in sharp relief.

High on the cliff ahead, tailings drizzle down the slope from John Hance's asbestos mine. When the great curtain with "ASBESTOS" emblazoned on it thudded down on the stage of a London music hall in the late nineteenth century, the asbestos likely came from Hance's mine— fire-resistant, asbestos theater curtains were much in demand in a time of open flame footlights. Asbestos is the common name for one of the serpentine group of minerals that occur in nature as green to yellow, silky smooth, more or less flexible fibers. Most asbestos fibers are short, slippery, difficult to spin and weave; only those a third of an inch or longer are suitable for weaving, and these are usually combined with a rough cotton for ease of handling. The fibers from Hance's mine were coveted for their three- to four-inch length. Ore ferried across the river was packed out by mule to the South Rim, shipped to San Diego, and thence carried around Cape Horn to London.

One in the long string of characters associated with the river, Captain "Honest John" Hance (his title presumably from the Civil War) first saw the canyon in 1883 while working at a ranch on the South Rim. In 1884 he improved an old Indian trail to the foot of the canyon. Although a prospector, he suspected that there might be more money in guiding tourists than in mining. As the "Münchhausen of the West," Hance enchanted guests with tall stories, vowing he once snowshoed across the top of the canyon when it was filled with clouds. Another time he claimed he couldn't save from starving the man whose new rubber-soled shoes kept him bouncing up and down in the canyon. As one euphoric guest wrote, after finding the Grand Canyon much grander and more sublime than Yosemite, Yellowstone, and Mont Blanc, "God bless our friend John Hance!"

129
—
Badger
Creek
and
Running
Rapids

The Hance Trail, until the Bright Angel Trail opened to the public in the 1920s, gave the only decent access to the river and boasts some notable "firsts." The first woman to hike into the canyon, Emma Burbank Ayer (after whom Ayers Point is named), came down the Hance Trail in May 1885, a year after it was finished. C. Hart Merriam used this trail when he camped in the canyon, working out his theory of life zones. S. B. Jones, a park ranger, saw an eagle splashing in a pool at the top of the Redwall and wrote that "this is the first definite record that we have of our National Bird in Grand Canyon." When the Birdseye Expedition was resupplied here in 1923, head boatman Emery Kolb took advantage of the supply train to bring his daughter Edith down. The river was so low that pack mules had to carry supplies to the foot of the rapid so boats could be run empty. When Emery let Edith ride on one of the unloaded boats, she became the first woman to run a major rapid in the Grand Canyon. Colonel Birdseye, horrified by the hair-raising run, disallowed any more women on *any* of the expedition's boats.

Flavell and Montéz were debating whether to run or to line Hance Rapid when three tourists came down the Hance Trail and said they wanted to see some action. Flavell's vanity got the best of him. In transit he broke and lost oars, tore out oarlocks, wedged in the boulders twice, and went down "sideways, endways, and every way," but he remained upright, thus being the first to run Hance.

The entrance of the rapid is forced far to the right. There is no neat tongue, no neat tail-wave train, no neat eddies, no neat run-out. There's no good cushion of water and not much margin for error, and the crack of a snapped oar signals that you're in the wrong place at the wrong time but it's too late now. George Bradley, with Powell in 1869, thought it "the worst rapid we have found today and the longest we have seen on the Colorado. The rocks are seen nearly all over it for half a mile or more—indeed the river runs through a vast pile of rocks." True. For Ellsworth Kolb it was the measure of a "nasty" rapid:

While reading over our notes one evening we were amused to find that we had catalogued different rapids with an equal amount of fall as "good," "bad," or "nasty," the difference depending nearly altogether on the rocks in the rapids. The "good rapids" were nothing but a descent of "big water," with great waves . . . the "bad rapids" contained rocks, and twisting channels, but with half a chance of getting through. A nasty rapid was filled with rocks, many of them so concealed in the foam that it was often next to impossible to tell if rocks were there or not, and in which there was little chance of running through without smashing a boat. The Hance Rapid was such a one.

True again. Running Hance is like going down a river-sized pinball machine. The difference is that rocks don't go "ding" when they're hit but broadcast "blang" when a propeller contacts an underwater chunk of basalt, or emit a rich, ripping sound when a raft pontoon is sliced open by a can-opener edge, or crackle sharply when a dory's wooden hull confronts a boulder and loses. Some very good boatmen have gotten hung up in Hance and remember the occasion with no joy.

To look back up from the bottom is to wonder how anything larger than a toy duck can bob through. Most rapids can be and are run in less than a minute and a half. Hance takes almost three.

As in three lifetimes.

across from Grapevine

9

As the rain increased, I heard some rock tumbling down behind us, and, looking up, I saw one of the grandest and most exciting scenes of the crumbling and falling of what we so falsely call the everlasting hills. As the water began to pour over from the plateau above, it seemed as if the whole upper edge of the Canyon had begun to move. Little streams, rapidly growing into torrents, came over the hard top stratum from every crevice and fell on the softer slopes below. In a moment they changed into streams of mud, and, as they came farther down, again changed into streams of water, mud and rock, undermining huge loose blocks of the harder strata and starting them, they plunged ahead. In a few moments, it seemed as though the slopes on both sides of the whole Canyon, as far as we could see, were moving down upon us, first with a rumbling noise, then an awful roar. As the larger blocks of rock plunged ahead of the streams, they crashed against other blocks, lodged on the slopes, and, bursting with an explosion like dynamite, broke into pieces, while the fragments flew into the air in every direction, hundreds of feet above our heads, and as the whole conglomerate mass of water, mud, and flying rocks, came down the slopes nearer to where we were, it looked as if nothing could prevent us from being buried in an avalanche of rock and mud.

Robert Brewster Stanton, 1920, *Down the Colorado*

Granite Gorges
and Spinning Spiders

To enter the Upper Granite Gorge under the silence of oars, the ominous growl of the first rapid floats upstream long before one becomes visible, the sound concentrated and amplified by the walls, more vocal than rapids upstream where the canyon is more open and vegetation absorbs some of the reverberations. The reach sustains two and a half more major rapids than any other comparable stretch of river, averaging only one and a half miles apart. The challenge with most rapids in the Granite Gorges is that boats can neither be lined nor portaged through, there being no long beaches or boulder aprons above them for a boater to walk. They have to be run. As Flavell remarked, "nothing but bail and shiver all day."

The Upper Granite Gorge begins at Mile 77.5, less than a mile beyond Hance. Three "granite" gorges grace the Grand Canyon, the upper extending from Mile 77 to 119, the middle but three miles long from Mile 127 to 130.5, and the lower from Mile 216 to 261. Powell's name for these gorges is a misnomer since the predominant rocks are metamorphic schists and gneisses, with igneous granite intruded only in dikes and plutons. But "Upper Schist and Gneiss Gorge" sounds awkward and, if anyone did, Powell had an ear for the sonorous, melodic name. Vishnu Schist rises beneath the Grand Canyon Supergroup shales and limestones, separated from them by what Powell called the Greatest Angular Unconformity, a gap of 825 million years. When the Grand Canyon Supergroup drops out and Tapeats Sandstone rests directly on Vishnu Schist, the missing 1.2 billion years earmark the Great Unconformity.

In the Upper Granite Gorge, panels of Vishnu Schist gleam and shine in the sunlight, fluted and scooped, glossy as a raven's wing. The hollows cradle flickering stripes of river reflections. Huge fins rise like polished scimitars, slice into the water, and force the river to hiss around them. Where seeps drizzle down from high on the wall they leave salt-streaked banners like pennants. In some of these spectacularly twisted and torqued rocks are relict pillow lavas, the same as those being spewed into the water off Hawaii today, cross sections of lava tubes formed underwater 1.74 billion years ago.

In summer, passing close to these sepulchral walls is like skirting the flank of a dragon. Rock made of seething, molten magma still pulses heat out more than a millennia later when its flat faces tilt to the sun like solar collectors. The hardness of the schist seems to defy the river. The river wheedles, nibbles, and laps, whispers, cajoles, and slaps, and makes little headway. If there is anywhere in the canyon that rock ignores the river's insistence, it is in these gorges.

The muttering of Sockdolager, the first rapid in the Upper Granite Gorge, drifts upstream long before the rapid reveals itself. A nineteenth-century slang word meaning "knockout blow," Sockdolager was named on the first Powell Expedition. Although not considered as difficult as Hance, Sockdolager still displays a pile of bad-tempered water as lateral waves rebound off rock walls, intersect in a rampant confusion of herringbone patterns. Stanton tried lining through and smashed up his lead boat. Hum Woolley ran it stern first with cousin Sanger clinging to the deck, most of the time completely underwater and "sick and dizzy with fear." Sumner, on Powell's first journey, declared that this rapid "made my hair curl . . . a white foam as far down as we could see, with a line of waves in the middle fifteen feet high." Trying to row and bail at the same time, and facing backward, Frederick Dellenbaugh and photographer Jack Hillers, who thought it "a hell of a looking place," manned the *Emma Dean* while Powell, on his second trip, shouted directions::

> I pulled the bow oars, and my back was toward the terrific roar which, like the voice of some awful monster, grew louder as we approached. It was difficult to refrain from turning round to see what it looked like now, but as everything depended on the promptness with which Hillers and I handled our oars in obedience to Powell's orders, I waited for the plunge, every instant ready to execute a command. We kept in the middle of the stream, and as we neared the brink our speed began to accelerate. Then of a sudden there was a dropping away of all support, a reeling sensation, and we flew down

the declivity with the speed of a locomotive. The gorge was chaos. The boat rolled and plunged. The wild waters rolled over us, filling the open spaces to the gunwale.

But to give the devil his due, some boatmen love Sockdolager. Norm Nevills was one of them. It was his "firm conviction that no one has ever lived until he or she has had a first view of Sockdolager—looking down into that fury of water, knowing he has to go through it in a boat— taking off, pausing on the brink and then, with what seems like express train speed literally hurtling down into the lashing waves. It's fearful— quickly changing into a perfectly thrilling exhilaration."

137
—

*Granite
Gorges
and
Spinning
Spiders*

Just above Grapevine Rapid at Mile 81.5, a peregrine falcon rockets upstream and strikes a swallow; feathers fly, all so quickly that the mind takes a second to catch up with the eye. The falcon lands on a rock ledge about thirty feet above the water, one of the nesting population that inhabits the canyon, in some reaches spaced a nest per mile, one of the highest known densities in North America. They have increased with the growing population of violet-green swallows and swifts available as prey, as well as with the expanding numbers of migratory waterfowl, all of which have responded to the greater overall aquatic productivity brought by Glen Canyon Dam. Seeing a falcon always enchants me, and I reflect on the keen interest they cause because they are "endangered." While I too treasure every glimpse, my heart also runs with the common folk, the red-spotted toads, the case-lugging caddis fly larvae, the water tigers and the brittlebushes, no less remarkable because they are more common, and no less important in the ecosystem because they are small.

At the back of Grapevine Beach slats and fins of schist anchor into the sand, framing a series of narrow V-shaped niches. As new land formed at the edge of the North American protocontinent, shear zones occurred where western plates thrust over eastern plates. The broken walls at Grapevine belonged to one of these zones, a niche of which provides web space for an orb-weaver spider. Across the two-foot opening of one of the niches the spider has made her first bridge line by fastening silk to one side and wafting to the other wall, attaching and stretching the line taut, setting out spokes, weaving a web now a foot across and guyed from all edges, in which she now hangs head down in the middle. Her silk is one of the strongest of natural fibers; a strand can pull out as much as a fifth of its length before snapping. These gossamer filaments were once used for dressing wounds because they were so efficient in stanching the flow of blood. The spider's silk is a fibrous protein insoluble in water that hardens as soon as it hits the air, and she is able to spin plain threads, sticky web threads, and egg-sack silk. The web rays are simple silk, but the spiral strands are viscous, and these she holds clear with a hind leg as she lays them.

When Madame scuttles outward to answer some unseen disturbance in her net, I have a glimpse of a rusty brown carapace, brown and tan striped legs, and two yellow spinnerets. Her shield-shaped abdomen with pointed corners identifies her as a spiny-bellied orb-weaver, the spines making her rather unpalatable to birds but not to solitary wasps, who like to stuff their cells with such as she. After her foray to the outer edge she returns to center, fastidiously picking at the strands to settle her weight, and snuggles back into an upside-down vigil.

At first light I check the web. In the night she has connected all the radii neatly and fashioned an elegantly symmetrical web. She dangles in the center, waiting for just the right message to signal breakfast so she can scuttle out to the entangled prey and inject her venom. Orb-weavers have such poor vision that they sense their prey by the vibrations of the web set off when a meandering midge or a cartwheeling caddis fly blunders into it. Under my hand lens, I note that some flighty victims escaped, leaving their hairs and scales on the net but not themselves, while the other tiny bodies caught in the web this morning speak to the exquisite efficiency of her efforts. Traditionally orb-weavers have been thought of as passive "sit-and-wait" hunters, garnering whatever happens to come their way. New research suggests that orb-weavers actually determine the type of prey they take with some precision by where they place their webs and by the size of its openings. As a breeze filters by, her gossamer construction shimmers with early morning light.

One hot July afternoon we camp just above Granite Rapid at Mile 93.1, in the deepest section of the Upper Granite Gorge. The walls are predominantly rough-grained Zoroaster Granite, bright Venetian red from their preponderance of feldspar, shot with ashy grays and coral pinks. Almost everyone recognizes granite for its coarse crystalline texture of microscopic minerals—pink feldspar, flakes of mica, and white or pink quartz. In addition to these, tourmaline is common in these granites, and the faces of small garnets and beryl flash when they catch the light.

Camp at Granite Rapid fills a long thin ledge on river left, continuing almost to Monument Creek at Mile 93.3. Monument Creek, when it runs, warbles down a steep, tight corkscrew canyon. Water has scooped the rock into chutes so narrow that sometimes the walls are but an arm's width apart, carved into the voluptuous polished curves of a Gaston Lachaise sculpture. Monument Creek is a quintessential Grand Canyon tributary, constricted and steep, a "hydrologically flashy" stream that responds quickly to storms and has had at least two major debris flows this century. It has all the requirements for huge flows: steep relief combined with rocks of varying stability and size, and a big supply of talus. All it takes to set one off is a localized, torrential rainstorm, one of which arrived in 1960, and another in 1984 that massively rearranged Granite Rapid. That year an isolated storm on July 27 set off a huge debris flow that freighted rocks all the way to the river. Hermit and Bright Angel shales contain clays that swell when they get wet and slide easily, removing support from the sandstone and limestone cliffs above them, which give way in massive falls. In this case, the Hermit shales failed and undercut the Supai Sandstone, two thousand feet above the river.

In less than three minutes during the first pulse, the debris flow dumped a twenty-foot-high dam across the creek near its mouth. Its peak discharge, around 3,800 cfs, equaled low flows of the main river. Robert Webb, a USGS geologist who studied this flow, estimated the total volume of sediment transported at 300,000 cubic feet. The slurry, with the consistency of wet concrete, skidded boulders down the canyon, one of which was estimated to weigh thirty-seven tons. No particles smaller than the size of a pea were found, which suggests that all the fine materials flushed straight into the river. Such debris flows may be brief, involving a single shot of debris, or last for hours, kept alive by continuing but separate pulses. Stochastic events, coming at unexpected intervals of twenty to fifty to five-hundred years, debris flows are the dominant process in clearing sediment off the walls and one of the most important processes in widening the canyon over time.

Given the steamy hot July afternoon, I put a bucket of water out to warm, thinking of a hair wash when the afternoon cools down and the water heats up. While I wait I watch a slender whiptail lizard with an extravagant tail still the bright blue of a young animal. A deep metallic teal blue burnishes its head and yellow stripes its back. It shuffles along the edge of the shade against the cliff. Its jerky gait alternates with quick steps and stops to look about, its head sweeping from side to side like a whisk broom. Whiptail lizards are always on the prowl, sometimes to the point that harvester ants take to their nests. Their speed allows them to elude all but the quickest predators—some snakes and the lizard's archenemy, the roadrunner, which it doesn't have to worry about down here.

In the midst of my lizard watching, frenetic chirping begins in a big tamarisk where a mother blue-gray gnatcatcher feeds three young perched high in the branches. They remain quiet until she approaches, then squeak and mew as loudly as a rusty gate hinge. If quiet and secrecy are the game, they're not playing. Each baby quivers its wings rapidly, stretching up with its mouth full open, calling, "Me first! Me first!" in a classic display of sibling rivalry. The mother's forays last but ten to twenty seconds—so clouds of insects must be available in the tamarisks and she, an efficient hunter.

I check the warming water and find two brilliant, iridescent green sweat bees struggling on the water surface (some species of these semi-social sweat bees respond to human perspiration, hence their name). Still water attracts bees, who lose tremendous amounts of water in flight stress exacerbated in this dry air. Although they nest communally, they have no contact with each other and, like sand wasps, may simply respond to pockets of appropriate habitat. Like many bees and wasps, they are brightly colored, a visual warning that goes along with the ability to deliver a wallop of a sting—a vertebrate predator soon learns that their color means unpleasantness. They have the large eyes associated with evening or night flight and can sometimes be found sampling evening primroses opening at dusk, long after bees usually fly. I offer them a grass sprig and place them in the sun. They vigorously wipe their abdomens with their back legs, vibrate their wings, flick their antennae and, when dry to their satisfaction, zip off.

Ravens awaken me at first light. From immediately across the river issues an incessant screeching as unmelodic as a garroted clarinet, an unholy racket that no amount of good parenting can silence, the raven version of the "terrible twos." A parent flies over, its wings wheep-wheeping, loud enough to hear over kitchen sounds of spatula on grill and whisk beating eggs. Ravens are one of only two raptors known to build nests in the canyon, the other being red-tailed hawks (peregrines and kestrels simply lay their eggs on bare rock). Ravens rotate their nests, probably because of parasites, leaving a nest empty until the parasites die out, then reusing it. The insistent wheedling quiets, the siblings presumably fed and down for their morning nap.

Running Granite this morning I forget everything I ever knew about water, such as that it's liquid and flows downstream. Water, as it smashes upstream, lands in my lap like a truckload of pig iron. Lateral waves bounce off the cliff, one from each side, flip one boat, dispersing hats and gear, up-ending psyches, generating enough adrenaline to stock a pharmacy. Below the rapid, strings of bubbles form, swirled by a turbulence of residual anger. Granite is an unreliable, treacherous rapid. I would not buy a used car from this rapid. Nor is the eddy below of good reputation. The first person to write about getting stuck in it was Norm Nevills. Sometimes called Forever Eddy by river guides, it boasts an unusually powerful eddy fence, strong enough to keep the eddy clear and green when the river is clouded with silt.

John Wesley Powell did not mention Crystal Rapid at Mile 98. Neither did Robert Brewster Stanton in 1900, Julius Stone in 1909, the Kolb brothers in 1911, or Birdseye in 1923. Buzz Holmstrom reported it as "long, wide and slow at first, steep and clear at the last." As late as 1965 a U.S. Geological Survey noted nothing significant. Until then Crystal Rapid existed only as a modest little riffle punctuated by a few large boulders that could be finessed at any water level. Now, Crystal Rapid in its short lifetime has been more lethal than Lava Falls (no one's ever been killed in Lava Falls) and at times, in its adolescence, has been un-runnable.

The night of December 3, 1966, was an archetypal dark and stormy night. An intense, unseasonal storm, originating in the North Pacific, slid across southern Utah and into northern Arizona. Over the next three days at least fourteen inches of relatively warm rain drenched the North Rim, concentrated at the heads of Crystal and Bright Angel Creeks. By Grand Canyon standards, with an average annual rainfall around eight inches a year, that was hellaciously extravagant. The warm rain also dissolved approximately six inches of snow blanketing the North Rim. Such a massive discharge of runoff and snowmelt, in less than half an hour, occurs maybe once every five hundred years.

Water rilled, riveleted, and gathered into a flood-force flow that raced over the canyon rim and into Crystal Creek, cantered thirteen miles to the river 6,500 feet below, slammed down slopes already waterlogged and unstable. That night innocent little Crystal Creek, named for the clarity of its water, transformed into a screaming, ranting virago. First the soft Hermit Shale and Supai Group rocks gave way and peeled off the wall. Tons of free-tumbling loose rock mixed with a slurry of soil and water in an exploding debris flow that carted thousands of tons of gravel and rock with a sound John Muir once described as "roaring like lions rudely awakened."

Boulders up to 14 feet in diameter, and weighing in at nearly fifty tons, blasted down the slopes at speeds that sometimes reached 50 mph, an unimaginable clamor of rocks banging and knocking together. In places the flow ran the height of a four-story building, 44 feet deep, torrents running between 9,200 to 14,000 cfs, a flow volume the same as that released from Glen Canyon Dam for the whole river on many days. It splintered and snapped big cottonwood trees, despoiled Anasazi sites untouched for eight hundred years, and cleaned out the creek's entire mollusk population. The flow shot hundreds of tons of chaos into and across the river. Undoubtedly reaching the opposite shore, it may have initially dammed the river until the impounded water broke over the top and bored a new channel down the left side. The previous river channel of around 280 feet was narrowed to 100 feet. In contrast to the consistent 2:1 constriction ratio of river channel width to normal channel width, the constriction ratio of Crystal after 1966 was a stringent 4:1, which approaches unnavigability.

Boatmen figured out how to run Crystal, albeit with a few dunkings. In newly formed rapids like Crystal, the prediction of wave behavior is particularly difficult because unstable boulders constantly shift in the channel. River guides still reminisce about the huge "Crystal Hole" that made passage through Crystal a nightmare—even if it has tripled in size with the telling, it was still a monster. Then came the 1983–84 floods, when Glen Canyon Dam operators increased the outflow to 92,000 cfs to keep Lake Powell from overtopping the spillways, a discharge triple that of any flow discharge through Crystal since 1966.

Crystal reacted. At around 40,000 cfs, a standing wave formed across the entire channel. At 50,000 cfs the trough-to-crest height reached twenty feet. At 60,000 cfs the wave became as impenetrable as Hadrian's Wall and higher, blocking the river just above the narrowest part of the rapid—a photograph exists of a thirty-foot raft in the wave's curl with wave to spare above it. Observers said the sound of the rapid reverberated like a jet engine, punctuated by sonorous booms every few seconds. At 92,000 cfs, the power of the flow rearranged the rapid to its present configuration, shunting all the smaller cobbles and pebbles downstream into a large rock garden. It lengthened the rapid and now over a half-mile intervenes between the beginning of the rapid and the end of the rock garden. The high discharges widened the channel and the old Crystal Hole lost some of its punch, but the lateral waves at the head of the rapid intensified and now present the main challenge to boating.

The unusually high releases from Glen Canyon Dam in 1983 presented hydrologists with a unique chance to see how channel shape changed at high flows that approached, although did not equal, predam flows. Geologists gained insight into some of the huge debris flows of yesteryear, like that in Prospect Canyon downstream, which formed Lava Falls at Mile 179. Researchers spent days sending inflated toys as markers to study Crystal Rapid, to the confusion and amusement of tourists. The conclusions were sobering in their implications for future river runners. Debris flows are not uncommon in the canyon. Every twenty to fifty years one reaches the river. Flows the size of the 1966 one are bound to occur again, capable of shipping debris into the river. But flows able to clear the channel no longer exist. Releases through Glen Canyon Dam's generators cannot exceed, and indeed seldom reach, 31,500 cfs, nowhere near enough to clean out big boulders or clear a newly narrowed channel beyond one-quarter the width of the main channel. Water must have a velocity of at least twenty feet per second (a current of around 13 mph) to move a two-foot boulder or thirty feet per second (around 20 mph) to nudge a three- to seven-foot boulder. The river seldom runs over 5 mph now.

The best the river can do now is shoulder smaller boulders downstream into a rock garden and winnow out the fines. Monster boulders may rearrange themselves as their support is removed, but most remain in place as insolent obstacles. In calm stretches boulders interrupt flow and send up boils of water that break and burble the surface; in rapids their placement determines where the big holes and backwaves will form.

Hydrologists hypothesize that to increase the ratio of Crystal, or any newly emplaced rapid, to the 2:1 constriction ratio common to other Grand Canyon rapids would require a flow of at least 400,000 cfs, unlikely for the foreseeable future—though it's unsafe to make predictions when it comes to the Colorado River. Crystal will be around for a good while, its name linked with that of Lava Falls as the two most difficult rapids on the Colorado River.

Seldom if ever does Crystal go unscouted. Watching Crystal perform is hypnotic and fractures a lot of equanimities. The fast tongue is as slick as satin, reflecting a big, rough dike of orange and carmine red Zoroaster Granite, like the water—big, rough, and chunky. Huge waves heave up and fall back, flounce and slam, spew spray and churn like a giant washing machine gone fearsomely berserk.

I sit watching until dusk, hypnotized. I think of the sea as continually sloshing back and forth, back and forth, repetitive; but my psyche goes with the river—always loping downhill, purposeful, listening only to gravity, always going on and on and never coming back. A string of seven long-winged nighthawks serpentine back and forth above the river in flowing ribbons of flight. Crystal booms between the silences. The river world flows but does not ebb, and tonight Crystal will insinuate itself into my dreams with an animate and foreboding presence.

A night at Crystal is not a quiet night. The garrulous rapid mutters and harangues incessantly. A cricket goes nonstop, as annoying as the bleep of a computer telling you you're wrong and refusing commands. Tiny winged things come to my headlamp, stagger into my eyelashes, crash-land onto my ground cloth, live a lifetime in hours. Fie on Zane Grey, who came out in 1907 to hunt mountain lions and rhapsodized about the "silence" of the canyon: "when twilight steals down gray and gloomy, and when the chasm sleeps in mystical Plutonian night there is always that same silence—a silence that keeps its secret." He never spent a night at Crystal, where even the gnats thud when they land and sound like helicopters with engine trouble when they take off.

In the morning two ring-billed gulls with black wingtips fly down Crystal, and a yellow swallowtail flutters across the river, messengers from the gods—good ones, I hope. I wonder whether I have neglected to make any necessary obeisances.

A robber fly, poised on the tip of a coyote willow branch oriented to the sun, drops down after a small fly. They are unmistakable flies, sturdy, with long abdomens and forward landing-gear that makes them look like 737s. Their big eyes take up most of the head, separated on the top by a deep and characteristic trough. As my eye becomes accustomed to the pattern of the willow, I spot more flies at work. They chase anything that moves in a way that says "food," attracted by the movement itself rather than any particular image of individual prey. Each fly in its turn darts out and grabs an insect (in one case a very large one), locks the insect between bristled legs, and thrusts its proboscis deep into its victim's tissues to suck it dry, a daylight Dracula. A moustache of stiff bristles keeps its struggling prey from damaging its eyes. I am so fascinated watching their forays that I almost miss a katydid, dressed in apple green with elegant, red, saw-toothed legs, as colorful as a medieval court jester, with a large sword-shaped ovipositor, making her a court jesteress.

The willows also hold a dozen cicada skins, little crisp carapaces of the singers that now sizzle away the summer. Pencil-sized holes dot the ground around the foot of the shrubs where they emerged, and from the cleanness of the openings, fairly recently. If you approach a cicada, he stops singing (only the males sing), making one almost impossible to find. But a stub of branch at an odd angle on a tamarisk proves to be not only a cicada but also a catchable one, still sluggish from cool night temperatures. When in the first violinist's chair at midday, a cicada fiddles while more sensible creatures like birds rest rather than hunt; the lucky cicada keeps its body heat down by "perspiring" through multiple pores, made possible by having a ready source of liquid from the plants it imbibes.

When I hold him in my hand he whirrs and buzzes and continues to do so as I sketch him into my notes. The most sophisticated singer of all insects, he is sturdy, with a wide, blunt head and big eyes, clear wings that extend beyond his body, and on his underside what looks like a tuxedo vest that serves to cover and protect the air cavities from which the buzzing emits. Muscles vibrating in these hollows in the thorax produce the sound, not drumming or stridulation as with katydids. I release him to his chorus line, having forgotten for a moment the insolent imminence of running Crystal.

Loading up the boat, lashing in, finding lines to hold on to, goes on with somnambulant oblivion—things done before, done again, habit. Don't pay attention to the roar. Concentrate on the menial. As a consequence, as I pass through Crystal, my mind never shifts out of slow motion. Drops of water freeze against the sky, rotate to separate sunlight into the hues of a rainbow, caught in a momentary interface between water and air that holds a vast and timeless space all its own.

Water hisses by, set rotating by rock ribs slanting into the river. Blue-gray highlights race over the putty surface, and ripples garner the salmon of the granite so that the river flows with flames. That's what brings us all back again.

basalt pourover above
Pumpkin

10

———

The head of the dam of boulders [of Lava Falls], where the previous day there had been a series of abrupt falls, was now completely submerged. Over it rushed a broad, solid chute of wildly running water which did not begin to break into waves until halfway down what had formerly been the rapid. From there on the combers were tremendous—the largest we had seen. They culminated in an enormous uptossed mass of churning, surging water just above where the boats were moored—a point where yesterday there was only a swift but comparatively smooth stretch of current. . . . The illuminated strip of rollers was a ghostly gray and the effect curiously like that of wind-billowed canvas.

Lewis R. Freeman, 1924, "Surveying the Grand Canyon
of the Colorado: An Account of the 1923 Boating
Expedition of the United States Geological Survey,"
National Geographic

Travertines and Lavas

Cauliflowers of turquoise fume into the putty-colored Colorado, cusps of bright blue Havasu Creek water marbling the tan river and swirling back upstream—Havasu Creek, at Mile 156.7, is second only to the Little Colorado in the amount of water it carries to the river. It is also derisively called "Have-a-Zoo," for the numbers of people that crowd its pools in the summer time. And with good reason—water of a divine temperature fills the travertine-formed pools, which have every depth and water flow necessary to entice bathers of every age and persuasion.

My first time at Havasu I relished sitting right at the edge of the creek where the water's rushing constantly rearranged and moved the green out of its way. Slender green grasses, horsetails and rushes, and trees with fluttering thin leaves were arrayed with a greenery so variegated that this small niche looked designed and planted, tended and manicured, by a master gardener bent on creating a pocket park with every shade and shape of green possible. It was so stunningly beautiful that it almost looked artificial, like a Disneyland fantasy, as if someone could cut off the faucet and stop the whole scene. In fact, just the opposite happened—somebody turned *on* the faucet.

In the fall of 1990 a flash flood ripped through Havasu Canyon, pegged by the U.S. Geological Survey at 22,800 cfs as against the creek's usual flow of 50 cfs. It ripped out the verdure, split trees to kindling, broke, mowed down and carted away every vestige of the beautiful shade, harvested velvet ash trees a foot in diameter and shuttled them downriver to the sawmill at Lava Falls. It wedged debris on ledges fifteen feet above the present stream bank. The flood rolled up the path along Havasu Creek and sent it elsewhere.

Remembering the shuttered shade of the old Havasu, the startling open brightness discomfited me as did the onslaught of canyon grape. The only large vine in the canyon, it flourishes between Havasupai Village and the river. The symbol of eternal life carved on early Christian sarcophagi, it clotted the bare spaces with Medusa-like stems that looped, enveloped, and choked every cranny with greedy green tendrils.

On the next visit to Havasu I experience the unbelievable: a cul-de-sac where no one else is in sight or appears the whole morning I am there. It is a small place, difficult of access, a modest price for solitude. Effects of the flash flood remain legion. A velvet-leaf ash trunk broken four feet off the ground typifies the slowness of recovery. It has spurted out clusters of green stems like a witch's broom. Insects, finding slim pickings this year, have totally riddled their meager leaves. Near by a foot-high coyote willow tries again with two spiky sprouts.

Six feet below this small terrace spreads a silty flat stuffed with cobblestones and figured with small flickering pools and miniature travertine terraces that direct the water, split the flow, double the bubbles, triple the froth, ruffle it around pads of watercress, shove it over the next fall. Loose travertine-encased rocks look like a child's mud pies, studded with rock raisins, iced with red-brown silt. In the quiet corners watercress proliferates and speedwell flowers brighten with flecks of periwinkle blue. Big tadpoles fan the water with their tails. Toad eggs sometimes cluster, sometimes rest separately, some with occupants vibrating vigorously, trying to break out.

In the quieter rills, travertine coats anything stationery with an odd turquoise tan, laid in curls and ruffles and thin crusty potato chips that snap off easily. It encases twigs, swathes grass stems and leaves, any surface below the waterline. Travertine coated a small leaf before it could disintegrate, creating a blade as crisp as if cut out of sheet metal. It surrounded sprigs of moss, leaving only the growing tips to retain their familiar clean green points, and cloaked the bases so thickly that they turn into small gritty globules.

Twenty feet away, a high wall of cleanly layered Muav Limestone curves above a small pool. Once water ran over about half of it and left a syrupy travertine-coated panel. The incrustation creates an undulating surface full of open-mouthed holes, an Edvard Munch scream in stone or a grotesque head in a baroque garden so badly weathered that you can pick out the features only if you know what to look for. Bunches of stonewort, an alga peculiar to travertine pools, root to the bottom and carpet the edge of the backwater, looking like a cluster of toy parasol frames turned wrong side out. Calcium carbonate constitutes almost a third of its dry weight, endowing the stems with their distinctive brittle roughness.

Packs of ripple bugs, tiny water striders, dart and swarm on the protected side of a clump of water speedwell. They look like miniature versions of the larger, more familiar striders, but they are wide enough of body to also be called "broad-shouldered water striders." They are so small they look like grains of pepper ground onto the water surface. Every pulse of water totally disarranges them. They move so quickly that they resemble electrons in a nucleus being bombarded by more electrons, sending them shooting off into their own orbits. When I scoop some up more than a dozen occupy the teaspoon of water in my palm.

Like the larger striders, they have extra "pre-apical" claws placed above those at the tip of their feet, which allow them to move swiftly without breaking the surface film, and a velvety water-repellant pile covers their bodies. They aggregate in spinning groups like this for protection—many eyes are better than two, and the random fright movement of one who bumps into a neighbor quickly activates the whole swarm, a phenomenon called the "Trafalgar effect" for its resemblance to the kind of signals Admiral Nelson used to communicate with his ships before battle. The striders accomplish their swift, skittery glides across the water by discharging saliva backward from their beaks, which chemically weakens the surface tension and, as the water surface "contracts" behind them, propels them forward. They constantly scatter, regroup into the safety of the cluster, rearrange, reform, stay in touch.

The last time I see Havasu, the stonewort and minute striders and the nice benches to sit on exist only in my field notes. All are gone, silted over by piles of sand and silt brought in by yet another flood.

Below Havasu the river widens and shallows for the next fifty miles, a reach of the river bereft of any native fish population. Ocotillo stalks the high river benches. Three or so times taller than other plants, they look like gigantic tufts of yarn on some immense quilt. Barrel cacti, like unstrung fence posts, space up the slopes. Yellow Hooker's evening primroses, named for the great botanist at Kew Gardens, Joseph Hooker, bloom on the beaches. Tumbled blocks and rock trash clutter the slopes, the middens of the cliffs. When cliffs step back from the river, mesquites find footing, their branches hung with balls of mistletoe. Clumps of bear grass become more frequent. Thick stands of horsetails fence the beaches with dark green while behind them fringes of Bermuda grass grow an unnaturally brilliant green.

A cable strung with a big orange ball stretched above the river marks the approach to National Canyon at Mile 166.5. A fatal helicopter accident in 1983 involving the cable caused the Federal Aviation Administration to establish a flight-free zone below 14,500 feet over almost half of Grand Canyon National Park; the agency now "requests" that pilots remain 2,000 feet above the ground over the rest of the park. Helicopters over the park remain an ongoing and fairly acrimonious controversy.

The beach at National affords many small cul-de-sacs between boulders in which to throw a sleeping bag. On a coyote willow near my sleeping space, mourning cloak butterfly caterpillars munch their way to satiety. Black, two inches long, with fine white dots and harmless bristles covering every segment, these methodical munching machines clutch the willow stems and leaves. Clinging with four pair of red prolegs, they begin feeding at the base of a willow leaf and scallop along the edge as they move outward, proceeding as efficiently as a threshing machine. Anchored by their rear ends at the joining of leaf and petiole, they chew only so far as their length, retreat, move to the next leaf and start over again. After the larvae have eaten their fill, they construct a chrysalis from which a butterfly emerges within a week. The adults are active most of the year, distinctive monarch-sized, dark purplish brown butterflies with a band of Naples yellow on the wing edge, the only butterfly so marked.

Newly hatched caterpillars, which need to find the proper food plant to survive, smell through their antennae, searching for the proper chemical vapor mixture from a leaf, as well as taste through their mouths. A plant may have more than 12,000 identified molecules from which a herbivore has to make sense and evaluate the nutritional content of the sap before it begins to feed. Perhaps most helpful is to have your mother lay your egg on the plant you will feed on as an adult, as the female mourning cloak does, in a collar on a willow twig. Ah, motherhood: food choice is so important to the survival of the larvae that a female adult uses all possible ways of finding the proper plant, a process of search and assessment during which she checks various plants before laying eggs or feeding. Rather than responding via "hard wiring" to a few key stimuli, these insects more likely react to an overall impression, a plant "gestalt."

For some reason National Canyon is often windy, and in summer the wind does not cool but blasts as if someone had opened a furnace door.

The wind drives in long pulses, hard enough that sand smokes two feet off the ground, fumes into dervishes that bend the bushes to their knees. When it's well over 90°F in the shade and hot sand dusts everything, there comes the kind of quietly desperate afternoon on which the sun can't go down soon enough.

About one minute before blessed shade touches the sand, five yellow sand wasps arrive. A few feet from the present water line, they conduct quick test adits, spewing out little spurts of sand as if prospecting. Females often shelter in an antechamber in the brood burrows while males dig their own shallow burrows for night protection. Just as shade arrives, three have found the right motel, register, dig in, and disappear. Sand continues to come out of each hole, gathering in little fresh piles, and then stops, leaving dime-sized depressions. Into this closed-down scene a late arrival alights, dredges diligently, vanishes.

They are the lucky ones. The hot wind, like a schma'al, blows well after midnight, and the temperature stays up at 92°F. I wait for the moon to rise over the ridge line and it never does, untrustworthy moon. A momentary calm and then, at 4:00 a.m., one of Mark Twain's scriptural winds gusts through, turvies everything, a typical, contentious down-canyon wind generated when cool air from the rim above sinks, picks up speed, and freights down the defile of a canyon at locomotive speeds, the kind of wind I could easily learn to hate.

In the morning fine sand traces every crease and crinkle of my ground cloth, every stitch in my sleeping bag. It filtered into hand cream and toothpaste. As I try to clean sand out of cracks and creases, two robust bumblebees sample the sand close to the water. Their abdomens are bright cadmium yellow except for the black on the tip and sooty wings. Each insect inserts its proboscis into the damp sand for a couple of seconds, siphoning up water. Yesterday noon bumblebees landed at the drip of the water cooler. When I put a teaspoon of water on a rock, they gathered, delicate red tongues splaying out like soft brushes on the rock to siphon up every last minim. These bees require large amounts of water. The effort of flight can heat their body beyond tolerance, and this combination of heat and wind must try them to the utmost.

Clouds that scudded across the sky last evening moved in to stay this morning. Bats, because of the crepuscular light, still barrel-roll after insects. There are fewer swallows this far down the river and, it seems to me, more bats, filling the same food niche. They fly in brisk, jerky patterns, as they peel off and dive after moths in a swift dance of death. Their gyrations suggest partners invisible to me, some of whom are eaten, some of whom escape. Many moths have "ears" with which to hear a bat's beeping radar far enough away to take evasive action. In response many bats have developed "whisper" sounds to fool the moths into perceiving them as farther away than they are. Neglecting to flee, they get gobbled up. Some moths can generate their own acoustical transmissions that turn a bat away in midswoop once the bat has learned to associate that sound with a distasteful morsel. Each plays out its hour upon the stage, lunging and feigning, feinting and spinning, a dance card filled with partners who may become dinner.

Undulating walls of Muav Limestone define National Canyon itself. If I were pushed to choose the handsomest formation along the river, I'd probably settle on the Muav as it walls National and Matkatamiba Canyons, its warm cream and honey colors interlined with smoky grays and slate blues. Water has carved it with a firm hand into elegant curving panels, picking out the fineness of its layers, the result of being deposited in the quiet subtidal environments and offshore shoals of the last Cambrian sea.

As I poke up the canyon I find rock nettle growing in big clumps, a reminder of how far down the canyon National Canyon is. At 166.5 miles downriver, the flora of National Canyon has more affinities with the Mojave Desert than with the Great Basin, and the latter's plants have largely disappeared. The lovely ten-petaled creamy white flowers look like an exotic hothouse plant, but the rest of the plant is a nuisance, its sticky, sandpapery leaves clinging to clothes like crazy, refusing to be peeled off, even adhering through the turmoil of a washing machine. On the bottom of one leaf, its big sharp hairs trap a tiny mayfly who would have joined a mating swarm this evening. This one will sit out the party, unwittingly snared and held in the grasp of the Wicked Nettle of the West.

A tiny intermittent stream trickles over sand and fine gravel, splays out over bedrock. Puddles and pools, from a few to many yards long, each have a complement of inhabitants, depending on substrate and flow. Water flutters and flickers for fifty feet over the limestone, widening and narrowing, sometimes smoothly surfaced, sometimes scalloped with light when it resembles nothing so much as a baby green-scaled dragon, each scale outlined in chartreuse. A brilliant cinnabar dragonfly hawks over and back, patrolling its kingdom. Water in one pool is almost gone, a plum of damp in the center ringed by cracked silt. When it dried, it took with it its store of new tadpoles. Now they are little black crescent moons, locked in a shattered silt sky.

Live tadpoles, usually dressed in basic black, here sport streaks of iridescent salmon and bronze paratoid glands on coppery heads, garbed in leopard-skin Georgie White tights—the flamboyant Georgie White was the first boatwoman of the canyon. Stubby dragonfly larvae hang by the dozen in diaphanous skeins of algae, and small tan water boatmen rest like empty sculls on the silty bottom, clinging by a claw. On the rocks in midstream, eighth-inch midge pupal cases nestle in minute indentations of the limestone like grains of black rice.

Buffalo gnat larvae cluster both on rocks and limestone ledges, little black threads, buffeted by a rapid current that delivers oxygen to their door but requires that they be anchored firmly by a posterior sucker. Buffalo gnats belong to a fly family, the Simuliidae, the Cosa Nostra of the insect world, which by any other name would still be nasty, miserable, craven, contemptible, blood-sucking demons. The adults are small, usually dark, somewhat humpbacked flies with short broad wings, sturdier than most midges and gnats. Heavy wing veins concentrated near the leading edge give them extra flying strength to maraud the neighborhood.

Like mosquitoes (little darlings by comparison), buffalo gnat females feed ravenously, looking for blood meals during the daylight hours and sometimes into the night, locating victims by their acute sense of smell, needing a blood meal for egg-laying protein because the larvae, being vegetarian, do not supply it. They don't bite, they stab. Females have mandibles like rapiers. After they lancinate the skin, their blades dice up the unhappy camper, sometimes leaving a red welt, other times raising exasperating blisters on the head that don't heal for weeks. Since closure of the dam, they have been discovered as a food source by the beach-dwelling harvester ants. They deserve each other.

Sometimes the quarter-inch larvae cluster in masses that cover the rocks like moss. The current delivers food, which the larva's large, paired mouth brushes spread out to strain. They require a minimum current of around two-thirds of a mile per hour to provide sufficient aeration and keep their heads pointed downstream. If need be, they can move about with a looping movement like an inchworm. To move farther, they anchor themselves by means of silken threads that keep them from being swept completely away.

When it comes time to pupate, the larva spins a cocoon and glues it to a firm surface, still able to breathe through a respiration tube to the water surface. The cocoon remains under water until hatch time. At the moment of emergence the pupal shell fills with air and the tiny adult fly is released in a bubble. When it reaches the surface, the little vampire wastes no time hardening its wings but sets out immediately to ravage and pillage a countryside of innocent, warm-blooded bodies.

In the morning, when I lift my waterproof bag leaning against a rock, two dozen minute daddy longlegs, with bodies the size of a lowercase *o* and inquisitive little faces and high-kneed threadlike legs, scramble for safety.

Loading up takes a little longer this morning. The boatmen take extra time to tie in duffles: we'll reach Lava Falls in twelve and a half miles. There is something sobering about watching an experienced river guide rig flip lines—the nylon straps fastened around the dory either side of midships. In the case of an upset, the theory goes, you scramble your way to the top of the upturned boat and, with a mighty heave on these lines, right it. I've watched flip lines being rigged before and it always strikes me as a very sensible thing to do. Today it's the rapid they're being rigged for that makes me queasy: Lava Falls.

One mile above Lava Falls, Vulcan's Anvil at Mile 177.8 broods sixty feet high in midriver. Someone should hang a banner from it that reads: Worry *now*. Gustave Doré, illustrating Dante, would have etched "All ye who enter here, abandon hope" on Vulcan's Anvil. Seventy feet in diameter, sixty feet high, it is no nice sedimentary block of Supai Sandstone or Muav Limestone fallen off an orderly wall but the remains of a living, spewing, spouting volcano, part of a Pleistocene dike-and-sill system that likely extruded within the canyon itself. As volcanic basalts resist erosion better than the surrounding sedimentary layers, it has remained smack in the center of the river as a portent of Lava Falls.

The serene horizontal logic of Marble Canyon is gone, replaced by walls made out of hell's fire and brimstone, leaving calling cards like Vulcan's Anvil and stuffing Toroweap and Prospect Canyons with lava. This massive black rock with its complex columnar joints has no relation to the neat layering that walls the river upstream. This rock is diagonals on the loose, crystallized mayhem, and controlled chaos.

Volcanic eruptions at the western edge of the Colorado Plateau migrated eastward about one centimeter a year, eventually blanketing 15,000 square miles of the steaming plateau with volcanic rock. When volcanic activity reached the Toroweap Plateau, within which Lava Falls lies, at the earliest around 1.2 million years ago, it cascaded over the rim and created this stunning landscape of black rock. The flows remain plastered on the walls, chronologically stacked, lava smothering the orderly sedimentary rocks, draped over the walls like black crepe over a catafalque. In hand, a chunk of basalt is dense and dark, salted with pale green glassy specks of olivine, close in color and composition to the basalts of the Hawaiian Islands.

Each of these flows was molten hot and rode down into the canyon with a mass of steam and flame and searing, galloping heat. The lava dams changed the river just as man-made dams do, and the slowing river dropped its gravels and silts entering the reservoirs behind them. The flows plugged tributary canyons like Toroweap and Prospect Valley and dammed the main canyon four times, once setting a dam that may have flooded the river 189 miles upstream as far as Lees Ferry, depending on how long the dam lasted, and another time sending a single flow unit 84 miles downstream from Lava Falls to Mile 263, nearly to Lake Mead.

The lava marks this reach of canyon as completely different from any other along the river, elegant and powerful, replete with visual splendors distinctly its own. Most lava flows erupted on the Esplanade, the high platform developed on the Supai Sandstone that follows the river. The lava oozed over the rim and into the canyon and, since it cooled slowly, created these distinctive handsome walls: a well-defined basal colonnade beneath a wide entablature of thin, sinuous columns. From the river below, a columnar wall appears neatly accordion-pleated, but close up the wall often looks like long railroad ties, haphazardly stacked vertically. Many lean, half-attached, and many have split cleanly away. Fallen columns cluster on the ground like faggots of firewood tied together.

On several panels, fans of fine columns splay outward with the elegance of a peacock's tail. Other panels are so delicate they seem sketched in India ink with a crow-quill pen, and still others are carved as beautifully and intricately as an ebony Louise Nevelson sculpture. The lavas caparison the canyon walls with a new vocabulary of rock color and shape, a notice of what heat dispenses and cooling composes.

It is ironic that one of the most astounding locales on the river is overshadowed by a rapid—who *ever* thinks of lava flows, blocked canyons, dikes and plugs and cinder cones when confronted with Lava Falls? Who ever camps just *above* Lava Falls? Who ever even *stops* on the left above Lava Falls?

Almost from day one the thought of running Lava Falls looms. A lot of Lava Falls is hype. A lot of it isn't. Lava Falls *is* different. It sounds different. Its voice growls, ominous and throaty, guttural noises from a dragon just awakened from a pleasant snooze by some upstart knight-errant whom it will dismember sinew by sinew. Lava Falls is like the nightmare that you remember vividly for a few minutes, washed with relief that it wasn't so, and then awake to find it *is* so.

Besides the urge to get Lava Falls over with, boatmen may in uneasy moments recall the predicament of the Birdseye Expedition in 1923, an easily repeatable near-disaster, given that the flood came from below Glen Canyon Dam. By the time Birdseye and crew reached Lava Falls, their radio had stopped working and they did not receive the warning of a heavy rainstorm in the basin of the Little Colorado River and possible flooding. Consequently they did not look for high ground on which to camp at Lava Falls. Emery Kolb, the boatman in charge, decided to line the boats down the left side of Lava that evening, the way he and Ellsworth had done a dozen years before in the dead of winter. At that moment, someone noticed that the river was rising ominously, already on its way to the 98,500 cfs that translated to a vertical rise of more than twenty feet and a tenfold increase in cfs. As Birdseye described it,

> The river continued to rise at the rate of about 18 inches an hour and reached the peak of 21 feet the following afternoon. No one had expected such a rise, and we were up all night pulling one boat or another to a higher place on the bank. The rapid, which had been a very short, sharp-crested fall before the flood, now stretched downstream as far as the eye could see, a tumble of racing water, some of the big waves running fully 20 feet high and throwing spray much higher. Immense quantities of driftwood, including many large logs, were carried downstream.

When I slog fifty feet up the sandy terrace on the left bank above the river, I have a view that most river passengers are seldom privy to: lava-choked Toroweap Canyon across the way, cut on the line of the Toroweap Fault, Prospect Canyon immediately downstream, and remnants of the biggest debris flow on the river, which once charged down Prospect Canyon and pushed the river toward the right wall, creating the churning dynamo of Lava Falls. It is that debris flow, not a legendary basalt ledge, that makes Lava Falls so dire. Prospect Canyon's wide level floor slopes gently toward the river. It does not enter the river on grade but ends in a precipitous, near-vertical cliff, for erosion has not had enough time to cut down to the base level of the river. Just downstream, the present mouth marks the river level of an older, wider, deeper canyon that, after its original incision, was filled with new basalt flows up to seven hundred feet thick. The thickest, oldest flows remain here, around 350,000 years old. Originally they formed the highest dam in the canyon, the top of which reached an elevation of 4,000 feet (making the dam height 2,330 feet, compared with Glen Canyon Dam, which is 638 feet above the original channel), and backed up the largest and deepest lake in the Grand Canyon. If the dam stood full height long enough, its lake would have taken 23 years to fill (Lake Powell took 15) and another 3,018 years to silt up.

Dams began to destruct as soon as they formed, even while the lava was still hot. Although basalt itself is extremely resistant to erosion, its structure of vertical columns make it weak at the jointing, and the columns separate. A dam of these discrete columns could be destroyed fairly easily. Because lava lay directly on a sand or gravel bed, the force of the waterfalls simply undercut the dam, and waterfalls migrated upstream rapidly. When the river overtopped a dam, a waterfall of abrasive, sediment-filled water formed that, given the structure of the basalt, breached the dam in short order, destroying most relatively soon after their formation.

The dams that formed on the Colorado River occupied the canyon probably no more than a total of 240,000 years, a mere hiccup in geologic times. Large river systems such as the Colorado tend to establish a state of equilibrium and when their equilibrium is disrupted set about quickly reestablishing it. After base level is reached, downcutting proceeds much more slowly. That process of reexcavation in the canyon took place at least twelve times and, with slope retreat, removed the rest of the basalt in the Inner Gorge.   •

Each time, I say I'm not going to run Lava Falls again. I am going to watch other people get banged around. I have given at the office on Lava Falls. No more. But here I am, on a hot, cloudless July day, cinching up my life jacket to suffocation, checking waterproof fastenings, thinking about letters I wish I'd written and kind, loving words I wish I'd said, and wishing devoutly I were someplace else.

I've gone through Lava Falls in a thirty-foot motor-driven raft without stopping to scout. I've gone through Lava Falls in January and February, March and May and July, August and September and November, without stopping to scout. But scouting is obligatory in a small raft, and *certainly* in a dory—a lot of looking and talking and pointing at churning water, which only engenders churning stomachs.

A trail like that to the River Styx, horribly well-worn and much too narrow, cuts into the black abrasive cindery lavas. Hung with boulders that have been poised on the same steep talus slope for millennia, they look ominously ready to fall the minute *you* pass beneath. Standing on the path high above the rapid, you look down into the rapid's maw, into the dark and ugly bunch of black boulders hurtled down by angry gods from Prospect Canyon and Toroweap Valley.

George Flavell made the first run of Lava Falls in 1896. Although tempered now by Glen Canyon Dam, the runs of Lava Falls can still change even as you watch, a living, breathing monster capable of getting harder or easier depending upon its temper at the moment. As water pours over massive underwater boulders, it curls into malevolent boat-smashing backwaves trying to fill in two humongous holes. The river falls fifteen feet in two hundred yards with most of the fall in two short increments, hence the epithet "falls."

The ideal running stage lies between 14,000 and 16,000 cfs, when a convenient slot appears with an entrance to the right of center, the "follow the bubbles" run. At 18,000 cfs a tremendous punching wave forms near the top that tends to throw a boat askew and, once out of line, does not allow a rower time to take the few precious strokes to miss the bottom hole. At 22,000 cfs water is high enough to cover the rock garden on the left and open up a thirty-second left-hand sneak run for small boats. The currents at Lava bore so strongly and so deeply, and travel at such high speed close to the river bottom, that they emerge as big, burbling boils as far as a quarter-mile downstream. The surface of the upwellings may elevate inches, sometimes as much as a foot, above the normal river level. Currents even go in opposite directions separated by a vicious shear line: Lava rearranges the river to its own designs.

After you've watched your life pass before you in half a minute, had some vertebrae rearranged, bruised an elbow, drenched a sketchpad, and wondered once again why you voluntarily put life and limb at hazard, there's the lower beach for lunch and obligatory champagne and mafficking. I don't partake. I am scheduled to run it again in a few weeks and have no interest in tempting the river gods that be.

And, if in the thrall of bare fear, you missed the lava-filled canyon show at Lava Falls, there's another one at Whitmore Wash. The original Whitmore Wash at Mile 186 was incised eleven hundred feet deep and three thousand feet wide through Muav Limestone. Nine flows of basalt filled the canyon and created a dam a half-mile long. Its lake may have stretched all the way to Hance Rapid at Mile 76.5 and a mile into Havasu Canyon. Today the remnants of those flows block Whitmore Canyon and separate it from the present river.

Camping at Whitmore one hot, sleepless, end-of-July night, I awaken to light splatty taps crossing my back, ja-bup, ja-bup, ja-*bup*. After the little trekker reaches the sand, I raise up on an elbow to watch a fat red-spotted toad on its uncertain journey elsewhere.

Wide awake now, luxuriating in the quiet dark, I ponder that no matter how many times I travel this river, there will always be places I miss—rock formations not pried into, streams not looked under, cliff doors not opened—but no rapids left unrun. If for any reason I cannot be here a century from now, the river will be and that's good enough for me. I appoint it my executor without instruction except to keep on doing what it's doing, sluicing down a limestone-walled canyon, pounding down a rapid, laving a sandbar, throwing spray twenty feet in the air, rounding cobbles, chastising foolish boatmen and honoring the skilled ones who devote their days to preserving and protecting two molecules of hydrogen and one of oxygen and fifty of silica and twenty of sodium and three of chloride, and ten of calcium.

All I charge it to do is to sustain the enchantment, the rosy pink reflections, the silvery evenings, the platinum dawns, the gilded days of summer.

just above Parashant Wash

11

At dusk it is different. The gorge banks full of purple and violet shadow as soon as the sun has gone down, and when night has set in it becomes densely dark, fathomless, formless. The only light comes from the sky overhead—the ribbon of sky that now takes on a night blue and is spangled with stars. The stars seem near, and the illusion of their nearness is helped on, perhaps, by their being seen at dusk from the gorge just a little before they are seen at the Rim. Stars from the bottom of a well and from the bottom of the Inner Canyon have a similar appearance. They are not visible from either place at noonday, but at dusk the well and the wall cut off the side-lights and thus make visibility greater overhead.

John Van Dyke, 1920, *The Grand Canyon of the Colorado*

Humpback Chub
and the Little Colorado

———————

Across from the mouth of the Little Colorado River at Mile 61.3, this month's humpback chub research crew unloads their gear. Last month's trip was a catch-and-implant trip. This trip that I join will focus on monitoring the ten transmitter-implanted fish plus continuing investigation of humpback chub behavior patterns. This takes two raftloads of equipment. Researchers carry lists of lists, constantly redefining their needs, aware that forgetting something essential, no matter how small, can prejudice a complicated, expensive project. So the dunnage contains fresh batteries and backup batteries; mesh bags and more mesh bags; extra motors; rigid gray cases with thick padding inside to protect the fragile radio receivers and fine, precise equipment like dissecting instruments; and heavy gear like the two small sport boats, to be unfolded and inflated on site, motors mounted. Quick and maneuverable, they afford the only means by which researchers can cover the necessary river miles.

By August the summer monsoons have set in. It has sprinkled off and on since noon and as soon as I get my tent pitched, pop on the rain fly, and toss my gear inside, the gentle peppering begins in earnest, punctuating the river with exclamation points, ticking on the nylon, dripping off the fly edge in syncopation, rain taking off in a jazz riff.

Thunder rolls, a soft muttering that begins behind, stumbles and lurches over, passes on in a fine curmudgeonly muttering. Suddenly a sharp flash, followed by a Zeusian bang of thunder that echoes like a rockfall, probing every corner of the heavens. Zeus may be a petulant, selfish, adulterous, lying, dirty old god, but he certainly hurls thunderbolts with panache. As the rain quickens, the drops leave platelets on the sand, indented in the center, rimmed, darker, beginning to cohere. Drops bombard the beach, as rain shells the ground. Sand flies into the air like miniature explosions. The cannonading lasts only until the sand becomes wet enough to stay put. Despite the pelting, rain wets the sand less than a quarter-inch deep.

Just in time to start dinner the rain passes on. A magnificent light washes the canyon, turning the Tapeats Sandstone to gold against a fuming, sooty sky, lit from beneath, a view Turner would have loved. The canyon walls darken while the sky vibrates, as luminous and alive as northern lights.

Most native fish species had been identified and named by 1900, but humpback chub, as a distinct species, remained undescribed until 1942, when an ichthyologist, Robert Rush Miller, looked over the natural history collection of Grand Canyon National Park and spotted an odd-looking, unnamed fish, caught near Bright Angel Creek ten years earlier. He called it *Gila cypha*, the specific Greek name for "humpbacked." Humpback chub are one of the eight native species that originally inhabited the Colorado River system, a distinctive endemic piscifauna developed over time—nowhere else in this country does a single drainage contain fauna that is three-quarters endemic. Most of the genus *Gila* developed in this ancient western river-and-lake system around 5 million years ago. When the lakes dried up and separated into island habitats, speciation occurred. The largest population of humpback chub now remains in the reach of the Colorado bracketing the entrance of the Little Colorado River and in the lower miles of the latter.

Humpback chub, with their pronounced forehead bump, are unmistakable fish, superstreamlined with a fusiform shape that minimizes drag and damps turbulence, also common to fast ocean swimmers like barracuda and tuna. The connection between tail and body elongates into a thin stalk that aids in quick acceleration, reduces recoil in swimming, and stabilizes the fish's body. A chub's skin is thicker and smoother than that of most fish, with scales embedded in the skin, typical of swift swimmers, a leathery covering that may also reduce friction and avert abrasion from the constant silt of the old river system. A chub intuits underwater vibrations from moving objects via a group of sensors located in a line along its flanks and has an incredibly developed sense of smell.

But such drastic adaptation can be a fatal disadvantage when it renders a species less able to adapt to rapid change. When Glen Canyon

Dam was closed, the habitat to which chub were so elegantly adjusted literally changed overnight. The cold, clear water interrupted natural reproduction. Plentiful shoreline eddy habitats, needed by young-of-the-year, disappeared, replaced by short-term fluctuating flows that decreased larval survival. This radical change, plus the stocking of predaceous non-native fish, has nearly destroyed the native fish fauna of the lower Colorado River. Trout and catfish are frequently caught with the bones of tiny chub in their stomachs, and adult chub sometimes have bite marks, presumably from channel catfish, the only species big enough to attack them. Numerous carp frequent the confluence area, possibly preying on egg and larval stages, but the biggest threat is the invasion of striped bass from Lake Mead.

167

—

*Hump-
back
Chub
and the
Little
Colorado*

In the waiting quiet of daybreak, the sound of a coffeepot lid being lifted and reset works better than an alarm clock. While it is still middling cool, I walk the perimeter of my territory. Yellow rayless daisy heads bedeck a big three-foot-high sweetbush, the involucral bracts (the cup that holds the individual flowers in the head) tipped with glands. Small bee flies with narrow cream-and-black striped abdomens wrap themselves around the half-inch flowers to feed. At water's edge yellow Hooker's evening primroses, accented by scarlet Indian paintbrushes, grow as tall as I. Bushes of dogbane with red stems nod over the water. The usual seep willow. The usual coyote willow. The eternal tamarisk, dripping strings of tiny flowers, soon to loose untold numbers of seeds upon an unsuspecting world.

Here, sixty miles from Glen Canyon Dam, it takes about nineteen hours for a release from the dam to reach us (the water travels about 4 mph). The river falls during the day and begins rising between midnight and 2:00 a.m., with highest water in early morning. At the moment, the river-edge apron of boulders lies uncovered and three, quarter-inch planarian worms wriggle in a small pool between the rocks, tiny snippets of wet, brown velvet ribbon. Photosensitive, they spend most of their time safely under rocks and are very vulnerable to predation in full daylight, probably saved by their slimy coatings, which gum up the mouthparts and antennae of insects that might otherwise feed on them. They live a hermaphroditic existence, a him/her searching for a her/him.

A handsome, iridescent dark green tiger beetle stalks the sand, its brilliance caused by innumerable, minute raised ridges striating the stiff elytra so that the surface works on the principle of a diffraction grating. Its common name comes from its voracious ways and lethal mandibles, its stealth, its ability to spurt up to three feet per second, enough speed to escape most predators. Tiger beetles withstand high sand temperatures by running on stilted legs, but when it's too hot, they survive by digging shallow burrows where females also deposit their single eggs.

On hatching, the S-shaped larva, often called a doodlebug, digs a tunnel in the bare, hot sand and latches itself in place with curved hooks on its back. It holds its flattened shieldlike head, usually colored to match its surroundings, at right angles to its body, blocking the opening. There it waits until a small insect blunders by, snapping it up without having to forgo the protection of its tube. A small wasp ingeniously parasitizes a doodlebug by decoying it into thinking it has a meal. The wasp allows herself to be seized, then stings the larva in its vulnerable extended neck. She enters the burrow, draws in the immobilized larva, lays a single egg on it, seals the opening, and departs.

By midmorning, the red line of the thermometer hung on my tent zipper can't go any higher. I repair to the river to pour water on an overheated head. I rinse, wait a second for the ice-cream headache to start, endure it until it stops, pour over another cupful, pause, endure. It helps.

Near my tent a beautiful boulder of limestone sits imbedded in the beach, sculpted with fluting that ranges from the most dainty channels to gouges an inch wide, carved in overlapping fans. A collared lizard, an exquisite creature with a double black color, bounds across the searing sand, launches itself into a series of grandiose jetés, and lands on this boulder in the filmy shade of a tamarisk. Fluorescent chartreuse washes its haunches and stamps it as a male. The black spots that dapple his legs diminish to dots on his back, spattered on a sulphur yellow ground. His tail, longer than his body proper, languishes over the rock. His dainty spidery toes flow into the fluted contours of the rock. He stilts himself up away from the heat-radiating rock, courting as much circulation as possible under his body. Watching him, I wonder what the lizards looked like that left footprints a yard apart in the sand of the Coconino Sandstone.

In the middle of this stultifying noontime heat, a canyon wren with a cinnamon brown tail and back and clean white bib searches cracks in a boulder close by. It chatters and tsks about the availability of insects, the vicissitudes of life, and the vagaries of a summer's day. I retreat to the river to slosh another bucket of water over my head, wait for the ice cream headache to begin and abate. If I have to have one I'd prefer to get it eating ice cream, but it's the only alternative to boiling over like a radiator.

In this enervating heat, my brain turns to mush after lunch. I head for the shadiest place in town, which is the kitchen. As I settle under a tamarisk I dislodge a side-blotched lizard, named for the oval black spot on each side just behind the front leg. The smallest, most generalized of the canyon's riparian lizards, they are as numerous as house sparrows. Insectivorous, they prefer ants and flies and snag them either by aggressive stalking or by a sit-and-wait strategy, according to need.

Tiny two-inch young predominate among those that scamper around the kitchen. This noon I watch two that stay in the fragile shade of a snakeweed, fortuitously on the foraging path of some red ants. Oftentimes rodents burrow beneath bushes like this snakeweed, and lizards use them for a hasty retreat, and in some places side-blotched lizard numbers depend upon the frequency of rodent nests available for quick haven. They are a delight to watch, quick and wary tail flickers, always on the qui vive. While I sit sweaty and lethargic, they remind me that others thrive in this turgid heat.

In the sky antimacassar clouds avoid the sun like the plague. Cicadas heat up to band-saw intensity. I try to lose myself in reading *Don Quixote*. The don's housekeeper, curate, and niece are having a fine, righteous time heaving all of the don's "romances" out the window. Sweat trickles down my nose and dots the page. Even reading is too much exertion.

I switch to watching the resident yellow-backed spiny lizard, whose sit-and-wait technique more fits my state of stasis. Two desert spiny lizards habitually hang out around the kitchen. One has more bright yellow dotting its body and head plates, while the other is more orange, the deeper color that usually indicates a male. Today only the male is on duty. He remains on his elevated survey perch for minutes on end before scrambling off to scarf up a dozen red ants. A big healthy lizard, he looks as if he lifts weights in his spare time, a solid, portly sort that would not look out of place with a watch chain and spats, a sophisticated boulevardier. When he spots an ant carrying a kernel of corn, his pell-mell dash is so tempestuous that it tosses ant and burden into the air and they disappear in the sand. The lizard stands there for a moment, swings his head back and forth, then waddles with a certain insouciance back to his station.

On one of his periodic forays he patters close to my chair. As I shift to get a better look, he darts into a plastic milk crate turned on its side that I've been using as a footrest. He dashes back and forth, sticking his head through one after another of the one-inch-square openings on the now vertical bottom that faces his home tree and safety, never turning around to see the wide open freedom behind him. Finally he discovers one of the larger oval openings on the side and flees to his sandy perch under the tamarisk, turns around, raises himself so far up on his front legs that he resembles a sitting dog, probably having had more of an adventure than he bargained for on a simple trip to the market.

Another noontime a tiny tree lizard winds by my chair so slowly that I reach down and pick it up, a baby barely an inch long with a tail half that length. Despite the name, tree lizards are found not in trees but usually on rock walls right above the river. This one's an elegant little creature: two rows of enlarged scales stripe its back, divided by a line of smaller ones, and a narrow fold of skin extends along its flanks, an impervious skin that made possible its reptilian trip to dry land, the first vertebrate to invade a terrestrial habitat. On its eyelid are two vermillion mites, firmly attached. Mites are everywhere, in soil, moss, fungi, from tundra to tropics, on land and in water, and only one of many parasites that affect lizards. Under a hand lens this pinhead of red has body segments completely fused into a single unsegmented disk hung with eight legs, four forward, four back, its mouthparts adapted for sucking blood. Its brilliant red color may be a warning, for although spiders gobble them up, almost any other potential predator tends to avoid them.

Tree lizards, coming up from mainland Mexico, probably ranged much more widely in previous epochs. Now their present distribution is an odd one, restricted to the riparian habitats of the Southwest deserts and to rocky habitats on isolated mountains. Adults are small, under three inches in length, much the same size as side-blotched lizards, with which they avoid potential competition by exploiting different habitats. Here in the canyon tree lizards prefer water's edge with large rocks and overhead cover, while side-blotched lizards seek boulders with sandy spots between. Both tree and side-blotched lizards belong to that group of "annual" lizards that are short-lived, mature within a year, and produce multiple clutches.

When summertime temperatures become too high, lizards seek refuge in cooler places, for they have no sweat glands or other method of lowering their temperature other than panting, an expensive, last-resort way to cool because it expends so much precious water. They effectively conserve water by not excreting liquid urine and by metabolizing extremely efficiently. Their water conservation is ten times higher than that of desert rodents, and their energy requirements, 10 to 20 percent lower than that of mammals and birds, is impressive.

The tree lizard moves to the edge of a flat rock, smacking up tiny ants with its darting tongue. It saves energy by allowing the ants to come close by rather than chasing after them—any ant coming within two inches is a goner. Two ants appear on the scene from opposite directions. The lizard eyes each in turn as if deciding which to snatch first, then, thsp-thsp, it nails them both.

In the fascination of watching the lizard I have forgotten about the ten-ton heat, which now registers again. Cicadas sputter like a static-filled radio that I can't turn off. I have no idea what time it is. My heat-registering chromosomes may have melted like butter on a hot rock.

Powell's Rio Colorado Chiquito, the Little Colorado River, drains more than 24,000 square miles, the largest tributary to the Colorado River south of Glen Canyon Dam. Scouring such a big area of bare-bones country makes it a major transporter of silt, an average of ten megatons of suspended sediments a year. During a big storm it can flush an equivalent of nine inches of topsoil per square mile into the Colorado and become, as George Bradley judged it in 1869, "a lothesome [sic] little stream, so filthy and muddy that it fairly stinks," and Jack Sumner on the same trip found it "a miserably lonely place indeed, with no signs of life but lizards, bats, and scorpions. It seemed like the first gates of hell. One almost expected to see Cerberus poke his ugly head out of some dismal hole and growl his disapproval of all who had not Charon's pass."

Without storms upstream, the Little Colorado runs an astounding, opaque, blatant turquoise blue. Fed by Blue Springs, it is milky from a high mineral content of chloride, sodium, calcium, and bicarbonate. Only a few algae grow in it because little sunlight filters through its opacity, its flow is so variable, and its salt and sediment load so high. Despite temperatures and salinity inimical to most plants and fish, humpback chub spawn in the Little Colorado in June and July. Low-velocity recirculation zones around its mouth and its backwaters, at around 70°F, are markedly warmer than the main channel and serve as important nursery areas for native fish. Female chub release sticky, BB-sized eggs, sometimes several thousand, and incubate them for five or six days. Swim-up occurs about twelve hours after hatching, resulting in a swarm of little transparent wigglers not yet half an inch long. Since trout will not enter the warm, saline waters, the young are shielded from one of their severest predators. As far as is now known, young chub shelter in the Little Colorado until they are mature enough to cope with the dynamics of the big river and to avoid predators in the main channel.

On the other side, a trail strings down the Little Colorado, tops out on the Tapeats Sandstone, and follows the Colorado River's left bank until a slot allows access down to the salt that drizzles out of the lower layers of the Tapeats. As water moves horizontally through the Tapeats layers, it leaks out in an almost continuous band forty to fifty feet wide, depositing a fairly pure sodium chloride, which the Hopi traveled over a hundred miles to harvest. Hopi legend tells of the Twins who discovered the salt, and the elder Twin, who, as he walked along the ledge, rubbed his fists against the sandstone, "turning everything he touched into salt."

One steamy afternoon I clamber up a tiny rough draw downstream from camp, climbing until I reach a small amphitheater, blessedly all in shadow from a Tapeats Sandstone wall that curves sixty feet above. Desert varnish blackens nearly all of the sandstone as if some giant had torched the amphitheater and sooted the walls. But on the unvarnished underside of ledges, the clean pale honey beige crossbeds curve sinuously, typical granular, rough Tapeats, deeply slotted between layers where coarser grains as big as tapioca stud its surface. In many places pale orange washes the sandstone. Elsewhere thin light green layers, characteristic of the basal strata of the Tapeats, show. These green clay layers often coat the bottom of an overhang and frequently contain worm burrow casts. An impervious clay layer beneath prevented the worms from burrowing deeper, and when the clay disintegrated on being exposed to air, the negative casts remained, describing the pushings and hitchings and snorkelings of a search for food 600 million years ago.

All the plants have paper-crisp browned leaves, as if heat radiating off these walls bakes them like an oven. Scraggly leftovers hang on by a single stem or two: shreddy Mormon tea, disconsolate looking mallows, datura skeletons that are all elbows and knees. Against the wall, two huge spiderwebs, starting about five feet up, drape downward and affix to the ground. They appear spun in two loose layers, connected on one edge so that the web at the bottom forms an open-sided funnel. The silk is so extremely fine that it would be invisible but for the trash of leaf bits and seed heads and wind wisps caught in it. These slovenly webs are the work of female black widow spiders, which usually hang upside down in the web or lurk under stones or debris nearby. Their venom may be among the most toxic of all venomous creatures, about fifteen times as strong as that of a rattlesnake. Although usually not fatal, a single spider's venom may contain a hundred or more toxins, many of which home in on and block human nerve cells with matchless precision. Black widows are the largest of the comb-footed spiders, named for the serrated bristles on their hind legs, an adaptation that makes it possible for them to wrap their prey in silk without becoming entangled themselves.

173
—
Hump-
back
Chub
and the
Little
Colorado

Meanwhile, the witch in *Hansel and Gretel* closed the oven door while I wasn't looking. I scramble down to the river, pull off my shirt, slosh it in the river, put it back on dripping wet, and feel my temperature lower on the instant. As the river begins its daily down, little knuckles of rock that weren't there a moment ago break the surface. The river glimmers and shimmers beneath the willows like a Monet painting. No lily pads, but the blowing willows and flickered reflection wouldn't be out of place at Giverny. Dimples in singles and in clusters rotate by, tiny vortices spinning off a submerged ledge. The knuckles become a miniature volcanic archipelago with two craters and its own encircling coral reef. The silt on them dries. The afternoon shrivels to an end.

In the ending daylight that begins starlight, two researchers and this volunteer burr upstream in one of the small research boats, running on dark water beneath dark cliffs. The river flows thickly dark and mysterious. A half-moon slathers the cliff tops with moonwash, as thickly as the paint in an Albert Pinkham Ryder moonscape. We are scheduled for an all-night watch to monitor a humpback chub known to be upstream near Sixty Mile Rapid. Our night's beach is a treasure, diminutive and unfootprinted, the perfect beach one almost never gets to camp on because it's so tiny. Tonight, toward the ending of summer, coyote willow tufts out seeds, a sphinx moth probes a white evening primrose, and a datura opens opulent, voluptuous blossoms with an odor reminiscent of petunias.

To track a humpback chub you first have to have caught and implanted one with a transmitter. No. 40.650 was implanted last May with a nine-gram transmitter (four dimes in weight) and an exterior antenna. The chub has been located, as they usually are, within half a mile of where it was tagged. It probably moves right at the edge of the main current, drifting downstream and swimming back up, close to but not in the swift water, in a narrow channel between the mainland and a small sandbar. Experience and netting show that they commonly swim in water between eighteen and forty-five inches deep. Probably others swim with it since humpback chub tend to be gregarious.

Profiles of the riverbed give the big picture, but humpback chub, bless them, use unmapped microhabitats. Humpback chub do not spend time in fast turbulent water but hover on the periphery of the high-velocity currents that create eddies around big boulders, in energy-saving minihabitats, where they use water currents as soaring birds use air currents.

As darkness comes, the canyon takes on a mystical aspect—an old picture album, bound in Victorian red velvet, holding a daguerreotype river. The deepening reds and roses at dusk are an illusion that depends on the structure of the human eye, the so-called Purkinje shift, something one is seldom aware of in the everyday world, where we flip on lights as soon as it gets dark. To appreciate this aberration of the human eye, one needs to be out-of-doors for the lovely, subtle transition between dusk and dark. Purkinje, the nineteenth-century Czech physiologist, noticed that the relative brightness of reds and blues changes with the onset of twilight. Daylight vision depends upon the cones in the retina, nighttime upon the rods, and they differ in their relative sensitivity to different wavelengths: the rods pick up blues better, the cones reds. When daylight fades, during the shift from cone to rod vision, one sees the world through rose-colored glasses.

Before I go to bed (my watch begins at 1:00 a.m.), I review how to use the telemetry system, how to read the water gauge (at lowest slosh), how to line up with the flagged stakes in the sand that give two lines of sight to the fish to allow for triangulation. Half-hour notations about fish activity are paired with readings of river height to determine if fish movement correlates with flow change. As I walk with the receiver in hand, I feel like a Roman soldier marching with the legion's labarum, for the receiver is a square paddle about fifteen by fifteen inches, cut out in the center, mounted on a staff that makes it about five feet tall. Each side of the square is a separate antenna, and readings are taken first from one side, then the other. The direction of the fish lies at nullity, where the two signals cancel each other out.

Cool drafts tiptoe across the beach, and warm air snakes down from the cliffs. The river is on the rise and it seems to me, trying to sleep, that the rush of Sixty Mile Rapid intensifies, as intrusive as if a shower had been left running full bore. Sixty Mile was hammering when we arrived, when I went to bed, and when I get up, a rumble instigated by a gravity that never turns off, an eternal, no-nonsense, high-level noise, sometimes more, sometimes less, but always, always there. Unable to sleep, I get up at midnight.

The Tapeats ledge on which all the telemetry equipment rests is markedly warmer than the beach only a few feet lower. Waves lave the ledge beneath my feet, lapping and smacking, glugging and gargling in the darkness. Light dollops of foam swirl in on rising water. A bat swoops overhead and in the quiet I hear its high-pitched squeaking.

As my eyes adjust I begin to see the world about me—the paleness of the Tapeats, how much the river has come up, the glowing white datura flowers. This night I will come to appreciate our marvelous human vision, which enables us to operate both day and night. Statistically, after being in the dark for only half an hour, my eyes should have adapted enough to be able to pick out an object whose brightness has diminished in the dark to only 1/100,000th of what it had in daylight. Even if I access only a fraction of that, it gives this night a warm and encompassing friendliness.

175
—

*Hump-
back
Chub
and the
Little
Colorado*

One o'clock: fish is in its accustomed place.

One-thirty: same. Water up another couple inches. Temperature, 69°F.

By two o'clock the cliffs stop holding up the half-moon and drop it into a box of darkness behind them. Before it went, the moon altered all the cliff faces so that they looked as if a gray gauze had been draped down from the South Rim, its soft folds enveloping the prows and crags as spiderwebs swath the walls of Redwall Cavern. I am reminded of H. C. Hovey, writing in 1892 about his first night in the canyon, when "the sky was azure and the full moon flooded the mighty walls with silvery sheen. A bright planet hung above a tall cliff at our right, and the stars in Orion's belt guarded another on our left, looking like electric lights along the ramparts. The hues that had seemed glaring by day were exquisitely softened, while the recesses not touched by the moon were enwrapped in solemn grandeur."

The river upstream reflects the night sky in a gunmetal gloss. The stars multiply, expand into all those invisible stars without names, from whom we receive more light than from the six thousand we can see, masses of stars floating beyond mindsight. The sky becomes as full of movement as the river, a wild varying number of cubic feet per second of whirling universe, swarms of stars adorning a glittery night.

Two-thirty: fish in precisely the same place. Temperature still a pleasant 69°. A silky, pure-white moth flits into my light's beam, *Pronubis*, the singular pollinator out servicing her yucca flowers. Modified mouthparts enable her to gather pollen but not to feed, and she performs her services without recompense except that of ensuring the survival of her offspring. She deposits her eggs in the flower's ovary, and when it ripens into a pod, the larvae will eat a few of the seeds while leaving most of them to survive. Each species of yucca has its own species of yucca moth, a mutualism developed over untold millennia.

A shooting star arcs across the sky. We are at the end of the Perseids and a shower of cosmic debris zings into our atmosphere and explodes. The ancients saw the night sky as a dome perforated with holes behind which the fires in the palaces of the gods were visible. When the gods got bored they tossed hot coals through the little apertures to see if they could hit Earth, hence shooting stars.

The Big Dipper wheels on its bowl. In years hence it will have stopped looking like a saucepan and will resemble a sugar scoop as the earth continues to wobble and the dipper's seven stars speed in different directions. Nor will other constellations remain as they are. Brilliant Sirius is now far from where the astrologer in a pharaoh's court saw it, and twelve thousand years from now our pole star will be Vega.

Three o'clock: fish stationary. Pisces, two fish in the heavens, the pair, the Northern Fish and the Western Fish, comes round again, and on this silvery summery evening, sky fish becomes river fish. I pull my knees up to my chest and rock back, scanning the stars, bringing back the ancient names like incantations. During the scientific blackout of the Middle Ages, celestial knowledge was kept alive by the Arabs, and many stars still bear their sinuous, sibilant names: Deneb, Altair, Betelgeuse, Mintaka, Alnitak, and "the star for which all evening waits," Aldebaran.

Three-thirty: fish squarely in the same place. The sky is a meadow of wildstar flowers. A cricket chirps continually, transmitting twenty to thirty chirps, pausing, then embellishing its plainsong with a syncopated triple tongue. The receiver chirps too. Picking up the fish every half-hour in the same place gives me an odd and inexplicable comfort, a quiddity with which I communicate in the night, not through words but through invisible pulses, electronic heartbeats.

As I enter data on the chart a tiny pink-eared cactus mouse with an extravagant tail longer than its body snuffles a beer can about ten feet away. I focus my headlamp on it, which disturbs it not. It springs up on the can for a taste, circles around and about, but always comes back to explore the can. It runs back under a ledge behind me, dashes out again, making in all eight forays. Of the thirteen species of rodents in the Grand Canyon, seven of them live in the riparian zone, despite the fact that beaches have a colder harsher habitat.

In 1890 W. H. Merriam, who was working out his theory of life zones, spent a short time camping in the Grand Canyon, where he encountered these plentiful little mice: "During the two nights spent in the cañon, these mice came about my blanket in great numbers and I was forced to place my scanty stock of provisions in a small tree for protection; but even there it was not safe, for the mice are excellent climbers." Cactus mice are the dominant mouse species along the river, and many a dinner is punctuated by the frantic scrabbling of one when it falls into an open food box.

177

Hump-
back
Chub
and the
Little
Colorado

Cactus mice are mainly active around dusk but when ambient temperature is as warm as tonight's, they're out bustling all night long. Apart from those occupying this riparian habitat, cactus mice live almost exclusively in desert habitats. When they live along the river, they adjust their home range from an irregular territory to a linear one that parallels the river. Being nocturnal, they orient themselves aurally, not visually. These little listeners have developed the capacity to put a sequence of signals into a spatial concept, to rehear and translate them into a perception of space.

Four o'clock: the river has risen over two feet in four hours. As I turn the antenna, it focuses dead on the line of the triangulation stakes. Typically, the fish has not moved. "Bunga bunga" goes the water under the ledge, like a bass fiddle plucked and plunked and amplified.

Four-thirty: *no fish*! Usually the receiver begins tweeting the second I turn it on. This time, *nothing*! I am dashed, dismayed, caught completely unawares. The fish has been so reliably there that I feel, irrationally, as if it is deliberately being difficult, a child hiding because it doesn't want to go to bed.

An odd and lonely petulance plops down beside me on the ledge. I *counted* on its being there. A creature I never saw—never shook hands with, never made a salad for, never shared a glass of wine with—just went out of my life without a by-your-leave. I sit, hands on knees, annoyed and bemused at my reaction. It seems very dark. The water rises ominously close. A chill breeze binds my head.

Five o'clock: still no fish. I spend a long time pacing, turning the receiver, listening. I stifle the urge to listen every ten minutes. Orion's right shoulder rises over the South Rim, marked by red Betelgeuse, the autumn sky beginning. As dawn leaks into the sky it edits out the stars like excess punctuation marks, deleting asterisks and periods, commas and semicolons, leaving only unhinged thoughts rotating and pivoting, and unsecured words. With the tactless insistence of daylight, shapes materialize, the world develops outlines.

At five-thirty all of Orion is up, fall on the stride.

I make one last reading.

No fish.

Gone.

And, so is summer.

Autumn

near Mile 267

12

To know the Canyon is to love it? Not necessarily. Crawling up the Tanner Trail some moonlight night in August, without food or water, you will hate the Canyon. Bitterly. That pale rim so far above, higher than five Empire State Buildings piled one upon another, seems inaccessible as Heaven, remote as salvation. But if you survive . . . Who could ask for a finer place than our Canyon in which to taste life deeply by risking life? By hanging it over the edge?

Edward Abbey, 1982, *Down the River*

Tanner Trail
and Mean Mesquite

The Tanner Trail reaches the river at Mile 68.6. Sid and Marie Davis, two soil geologists, and I walk down it to join a group of USGS geologists mapping recent deposits along the river between Lava Creek at Mile 65.2 and Unkar Delta at Mile 73. For those who work in the bottom of the Grand Canyon, there are only four ways to reach the river, not counting vehicle access, which exists only at Lees Ferry, Diamond Creek, and Pearce Ferry. The first is by boat, often the only way that many places on the river can be reached. A second is by helicopter, extravagantly expensive and limited in the places one can be put down. The third way is on foot, down a maintained trail. In nearly 300 miles of river there are only two well-kept and traveled trails: the Bright Angel and South Kaibab from the South Rim, both reaching the river at Mile 89, the latter continuing across the river to the North Rim as the North Kaibab Trail. The fourth way is via the more plentiful, unmaintained old mining trails: Tanner, Bass, Hermit, and Hance, most without water, all requiring a degree of trail finding. Take your choice: any way takes time and effort and, occasionally, risk.

The Tanner Trail begins at Lipan Point, about twenty miles east of Grand Canyon Village. The trail drops from 7,300 feet to 2,700 in nine miles, cantankerous, steep, occasionally obscure, usually difficult. Somewhere nearby, in September 1540, the first Europeans looked down between their toes into a gorge deeper than any they had ever seen. In that year Hopi Indians led Garcia López de Cárdenas, heading an exploring party sent out by Francisco Vásquez de Coronado, to the rim of the canyon and, according to the account of the trip's recorder, Castañeda, who not only did not accompany Cárdenas but wrote from memory twenty years later, they "spent three days on this bank looking for a passage down to the river which looked from above as if the water was 6 feet across, although the Indians said it was half a league wide." The Hopis, who surely knew how to get down to the river, did not lead the explorers there, and the Spaniards' attempts to get themselves down were futile. Nor did Father Francisco Tómas Garcés fare any better. In the summer of 1776 Garcés looked down into "a deep passage . . . steep-sided like a man-made trough," and called it after its color: Rio Colorado.

Seth Tanner, a Mormon prospector, developed this old Indian trail down to the river in 1882 and subsequently discovered copper and silver in the area. Later it connected with the Nankoweap Trail across the river, a route developed in 1882 for geological exploration under the direction of the head of the new U.S. Geological Survey, John Wesley Powell. The connection also provided ingress and egress for horse rustlers, who could cross the river at low water and usually took time in the seclusion of the canyon to do some imaginative brand doctoring. On this side of the river, the Tanner Trail meets the Beamer Trail, which wavers northward along the river and links with the Hopi Trail up the Little Colorado River. The Grand Canyon rattlesnake was first collected here, which makes the Tanner Trail its type location and makes me very judicious indeed about where I place my hands and feet.

By noon we reach the top of the Redwall Limestone where the view opens down to Tanner Beach across the river, lying like an open peach half, across to Tapeats Sandstone ledges and Cardenas Lava dark as the ashes of a doused campfire. The Redwall sharply curtails access to the canyon. Very few breaches exist through this formidable limestone front. Shales crumble into slopes, often slippery, with an angle of repose that usually permits one to ascend or descend with impunity. But the Redwall rises sheer, immutable, allowing no way up, no way down, no way across. Only where a fault has shifted, only where a major stream has cut, do breaks form, and the Tanner Trail makes use of one of these.

The high impromptu steps chopped into the limestones are no problem for a six-footer's long legs, but a five-footer must endure a continual thud and jar. The alternative is unthinkable—going down on the seat of my pants—although the precedent to do so was set by adventurer-lecturer Burton Holmes, who took the difficult parts of the Hance Trail in that position in 1898.

The last few miles of the trail cross the pulverized slopes of Bright Angel Shale and Dox Formation, named (for heaven's sake) after Miss

Virginia Dox from Cincinnati, Ohio, the first lady visitor that William Bass guided to the bottom of the Grand Canyon. The layers of brick red sandstone, siltstone, and mudstone of the Dox Formation, part of the Grand Canyon Supergroup deposited a billion years ago, erode easily, giving the landscape an open, rolling character very different from the narrow, limestone-walled canyon upstream, both in lithology and color, fully fitting Van Dyke's description of "raspberry-red color, tempered with a what-not of mauve, heliotrope, and violet." Sediments flowing in from the west formed deltas, floodplains, and tidal flats, which indurated into these fine-grained sedimentary rocks thinly laid deposits of a restful sea, lined with shadows as precise as the staves of a musical score, ribboned layers, an elegant alteration of quiet siltings and delicious lappings, crinkled water compressed, solidified, lithified. A loose fragment of shale the size of a quarter starts a stream of little stony pumpkin seed chips with a quiet rustling and whispering.

185

—

Tanner
Trail
and
Mean
Mesquite

At the base of these toasted slopes the bone-dry bed of Tanner Creek shirks to the river. Here, on January 22, 1900, Robert Brewster Stanton, with more faith than good sense, entrusted all his exposed film to a prospector who promised to carry it out and mail it to Denver for developing. Stanton did not know, until March 1 when he reached Diamond Creek nearly 160 miles downstream, that his rolls of film had turned out beautifully.

On the beach across the river, I can see my two big blue river bags, which came down on the raft from Lees Ferry, stuffed with all I will know of home for the next few weeks, and reflect that sometimes it's easier to get my gear here than it is me. The river surface rumples with afternoon wind, a raven on beach patrol beats overhead against a deep blue sky. Tamarisk tarnishes like brass, giving on to autumn.

From Tanner Beach sun skims the top of the Palisades across the river, by seven o'clock puts a blush on the creamy walls. No wonder Clarence Dutton called them "palisades" when he saw them in 1886. With their tightly packed vertical shadows they look exactly like a fence of stakes.

Camp on river right occupies a huge sandbar that fills the inner curve of the river. Upstream a small dune has piled up on the beach. A 1:3,000 aerial map, taken six years ago to the month, records the tamarisk and driftwood piles in precisely the same places, but the dune itself has migrated upstream about three hundred yards.

Some of the plants sparsely scattered across the sand still bloom— white evening primrose, pink skeleton plant, magenta windmills, tangerine mallows, brittlebush, ricegrass, and the camper's plague, camel thorn. It's the first time I've seen this recent invader in numbers, and I would not be grieved were it the last. It grows in brakes waist to shoulder high, and its inch-long, needle-sharp spines make it a misery to walk through. It can pure ruin a beach for camping. It arrived in the general proliferation of riparian vegetation since dam closure, which brought many introduced species into these riverside areas. Although introduced exotics may not compete well with established native plants, their ability to colonize swiftly gives them an advantage when disturbance weakens native plant populations. The thousands of people coursing through the canyon aid in dispersing camel thorn, while their tramping keeps it from forming barbed-wire thickets. Two other troublesome plants have recently invaded: peppergrass, a mustard that spreads rapidly by underground roots, and Ravenna grass, an ornamental that the park uses in landscaping.

Walking inland, I slog up a coppice dune studded with a fair stand of arrowweed. Heaps of sand collar their stems, the dune still mobile and meddling with its inhabitants. Although dune soils drain well, they hold lenses of deep moisture in suspension by capillary action. In fact, dunes supply better habitats than those offered by saline soils or unstable talus. Annuals may dominate briefly after a rainy period, but over the long term perennials like arrowweed have best solved the challenges of drifting sand, with long, anchoring root systems that can undergo periodical burial and leaves able to endure intense reflected heat, covered with silky hairs that help curtail water loss. Many spiders and lizards prefer a loose sandy habitat into which they can burrow easily to avoid heat and desiccation, and omnivorous species that feed on detritus find it on the dune's unstable slip face where windblown debris accumulates.

Arrowweed illustrates its name with straight stems of uniform diameter, a bare shaft also used in basketry. It flowers frequently throughout the year with thimble-sized clusters of small lavender flower heads displayed against grayish leaves. Arrowweed, like another native plant, coyote willow, has multiplied rapidly on beaches since dam closure. All botanical surveys have noted it, beginning with that made by Lieutenant J. C. Ives, who found it along the banks as he boated up from the Gulf of California to Diamond Creek in 1858.

Arrowweed colonizes in somewhat drier habitats farther away from the water than willow and tamarisk. It reproduces by sending out runners from which new sprouts rise and hence forms thick, hedgelike clones. A fine duff of arrowweed leaves pave the sand, crunchy scraps of tan and gray overlaid with a plaid of narrow shadows. In the river-edge desert, organic input is so low and gets so quickly blown away that little collects to enrich the soil. Arrowweeds' dense growth pattern forms a windscreen so that leaves dropped on the ground are protected from wind and remain to disintegrate in place.

At the upper end of the beach, I begin a sketch and give up, in danger of becoming the core of a sand dune myself. Sand streams along the ground like a tan smoke and lays a film on my sketchpad. My pen grits on the paper and the ink dries before it touches the page. Gusting from downstream, wind corrugates the sand. A peppering of darker, heavier sand on the upstream face of the ripples visually exaggerates the contour. Sand grains that lift this easily range between 0.15 to 0.27 millimeters— the diameter of a fine drafting pencil lead.

187
—
Tanner
Trail
and
Mean
Mesquite

The sound of the wind changes from a freight train barreling through a tunnel of canyon walls to the stentorian breathing of some horror-movie monster. Fingers of wind scribble across the river, leaving graffiti on its surface. Slots of calm contain lozenges of blue sky outlined in tan, ripples as Renoir painted them. Another gust crosshatches the ripples, faceting them finer, and I remember the meticulous color notes Raymond Cogswell made for the photographs he took on the trip with his brother-in-law, Julius Stone, noting that "waves in mild rapids and riffles have a decided lilac tint, intensified by the mud color of the water." A blast hits shore, grabs a piece of beach and catapults it up into the air, then swirls it across the water like a sand-colored wraith, a ghost of sandbars past.

On my way back to camp I skirt a coyote willow thicket. Coyote willows have very narrow leaves with a strong midvein, much narrower-leaved than any other willow along the river, grayed with fine hairs in proportion to the aridity of their habitat. Like arrowweed, coyote willow clones by means of creeping rootstocks, a more effective means of reproducing than by seeds, for willow seeds are short-lived and must instantly land in a hospitable habitat, sprout quickly, and survive both flooding and desiccation, a formidable list of requirements for a tiny seed in a big desert river canyon.

Pinecone galls tip some of the willow branches, aberrant growths that look uncannily like miniature pinecones, caused by a tiny midge, *Rhabdophaga strobiloides*. In early spring the midges' first generation of the year produces galls on male willow catkins. The second generation attacks the leaf buds, causing this multiplication of miniature bud leaves, forming these distinctive galls. The cycle begins when a female lays an egg on a willow bud and the salivary enzymes she inserts during egg laying provoke the plant to proliferate tissue to isolate the newly hatched larva. This legless white comma of a larva may look totally nondescript—no eyes, no nose, no face—but when it plugs into the plant's vascular system, it becomes a sophisticated manipulator: it stimulates the plant's cells, both mechanically, through its feeding, and chemically, through its saliva, causing the tissues upon which the larva sups to differentiate from tissues in the rest of the plant. Within a couple of days all plant cells involved with nourishing the larva withdraw from the plant's normal growth cycle and usurp nourishment from the rest of the plant. Controlled now by the minute gourmand, their sole purpose is to feed and shelter the greedy little freeloader.

Gall makers, usually minute midges and wasps, are plentiful along the river, as their various designs: nubbins on hackberry leaves and furry balls on saltbush stems, red peppercorns on willow leaves, stem swellings on rabbitbrush, and fringed balls on sagebrush stalks, little nurseries of intricate sizes and shapes, housing oblivious sucklings against a treacherous and uncertain world.

One of camp duties is to settle, purify, and pump water for drinking and cooking. Boiling uses large amounts of fuel and generates a lot of heat on a warm day. Chlorox adds nothing to the taste of the water, although it kills most germs. Since filtering removes giardia and salmonella, a pump provides an efficient way to purify our water.

River water sits in big buckets overnight to settle out the silt. Upstream storms caused both the Paria and the Little Colorado to flood recently, spewing mud into the river, and this morning silt lies over an inch thick in the bottom of the buckets and tints the water pink. The little pump shudders and leaks with the effort of forcing Colorado River gravy through. When I remove the filter to clean it, a quarter-inch of velvety-fine silt coats it.

I spend half an hour alternately pumping and cleaning. You use water *very* judiciously when you have to replace what you use. Turning on a faucet and letting the water run while you brush your teeth seems an incomprehensible and flagrant waste of the rim-world. Down here it's "Water, water every where. Nor any drop to drink."

On the downstream side of Tanner Creek, archaeological sites around twenty-one hundred years old wreath a big dune. The crest of the dune is a popular campsite. This morning a National Park Service work crew stabilizes the loose sandy slopes that lead up to the campsite, an area heavily disturbed and eroded from overuse. The angle of repose of the dune sand lies at about a 25 percent angle. When the slope reaches 30 percent, which happens when footsteps momentarily steepen it, sand begins to avalanche. To control this erosion the crew embeds two-foot logs connected by cables into the slope. Logs and cables are not yet buried in the sand but, when hidden, will scarcely show and will provide a directed and firmer path for the hundreds of people who traipse up the dune's unstable slope. Crews have done their work so skillfully that most people are not aware that, for instance, popular camping beaches like those at Nankoweap and Cardenas have already been considerably stabilized, nor that the simple and ingenious "planting" of dead shrubs to block unsightly multiple paths has allowed them to recover.

189
—
Tanner
Trail
and
Mean
Mesquite

Setting steps like this and providing other visitor guides are controversial. Some people feel that the Park Service unnecessarily tampers with the natural landscape. Uncontroversial is the fact that these devises help to stabilize and focus the traffic of 18,000 to 20,000 visitors per year to specific areas strengthened to withstand it.

A huge, half-moon cobble bar downstream supplies the dune with its sand. During high predam flows, the river probably covered the cobble bar, filling the spaces between the imbricated cobbles with wilts and sands. The stones, like those in most rocky river beaches, overlap one another like shingles, all tilting downstream. The bar sits high enough to have escaped inundation during the high flows of 1983–84, when only a tiny channel snaked in along the foot of the dune, but it was obviously overtopped in predam times, for the river has cut away the river terraces that once covered it, leaving twenty- and thirty-foot terrace walls that give valuable insight into Anasazi settlement patterns and land use, as well as how the terrain along the river has changed over the last few thousand years.

The walls of the terraces, sliced through by drainages, display a neat alteration of rusty red and beige layers. Wind-carried and water-carried deposits usually lie in discrete layers whose area can be mapped. Eolian sands are more uniform in grain size since the smaller grains have been blown out. Alternately sent downstream or momentarily stored in a sandbar, sand is the most plentiful sediment in the river ecosystem, moving through in the sequence of deposition and scour. Water-carried deposits may be both alluvial, brought in by the river, or colluvial, washed down from hillsides above. They are finer, often velvety, silt. Wet silt adheres to your skin, while coarser eolian sands feel like sandpaper and brush off cleanly. The extent and placement of these deposits has significance in management decisions for the Colorado River.

Layering of the two kinds of textures, colluvium enriched with minerals alternating with porous, well-drained sandy soils, made good agricultural soil for prehistoric farmers. A reliable correlation exists between Kayenta Anasazi occupation of A.D. 1050–1150 and one of these alluvial units, a layer geologists call the "striped layer" for its clear alternation of pale tan layers brought in by river flow and red layers sloshed down off the hillsides. These distinctive Roman-striped layers lie above the old high-water line of mesquite and cat's-claw acacia, held in a terrace estimated to have developed over a 400-to-500-year period of deposition.

If this area was farmed, and it undoubtedly was, it profited by being enriched with influxes of sediment during spring floods. But over time, salts accumulated as rocks broke down, their contents of sea salt dissolved and percolated into the soil by rainwater, concentrated by high evapotranspiration rates. After the river overflowed and renewed the land, it could be farmed again. Interspersed with the layers of alluvium are thin lines of charcoal, likely from burning native vegetation to clear the land and perhaps crop stubble burning. Carbon dates on this charcoal also correlate well with periods of Anasazi occupation.

At the foot of the terrace, the cobble bar stretches to the river. Midway an island of tamarisk casts a parsimonious shade that a light breeze constantly rearranges. I eat lunch here, directly across the river from an eye-stopper graben in which a large section of the earth's crust dropped between two fault lines, "drop" being a relative term since the slippage required millennia. Grabens are often huge landforms, too large to see in their entirety, but this one is seeable in one glance. Named the Basalt Graben, its wedge shape makes it look like the keystone of a gargantuan masonry arch. Faulting, which began after the dark Cardenas lavas flowed out 1.1 billion years ago, displaced strata on the downstream side about seventeen hundred feet. The Basalt Canyon Fault brought the black basalt down to abut against the neatly layered red Dox. The Butte Fault forms the upstream side of the graben, the same fault visible a few miles upstream in Kwagunt and Nankoweap Canyons. This stunning panorama is a gift of the river that cut through it and made it manifest.

From a distance the cobble bar looks flat but as I continue to walk across it, I find it corrugated as a washboard. Silt cracks reticulate a narrow channel recently muddy. Drying slowly, the edges of the individual plates curl upward, splitting between layers. A big cottonwood log lies far up from the river, lofted in by a predam flood. Cobbles and pebbles stabilize and shade the sand, and between them grow bristly little sprouts all under four inches high, the river version of a rock garden. A Plimsoll line of tenuous green algae scribes many of the translucent quartz pebbles.

Some of the stones are beautifully rounded, those between one and two inches long the most whole and symmetrical. Above that size, they still betray their original irregular form with odd angles and hollows. Below that size they are generally shattered. It is as if between one and two inches the integrity of the rock and the abrasive power of the river reach eloquent equilibrium in a harmonious ratio of surface to volume, creating the perfect oval. Wrapped in autumn sunshine, I give thanks for river edges and the light that sparks off the ripples and a row of near-perfect river cobbles that the river once carried in its pocket.

191

—

*Tanner
Trail
and
Mean
Mesquite*

The next day I wander up an arroyo, enticed by what's beyond a huge chunk of conglomerate that nearly stoppers its mouth. Nothing much grows in the flat gravel base of the arroyo, freshly washed and plaited with little sharp-edged, inch-deep channels. Masses of river gravel cemented by calcium carbonate band the creek walls, and chunks of it lie in the creek bed, a local phenomenon, a continuation of the well-cemented gravel along the left bank of the river since Kwagunt Creek. The pebbles, probably relic deposits from the Pleistocene, may be up to thirty thousand years old. When the Colorado River ran an estimated seventy-five to eighty feet higher, these gravels dropped on top of an impervious Dox Sandstone layer. Water percolating through the ground leached out the minerals that cemented the hodgepodge together.

Gray lines crisscross maroon layers of Dox as if the wall were tiled and grouted. These marked changes in rock color, often associated with rock fractures, sometimes limn the cracks or freckle the rock with "reduction spots" where ferrous oxide, the red iron ore contained in the rock, loses a molecule and is "reduced" to ferric oxide. Ferric oxide is grayish green, while ferrous is rusty red to burgundy. Farther up, thin cards of Dox Shale pave the slope—note cards, playing cards, calling cards, potato chips of shale holding at a steep angle of repose, some ripple-marked and mud-cracked, floodplain deposits that filtered down a billion years ago. Shallow, regular ripple marks scallop the larger slabs, docile fossil waves on peaceful fossil shores. I pace the shallow sea, walking the time between, reflecting on the kind of fossil I'd like to be. I guess I'd like my bones to be replaced by some vivid chert, a red ulna or radius, or maybe preserved as the track of a strange lug-soled creature locked in the sandstone—how did it walk, what did it eat, and did it love the sunshine? I step in the wrong place and the slope disappears beneath my feet in a clatter of stony imprecations.

Only the slightest of air movements nudges a sweetbush stem or tickles a brittlebush leaf. A small checkered butterfly samples summer's late bloomers. Dozens of grasshoppers clatter and ratchet, Chinese firecrackers in an Arizona desert. Bee flies zip between open flowers, all small tickings in this spread of timeless landscape, where the second hand moves but once a century. Chalky gray brittlebushes stand out dramatically against the dark shales. Brittlebush, *Encelia farinosa*, was named for Christopher Encel, a German naturalist; *farinosa* refers to the pale gray, mealy covering on its leaves and stems, an adaptation to prevent water loss. The stems secrete a fragrant resin that explains the Mexican name of "incensio." Prehistoric Indians chewed the resin and coated their bodies with its numbing sap to relieve pain.

Brittlebush twigs match the gray of the leaves, until I pass one small bush whose twigs shine amber and an uncharacteristic glitter coats the gritty sandstone beneath, the honeydew of hundreds of aphids that encrust the tip ends of the stems and cover the undersides of the leaves. Most cluster on the veins of young leaves, pinheads of off-white fuzz with horsehair legs, threadlike beaks plunged into plant tissue from which they siphon the plant's phloem, an arrangement at least 300 million years old. They eschew the tiny, brand new, just unfurled leaves but crowd those an inch down from the tip, in the end affecting the whole plant since photosynthates must be shunted from growth areas to infested areas.

This flocking of aphids results from parthenogenetic reproduction. Females produce the year's first young without fertilization and continue to do so until some trigger occurs—a shift in the weather, shortening day length—or the plant stops providing nourishment. Then males hatch, mating occurs, producing offspring capable of wintering over.

When I dislocate an aphid from its chosen vein, it looks like some Lilliputian lunar vehicle under my hand lens. It stalks its way to the leaf margin, tests the abyss, and stops. Its characteristic cornicles, which stick out like twin tail pipes from the end of the abdomen, may have developed for defense, for they secrete a sticky substance that dabs a predator or parasite on the head and clogs up its mouthparts. Most aphids also emit alarm pheromones from their cornicles, a powerful message to which the rest of the colony reacts on the instant, dropping off the plant en masse. Oddly, since pheromones tend to be very specific communicators, the aphid alarm pheromone also energizes any tending ants.

Plant sap, when processed through the aphid's gut, becomes a more complex substance called honeydew, a sugary, energy-rich liquid of surplus ingested sap plus excess sugars and waste materials, which may come close to fulfilling the complete dietary needs of attending ants. Aphids produce copious amounts of honeydew, up to 133 percent of their body weight in an hour. If the sugary stuff collects on their bodies, it can mold and fungal infection may wipe out a whole colony. When an ant worker, which requires liquid food, palpates an aphid, the aphid produces a drop of honeydew that the ant imbibes.

193
—

*Tanner
Trail
and
Mean
Mesquite*

The third party to this mutualistic arrangement is the brittlebush itself, which manipulates the aphids by speeding up or slowing down its productivity, and stimuli from the leaf determine whether an aphid prefers the shaded or the sunny side. Although in the long run aphids are not beneficial to plants, there may be a quid pro quo: if ants tend a plant's aphids, they may prevent other plant chewers and siphoners from attacking.

Despite the infestation, the brittlebushes look amazingly healthy. If they weren't, the aphids would have gotten the message and left. In my rim-world garden, aphids on my peonies and columbines offend me. Out here, where I have the time to observe, I appreciate how these little clockwork creatures perform their intricate, nefarious business in the most efficient aphid way possible.

The mouth of Basalt Canyon looks as if a road grader growled through and never came back to clean up the mess. Rocks pile in untidy heaps. Plants bend every which way, whacked crooked by recent storm flow in the canyon. A white cabbage butterfly dotters past, followed by its equally erratic shadow. I start up the canyon, dressed in sheer indolence with not one whit of foreboding about how the day will end, simply relishing the sunshine and "October's bright blue weather."

As the canyon cuts through the fault that bounds the downstream end of the graben, rosy sandstones give way to black basalt. The Cardenas Lava was discovered and named for exposures in this canyon. The resistant basalt rises almost vertically, and Basalt Canyon has a darker, more rigorous aspect quite unlike the scoop-shaped canyons and tributaries cut in softer rock. The rill of Basalt Creek gradually becomes a rivulet that trickles into a neatly woven, four-strand braid. It may only drizzle today but the high-water salt lines on the walls verify that when it flashes it runs feet deep, reams out the narrow places, scoops suck holes in the sand around the monstrous boulders it can't budge, and flings rough clasts in flagrant furrows.

Salt crusts every surface and outlines every crack and crunches crisply underfoot. Narrow lines of salt thread the walls, widening into raised welts that rub off at a touch. The basalt exudes so much salt that some segments of the wall are completely spiderwebbed by it. A hundred feet farther, an iron salt colors the rivulets brilliant rusty orange and leaves a fuzzy, flocculent surface deposit up to a quarter-inch thick, a soft and mushy burnt orange carpet. Pure iron is not soluble in water, and what colors the water orange is probably a salt such as ferric or ferrous phosphate. Where the coating thins to a skim, it turns the water surface as iridescent as an oil slick.

I walk upward until a high, curving travertine wall, hung with pennants of dark algae, glimmers with water and momentarily blocks passage. Here at the bottom of the canyon all is in shadow, but sun blazes the upper walls a ruddy cinnamon. A rust-red dragonfly and a tiny blue butterfly patrol. A big paper wasp, iridescent blue black with henna wings, landing gear dangling, hums by. The time it has taken to get here marks this as the turnabout if I am to get back by five o'clock, as I said I would.

When I get back to the mouth of Basalt Creek I turn left, upriver. As I round the beach two ducks lift off, quacking. A small channel separates an island from shore, and in the quieter waters waterfowl land and feed. Ahead the beach ends in a five-foot drop directly into deep water—no rocks stick up, no ledges shelve out of the water to walk on or hold onto. I have no choice but to clamber up, batting through a thicket I can't see the end of. I bushwhack through a dense apron of tamarisk thicket, a horrid mass of dead trunks and thick branches interwoven like a steel mesh. A deadfall of branches hides channels gouged out by old flows. More than once my foot goes through and branches lock around my leg like a bear trap. When I pause to get my breath I'm conscious that blood drizzles down both legs. So much for wearing shorts.

Ahead and above the tamarisk grow the old high-water-line mesquites, a no-man's-land of interlocked trunks and barbed branches. The slope, a sliding slithering pile of shale, gives me nothing to grab onto except mesquite branches full of thorns that rake my shoulders like tiger's claws. I gingerly use thumb and forefinger to grasp each spiky branch and put it aside with great care, as slow as crawling through coils of barbed wire. I manage only a few feet before I give up. Only the mindless devotion to getting back when I said I would drives me forward.

I break the mesquite screen and surge back into the tamarisk, then through to the arrowweed, not the friendly open stems of our beach but a palisade of tall, tensile shrubs. Once, near eye level I spot a katydid the size and color of an arrowweed leaf. Ninety years ago, when I left this morning, the sight of a katydid this close would have riveted my attention. But not this afternoon. Without a second thought I bat it out of the way. It soars to another stem a foot away, unbound by what trammels me.

The light dims faster than makes sense. I occupy a high-anxiety nightmare in which I can never get to where I'm going, everything takes twice as long as it should, I forgot my airline ticket, I have no suitcase, no clothes, no money, and my flight is being called. After what seems hours of pushing and shoving, getting swatted and lashed, the breakthrough of the last screen comes so suddenly that the merciful beach opening below stuns me. In the deepening darkness I recognize the tail end of our beach, an endless quarter-mile from camp. I begin to jog, hitching along like a poorly articulated puppet. Ahead shrubs turn into people. I lift my arm in greeting. It hurts.

Enough scratches crisscross my shins for a dozen games of ticktacktoe. Disinfectant stings unmercifully. I feel flagellated, flayed alive, splinters of bones strung together by bits of sinew and shreds of muscle, an ancient stylite of the desert, doomed to spend the remainder of my days bound to a mesquite tree, holding my unsaintly symbol, a bottle of iodine.

I worm my way into my sleeping bag exhausted, yearning for sleep to soothe. But sleep does not come. Tonight this canyon is too much— too much wind, too much river, too much sand, too many thorns, too many puzzles, too far to reach, too beyond to find.

195
—

*Tanner
Trail
and
Mean
Mesquite*

Basalt Graben, right drainage

13

Now, a sunrise in the Grand Canyon lasts as long as you please. Each hour is a sunrise for some cavern deeper than the last, and in fact there are many where it has yet to rise for the first time since the canyon was made by those ages of running water. So all this time we two sat on a flat ledge, with our heels dangling, our elbows on our thighs, watching while the clock and the sun and the shadows went round. But the human mind thinks largely by comparing one thing with another, and since there is nothing like that infinity of red-and-yellow cliff and pinnacle and palisade which we watched so long and silently, I know of no way to describe it after all our looking.

Benjamin Brooks, 1905, "Over Night at the Edge of
the Grand Canyon," *Scribner's Magazine*

Hilltop Ruin
and Beaver Burrows

———

At Mile 71.2, Cardenas Creek, I awake to a 37° hand-numbing November cold. Last night's sunset was vintage Grand Canyon: sun shafting like a klieg light through the clouds beaded over it, focused on the pink stucco facade of the Redwall, plunging the rest of the landscape into a brooding silhouette against an extravagant orange-and-purple silk batik sky, a John Van Dyke description incarnate: "vermilion-red" against "fire-green . . . so subtle is the blend that you cannot draw a line between gold and orange or purple and mauve . . . a silver, a saffron, a pink, a heliotrope." Coyotes called late into the evening, three or four barks drawn out into thin silver wires of rising sound. A gabbling flock of Canada geese flew over in the predawn blackness, their cries pulsating in the darkness, their wings whispering snow.

This morning as the sun intensifies behind the Palisades, sharp shafts of light stripe the beach, and I realize how aware I've become of those first beams of light cracking the brittle cold. The rising and the setting of the sun in the canyon becomes a matter of importance: here sunrise and sunset bracket the days of my life in a way they do not do in a thermostat-set, electric-lighted rim-world. Here sunrise and sunset receive their daily obeisance because there is no intervening wall and window, only the enfolded, immediate, imposed reality. Every morning this week, as the sun rises out of a new cliff notch, I register how soon it appears, clasps my wrist, warms my hand, when the beam strikes my retina. Down here one genuflects to the sunrise and absorbs the cadence.

A debris flow, or more likely several, created an isolated prow 425 feet above the river. A former stream bed of Cardenas Creek provided a chute for the slurry of Supai and Dox that freighted down from the south or southeast. Most dry creek beds in this area closet old debris flows that were activated during the massive melting sometime after the end of the Pleistocene Ice Age, around ten thousand years ago.

Partway up the ridge, well-rounded river pebbles erode out of the slope, dropped by a slowing current when the river ran this high. Then the slope steepens, the soil whitens, the flow differing in color and lithology from the terrain which it covered. From the crest, the view is splendid in every direction. Downstream a patch of deeper green marks a pocket marsh. Across the river pinyon and juniper serrate the Walhalla Plateau. Behind me the Palisades form a phalanx two miles or more back from the river. Below, the river swirls into smoky jade moiré patterns. A wispy high cirrus layer blurs the sharpness of the shadows. Two condensation trails form a huge cross in the sky, the Emperor Constantine's *In hoc vinces* reincarnated.

Granted the wind hoots and hollers up here, but taller, bushier plants belie the impression that life is as tough as it is on those granulated Dox slopes below, where plants are far-spaced and wind-trimmed to hemispheres. Up here tiny yellow dogweeds pop out of cracks in limestone boulders, shrubs of wolfberry and Mormon tea flourish, and generous amounts of fluffgrass grow among scattered river pebbles that could be 700,000 years old.

A small bird hops from rock to rock a few feet away. It has a longish insect-probing bill and grayish brown color but lacks distinctive markings except a dark stripe through its eye and a light gray streaked breast. When it alights, it bobs its tail like a sandpiper: a rock wren, ever-present this fall, wren-busy and wren-cheeky, repeating "ta-peat, ta-peat peat peat."

Here on this place of far view, the Anasazi built a small enclosure now called Hilltop Ruin, discovered by Robert Stanton in 1890. The hilltop is too small and too far from the water to be farmed, and no wastage has turned up that would suggest a tool-making site. No evidence of daily living such as fire pits endure, although a few meager shards found date between A.D. 1100 and 1200. This enigmatic site has never been excavated. If built for communication or defense, with its obvious advantage of long views to the cardinal points of the compass, no evidence of that use remains. Farming settlements scatter far up and down along the river here. Defense a priori would have been an exceedingly haphazard affair, and no signs of warfare mark the Anasazi years.

Neurobiologist-author William Calvin speculates that the Anasazi used Hilltop as a sun calendar. Such sun calendars were in use throughout the prehistoric world, as far back as Stonehenge in England. In the Southwest sophisticated levels of observation went on at large sites like Pueblo Bonito, at Chaco Canyon in New Mexico. Sun observatories still standing at places like Hovenweep, in Utah, have ports or slots built at an angle that dictate a precise position for an observer at a precise time. Calvin suggests that here the landscape itself provides the wherewithal to make a "horizon calendar": an observer can move each morning to keep the rising sun in the *same* notch of the Palisades marking his position daily, say, with a rock placed on the ground. Over a season, rocks in that line become closer spaced as solstice approaches, and at solstice the string of rocks describes a small loop at the end, the eight-day period of actual turning when the sun appears to pause—indeed, "solstice" means "sun stands still."

Today Hopi people, the direct descendants of the Anasazi, use the winter solstice to set the time of religious festivals and corn planting, and so too the Anasazi may have watched the sun to time their ceremonies and lives. At this time of year, as the Hopi express it today, "the sun is in his winter house," and they make prayers for his prompt return to his summer house, ceremonies to hasten his foot-dragging passage across the horizon, to bring back warmth, to heat the soil, to sprout the seed.

Into the contemplative silence yet another scenic helicopter flight drones over, on the way to see if the Little Colorado is blue. How much those remote passengers miss of the extraordinary privileges of cool sandstone and layered limestone, the joyful puzzles, the resonate stillness, the grandiose operatic landscape distilled into a perfect river pebble buried half way up a slope, the sense of being intensely human with all its concomitant glories and disgraces, the insights into an ancient mind puzzling out the sun's walk and the moon's path. Down here one comes to nodding terms with what went before, how slow the eons, how quick the riffle, how incredible the sky.

When the annoyance fades away, the great quiet of this solitary morning is such that small sounds—a wren's footsteps, a fly's inhalation, a butterfly's wings on the downstroke, limestone weathering, solstice coming—make themselves heard like an ancient canon.

Even with the most meticulous kitchen keeping, there's always one suicidal cantaloupe seed that throws itself off the table in a fit of unrequited passion and winds up the trophy of usufructuary ants. Why not—all

201
—

*Hilltop
Ruin
and
Beaver
Burrows*

by itself, one seed may contain enough water to meet one ant's water needs. A bright orange harvester ant, with large head and mandibles, explores the sand in haphazard spurts, a search pattern that brings it to the fresh seed, which it tests and then hoists up like a longshoreman with a sack of grain. It trudges fifteen feet across the beach, falls down a footprint, staggers up the far side in fits and starts, leaving a lacy half-inch-wide trail. In all, it takes fifteen minutes to drag, shove, and tote its seed twenty feet. Since closure of Glen Canyon Dam, harvester ants have heavily invaded the beaches. Previously spring floods washed out nests too close to the water. Now ants can colonize nearer the river's edge.

Later in the morning, on a dry terrace above Cardenas Creek, I watch a nest of working harvester ants, fascinated by their orderly communal comings and goings. Of the hymenopterans that live in deserts in numbers—bees, wasps, and ants—ants are surely the most successful group, having staked out their claim to success a 100 million years or so ago. Now they are one of the most important inhabitants of the desert Southwest. Tiny as they are, the total biomass of ants in the desert is significantly greater than that of much larger mammal herbivores. Biologist E. O. Wilson calls them "the little things that run the world" and believes that "if humans were not so impressed by size alone, they would consider an ant more wonderful than a rhinoceros."

The common harvester ant in the canyon is *Pogonomyrmex barbatus*, the California bearded harvester ant, "bearded" by virtue of long hairs on the underside of workers' heads. Harvester ants forage during the day this late in the year, but in summertime they switch to early morning and late afternoon, even though some can travel on soil surfaces hotter than 120°F. Largely a Western genus, harvester ants build mounds often several feet across, and often the workers clear off vegetation around the nests, which makes them conspicuous even from an airplane.

The ground twinkles with ants, this morning all working the nest's westward quadrant. They go out empty-footed and come back with a fluffy seed held up in front like supplicants with an offering. Group foragers, they travel out straight and purposefully, take no detours other than those necessary to avoid a big rock, mostly just going up and over even good-sized stones. They return with the whole seedhead and shuck it at the nest. The discarded trash of tiny tufts of white hairs surround the nest: no litter laws here.

A definite protocol accompanies nest opening in the morning. The first ants out begin a concentrated search for seeds. The second wave assumes maintenance responsibilities, repairing any holes in the nest. The third wave, which I've been watching, are harvesters who take their clues of where to forage from the first ants out, who do not continue to forage once they have set the day's direction. Although these first ants may go every which way on an outbound trip, they zip home by the shortest route, establishing trunk-trails and marking them with pheromones delivered through their stings. Actually they are not so much trails as half-inch-wide cylinders of scent. As Wilson points out, while we live in a sensory world of sight and sound, ants operate in a chemical world. In most species, a worker carries between ten and twenty exocrine glands, which release pheromones that, among other messages, alarm, recruit, and identify.

203
—
Hilltop
Ruin
and
Beaver
Burrows

This nest, which houses a mature colony, is an impressive structure. It may last years, enriches the soil, and can be passed to the next generation. The entryway leads to branching shafts deep in the ground, which provide surcease from the physical extremes of temperature and desiccation of the canyon, as well as from surface predation—lizards *love* ants. Climate-controlled oval chambers connect to the main shafts, the larger and uppermost acting as nurseries where the queen and nurse-workers raise the young, the smaller and lower compartments serving for hibernation. Because of nests ants can thermoregulate, go out to forage when it's too cold for predators to be about, and return to get warm again.

Nests also have storage rooms for seeds, which ants coat with an antibiotic saliva and, to prevent their molding, rotate as necessary, protecting their food supply in which seeds may not be available all year round. Sometimes harvester ants living on the beach with a goodly supply of buffalo gnats take those they've captured back to the nest, dry them in the sun, and then stash them away in storage chambers.

From a plant's point of view, nests better their environment of impoverished canyon soil. Nests improve soil texture, humidity, and acidity and contribute nutrients from the accumulated waste materials and ant graveyard. Seeds that land there and become covered, out of the reach of birds and mice, stand a better chance of survival. Seeds often sprout and establish fairly dense patches where they are of further benefit to the ants because they require less travel to harvest. Both plant and ant benefit: the ant secures a reliable food supply, and the plant extends its range. Plants take advantage of the richer soil by making their seeds and fruits attractive to ants. "Ant plants" keep their seed stalks relatively low and often the seed-bearing stems curve down at maturity so that seeds are easier for ants to reach. Seed capsules do not pop open all at once but do so slowly over an extended time, luring ants to make repeated visits. Plants may also benefit from ants on patrol for they may control populations of other insects that beset leaves and stems.

I track a worker thirty feet out until it picks up a seed and starts back. While I supervise such busy trucking in and out, I also watch that I don't host any workers on my foot. *Pogonomyrmex* is the only ant genus to have an autonomous sting, more lethal to humans than hornet or honeybee venom. The worker ant's ovipositor, no longer used for depositing eggs, has become an efficient syringe that punctures the skin, then forces venom in under pressure. Such formidable defense allows ants to patrol across open ground, where they could easily be preyed upon were it not for this efficient defense.

The pain from a harvester ant's sting is considerably greater than that from other ants and bees and lasts a lot longer. A sting feels like getting smacked with a red hot two-by-four. It hurts for days. The venom contains considerable pain factors, as well as those that break down blood cells, and is saved from being worse because the ant can administer only an infinitesimal amount. For a vertebrate predator, often the immediate shock is enough to allow the ant to escape. For me, the only remedy is standing in the cold river until my leg goes numb. Nothing else helps.

It is a desultory Sunday morning, albeit no one delivered the Sunday papers. Someone whistles "Amazing Grace." An American coot, a small, stolid black duck, stalks the far end of the beach with ministerial dignity. Camp has an air of general indolence although everyone is working—they're just getting started later. Even though we are on a seven-day workweek, it is as if we're timed to a six-day-on-one-day-off cycle whether we observe it or not. Someone else searches for the empty cans carried off last night by the resident wood rats, doubtless sleeping off an orgy brought on by having absconded with an almost full case of avocados. Half a dozen evening grosbeaks dart among the trees, their yellow the color of the turning willows, wings black as tamarisk trunks. A small flight of midges centers briefly over my head, two fall on my notebook *in flagrante delicto*, separate, waft off.

In the stillness a raven calls like a bad omen on the wing. It rains not, neither does it sun. The river rises not, neither does it fall. The sky leaks patches of blue. The raven calls twice. November drizzle permeates the canyon, filling it like a broth, beading everything with moisture. Pinpoints of water pucker my notebook page. Mists festoon the rim to the east, but the sun blazes like a white spotlight behind a scrim of clouds. Then shreds of blue sky show to the southwest, and sun seeps between the two weathers. Again rain closes in, lowering and drifting, diaphanous, slow, nudged by a witless breeze.

I dig out my rain suit and head for the small marsh downstream. The breeze freshens, this morning's clouds disappear, dragging fingers of white as they go, flaunting perfidious tags of blue sky. In the thicket behind the beach, thirty-foot-high willow trees with narrow filmy foliage rise above a band of tamarisks a third their height. The only large willow growing on the Colorado River below the dam, Goodding willows may grow to fifty feet with a trunk three feet in diameter. They were once more common but happen to be favored beaver food. The only stand of these big willows survives here at Cardenas Marsh.

205
—
Hilltop
Ruin
and
Beaver
Burrows

Down the beach reed grass seed heads nod six feet above an oval of damp mucky sand. The leaves rustle, interlock, separate, stridulate one against the other. Dried canes rattle. Their faint shadows figure the sand, fade and sharpen, fade again. In places the muck, webbed with roots, cracks a foot deep, too squishy to walk on. Reeds and bulrushes and sedges ring the sink, each staking out its own preferred regimen of moisture. The dead stalks of big bulrushes arch over in a confusion of wickets through which fresh green stems poke, breaking open to expose a snowy white pith. Torrey's rush bands the edge, long stems extending beyond the stiff ball-like flowering cluster. Disjunct clumps of bulrushes with bluish stems shake open loose heads like tassels at the top. The stems are so big and thick, at least an inch in diameter at the base, that they wedge open deep cracks in the sand. Speedwell and alfalfa, finished blooming a month ago, insinuate themselves around and between the big plants, groupies at a bulrush concert.

Cattails have their wetter ring of beach, where the rhizomes can enjoy regular immersion. The cattail marsh provides shelter for two endangered songbirds, yellowthroats and willow flycatchers, both of which breed in the marshes of the new riparian zone. The rarest of nesting birds in the canyon, willow flycatchers visually fall into the "little gray bird" category. Aurally they make a distinctive "fitzbew-fitzbew." Recently the numbers of willow flycatchers have declined in the canyon, although the population is still the largest one in Arizona. Ornithologists think that loss of habitat, like Goodding willows for high perches, and the breaking up of once contiguous habitats into smaller islands, along with heavy cowbird parasitism, may be causes for their decline. As obligate riparian nesters, they need modestly dense shrubs with nesting niches ten to twenty feet off the ground. Ornithologists have established that along the river willow flycatchers nest only between Miles 47.1 and 56, from Saddle Canyon to Kwagunt Creek, and at Cardenas Marsh, which suggests that influences besides habitat affect nesting pairs. This small marsh at Cardenas is their prime breeding habitat, and to protect these birds Cardenas Beach is closed to camping from mid-June to mid-July, their breeding season.

The floods of 1983 wiped out all those riparian nesting birds that nested three to five feet above the water, a height reached at 41,000 cfs—yellow-breasted chats, Bell's vireo, and common yellowthroats. The chats and vireos lost half of their nests, and yellowthroats lost all of them, because the flood hit when nesting was at its peak. Many renested, again unsuccessfully, when high flows continued. Since then the Bell's vireo population has recovered but the common yellowthroat, which prefers cattail marshes, has continued to decline.

Farther down the beach a dark thicket pushes right to the water's edge. After crabbing my way through some twenty feet of thicket I suddenly come upon a well-traveled beaver passageway down to the river, grasses broken and packed down, overlaid with sand, not as smooth as a slide but clearly well trafficked.

Trappers heavily traveled other streams and rivers in the Colorado River system during the mid-nineteenth century to service English gentlemen's demands for beaver hats. The Grand Canyon was spared, largely because of its difficulty of access. Although James Ohio Pattie may have trapped the river in 1826, his exact route is not known and he likely would have touched the river only at its quite far apart points of access. When trappers George Flavell and Rámon Montéz, men who certainly had an eye keyed to seeing beavers, ran the river in 1896, they mentioned none. Only a few months later, when Nathaniel Galloway came down the river in the fall-winter season of 1896–97, he got a few pelts, affirming that a sharp-eyed trapper could still find beaver albeit not many. Trapping has never been a major enterprise within the canyon and beavers here have existed relatively undisturbed.

The spring spates of the predam river limited beaver populations. They decimated the riparian vegetation that is beavers' main food supply and often drowned young beavers in their dens. Stream beavers build lodges and dams and assiduously maintain them, but beavers along the Colorado den deep into the vegetation at the edge of the river or burrow into the riverbanks. The entrances to their excavations usually lie below the normal high-water line. When the river is low, the dark holes punctuate the banks along shore, another syntax of survival. Now the calmer postdam waters have allowed more young to mature and a 1977 census suggests a solid population in Marble Canyon. The expanding beaver population and its depredations may be the major reason that

Goodding willows and Fremont cottonwood are not now reestablishing themselves along the river. Coyote willow, also the beaver's favored plant, maintains its abundance by cloning.

I turn left and pad up the beaver runway under a ceiling of thatch. Thumb-sized willow stems gleam, cleanly cut on a slant a few inches off the ground. The alley narrows and fallen branches, caught knee-high, blockade the passage like a series of sawhorses. Thwarted, I stop thinking like a human and begin thinking like a beaver, drop down on hands and knees, crawl and, finally, squirm through on my stomach. When I reach a cul-de-sac and can sit up, I feel as Alice must have felt when she landed with a soft thump at the bottom of the rabbit hole. At least two dozen trees fell to create this little clearing, and from it trails fizzle out in every direction, deeper into the thicket. If a beaver were to look up, it would see fluffy seed heads of grass and feathery boughs of tamarisk and a sky filtered through crosshatched leaves of reed and willow, grays and tans freshened with an occasional green sprout, a world shuttered and dimmed. Dried leaves and fine twigs net the ground with a soft, dry duff. No horizon, no rim lines, no reference points, just now and then a whisper of flowing water. Pretty nice digs if you're a beaver.

Here a beaver recently cut a three-inch-diameter willow a foot off the ground. Fresh cream-colored wood chips lie all around. No trace of the trunk remains, although the upper twigs still hook into the reed grass where they fell. Cut willow stalks—both old and darkened, and new and bright, often on the same stump—form the basis of a diet that includes the tuberous roots of the marsh plants just upriver, as well as cat's-claw acacia and mesquite. Beavers have obviously been hard at work here for many seasons.

On hands and knees I slowly hitch back out, nose to soil, eyes on the ground. Something nudges the dirt beneath my hand in response to pressure, only an imperceptible shifting of dark sand but movement nevertheless. An eye. A baleful eye with a boss behind it. Two eyes, unblinking, bulging and lugubrious. I gently pull the sand away and there hunkers Toad of Toad Hollow, the biggest toad I've ever seen. Its olive brown color and irregular camouflage blotches, the pale cream stripe down its back, its warty surface, and its portly size identify it as Woodhouse's toad, named after Samuel Washington Woodhouse in 1851, a Philadelphian who was the first naturalist to visit northern Arizona on an expedition charged with locating the confluence of the Colorado and Little Colorado Rivers.

We are literally nose to nose, and I'm thankful I don't look like food. A proper-sized image must move across a toad's vision before it will

207
—
Hilltop
Ruin
and
Beaver
Burrows

lunge for prey. If the image isn't the right size, even if what passes in front of its eyes is its dearest delight, the toad ignores the tidbit. What the eye sees, not what the brain discerns, determines the reaction, the connection between eye and brain and muscles fixed.

Scientists know little about these toads in the canyon other than that they need moist habitats and are restricted to the river corridor, although outside the Grand Canyon they have an almost continental range. At first glance toads appear obviously unsuited to an arid environment because their skin is moist and water permeable, their eggs lack any sort of shell to protect against water loss, and they require water for both the egg and larval tadpole stage. Overall, only a few amphibian species do live in arid regions, and those that do have various adaptations to survive, one being the ability to burrow. Flanges on the back legs of Woodhouse's toads enable them to dig themselves underground. Once there, they can remain sequestered for long periods, waiting for the right conditions before emerging.

Another defense mechanism that many species of toads have, as every kid used to know, is a coating of noxious substances on their skin. Most substances, if not vile tasting, produce unpleasant physiological effects on any predator bold enough to order toad pizza for lunch. Some are cardiac glycosides that have digitalis-like effects on both snakes and mammals; others induce vomiting. Since producing these compounds requires considerable energy, they must be of proven value in defense. Successful amphibian predators either become increasingly tolerant to the irritants, or find ways to avoid the most poisonous parts, or both. Increased predation pressure then leads to the survival of individuals with the best cryptic behavior and coloring, both of which characterize this recent acquaintance.

I brush the loose duff back over the toad and continue down the runway to the river. Outside the breeze whips up. The sky clears. A bird scolds. It takes a moment to adjust both eyes and senses, to stand upright, to declare myself bipedal and human, and forever forswear willow cuttings for dinner.

A waspish wind accompanies me as I walk back past the marsh, past the bulrushes and reeds with sunlight glossing their stems. Clouds thin and float, drift and shred. The bulrush shadows quiver, cross and uncross, whisper a song of shapes and shadows and chill change coming. I remember the recent warmth and quiet of the thicket, take comfort knowing that a cloister exists just yards from here where weather matters little, where even at noon it is dim and quiet, where night is as good as day, and willow both rounds and soothes the stomach.

Low clouds lie like jigsaw pieces on a blue table, negative and positive shapes slowly moving across the sky as if the wind were working the puzzle. A high-altitude jet, the canyon weather forecaster, leaves no contrail—despite the lower clouds, the upper air dries out. As the morning progresses the clouds contract, becoming a herd of sheep hurrying north, shepherded by a yapping wind.

Fifty miles upstream, pioneer boatman Bert Loper drowned in his eightieth year, and his body drifted downstream to Cardenas Creek, where it was found. Loper, recognizing his age and a bad heart but determined to row anyway, left simple and poignant instructions: "If anything happens to me on this trip I don't want you to try to get me out. You just take me above high water line and scoop out a shallow grave and cover me over and put some rocks on top and leave me. That's where I want to be. In the Canyon."

Spencer Towers

14

Then the cold air from Kaibab comes sliding down the russet-hued slope, and in the currents thus set in motion, whole flocks of dove-breasted clouds are netted. Sometimes they are packed close from rim to rim and in the whirl of hot and cold, struggle woundedly between the walls. . . . After such intervals, sometimes, the upper levels will be fleecy soft with snow, through which, far down, you can see the dust-colored cat-claw and the hot banks on which the gila monster sprawls; for never, never do the clouds get down to the river except they have been to the mountain and resolved themselves in rain. On that business almost any day you will see them feeling their way cautiously among the rock towers, or catch them of early mornings resting just under the Rim, behind some tall potrero.

Mary Austin, 1924, *The Land of Journey's Ending*

River Terraces
and Unkar Delta

———————

Eight hundred feet above the river around Mile 72, on river right, the black Cardenas lavas meet the cranberry Dox, and I make that joining my goal for lunch, climbing the slope via a two-foot-wide, flat-bottomed drainage that goes up in steep steps. At its edge grow salt bushes, one dotted with round marble-sized galls with a thin, fuzzy coating. No live larvae or eggs remain inside, but in several galls, imbedded in the inner green wall, are infinitesimal black wasps with long thread-like ovipositors, heads pointing outward, some species of ichneumon wasp that did not escape.

The wind sharpens, the day turns nasty. Mists drain down onto the gorge and snow squalls blur the distant promontories. The cloud cover behind me moves southward with magisterial slowness, lidding the canyon. Huge boulders of Tapeats have fallen off the slopes above, some as big as garages, but none offer surcease from the wind, which simply gathers speed and works around the boulder, snarls louder and snaps harder. A shaft of sunlight momentarily illumes the slope while rain sifts across the Palisades like curtains of silver mail.

Near the contact zone of sandstone and lava, the silty sandstone layers of Dox weather to form narrow shelves that give lousy footing. The Dox sediments were very close to sea level when, around 1.1 billion years ago, the lavas poured onto their sands and silts and shallows full of hyper-saline water, the rate of lava accumulation about equaling the rate of subsidence. Along six miles of river, lava layered nearly a thousand feet thick.

At the contact of sandstone and basalt, the Cardenas resembles a rich paint box, full of colors begat from the alteration of minerals—bright turquoise blue flecks, big orange cauliflowers, and shots of startling malachite green. As brackish water quenched the fiery lavas, it caused chemical alterations that created these spirited hues, a box of melted crayons, unlikely colors juxtaposed, brilliant, each intensifying the other.

From up here the panorama fans open across the river. The simple horizon one sees from the river disappears in a dozen horizons of rims and spires, walls and pinnacles, an array of juxtaposed, intersecting landforms, sloped and layered, striped and slanted. Below, the river is "without glimmer or sheen, a motionless surface," just as Dutton saw it, a band of bland porcelain in this otherwise overcomplex landscape. I disagree with Cárdenas: the river is not six feet wide. It is six inches.

Autumn's weather in the canyon shifts as quickly as spring's. The day calms beneath weak sunlight that shines but does not warm. Now that I don't have to fight the wind I come only partway down, to an ancient pediment surface, the gently sloping rock surface at the foot of a steep slope, usually thinly covered with alluvium.

These pediments afford both an understanding of where and how much higher the Colorado River once ran and a suggestion of sequence, since the oldest pediments lie highest and farthest from the river. They are most clearly seen in this seven-mile reach of river from Lava Creek at Mile 65.5 to below Unkar Delta at Mile 72.4. Only here do the soft shale walls of the Dox Formation step back, allowing the Inner Gorge to widen, revealing these large aggradational forms as seldom elsewhere in the canyon. In this splendid openness geologists find some of the clues to how the Colorado River functioned in predam times.

When the river downcuts it gnaws at the front of a terrace, removing not only part of what was previously deposited but also some of the bedrock beneath, incising a deeper trench that strands the older gravel deposit at a higher elevation, often above the flood stage of the current flow regime. When downcutting stops, a new cycle of aggradation starts to build a new terrace at a lower elevation, visible from this high vantage point as blue torn-paper shapes marching into the distance. Glaciation occurring not here but in the Rocky Mountains caused the cycles of aggrading and downcutting that built and cut these terraces, and the secondary climatic effects in the Grand Canyon correlate with the major glacial cycles farther north. The Colorado River has repeated these cycles of alternating erosion and aggradation several times.

The terraces are remarkably stable, lying above flooding, even extreme flooding.

When glaciers advance, they overload their runoff streams, more silts and gravels reach the canyon, and aggradation occurs. As glaciers retreat, they contribute less debris, the river receives less sediment, aggradation stops, and the river renews its downcutting. The latest change from a pluvial to a postpluvial climate occurred between ten thousand and twelve thousand years ago, a change also documented in wood rat middens and pollen spectra. Closest to the river, one of the youngest terraces visible contains an archaic hearth, which may date back over two thousand years. Since then river cutting has resumed. With Glen Canyon Dam trapping the river's sediment, the river is caught in a permanent warm-dry cycle, able only to downcut, never to build.

215
—

*River
Terraces
and
Unkar
Delta*

Here, away from the beat of the river, stretches a remarkable stillness of landscape, aurally and visually, a soothing repetition of landforms, the graceful, concave curves of retreating escarpments. The pediment on which I stand tilts gently and evenly toward the river. Neither gullied nor rutted, a close-fitting desert pavement of basalt pebbles protects it. Angular dime-sized tesserae abut as closely as if hand-set, enlivened by an occasional marble-sized chunk of white quartz or an exquisite vermillion-banded chert.

Even if the small smooth stones of the pavement were light-colored to begin with, desert varnish veneers them, as glossy black as polished jet. A mite, an infinitesimal round tan body, hurries across a black pebble. I rest pebble plus mite in the palm of my hand and fish out a hand lens. The mite goes round and round, over and under the pebble, using its front two legs like antennae, tapping, tapping as it goes. It leaves the stone, travels up my arm, a weightless atom.

Despite the heat radiation off this swarthy surface, dozens of half-inch seedlings of windmills sprout, and dwarf Mormon tea and brittle-bush checker the slope. Desert winds fling away and desert storms hose out the seeds of desert plants in places like this, but the pavement stones give seeds the modicum of protection they need to sprout and endure. The pebbles gleam softly, glazed black and gray and caramel: where river pebbles are, river was.

Fluting radiates down the curved crown of a sandstone boulder like chrysanthemum petals, tiny channels dissolved in the rock by millennia of rain. Basketball-sized boulders lock firmly into the soil, settled long enough to have eroded in place, some weathered to just a rim of rock or a pitted nubbin. Limestone boulders are rare on this side of the river, although they abound on the other side. I find but one here, almost completely buried, its exposed surface roughly turreted with bits of chert left standing in high relief, a characteristic geologists would like to be able to use in dating on the assumption that the higher the relief of the chert, the longer the rock was subject to erosion.

As I amble down to the river, I find Sid Davis filling in a pit he has dug on another high pediment, hoping to find a dating tool in the buried layers of white calcium carbonate called caliche. The pit wall reveals two and perhaps three layers of caliche, formed at different times. Each layer is a remnant of different age and paleoclimates that formed them. Wetter conditions prevailed in the Pleistocene Epoch, which carried carbonate from the upper zones to deeper levels, creating higher concentrations of caliche in the soil profile. Caliche, or secondary calcium carbonate, common in arid regions, may either develop *in situ* at the base of alluvial deposits with groundwater intrusion in the gravel/bedrock interface, or over time, on the surface that catches the influx of dust and carbonate-rich rain water.

Here in the youngest layer, caliche weathers out as chips or white carbonate rinds scattered among the gravel pavement, the result of sheet erosion, profuse wherever gullying starts. The next older layer begins about seventeen inches lower and in it are fist-sized concretions and nodules. Immediately beneath this layer is another carbonate-rich horizon, lighter in color, and probably unrelated to the layers above. Well-developed rinds enclose buried basalt rocks like a grapefruit skin.

After caliche on the surface has been transported deeper into the soil, new caliche begins to form at the surface, as thin filaments a quarter of an inch or so long that line abandoned root channels in soft masses, or coats the underside of gravels and pebbles like thin skins. Over time these features grow, and eventually dominate the soil profile, typical of arid environments in the West. Since essentially no readily available source of calcium carbonate from limestone rocks exists on this side of the river, this pediment must be very old to have had this much caliche development.

With this stupendous panorama before me I wish—but only briefly —that I had a camera. There is no way to catch in a photograph (or in a drawing or in words, for that matter) the breath and breadth of this river valley, the cutting bite of the wind, the clouds layered with shafts of sunlight, the flicker of Mormon tea, the snow wedges on the horizons, all the sweep and vastness. No single picture, no matter how elegant and comprehensive, can capture this riverscape—the delight of moving water, persimmon and lavender cliffs, the sound of freight-train rapids or the silence of a dune, the sassing of a rock wren. Nothing can capture the coolness of a spring beach, the odor of turpentine bush on your fingers, the chill of the river, the heat of the rock, the constant change. This landscape is animate: it moves, transposes, builds, proceeds, shifts, always going on, never coming back, and one can retain it only in vignettes, impressions caught in a flash, flipped through in succession, leaving a richness of images imprinted on a sunburned retina.

217
—
*River
Terraces
and
Unkar
Delta*

The sun comes out, the river shoots sparks of light that swing around the corner in moving torsades, like horizontal fireworks. The breeze gutters like a flame. When it stops, a yellow jacket drones by on its scenic overflight and, when it has passed, my ears ring with the sunny silence, a soundless world defined only by light and movement, as if all other senses were blocked, rendering vision and this river canyon all there is in the world.

At Mile 72.4 the river turns westward. The mass of the Kaibab Plateau forces the river to run generally south from Lees Ferry before it loops into a big S-curve starting at Cardenas Creek. At the bottom swing of the S, the river describes a 180° arc. The current, flowing fastest on the outer side of the curve, cuts a handsome cliff and breaks into a double rapid. Along the inner curve the current slows and the river has, over time, dropped tons of sediments, adding its silts to the sand and cobble and boulder debris brought in by Unkar Creek, forming a 125-acre delta, although not a delta in the strict sense of being formed only of creek-carried materials. Unkar is a Paiute word meaning "red creek" or "red stone," doubtless referring to the dominance of Dox shales walling the delta.

This sunny November morning, freed from the usual press of river scheduling, I am blessed with a morning of beautiful solitude at Unkar Delta. Goldenweed and magenta windmills tapestry the ground, sunshine polishes the prickly pear pads, typical lower Sonoran Desert vegetation I've seen a hundred times, but this morning it is all festive and fresh because I own the untrammeled time to enjoy it.

With its fifty-two archaic sites, the delta held the largest gathering of prehistoric peoples along the river. Between 1966 and 1968 a team of archaeologists from the School of American Research in Santa Fe surveyed the delta. Researchers endured unrelenting summer heat, difficulties of supply, and miserable and disruptive winds but kept careful and detailed records on the excavations despite these daunting conditions. They sampled as many sites as possible and numbered them in the sequence of excavation. They excavated as time allowed, collected, cataloged, and classified nearly 10,000 stone tools and over 27,000 shards and other artifacts left from decades of habitation. And in their apocryphal spare time, they planted and tended their own experimental gardens.

Out of all their data they established a sequence of four occupation periods. The first group, the Cohonina, came from the South Rim about A.D. 900. Around A.D. 1050 the second group of immigrants, this time Anasazi, also came down from the rim and remained two decades, enjoying a well-documented period of increased and effective moisture in the canyon. The third settlement, from 1075 to 1100, was immediately succeeded by the fourth and last phase, which continued until 1150, when the delta—as well as the rest of the Grand Canyon—was abandoned.

Near the mouth of Unkar Creek, the Cohonina, for whom fording the river at low water would have been no problem, established the oldest datable settlement less than twenty feet above the river. Although prehistoric people must have trekked into this delta earlier than the first substantiated date of A.D. 900, the doubling and tripling of Cohonina populations between A.D. 700 and 900 goaded them to establish outlying settlements as an immediate solution to overpopulation. These Cohonina settlers farmed the same crops as the Anasazi, but their pottery was not as well made nor were their dwellings as well constructed. The similarities of lifestyle may simply have been those imposed by the stringent conditions of the canyon world. The Cohonina fashioned distinctive pottery, fat ollas and squat bowls manufactured with the paddle and anvil process, in which they modeled the pot in its entirety (traditional Anasazi pottery is coiled). They abandoned the area by the early tenth century, and all traces of their civilization vanished after A.D. 1200.

To get an overview of the later Anasazi settlements of the delta I climb to the highest and oldest river terrace south of Unkar Creek, following the dry creek bed, a confusion of channels and a jumbled chaos of rough cut rocks, piled with driftwood, blocked with boulders. The channel narrows here and widens there, like a boa constrictor that swallowed a pig. The creek provided tools and building materials for a small pyramid—limestone and shale slabs, clay for adobe, cobbles for tools, unlimited pebbles for chinking, and pieces of chert washed down out of the Redwall to be knapped for knives and points.

The terrace I walk toward rises almost two hundred feet above the river and dominates the delta. Its thirty-five acres spread high and dry, studded with rough limestone boulders, pitted and fluted by past rains. The few wind-deformed mesquites witness that this is an inhospitable place to farm or live. When desert pavement does not cover it, the soil is spongy to walk on, typical desert soil where the top few inches are full of tiny air pockets formed during hot weather when rain hits heated soil.

Below, Unkar Delta spreads out like a map. Unkar Rapid bounds over boulders and piles into haystacks, its boom and bombast damped by distance. Along the creek, which today divides the delta into a northern third and a southern two-thirds, terraces rise in steps, varying in soil depth, exposure, amount of vegetation, and the runoff they retain. Thicker vegetation testifies that the older and higher terraces have the best growing conditions, but over time prehistoric peoples farmed nearly every arable square inch on the delta. The regular hand-set alignments of stones outlining rooms or set for water conservation stand out against the natural disorder of the landscape. All the sites at Unkar Delta were back-filled, and now only the edges of walls show above the surface, a stony grid of places to sleep or store grain, places to grind corn or make pottery, places to build a fire and cook, places to huddle against the chill of a river morning, and places to make prayers for planting. As I walk down toward the area where the second group of colonists settled, I ponder their cunning exploitation of a meager environment that in the end and after all was, and still is, the winner.

For a century and a half after the Cohonina left, the delta remained unoccupied. Intervening dry periods shrank the area available for farming, and people simply moved out, not to come back until the climate again promoted farming. Anasazi movement down into the canyon closely tracked wetter periods. A well-documented period of benign and beneficent moisture in the Southwest, from A.D. 950 to 1150, brought higher water tables and greater fertility. Better climate favored a better yield from new or improved domestic plants and perhaps the addition of exotic species. At the same time marmots, bison, and scaled quail species also extended their ranges temporarily.

A hunting and gathering lifestyle encouraged mobility across vast areas, but with growing numbers of people, the same amount of space had to be apportioned between more users. The decrease in access to traditional resources led to a greater dependence upon agriculture, which in turn led to a more sedentary lifestyle, a commitment that engendered profound cultural changes in almost every aspect of Anasazi life. In these decades the canyon suddenly bloomed with hundreds of small sites. At the same time, evidence exists that in many places the population was expanding enough to approach or breach the land's carrying capacity. An imbalance between natural resources and the population they must support seems to be a precondition of agriculture, and investment in agriculture seems not to occur until local population densities are high enough to support and require it.

Hunters and gatherers as a rule invest less labor and time in subsistence activities than do agriculturalists. Gatherers usually need work only two days a week to find enough food, and children and young adolescents generally are not pressed into hunting and gathering duties, while agriculturalists—including children and adolescents—work four to six days a week. Early domestic crops were not especially productive, and farmers often had poorer nutrition than that of the hunters and gatherers who ate a wider variety of plants.

But the advantages of agriculture became obvious to an Anasazi farmer when he could hold a hundred tiny seeds of goosefoot or amaranth in his hand and see them equal in mass to a single kernel of corn. Although corn provides less food value than pinyon nuts, pinyon trees are scattered and extremely fickle producers. A cache of corn in a well-sealed olla was worth two basketfuls of once-in-a-while pinyon nuts that took miles of walking to collect. So much energy was needed to gather wild seeds equal in caloric value to a small field of corn that pure stands of even modestly productive harvests were worth the effort. Eventually corn would produce as much or more food per unit of land than most customarily gathered wild seeds and, in time, corn and beans grown together came to equal the caloric content and protein of many wild seeds. Domesticated corn came to contribute 70 to 80 percent of diet during the time that Anasazi lived in the canyon.

The Anasazi had been raising beans, squash, and several varieties of corn since A.D. 700 and were now achieving enough surplus to need more storage space. As agriculture became more reliable, as skills with planting and tending increased, the continual trekking across the countryside gradually petered off. Hunting and gathering always added to the Anasazi larder at Unkar Delta, and crops probably supplied only 50 to 60 percent of their diet. Wild plants remained widely used, and hunting continued throughout the delta's inhabitation. Over time the Anasazi became first and foremost agriculturists. Domesticated plants came to form the backbone of their subsistence economy, and once they committed to agriculture, there was no going back.

When the second group of colonists arrived around A.D. 1050, they came on the winds of change. With them they brought the Tusayan Gray Ware and Tusayan White Ware typical of the Kayenta Anasazi. The commonality of pottery types across this whole area indicates a strong common culture of relatively open communities closely related to each other, without any significant linguistic barriers to block a broad, continuous exchange of goods and ideas. The new settlers built two dwellings in a semidune area at the base of the lookout terrace. Their large rooms were occupied but once, an anomaly at Unkar, where most sites were occupied over and over, built and rebuilt, during different settlement periods.

221
—
*River
Terraces
and
Unkar
Delta*

Fortunately for archaeologists, the rooms contained remnants of the posts that held up the roof. In the Southwest tree trunks used in construction offer tremendous help in dating prehistoric sites. When sap retreats to the tree's roots in the fall and the year's growth stops, a smooth line forms, separating the large thin-walled cells that mark spring growth from the heavier-walled cells that mark the growth of late summer. In the Southwest, where trees seldom have enough water to produce consistently broad, even growth rings, the width of the rings closely tracks both relatively small environmental changes and seasonal rainfall. Momentary increases in tree-ring widths correlate well with settlements of the delta.

The second group of settlers spent twenty years here, exploiting their total farming environment as well as hunting and gathering. The increase in the number of storage areas and the number of artifacts associated with milling corn, more above-ground, stone-walled living space, and an increase in the number of rooms per site evidence an increasing dependence upon agriculture. Gardening may even have made hunting easier, since cultivated fields and plots of second growth often attract deer and other animals. Fields dug up for cultivation also provided the perfect habitat for opportunistic plants like goosefoot, purslane, and tansy mustard, all used by prehistoric people.

By A.D. 1070 people again left the Delta. Tree rings indicate that an interval of drought occurred severe enough to dry out the ground and lower the water table. People returned when a pulse of precipitation enticed them back. Between A.D. 1075 and 1100, an estimated ten families moved into Unkar Delta and built UN-1 ("UN" for Unkar and "1" for the first site excavated), one of the largest and most striking sites on the delta. UN-1 sits seventy-five feet above the river with a splendid 360° view of the towers and turrets of the canyon, usually blessed with a breeze. The twenty-room complex forms a wide U, rooms at either end set at right angles to the main row, connected by common walls and opening to the southeast. The rectilinear style of these Pueblo II sites is so characteristic that one archaeologist calls them "almost maniacally modular."

At least two dozen storage cists were built during these twenty-five years. The proliferation of storage cists signals a happy increase in the amount of seeds to store, the blessing of reliable production. Corn is easily stored with kernels either on or off and needs only be kept dry and sealed off from rodents and insect pests. Even the seeds of short-lived plant species, under proper storage, can remain viable up to three years.

UN-1 and its close neighbor, UN-3, built between A.D. 1040 and 1160, had not only their own living spaces but also their own ceremonial spaces. These families built two of the few kivas found here. Kivas are subterranean ceremonial spaces with certain distinctive features, clearly set apart from rooms used for living and storage. Traditionally they included a bench on one wall, a fireplace with a ventilator, an ash pit, and a small opening in the floor called the sipapu, through which spirits entered this world and through which the soul of the deceased left, a characteristic arrangement that has persisted through the centuries and is still utilized by Hopi descendants today. Most ceremonies took place in the winter, when time was not consumed in caring for crops, and the appearance of kivas suggests that these family groups remained here throughout the year.

UN-1 burned and after the original walls collapsed, later settlers used the rubble to lay rock alignments and construct garden enclosures within and around the old rooms. By enclosing irregular areas with cobbles and clearing out the inside for moisture conservation, like the "waffle" gardening Hopis do today, farmers protected young plants from wind damage and conserved water. Alignments, strings of dry-laid stones, slow runoff and allow soil to build up behind the rocks. Terraces run parallel to the contours of the slope, often in lengthy lines of sixty feet or more, generally a yard or so apart.

Throughout the Grand Canyon low check dams occur near masonry ruins, and their use amply reflects prehistoric farmers' attention to water and soil management. Check dams, anywhere from three to twelve feet long, were constructed of somewhat larger limestone blocks placed directly athwart small water drainages. These dams did not divert and control water but simply attempted to slow runoff and curtail erosion, and to conserve what water was available whenever it was available. No evidence exists on Unkar Delta for formal irrigation works, which makes sense—a rampaging springtime river would have destroyed them on a regular basis, and the centralized social organization was not in place and the numbers of people needed for building and maintaining elaborate works was not available. The use of multiple small systems had an extra advantage: the failure of any one would not imperil the whole. Today water-laid silt and sand lie seven to twenty inches deep behind the stones, witness to the holding capacity of such modest devices. Their placement relative to other structures suggests that they belong to the last, and fourth, occupation of the delta.

Attempts to control water mark the onslaught of short torrential summer storms that frequently cause damaging runoff. The monsoonal pattern arises from convection storms spawned when heat rises rapidly from a hot ground surface. Reaching the upper air, the heated air cools rapidly and births violent local thunderstorms, usually in the afternoon. The suddenness and energy of these unpredictable storms often erode soil, gut fields, and damage crops. Water seldom "flows" in this country—instead it gobbles, rampages, breaks, topples, undercuts, gnaws, rips, gouges, falls, pounds, pummels, and hammers. "Average precipitation" is not a useful concept in the Southwest, where annual deviations are often extreme and not all the rain that falls, falls kindly.

223

—

*River
Terraces
and
Unkar
Delta*

By A.D. 1100 increasing population prompted expansion into areas seldom used previously, and for the last time settlers moved down onto the delta, bringing changes in ceramics, in building style, and in the way in which they used land. An influx of pottery from the Virgin Branch of the Anasazi, farther west, appears, and for the first time pottery shows evidence of local manufacture, a reddish brown ware fashioned from clays and tempers indigenous to Unkar Delta. Trade to the east, which had brought in Kayenta wares, waned, while that to the west waxed and local production picked up the slack. After 1100 all housing was built completely off the better farmlands. The fourth group of settlers clearly reserved the best agricultural land, betokening a new appreciation of its worth and a greater trust and reliance on what it could grow, an intensification that usually comes only when population has increased to a point that limits people's mobility and ability to expand.

One of the last settlement sites lies across the dry bed of Unkar Creek, up against the mahogany Dox cliffs. With the new storm pattern there may have been flash flooding from Unkar Creek, which would have dictated setting dwellings farther up on the slope, safely out of danger. This site, patently unfarmable, endures the full blazing sun. The little metal tag stamped "UN-6" is almost too hot to touch. The Dox crumbles into fine gravels that drizzle down cliff faces and fan out over the hard beige surface of the uppermost terrace. First erected between A.D. 1070 and 1175, this dwelling was built and rebuilt, a small site used over four different occupations.

Dramatic increases in hearths and bins, cists and alignments, all point to better harvests, correlating with a period of generally higher water tables between A.D. 1100 and 1150. The number of outdoor fire pits, like the presence of kivas, implies year-round residency. The simple inside fire pits of earlier settlements were elaborated into different shapes and linings, tailored to different uses: smaller, deeper pits focused heat for cooking, while a shallow saucer-shaped pit optimized heat radiation for warmth and light.

Shallow gullies wrinkle the Dox slope. A triangular, exquisitely thin shard nestles in a little crease of the bank, the same terra cotta color as the soil. Tiny black lichens pepper its raw edges. On it the potter drew five slender black lines with a fine brush and a sure hand: I created, therefore I was.

Cape Solitude

15

Suddenly the storm opened with magical effect to the north over the cañon of Bright Angel Creek, inclosing a sunlit mass of the cañon architecture, spanned by great white concentric arches of cloud like the bows of a silvery aurora. Above these and a little back of them was a series of upboiling purple clouds, and high above all, in the background, a range of noble cumuli towered aloft like snow-laden mountains, their pure pearl bosses flooded with sunshine. The whole noble picture, calmly glowing, was framed in thick gray gloom, which soon closed over it; and the storm went on, opening and closing until night covered all.

John Muir, 1902, "The Grand Cañon of the Colorado,"
Century Illustrated Monthly Magazine

Bright Angel Trail:
Coda

———————

For Christmas my eldest daughter, Susan, and I give each other a hike down the Bright Angel Trail, a couple of nights at Phantom Ranch. We will walk back up the South Kaibab Trail on winter solstice, the end of autumn, the beginning of winter, the rounding of the year when Sun prepares to leave his Winter House. We start down, knowing a major snow is coming in on a huge outbreak of polar air. Scathing winds. A wind chill factor of ten below. I question my good sense in going. There may not be enough clothes in the world to keep me warm.

The Bright Angel Trail follows the Bright Angel Fault, a fault that simply on the basis of accessibility is the best-known in the Grand Canyon. Walking inside it helps one understand the other great fault systems to which there is no easy access. Once below the rim the wind mercifully abates. Sun lights the Coconino Sandstone and snow outlines ledges on the damp Hermit Shale like chalk lines on a blackboard. Not quite ten miles from rim to river, the elevation drops from 6,860 feet at the South Rim to 2,400 feet at river's edge. With each footstep, we go back 20,000 to 30,000 years in time.

Because the path is so narrow, hikers must flatten against the cliff wall while the "scrawniest Rosinantes and wizened-rat mules," as Muir described them, pass by. The eighteen miles of trail that the mules travel are doused yearly with 8,000 gallons of mule urine and 117 tons of road apples. I shouldn't grouse: Charles Silver Russell, trying to do a photographic run of the river in 1915, had a steel boat built, which he and his helpers loaded on a dolly to cart it down the Bright Angel Trail. Every time the mules came by, the men had to jockey dolly and boat off to the side and cover them with canvas so as not to scare the mules. It took a week to get it down and then Russell wrecked it at Crystal. Twice.

Even in December the cottonwoods at Indian Gardens hold their leaves, although most fade to dirty yellow. They were planted by Emery Kolb, who maintained a darkroom here to avoid having to pay for pumping water to the South Rim (water issues from Roaring Springs, just below the North Rim, and runs by gravity to Indian Gardens). After taking pictures of tourists on their mules, Kolb would race down the trail to Indian Gardens, develop and make prints, and sprint back up to the top by the time the riders returned, all prints seventy-five cents each, thank you very much.

Clouds begin to filter across the sky. Sunlight washes the far buttes but shadows wallow in the canyon. We've picked up six more degrees. Even in December while snow garnishes the Kaibab, brittlebushes and one sweetbush bloom, both cheerful brassy yellow. The change from prehistoric path to commercial trail transpired in 1891, when miner Ralph Cameron and others improved it to allow access to copper mining claims. Cameron (it was originally called Cameron Trail) operated it as a toll trail. When the courts declared his claims invalid, the trail became, in one instant, the property of Coconino County, Arizona, and *its* toll road.

In 1902 the U.S. Geological Survey established a trail from the North Rim down to the river, connecting with the Bright Angel Trail, and called it the North Kaibab Trail. One crossed the river in a boat "lent by a friendly prospector" at the only crossing between Lees Ferry, eighty-nine miles upstream, and the Bass Trail, thirty-five miles west. By 1903 the trails had become such a regular route that the county upgraded the river crossing to a steel rowboat.

After the National Park Service took over administration of the Grand Canyon in 1919, it decided to replace the boat with a steel suspension bridge. Harriet Chalmers Adams, on assignment for the *National Geographic*, came down on mule back to write about its construction. Getting building materials down was a logistical nightmare. Eight mules carried the twelve-hundred-pound cables that were anchored into the walls eighty feet up. As today, wooden planking floors the bridge, and wire mesh cages the sides for protection. Adams took a canvas boat across to "Roosevelt camp" (now Phantom Ranch, which got its name from early surveyors who noticed a ghostly haze that often hung in the canyon in late afternoon), and exited by mule up the North Kaibab Trail.

Failing in its first attempts to acquire the Bright Angel Trail from Coconino County, the Park Service, from 1924 to 1928, built its own toll-free trail and crossing: the South Kaibab Trail, which connects with the North Kaibab Trail via the bridge. Upon completion of the South Kaibab, Coconino County, scarcely in a spate of public dedication, sold the Bright Angel Trail, which it had gotten for nothing, to the Park Service for $100,000, a *very* tidy profit.

We lunch at the top of a series of switchbacks called the Devil's Staircase, relishing the last sunlight before we enter the shadowy murk along Pipe Creek. Across the way the line of the Great Unconformity bears witness to what the earth did with its yesterdays, Tapeats against Vishnu, sandstone against schist, a familiar, friendly juxtaposition that has come to mark my eons in the Inner Gorge.

Pipe Creek chortles down the Pipe Creek Fault, a branch of the Bright Angel Fault system. The trail crosses a vein of salmon-pink Zoroaster Granite with big chunks of milky quartz, one of the proliferation of Zoroaster dikes and sills in the Bright Angel section. Lichens spatter paint a swath of deep red granite. Being damp intensifies the lichens' color, rendering them vivid gray green against the darker rock, ruffled edges markedly brighter with new growth. Scraps of brilliant chartreuse map lichen vibrating with color on this cloudy day, scabbing the surface with a near Day-Glo brilliance, growing above a webbing of cracks vivid with moss.

As Pipe Creek nears the river, Vishnu Schist begins to look like marble cake batter, swirled in ribbons and stripes: the Pipe Creek migmatites, a transitional stage between metamorphic and igneous rock. White lines swirl into dark gray rock with overtones of purple, undertones of navy blue, no orderly layers like a sandstone or a shale, but rock molded and welded, puddled and re-reworked, sunbaked and frost-split. Bands of white quartz flecked with red outline rounded knobs, and wider bands of crimson beribbon it. Sometimes the lighter lines are as steady as a stretched string, other times as quirky as a corkscrew, recording in turn a white quartz lizard, a red granite ankh, a silvery snake, a gray sneeze, a purple sniffle.

Wind shoots off the river and whips every bush and grass stem with a vicious, malevolent intensity, seeming to come from everywhere and all at once. Clouds bullet across the sky. I start across the old foot bridge over the river at Bright Angel Creek. Despite the cold I stop at midcrossing. The river makes a big curve downstream, posing that old evocative river question: what's around the bend? Horn Creek Rapid, that's what. For some peculiar satisfaction, I'm glad I know.

Susan and I hurry along Bright Angel Creek, eyes tearing from the wind, too chilled to talk. Bright Angel was originally called Silver Creek for the silver "float," although the source of the silver was never found. Trout are spawning, a month or so earlier than those in Nankoweap Creek, just forty miles upstream. Two ouzels fly along the creek, darting and jabbering. Despite the presence of ouzels in almost every tributary stream in the canyon, it is still a treat to see them parading underwater as easily and perkily as other birds do on the bank. Snow flares through the cottonwood leaves, flakes the size of chads. Chicken wire wraps many of the big cottonwood trees along Bright Angel Creek to protect them from beavers—by the time Phantom Ranch was established in 1922, beavers had pretty well cleared them out.

We straggle into Phantom Ranch in day-darkening, spitting rain, altogether foreboding weather. After dinner, the wind tunes up to gale force, a wild Walpurgis Night. The cottonwoods clatter. Wind shrieks in uneven pulses and jagged crescendos. The ragged intervals between blasts create an erratic, irrational, breath-holding tempo that breaks the easy rhythm of nightfall. The latest weather forecast comes in with the last hiker: a foot of snow on the rim, blizzard conditions, all roads closed in and out of the park. That night winter knocks on the doors of consciousness, flaunting all its chill and bleakness, darkness and bitter corners, full of vindictive winds and treachery.

Two mornings later, still afflicted with truculent skies, belligerent wind, and clanging cold, we start up the South Kaibab Trail, leaving the river as the Anasazi did, on foot. Just before the Kaibab Bridge, some Anasazi tucked a small living space between wall and river. When Powell stopped here looking for wood from which to carve replacements for his eternally broken oars, he noted this site and wondered "why these ancient people sought such inaccessible places for their homes." The answer is, of course, that these were no "inaccessible places" to the Anasazi, who traveled this canyon freely and easily. Constructed on a talus slope about thirty feet directly above the river, the site has the highest elevation available of any place on the delta of Bright Angel Creek, the first space along the river downstream from Unkar Delta amenable to settlement.

Twice between A.D. 1050 and 1150 small groups of Anasazi farmers located here, encouraged by the same temporary increase in annual rainfall that allowed marginal agricultural land to be taken up elsewhere along the river. Although the steepness presented some leveling problem for the builders, siting here substantially reduced the chance of being flooded out by living too close to the creek. They situated carefully to take advantage of solar radiation and to free up the largest amount of potential farming area. Even the floods of 1983 did not reach its masonry walls. But the benches they farmed a quarter-mile down the creek no longer exist, having been modified when Phantom Ranch was built as well as by the December 1966 flood that also created Crystal Rapid. At its peak, the population here never exceeded fifteen or sixteen people, still a group large enough to build their own kiva.

When I take my gloves off to take notes, my fingers sting with the cold. In this confined chasm, the lack of sunlight and warmth congeal my marrow. Focused on my own discomfort, I recall the miseries registered in one of the two skeletons found here, that of a middle-aged Anasazi woman of my stature. The burial, rare in the Grand Canyon, was unearthed quite by accident when a construction crew was working at Bright Angel Creek in 1982. Typical of this egalitarian Anasazi society, only two artifacts accompanied the bodies: a Tusayan Corrugated jar, a cooking vessel of no special or decorative significance, and a bracelet on the arm of the juvenile.

The woman's skeleton bore marks of unusual trauma and degeneration. The atlas, named after Atlas, the Greek Titan who carried the heavens on the back of his neck, and the base of her skull were fused at the junction of the first cervical vertebra and the backbone. This fusion, a birth defect known today as Klippel-Feil Syndrome, is often hereditary and accompanied by other physical anomalies. In addition, the second and third cervical vertebrae were frozen into a single unit (now called a block vertebra), which put greater than normal stress on the neck, surely exacerbated if she used a tumpline. These fusions can reduce the size of the neural canal, allowing bone to impinge directly upon the spinal cord, which normally causes numbness and pain in the arms, weakness in the legs, sometimes muscle control problems, headaches, and blurring or doubling of vision.

Her left leg showed two fractures, one a stress fracture, probably from a fall while the left leg was extended, such as might have happened by losing her balance and pitching forward while stepping off a height. The full impact of the shock traveled through the knee while it was in an extremely vulnerable position, and when it healed with only yucca poultices to damp the pain, although movement was probably restored, osteoarthritic degeneration set in.

All her life she must have lived in pain, unsure of her balance, always walking in a blurred landscape. She bore pain without medication, misery without surcease, no hope of feeling better tomorrow, a bitter lot in this place of cold leavings. And yet, my instinct tells me that somehow she was a useful working member of her family group and did the work that she could do. I give her honor.

A short way up the trail I turn and look back down across the river to that small site squeezed in between river and cliff. Its emptiness on this chilling day epitomizes for me the Anasazi's final exodus from the Grand Canyon, for by A.D. 1200 there were no beginnings, only endings. Land expansion ended. The Virgin Anasazi branch disappeared. The uplands were virtually abandoned. Because there *was* someplace else to go, the whole population picked up and filtered eastward to the Rio Grande drainage, where their ancestors still live today.

The Southwest is unique in having a body of data—geological, climatological, palynological, tree-ring, and radiometric—that establishes in extraordinary detail the fabric of prehistoric climate unavailable elsewhere. A preponderance of the Anasazi movements on the Colorado Plateau neatly match known environmental changes, and all evidence verifies the hypothesis that environmental stress combined with overpopulation *does* trigger the kind of socioeconomic change and population dislocation that beset the Anasazi in the middle of the twelfth century. No evidence of warfare or aggression, no massive epidemics, no other catastrophic causes can be documented. The massive movement eastward ties clearly and directly to environmental deterioration exacerbated by too many people.

When the climate turns bad, no one then or now can make an arroyo carry more water, no one can lengthen a growing season, or raise a water table, no one can gentle violent summer storms. Arroyo cutting destroyed fields and pulled chunks of arable land into the river, lowered the water table, and left remaining lands high and dry. In most canyon tributaries debris caught high in shrubs and trees tells of fearful and fast torrents that reamed out a creek bed, clawed out the banks, and rattled the cobbles, destructive rampages against which, even today, there is no protection.

The Anasazi already employed strategies to deal with a falling water table, such as more rigorous use of agricultural ground, and soil and water control features to curtail erosion and conserve summer's rains. Anasazi farmers engineered a more drought-resistant maize, incorporated more fields of more aspects into their system. Their technology produced reliable yields in places that cannot support agriculture today. The failure of prehistoric Southwestern farmers was not for lack of ingenuity or expertise but simply tells that the problems they faced were unsolvable.

Good times in the Southwest have a way of not lasting long; change blew in on a cruel, dry wind. Arroyo cutting begins when groundwater depletion is rapid, where valley floors are narrow and stream gradients high, a good description of most of the Colorado's tributaries here. No rain gauge recorded fewer tenths of inches over time, no data bank furnished comparative data, no climatologists forecast oncoming disaster or disagreed about global warming or global cooling. Tree rings narrowed in response to a less benevolent climate, a lowering water table paralleled diminishing rainfall, and an arroyo's steepening sides told of unmanageable erosion, narrowing the dry-farm belt to zero.

The mechanics of leaving, the breaking down of a settlement system, are complex. If enough people leave, the remaining population may be small enough now to be compatible with what the area can support, and those who remain gain more mobility, more territory, more lands upon which to hunt or gather. But there may be a point of no return beyond which a settlement cannot be maintained, when families choose not to be separated, when social relationships that depend upon contiguity cannot be held together long distance, when not enough people remain to carry out the necessary ceremonial roles, and when the exodus of people frays local exchange networks.

The casual nature of their leaving, taking some goods with them, leaving others, suggests an intent to return when conditions bettered as they had time and again in the past. But this departure was different. Even during short wetter intervals no one ventured back, perhaps because most arable lands were too damaged or were simply gone, washed down the river, along with a way of life.

Today is the winter solstice. Somewhere, far away, Sun begins a slow turn to the north, but here my boots squeak on the powdery snow. Body heat drains into an encompassing shuffling coldness, miles of growing cold, ascending into a colder, rougher-edged world, a shivered dark, always framed by those continuing icy vistas of such brutal starkness and terrible beauty.

The interminable zigzags of miles of trail unwind upward to a rim eternally out of sight, elusive, dangerously distant, perhaps unattainable. Blowing snow bites like pulverized diamonds across my face. The views build, illustrations in a wondrous fairy story of ice castles with cut-crystal spires, scrims of spun snow for ballets of ice crystals. Clouds canter into the canyon and out again with cymbal-clashing grandeur. Cold hones the world to a hypersharpness, as if it inhales the atmosphere and leaves this transparency, a gelid nothingness, the clarity of a vacuum.

We flatten against the cliff as the ascending mule garbage train passes us. For once I am thankful to see them. Their trail-breaking saves us from having to struggle through crusted snow drifted hip-deep. How such large four-footed animals make such a narrow track is beyond me. To stay in their path I mince and teeter, awkwardly placing one foot directly in front of the other.

At Cedar Ridge, a mile and a half from the top, a demonic wind explodes, unleashing razor blades of ice, ready to flash freeze a face on the instant. I jockey on a windbreaker over my down jacket. At the top when I take it off a quarter-inch of frost coats it inside like a frozen fleece lining. The temperature is 6°F.

I drop my pack and step to the edge of the canyon for one last look down into its shrouded silence. The sky dims early and the landscape shimmers with tender pinks and blues and whites. Frosty mists powder every turret. A stately pavane of snowshowers threads among farther buttes. Cold stings my nose and my eyes. In this terrible silence I see below me no silly lizards doing push-ups, no springtime bloom of redbuds, no little tree frog smiling smugly like a miniature Buddha, no bald eagle with a fierce yellow eye nailing a fat trout, no humpback chub ferreting out an existence between fast water and slow water, none of the animation of the canyon, only a final stillness, only a beckoning, deepening cold, an absence, beyond which there is no more beyond, and I step back, uneasy: in this terrible clarity of pure white light there is some kind of clarion warning.

Yet hypnotized by the singular beauty of the view, once more I step to the edge, wanting to make contact with the river just one more time. With the river out of sight and only this uncharacteristic preternatural silence, it takes an act of faith to believe that it even exists. Yet I know it is there, curling into back-eddies that chase upstream, nibbling at sandbars and rearranging beaches, always sculpting the perfect river cobble and fluting the limestones, dancing with raindrops, multiplying the sun in its ripples, taking its tolls and levies against the cliffs, pounding and pulsing with life that vitalizes anyone who rows and rides it, yesterday left upstream with a sixteen-hour lag, tomorrow waiting at the bottom of a rapid, today an intensity of being that runs with the river.

Into my cold-impaired memory flashes the picture of another ascent. One November, after two weeks on the river, I hiked out alone up the Bright Angel Trail. To keep warm I wore an outlandish assortment of layers, walked in scuffed boots, and labored under an ugly, bulging daypack. As I gained the asphalt walk at the top of the trail, the number of people dismayed me. After an idyllic two weeks spent at only two campsites, with time to wander far and alone every day, I felt as bewildered as Rip van Winkle must have: the world had gone on and left me behind. Maybe I didn't know how things like light switches and faucets and computers worked anymore. My head, my heart, my psyche lagged a dozen miles down in the canyon. I remembered John Burroughs quoting a lady tourist's comment that the canyon had been built a little too near to the lodge.

Out of one of the clusters of people stepped a nice-looking, neatly dressed, middle-aged woman, a question obvious in her face. I paused, uncomfortably conscious of how derelict I must appear. "Excuse me," she began, "is there anything down there?"

Sensing the sincerity in the question and wanting to be courteous, but overwhelmed by trying to put the richness I had always been blessed with "down there" into quick words, I could only mumble something about yes, there's a beautiful river down there, although the question so unseated me I'm not sure what I said.

The question haunted me, as questions like that often do, and the real answer came, as answers often do, not in the canyon but at an unlikely time and in an unexpected place, flying over the canyon at thirty thousand feet on my way to be a grandmother. My mind on other things, intending only to glance out, the exquisite smallness and delicacy of the river took me completely by surprise. In the hazy light of early morning, the canyon lay shrouded, the river flecked with glints of silver, reduced to a thin line of memory, blurred by a sudden realization that clouded my vision. The astonishing sense of connection with *that* river and *that* canyon caught me completely unaware, and in a breath I understood the intense, protective loyalty so many people feel for the Colorado River in the Grand Canyon. With that came the answer: there *is* something down there, and it cannot be explained in a listing of its parts. It has to do with truth and beauty and love of this earth, the artifacts of a lifetime, and the descant of a canyon wren at dawn.

Sometimes the "down there" is so huge and overpowering, the river so commanding, walled with rock formations beyond time, that one feels like a mite on a lizard's eyelid. And at other times it is so close and intimate: a tree lizard pattering little chains of prints in the sand around my ground cloth, a soldier beetle traipsing the margin of my notepad as I write by firelight, the trilling of red-spotted toads in iambic pentameter, cicadas singing a capella, the mathematical precision of leaf-cutter bees, a limestone cavern measureless to man swathed with yards of gauzy webs woven by tiny spiders. Often the "down there" encompasses contrasts between minute midge and pounding waterfall, between eternity in an ebony schist and the moment in the pulsing vein in a dragonfly's wing, a delicate shard lost in an immensity of landscape, all bound together by the time to observe, question, presume, enjoy, exaltate. The "down there" is bound up with care and solicitude, sunlight on scalloped ripples, loving life and accepting death, all tied to a magnificent, unforgiving, and irrevocable river, a river along which I wandered for a halcyon while, smelled the wet clay odor of the rapids, listened to the dawns, and tasted the sunsets.

Some of the things I know about the river are undefined, as amorphous as the inexplicable connection that seeps into my bones while leaning against a warming sandstone wall on an early spring afternoon, or the ominous rockfalls on a winter night giving notice of a canyon under construction, the ragged pound of a rapid that matches no known rhythm but has lodged in my head like an old familiar song, the sheer blooming, healthy joy of the river's refrain.

But one thing is defined and clear: the terrible life-dependent clarity of one atom of oxygen hooked to two of hydrogen that ties us as humans to the only world we know.

Reference Material

Appendix : Mileages

Mileages are based on George H. Billingsley and Donald P. Elston, 1989, "Geologic Log of the Colorado River from Lees Ferry to Temple Bar, Lake Mead, Arizona," in *Geology of Grand Canyon, Northern Arizona*, ed. Donald P. Elston, George H. Billingsley, and Richard A. Young (Washington, D.C.: American Geophysical Union), 1–47. I list only mileages pertinent to this text.

Lees Ferry	0.0
Paria River	0.8
Navajo Bridge	4.3
Badger Creek/Rapid	7.8
Soap Creek/Rapid	11.2
Rider Canyon	16.9
House Rock Rapid	17.0
Twenty-four Mile Rapid	24.2
Twenty-five Mile Rapid	25.0
Shinumo Wash	29.4
South Canyon	31.5
Stanton's Cave	31.7
Vasey's Paradise	31.9
Test Adit Dam Site	32.8
Redwall Cavern	33.0

Nautiloid Canyon	34.8
Buck Farm Canyon	41.0
Eminence Break Trail	43.7
President Harding Rapid	43.7
Saddle Canyon	47.1
Eminence Break Fault	49.7 (*at river level*)
Little Nankoweap Creek	51.8
Nankoweap Creek	52.1
Kwagunt Creek/Rapid	56.0
Little Colorado River	61.3
Lava Creek	65.5
Tanner Creek/Rapid	68.6
Basalt Graben	69.0
Basalt Canyon	69.5
Cardenas Creek	71.2
Unkar Creek/Rapid	72.4
Hance Rapid	76.5
Upper Granite Gorge	77.5–119.0
Sockdolager Rapid	78.6
Grapevine Rapid	81.5
Kaibab Bridge	87.4
Bright Angel Trail Bridge	87.8
Horn Creek Rapid	90.1
Monument Creek	93.3
Granite Rapid	93.4
Crystal Creek/Rapid	98.0
Shinumo Creek	108.5
Elves Chasm	116.6
Blacktail Canyon	120.2
Middle Granite Gorge	127.0–139.5
128 Mile Canyon	128.5
Stone Creek/Canyon	131.9
Tapeats Creek/Rapid	133.6

Deer Creek Falls/Canyon	136.2
Fishtail Canyon	139.0
Kanab Creek	143.6
Matkatamiba	148.0
Havasu Canyon	156.7
National Canyon	166.5
Vulcan's Anvil	178.0
Toroweap Fault	179.0
Lava Falls	179.0
Prospect Canyon	179.2
Old Whitmore Wash	187.0
Whitmore Wash	188.0
Hurricane Fault Zone	190.7–222.0
Parashant Wash	198.5
Granite Park	208.8
Lower Granite Gorge	216.0–261.0
Granite Spring Canyon	220.5
Diamond Creek	225.7
Separation Canyon	239.6
Bat Cave	267.0
Grand Wash Fault	278.0–278.5
Pearce Ferry	279.2

Notes

The purpose of these notes is to provide references, historical as well as current, for readers who would like to know more about the river and its natural history. They are not definitive, nor are all my sources cited, but indicate books and articles that were especially useful to me. Notes are indexed only if they add information to the text.

1 Prelude: Lees Ferry

Colorado River Compact: According to Steven Carothers and Bryan T. Brown, 1993, *A Natural History of the Colorado River in Grand Canyon* (Tucson: University of Arizona Press), 23–24, dam operation is subject to the requirement of 8.23 million acre-feet that the Upper Colorado River Basin is contractually bound to release to the Lower River Basin each year, as well as the multiple requirements of the Colorado River Compact of 1922, Boulder Canyon Project Act, Upper Colorado River Basin Compact, Water Treaty of 1944 with the United Mexican States, Colorado River Storage Project Act, and Colorado River Basin Project. Carothers and Brown provide the best all-around reference, recommended reading before *and* after for anyone running the river, written by two knowledgeable biologists, usefully and handsomely illustrated.

Mile markers: Lewis R. Freeman, 1923, *The Colorado River: Yesterday, To-day and Tomorrow* (New York: Dodd, Mead).

Commercial traffic: R. M. Turner and M. M. Karpiscak, 1980, *Recent Vegetation Changes along the Colorado River between Glen Canyon Dam and Lake Mead, Arizona* (Washington, D.C.: USGS Professional Paper 1132), 43; George H. Billingsley and Donald Elston, 1989, "Geologic Log of the Colorado River from Lees Ferry to Temple Bar, Lake Mead, Arizona," in *Geology of Grand Canyon, Northern Arizona*, ed. Donald P. Elston, George H. Billingsley, and Richard A. Young (Washington, D.C.: American Geophysical Union), 1. This volume, hereafter *Geology of Grand Canyon*, includes an excellent river guide with recent papers on the geology of the canyon.

Hamblin: Leland H. Creer, 1958, *The Adventures of Jacob Hamblin in the Vicinity of the Colorado* (Salt Lake City: University of Utah Press, University of Utah Anthropological Papers 33); Frederick S. Dellenbaugh, 1926, *A Canyon Voyage* (New Haven: Yale University Press), 153, accompanying Powell on his 1871 trip describes his meeting with Hamblin: "On landing we were met by a slow-moving, very quiet individual, who said he was Jacob Hamblin. His voice was so low, his manner so simple, his clothing so usual, that I could hardly believe that this was Utah's famous Indian-fighter and manager."

Notable visitors: Silvestre Veléz de Escalante, 1776 (1943), "Journals," *Utah Historical Quarterly* 11:97–98; Powell: George D. Vanderluis and Charles B. Hauf, 1969, "Road Log: Yaki Point (Top of the Kaibab Trail on the South Rim of the Grand Canyon) to Lee's Ferry, Arizona, via Cameron," in *Geologic and Natural History of the Grand Canyon Region*, ed. D. L. Baars (Durango, Colo.: Four Corners Geological Association), 211; Stanton: Robert Brewster Stanton, 1965, *Down the Colorado*, ed. and intro. Dwight L. Smith (Norman: University of Oklahoma Press), 108–9, whose Christmas menu lists "Oxtail, Tomato, or Chicken soup; Colorado River Salmon; Roast Turkey, Beef, Ox Heart, and for Entrees: Braised Chicken, Game Pie, Mashed Potatoes, Stewed Onions, Tomatoes, Rice, Potato Salad; Wheat, Corn and Graham Bread; Tea, Coffee, Chocolate, Milk; Plum Pudding, Hard Sauce; Mince and Apple Pie with Apple and Cherry Sauce; Bents Crackers and Utah Cheese; Arizona Apples, fresh Peaches and Pears, Raisins and Nuts (all grown at Lee's Ferry); Havana Cigars, Turkish Cigarettes"; Flavell: G. F. Flavell, 1987, *The Log of the Panthon: An Account of an 1896 River Voyage from Green River, Wyoming, to Yuma, Arizona, through the Grand Canyon*, ed. Neil B. Carmony and David E. Brown (Boulder, Colo.: Pruett Publishing); Woolley: David Lavender, 1986, *River Runners of the Grand Canyon* (Grand Canyon: Grand Canyon Natural History Association and University of Arizona Press), 38–40; Stone: Julius S. Stone, 1932, *Canyon Country: The Romance of a Drop of Water and a Grain of Sand* (New York: Putnam's Sons), 83, one of the best of personal river narratives; Kolb: Ellsworth L. Kolb, 1914, *Through the Grand Canyon from Wyoming to Mexico* (New York: Macmillan), 249–50; Edith Kolb, 1923, "Diary" (Emery Kolb Collection, Cline Library, Northern Arizona University, Flagstaff), series 2, box 1, subgroup 4, folder 1756, July 2 and August 1, 1923; Birdseye: Claude H. Birdseye and Raymond C. Moore, 1924, "A Boat Voyage through the Grand Canyon of the Colorado," *Geographical Review* 14(2):177–80; Hatch: Roy Webb, 1990, *Riverman: The Story of Bus Hatch* (Rock Springs, Wyo.: Labyrinth Publishing), 41; Nevills:

William Cook, 1987, *The Wen, the Botany, and the Mexican Hat: The Adventures of the First Women through Grand Canyon, on the Nevills Expedition* (Orangevale, Calif.: Callistoga Books), 63–64; DeColmont Expedition: Roy Webb, 1987, "'Les Voyageurs sans Trace': The DeColmont-DeSeyne Kayak Party of 1938," *Utah Historical Quarterly* 55(2):167–69, 179–80.

Lees Ferry name: Nancy Brian, 1992, *River to Rim* (Flagstaff: Earthquest Press), a carefully researched, reliable guide to Grand Canyon names.

Pearce Ferry: Ibid., 134, often misspelled "Pierce," the ferry was named after Harrison Pearce, who ran it.

Beadle: J. H. Beadle, 1873, *The Undeveloped West; or, Five Years in the Territories: Being a Complete History of that Vast Region between the Mississippi and the Pacific, Its Resources, Climate, Inhabitants, Natural Curiosities, etc., etc., Life and Adventure on Prairies, Mountains, and the Pacific Coast* (Philadelphia: National Publishing), 633–37, 645–53, 663, quotes, 33, 637, 653.

Emma Dean: Ibid., 634–35; Dellenbaugh, *Canyon Voyage*, 319, "Preparations for our descent through the great chasm were immediately begun. The boats had been previously overhauled, and as the *Nellie Powell* was found unseaworthy from last seasons's knocks, or at least not in condition to be relied on in the Grand Canyon, she was abandoned, and Lee kept her for a ferry-boat."

Emma Lee: Beadle, *Undeveloped West*, 637, characterizes her as "full of harangue," a description that matches that of others who dealt with Lee's seventeenth wife, who was tough enough to pull a handcart from Iowa City to Salt Lake City in 1857; however, Dellenbaugh, *Canyon Voyage*, 210, speaks more kindly of her as "a stout, comely young woman of about twenty-five, with two small children, and [who] seemed to be entirely happy in the situation," and praised the fresh fruits and vegetables she grew at Lees Ferry; E. O. Beaman, 1874, "The Cañon of the Colorado, and the Moqui Pueblos: A Wild Boat-Ride through the Cañon and Rapids, a Visit to the Seven Cities of the Desert, Glimpses of Mormon Life," *Appleton's Journal* 11:592, describes a woman who shepherded "seven children, the eldest of which was not more than ten years old. Here, in a miserable ranch, forty-five miles from any settlement, and divided only by a river, fordable in low water, from the most savage of Indian tribes—the Apaches and Navajos—lived this faithful woman with her little brood, subsisting, as best she might, on the milk of a few cows and what she could win from the unwilling elements."

John Doyle Lee: Juanita Brooks, 1962, *John Doyle Lee: Zealot-Pioneer Builder-Scapegoat* (Glendale, Calif.: Arthur H. Clark), 203, 314–20; William Wise, 1976, *Massacre at Mountain Meadows: An American Legend and a Monumental Crime* (New York: Thomas Y. Crowell). Lee's and Hamblin's falling out came over what Lee considered Hamblin's negligence toward Emma when she was about to deliver and Hamblin failed to send a midwife; Lee's excommunication was revoked in 1961, largely due to Brooks's efforts; according to Beaman, "Cañon of the Colorado," 623, Lee did not know Beadle was a reporter until he was gone and allowed that he "would have given the d——d Gentile a blast that would have lasted him home."

Glen Canyon Environmental Studies (GCES): U.S. Department of the Interior, Bureau of Reclamation, 1989, *Glen Canyon Environmental Studies* (Washington, D.C.: U.S. Government Printing Office) [hereafter *GCES*], 12–13; U.S. Department of the Interior, Bureau of Reclamation, 1993, *Operation of Glen Canyon Dam: Draft Environmental Impact Statement* (Washington, D.C.: U.S. Government Printing Office) [hereafter *Draft EIS*], 3; agencies involved in the GCES: Bureau of Reclamation (BurRec), Western Area Power Administration (WAPA), National Park Service (NPS), U.S. Fish and Wildlife Service, Arizona Department of Game and Fish, U.S. Geological Survey (USGS), and several Native American tribes; U.S. Dept. of Interior, March 1995, *Operation of Glen Canyon Dam, Final Environmental Impact Statement* (Washington, D.C.: Govt. Printing Ofc.) [hereafter *Final EIS*], 10. Phase 1 of GCES was 1982–88, Phase 2 is 1980 to present.

Environmental Impact Statement: Steve Carothers, 1992–93, "The Glen Canyon Dam EIS: Random Thoughts and Revelations," *The News* 6(1):6; now called *Boatman's Quarterly Review*, this journal is the well written and edited, informative publication of the Grand Canyon River Guides; see also Duncan T. Patten, 1991, "Glen Canyon Environmental Studies Research Program: Past, Present and Future," in *Colorado River Ecology and Dam Management*, proceedings of a symposium, May 24–25, 1990, in Santa Fe, New Mexico (Washington, D.C.: National Academy Press) [proceedings hereafter *Colorado River Ecology*], 239–40.

Cost: William H. Clagett, *Statement of Mr. William H. Clagett, Administrator, Western Area Power Administration, Department of Energy, before the Subcommittee on Water, Power, and Offshore Energy Resources and Subcommittee on National Parks and Public Lands, Committee on Interior and Insular Affairs, U.S. House of Representatives,* May 22, 1990, 2–3; at 6–7 Clagett explains that the estimated $16 million price tag represented WAPA's cost of purchasing replacement power to meet its contractual obligations due to the loss of generating capacity while limited flows were in effect for the GCES; WAPA, 1994, *Ideas That Worked: 1993 Annual Report* (Golden, Colo.: WAPA), 45, affirms that because of the Grand Canyon Protection Act of 1992, changes occurred in the allocation of costs for environmental impact studies and monitoring, and $60.4 million, previously booked as costs, are now recognized as income for fiscal year 1993.

Two excellent accounts of Glen Canyon Dam are Philip L. Fradkin, 1982, *A River No More* (New York: Knopf), and Russell Martin, 1989, *The Story That Stands Like a Dam* (New York: Henry Holt).

Time span of studies: David R. Dawdy, 1991, "Hydrology of Glen Canyon and the Grand Canyon," in *Colorado River Ecology*, 42–43.

Lack of predam studies: R. Roy Johnson, 1991, "Historic Changes in Vegetation along the Colorado River in the Grand Canyon," in *Colorado River Ecology*, 184, "The possibility of large scale changes that were to occur in the downstream aquatic and riparian ecosystems were not considered until they became obvious, after the completion of the dam." The exceptions are few: Ivo Lucchitta, April 1994, cites hydrographs for Lees Ferry; Henry A. Pilsbry and James H. Ferriss, 1911, "Mollusca of the Southwestern States, V: The Grand Canyon and Northern Arizona," *Proceedings of the Academy of Natural Sciences of Philadelphia* 63:174–99, made a predam inventory of mollusks.

1983–84 floods: Trevor C. Hughes, 1991, "Reservoir Operations," in *Colorado River Ecology*, 211–12; Jack A. Stanford and James V. Ward, 1991, "Limnology of Lake Powell and the Chemistry of the Colorado River," in ibid., 76, 79–80; Bryan T. Brown and R. Roy Johnson, 1984, "Effects of Colorado River Flooding on Riparian Birds Studied," *Park Science* 4(2):12–13; Bruce Babbitt, 1991, Foreword, in Carothers and Brown, *Natural History of the Colorado River*, xiv–xv; according to Carothers and Brown, 13–14, 25–26, BurRec now maintains the dam approximately 5 ft. below full; John C. Schmidt, [1992?], "Temporal and Spatial Changes in Sediment Storage in Grand Canyon," in *The Influence of Variable Discharge Regimes on Colorado River Sand Bars below Glen Canyon Dam: Final Report*, ed. Stanley S. Beus and Charles C. Avery (Flagstaff: U.S. Dept. of Interior, NPS Cooperative Parks Study Unit, Northern Arizona Univ.) [volume hereafter *Variable Discharge Regimes*], 6, 9, 13–14; *Final EIS*, 81–83, states that "if the reserve was near full when such hydrologic events occurred, floodflows would be difficult, if not impossible, to avoid."

Long-term monitoring/studies: *Draft EIS*, 1–3; Steven W. Carothers, Stewart W. Aitchison, and Roy R. Johnson, 1976, "Natural Resources, White Water Recreation, and River Management Alternatives on the Colorado River, Grand Canyon National Park, Arizona," proceedings of the first Conference on Scientific Research in the National Parks, part 1, 254; Luna B. Leopold, 1991, "Closing Remarks," in *Colorado River Ecology*, 256–57, "The need for a long-term, uninterrupted program of observation and measurement is the unassailable conclusion of the studies made to date."

Paria terraces: Stanley S. Beus and Michael Morales, eds., 1990, *Grand Canyon Geology* (London and Flagstaff: Oxford University Press and Museum of Northern Arizona), 413–15, where W. K. Hamblin, "Late Cenozoic Lava Dams in the Western Grand Canyon," theorizes that the Paria and Colorado dropped gravels as they entered the upper end of a lake formed by a lava dam downstream at Toroweap Canyon; Lucchitta, April 1994, thinks the lake did not last long enough for terraces to form and suggests they were more likely built by aggradation.

Coconino Sandstone: George H. Billingsley, 1978, *A Synopsis of Stratigraphy in the Western Grand Canyon* (Flagstaff: Museum of Northern Arizona Research Paper 16), 13–15; Larry T. Middleton, David K. Elliott, and Michael Morales, 1990, "Coconino Sandstone," in Beus and Morales, *Grand Canyon Geology*, 183, 192–94, 199; Edwin D. McKee, 1974, "Paleozoic Rocks of Grand Canyon," in *Geology of Northern Arizona with Notes on Archaeology and Paleoclimate*, ed. Thor N. V. Karlstrom, Gordon A. Swann, and Raymond L. Eastwood (Flagstaff: Northern Arizona University, Museum of Northern Arizona, and Geological Society of America, Rocky Mountain Section), 148–49.

Pangaea: Dave Thayer, 1986, *A Guide to Grand Canyon Geology along Bright Angel Trail* (Grand Canyon: Grand Canyon Nature Association), 16–17, although focused on the trail, is *very* useful elsewhere in the canyon.

Dam-caused changes: *Final EIS*, 6–7, NPS, 1992, "Influences of Glen Canyon Dam Fluctuating Flows on Spawning Rainbow Trout and Wintering Bald Eagles, with Observations on the Effects of Human–Bald Eagle Interactions on the Colorado River in Grand Canyon National Park, Arizona" (Final Report: Northern Arizona University to Grand Canyon National Park), 55; Luna B. Leopold, 1969, *The Rapids and the Pools—Grand Canyon* (Washington, D.C.: USGS Professional Paper 669-D), 144; W. E. Garrett, 1978, "Are We Loving It to Death?" *National Geographic* 154(1):23.

Sediment load: Dean W. Blinn, Lawrence E. Stevens, and Joseph P. Shannon, [1992?], "The Effects of Glen Canyon Dam on the Aquatic Food Base in the Colorado River Corridor in Grand Canyon, Arizona" (GCES/NPS Cooperative Agreement, GCES-11-02), 82; Schmidt, "Temporal and Spatial Changes in Sediment Storage in Grand Canyon," 3, 18–19; according to Carothers and Brown, *Natural History of the Colorado River*, 52, the 1927 flood carried a high of 27 million tons of silt measured at Bright Angel gauging station; Richard Hereford, Helen C. Fairley, Kathryn S. Thompson, and Janet R. Balsom, 1993, "Surficial Geology, Geomorphology, and Erosion of Archaeologic Sites along the Colorado River, Eastern Grand Canyon, Grand Canyon National Park, Arizona" (GCES Open-File Report 93, CUL800), 1, write that the dam now holds back approximately 5 million tons of sediment a year; Robert Dolan, Alan Howard, and Arthur Gallenson, 1974, "Man's Impact on the Colorado River in the Grand Canyon," *American Scientist* 62:394–97, give the pre-dam median suspended-sediment concentration at approximately 200 times more than today's; Gary M. Smillie, William L. Jackson, and Dean Tucker, [1992?], "Colorado River Sand Budget: Lees Ferry to Little Colorado River including Marble Canyon," in *Variable Discharge Regimes*, 1, 7, cite an average annual sand load of 790,000 tons a year, contributed by the Paria, which is not enough to prevent a deficit between Lees Ferry and the Little Colorado River; *Final EIS*, 89–96.

Cladophora glomerata: Draft EIS, v, 37–38; Dean W. Blinn and Gerald A. Cole, 1991, "Algal and Invertebrate Biota in the Colorado River: Comparison of Pre- and Post-dam Conditions," in *Colorado River Ecology*, 103–5, 111–12, 114–15; B. A. Whitton, 1975, "Algae," in *River Ecology*, ed. B. A. Whitton (Berkeley: University of California Press), 87–88.

Midge larvae populations: *River Ecology*, viii.

Diatoms: Blinn and Cole, "Algal and Invertebrate Biota," 103–6, 112–14; Dean W. Blinn, Robert Truitt, and Anne Pickart, 1989, "Response of Epiphytic Diatom Communities from the Tailwaters of Glen Canyon Dam, Arizona, to Elevated Water Temperature," *Regulated Rivers: Research and Management* 4:91; David B. Czarnecki and Dean W. Blinn, 1978, "Diatoms of the Colorado River in Grand Canyon National Park and Vicinity," *Bibliotheca Phycologia*, band 38 (Germany: Strauss and Cramer GMBH), 4; David B. Czarnecki, Dean W. Blinn, Terrill Tompkins, 1976, *A Periphytic Microflora Analysis of the Colorado River and Major Tributaries in Grand Canyon and Vicinity* (Grand Canyon: Grand Canyon National Park, Technical Report 6), Colorado River Research Series, contribution 35, 1; Blinn, Stevens, and Shannon, "The Effects of Glen Canyon Dam on the Aquatic Food Base," 82–83, state that diatoms form 90 percent of the diet of *Gammarus* and 60 percent of the diet of midge larvae, but only a quarter of the diatoms remain by Diamond Creek; *Final EIS*, 111–12.

Gammarus lacustris: J. V. Ward and B. C. Kondratieff, 1992, *An Illustrated Guide to the Mountain Stream Insects of Colorado* (Boulder: University Press of Colorado), 36–37, a good identification book for stream invertebrates; Steven W. Carothers and Robert Dolan, 1982, "Dam Changes on the Colorado River," *Natural History* 9(1):79–80.

Trout stocking: W. L. Minckley, 1991, "Native Fishes of the Grand Canyon Region: An Obituary?" in *Colorado River Ecology*, 142–45; Glen E. Sturdevant, 1928, "Inspecting a Possible Trout Stream of Grand Canyon," *Grand Canyon Nature Notes* 2(11); this publication, begun by Sturdevant and published between 1925 and the mid-1930s, is a good resource for information about the early years of the park; Robert T. Williamson and Carol F. Tyler, 1932, "Trout Propagation in Grand Canyon National Park," *Grand Canyon Nature Notes* 7(2):11–15; Angus M. Woodbury, 1960, "The Colorado River—The Physical and Biological Setting," *Utah Historical Quarterly* 28(3):198–218; J. P. Brooks, 1931, "Official Report on Stocking Canyon Streams with Fish," *Grand Canyon Nature Notes* 5(5):48, was convinced that though "the obstacles encountered in making the plants were greater than elsewhere the efforts are justified by the results obtained."

Native/non-native fish: Allen Haden, 1992, "Nonnative Fishes of the Grand Canyon: A Review with Regards to Their Effects on Native Fishes" (GCES AQU 901; on file at GCES Office, Flagstaff, Ariz.), 5–7, 13–14; Haden lists at least 12–14 introduced species; Carothers and Brown, *Natural History of the Colorado River*, 88ff., it would be "virtually impossible to eradicate trout without also decimating remaining native species"; GCES, 3–6, 12–13, the NPS cannot manage trout to the detriment of native fish, nor will it manage for native fish because of the massive changes required in dam operation; *Draft EIS*, 13, it would cost around $60 million to install multilevel intake structures, and warmer temperatures could allow non-native predators like striped bass to come farther upstream from Lake Mead; *Final EIS*, 14–15, 41–42, proposes trying to establish a new chub population because of the precariousness of the present one.

Quote: Clarence E. Dutton, 1879, *Tertiary History of the Grand Canyon District* (Salt Lake City: Peregrine Smith, reprint 1977), 260.

Predam flood regime: Alan Howard and Robert Dolan, 1981, "Geomorphology of the Colorado River in the Grand Canyon," *Journal of Geology* 89(3):271; Muniram Budhu, [1992?], "Mechanisms of Erosion and a Model to Predict Seepage-Driven Erosion Due to Transient Flow," in *Variable Discharge Regimes*, 2:2; *Final EIS*, 6.

Bald eagles: Bryan T. Brown, Robert Mesta, Lawrence E. Stevens, and John Weisheit, 1989, "Changes in the Winter Distribution of Bald Eagles along the Colorado River in Grand Canyon, Arizona," *Journal of Raptor Research* 23(3):112–13; Jon M. Gerrard and Gary R. Bortolotti, 1988, *The Bald Eagle: Haunts and Habits of a Wilderness Monarch* (Washington, D.C.: Smithsonian Institution Press), 29–31, have clocked eagles arriving within five minutes.

Immature eagle identification: William S. Clark, 1983, *A Field Guide to Hawks, North America* (Boston: Houghton Mifflin), 81–83, 88; Peter Dunne, David Sibley, and Clay Sutton, 1988, *Hawks in Flight* (Boston: Houghton Mifflin), 145–48, 151–54, 156.

Hermit Shale: Ronald C. Blakey, 1990, "Supai Group and Hermit Formation," in Beus and Morales, *Grand Canyon Geology*, 161–62, 164, 176–77; Stanley S. Beus and George H. Billingsley, 1989, "Paleozoic Strata of the Grand Canyon, Arizona," in *Geology of Grand Canyon*, 124.

Redwall Limestone: Raymond C. Gutschick, 1943, "The Redwall Limestone (Mississippian) of Yavapai County, Arizona," *Plateau* 16(1):1, 9; W. K. Hamblin, 1970, "A Summary of the Stratigraphy of the Western Grand Canyon Region," in *Guidebook to the Geology of Utah, Number 23*, ed. W. K. Hamblin and M. G. Best (Salt Lake City: Utah Geological and Mineralogical Survey), 84, 123, 124–26, 128, 142; plus two articles in Beus and Morales, *Grand Canyon Geology*: Stanley S. Beus, 1990, "Redwall Limestone and Surprise Canyon

Formation," 119–21, 125–28; and Andre R. Potochnik and Stephen J. Reynolds, 1990, "Side Canyons of the Colorado River, Grand Canyon," 472–73.

Naming: John Wesley Powell, 1875, *The Exploration of the Colorado River and Its Canyons* (New York: Dover Publications, reprint 1961), 238–40, "The walls of the cañon, 2,500 feet high, are of marble, of many beautiful colors, often polished below by the waves . . . As this great bed forms a distinctive feature of the cañon, we call it Marble Cañon."

2 Fishing Eagles and Spawning Trout

Nankoweap derivation: Stewart Aitchison, 1985, *A Naturalist's Guide to Hiking the Grand Canyon* (Englewood Cliffs, N.J.: Prentice-Hall), 90; this work is indispensable for canyon hiking.

Tamarisk: Steven W. Carothers and N. Joseph Sharber, 1976, "Birds of the Colorado River," in *An Ecological Survey of the Riparian Zone of the Colorado River between Lees Ferry and the Grand Wash Cliffs, Arizona*, ed. Steven W. Carothers and Stewart W. Aitchison (Grand Canyon: Grand Canyon National Park, Technical Report 10) [volume hereafter *Riparian Zone*], 119–20; Bryan T. Brown and Michael W. Trosset, 1989, "Nesting-Habitat Relationships of Riparian Birds along the Colorado River in Grand Canyon, Arizona," *Southwestern Naturalist* 34(2):261, 268; William L. Graf, 1978, "Fluvial Adjustments to the Spread of Tamarisk in the Colorado Plateau Region," *Geological Society of America Bulletin* 89:1491; Johnson, "Historic Changes in Vegetation," 180, thinks that tamarisk have increased the richness of the riparian community "apparently without deleterious effects often associated with non-native invaders"; compare with Larry Stevens, 1993, "Scourge of the West: The Natural History of Tamarisk in the Grand Canyon," *The News* 6(2):14–15.

Riparian vegetation: Martin M. Karpiscak, 1976, "Vegetational Changes along the Colorado River," in *Riparian Zone*, 1–2; R. Roy Johnson and James M. Simpson, 1988, "Desertification of Wet Riparian Ecosystems in Arid Regions of the North American Southwest," in *Arid Lands Today and Tomorrow, Proceedings of an International Research and Development Conference*, October 20–25, 1985, Tucson, Arizona, ed. Emily E. Whitehead et al. (Boulder, Colo.: Westview Press), 1387; Carothers and Brown, *Natural History of the Colorado River*, 120, contrast the rate of streamside vegetation growth between 1965 and 1973 at about half an acre per mile with the current rate of about a quarter-acre per mile; Lawrence E. Stevens, and Tina J. Ayers, eds., 1993, *The Impacts of Glen Canyon Dam on Riparian Vegetation and Soil Stability in the Colorado River Corridor, Grand Canyon, Arizona: 1992, Final Report* (Flagstaff: NPS Cooperative Studies Unit, Northern Arizona University), 2/1, cite a 90–95 percent loss of riparian vegetation in the last decades; *Final EIS*, 130–33; Johnson, "Historic Changes in Vegetation," 179, 189, 200, identifies the Grand Canyon as "the only major riverine ecosystem in the Southwest where there has been an appreciable increase rather than a decrease in riparian vegetation and associated animal populations during the 1900s. Since these Colorado River riparian lands are used by transients and wintering birds as well as breeding birds, they constitute one of the most important avian resources in the Southwest."

Debris flow/driftwood in Stanton's Cave: Karpiscak, "Vegetational Changes," 1–2; Donald P. Elston, 1989, "Pre-pleistocene(?) Deposits of Aggradation, Lees Ferry to Western Grand Canyon, Arizona," in *Geology of Grand Canyon*, 175, 178; Richard Hereford, 1984, "Driftwood, Stanton's Cave: The Case for Temporary Damming of the Colorado River at Nankoweap Creek in Marble Canyon, Grand Canyon National Park, Arizona," in *The Archaeology, Geology, and Paleobiology of Stanton's Cave*, ed. Robert C. Euler (Grand Canyon National Park: Grand Canyon Natural History Association, Monograph 6), 102–5, argues that a debris fall off the east wall dammed the river, making a reservoir with water high enough to wash logs into the cave; Lucchitta, April 1994, thinks the debris flow came down Nankoweap Creek because the matrix resembles that of debris flows downstream, and old river pebbles on top (indicating the river flowed here) intermix with rubble from the flow itself.

Trout diet/spawn: William Leibfried, personal communication, January 1989; Blinn and Cole, "Algal and Invertebrate Biota," 104–5, 112, 114; NPS, "Influences of Glen Canyon Dam," 8, 17–19, 21–23; Carothers and Brown, *Natural History of the Colorado River*, 90, spawning nets have not yet been analyzed for larvae but researchers suspect that spawning success is very low and larval survival is minimal.

Golden eagles: Dunne, Sibley, and Sutton, *Hawks in Flight*, 144–45, 150–51; Bryan T. Brown, 1992, "Golden Eagles Feeding on Fish," *Journal of Raptor Research* 26(1):36–37, goldens were present up to 80 percent of the time during the studies.

Disturbance: Bryan T. Brown, 1993, "Winter Foraging Ecology of Bald Eagles in Arizona," *Condor* 95:132–38; NPS, "Influences of Glen Canyon Dam," xii, xv, 103–4; Brown, "Golden Eagles Feeding on Fish," 36, disturbance precludes eagle feeding during about 10 percent of daylight hours. Motor trips are banned from September through December but currently there is pressure from fishermen to allow motors to give better access into Marble Canyon; and part of the eagle research addresses how this would affect bald eagle feeding.

Trout population: NPS, "Influences of Glen Canyon Dam," xii, 14–15; Bryan T. Brown and Lawrence E. Stevens, 1992, "Winter Abundance, Age Structure, and Distribution of Bald Eagles along the Colorado River, Arizona," *South-*

western Naturalist 37(4):404, there may be up to fifteen hundred trout spawning at a time; *Final EIS*, 122–25.

Precocious parr: Ring T. Cardé and Thomas C. Baker, 1984, "Sexual Communication with Pheromones," in *Chemical Ecology of Insects*, ed. William J. Bell and Ring T. Cardé (Sunderland, Mass.: Sinauer Associates), 373, precocious males occur in other mating situations, including insects.

Roosting/flight behavior/weather sensitivity: Clark, *Field Guide to Hawks*, 83; NPS, "Influences of Glen Canyon Dam," 58–59; quote, T. H. White, ed., 1960, *The Bestiary: A Book of Beasts being a Translation from a Latin Bestiary of the Twelfth Century* (New York: Putnam's Sons), 105.

Trout consumption: Bryan T. Brown, 1992, in "Halieatus Herald III," ed. Teresa Yates (Xeroxed paper), 1, documents that 888 foraging events, of which 684 were successful, and forages on live trout were more successful by adults than subadults; it appears that eagles are staying at Nankoweap an average of seven days each and if so, then some seventy eagles moved into and through Nankoweap during the study period; *Final EIS*, 137–38.

Pirating: David K. Garcelon, 1990, "Observations of Aggressive Interactions by Bald Eagles of Known Age and Sex," *Condor* 92:532–34; David L. Fischer, 1985, "Piracy Behavior of Wintering Bald Eagles," *Condor* 87:246–51.

Eagle time on perch: Gerrard and Bortolotti, *The Bald Eagle*, 119–20, eagles may spend as much as 93 percent of their time perching.

3 River Marshes and Familiar Faults

Quote: John Van Dyke, 1920, *The Grand Canyon of the Colorado* (New York: Charles Scribner's Sons, reprint Salt Lake City: University of Utah Press, 1992), 66; Van Dyke spent three luxurious summers at El Tovar, but some of his plant identifications give pause, such as finding trillium, a plant native east of the Mississippi, on the Bright Angel Trail!

Marshes: *Draft EIS*, 39; Lawrence E. Stevens, John C. Schmidt, Tina J. Ayers, and Bryan T. Brown, 1993, "Fluvial Marsh Development along the Dam-Regulated Colorado River in the Grand Canyon, Arizona," in Stevens and Ayers, *The Impacts of Glen Canyon Dam*, 4/10; *Final EIS*, 235–36, 245.

Travertine: Potochnik and Reynolds, "Side Canyons," 479–80.

Winter annuals: Richard S. Inouye, 1991, "Population Biology of Desert Annual Plants," in *The Ecology of Desert Communities*, ed. Gary A. Polis (Tucson: University of Arizona Press) [volume hereafter *Ecology of Desert Communities*], 27–28, 31–34, 38, 41; Donald L. Waller, 1988, "Plant Morphology and Reproduction," in *Plant Reproductive Ecology: Patterns and Strategies*, ed. Jon Lovett Doust and Lesley Lovett Doust (New York: Oxford University Press), 205–6;

Barbara G. Phillips and Arthur M. Phillips, 1974, "Spring Wildflowers of the Inner Gorge, Grand Canyon, Arizona," *Plateau* 46(4):149–156; Thomas D. Lee, 1988, "Patterns of Fruit and Seed Production," in *Plant Reproductive Ecology*, 181–82, 191, 195.

Bumblebees: Bernd Heinrich, 1979, *Bumblebee Economics* (Cambridge, Mass.: Harvard University Press), 198–99, and Heinrich, 1993, *Hot-Blooded Insects* (Cambridge, Mass.: Harvard University Press), 256, 273–75, 280, 351, 464–65; E. G. Linsley, 1978, "Temporal Patterns of Flower Visitation by Solitary Bees, with Particular Reference to the Southwestern United States," *Journal of the Kansas Entomological Society* 51(4):536–37, 539–42, and Linsley, 1958, "The Ecology of Solitary Bees," *Hilgardia* 27(19):552–59, 565–66, 571–73.

Clover/Jotter/Nevills: Cook, *The Wen, the Botany, and the Mexican Hat*, gives the full story of the expedition; P. T. Reilly, 1987, "Norman Nevills: Whitewater Man of the West," *Utah Historical Quarterly* 55(2):186–88; Elzada Clover and Lois Jotter, 1944, "Floristic Studies in the Canyon of the Colorado and Tributaries," *American Midland Naturalist* 32:608; Gary Topping, 1984, "Harry Aleson and the Place No One Knew," *Utah Historical Quarterly* 52(2):174, reports that Doc Marston, the patriarch of river historians and one of Nevills's boatmen, remarked that he could never figure out what Nevills's "balanced" menus were "supposed to balance, unless it was the Nevills budget."

Bessie Hyde: Lavender, *River Runners*, 38–40, 205, claims Hyde would have been the first woman to run the river all the way through had she lived—or did she? This, and Lavender, 1982, *Colorado River Country* (Albuquerque: University of New Mexico Press), are two scholarly and charming books by one of the best Western historians.

Botanical inventories: Stevens and Ayers, *The Impacts of Glen Canyon Dam*, Appendix 8A, "Preliminary Checklist of Plants from the Colorado River Corridor in Grand Canyon National Park," is the most recent (albeit incomplete); see also Barbara G. Phillips, Arthur M. Phillips III, and Marilyn Ann Schmidt Bernzott, 1987, *Annotated Checklist of Vascular Plants of Grand Canyon National Park* (Grand Canyon: Grand Canyon Natural History Association), with species along the river noted either by site or altitude; Michael E. Theroux, 1976, "Vascular Flora of the Grand Canyon," in *Riparian Zone*, 42, and Theroux, 1977, "A New Species of Flaveria (Compositae: Flaveriinae) from Grand Canyon, Arizona," *Madroño* 24:13, 15–16; Arthur H. Holmgren and Noel H. Holmgren, 1988, "Euphorbia Aaron-Rossii (Euphorbiaceae): A New Species from Marble and Grand Canyons of the Colorado River, Arizona," *Brittonia* 40(4):357–62; Peter S. Bennett, 1969, "Some Notes on the Vegetation of the Inner Gorge, Grand Canyon," in *Geologic and Natural History of the Grand Canyon Region*, ed. D. L. Baars (Durango, Colo.: Four Corners Geological Association); W. B. McDougall, 1964, *Grand Canyon*

Wildflowers (Flagstaff: Museum of Northern Arizona and Grand Canyon Natural History Association), is useful for the nonscientist, as is Arthur M. Phillips and John C. Richardson, 1990, *Grand Canyon Wildflowers* (Grand Canyon: Grand Canyon Natural History Association).

Alignments: Robert C. Euler and Walter W. Taylor, 1966, "Additional Archaeological Data from Upper Grand Canyon: Nankoweap to Unkar Revisited," *Plateau* 39(1):26–28.

Beavers: Glen E. Sturdevant, 1928, "A Reconnaissance of the Northeastern Part of Grand Canyon National Park," *Grand Canyon Nature Notes* 3(6):5.

Sturdevant's death: [No author] "In Memoriam and Our Sorrow," *Grand Canyon Nature Notes* 3(8):1–4.

Earthquakes: David S. Brumbaugh, 1990, "Earthquakes and Seismicity of the Grand Canyon Region," in Beus and Morales, *Grand Canyon Geology*, 438–39; Sandra Scott, 1992, "Regarding: Friday, April 13, 1992," *Grand Canyon Natural History Association* (May), 2–3, on recent earthquakes in April 1992 and May 1993; quote, John Muir, 1902, "The Grand Cañon of the Colorado," *Century Illustrated Monthly Magazine* 60:116.

Butte Fault: Thayer, *Bright Angel Trail*, 17–18, 41; Potochnik and Reynolds, "Side Canyons," 475; Donald P. Elston, 1989, "Middle and Late Proterozoic Grand Canyon Supergroup, Arizona," in *Geology of Grand Canyon*, 94, 98, 102; Brumbaugh, "Earthquakes and Seismicity," 438–39; Stanley S. Beus, Richard R. Rawson, Russell O. Dalton, Gene M. Stevenson, V. Stephen Reed, and Thomas M. Daneker, 1974, "Preliminary Report on the Unkar Group (Precambrian) in Grand Canyon, Arizona," in *Geology of Northern Arizona with Notes on Archaeology and Paleoclimate*, ed. Thor N. V. Karlstrom, Gordon A. Swann, and Raymond L. Eastwood (Flagstaff: Northern Arizona University, Museum of Northern Arizona, and Geological Society of America, Rocky Mountain Section), 50; Ivo Lucchitta and John D. Hendricks, 1983, "Characteristics, Depositional Environment, and Tectonic Interpretations of the Proterozoic Cardenas Lavas, Eastern Grand Canyon, Arizona," *Geology* 11:177–81.

Kaibab Monocline: Peter W. Huntoon, 1974, "Synopsis of Laramide and Post-Laramide Structural Geology of the Eastern Grand Canyon, Arizona," in *Geology of Northern Arizona* (see previous paragraph), 330–31, and Huntoon, 1990, "Phanerozoic Structural Geology of the Grand Canyon," in Beus and Morales, *Grand Canyon Geology*, 265, 273; quote, Dutton, *Tertiary History of the Grand Canyon District*, 260.

Canyon widening/cutting: Richard Hereford and Peter W. Huntoon, 1990, "Rock Movement and Mass Wastage in the Grand Canyon," in Beus and Morales, *Grand Canyon Geology*, 443–44, 448–49; Ivo Lucchitta, 1991, *Qua-*

ternary Geology, Geomorphology, and Erosional Processes, Eastern Grand Canyon, Arizona (Flagstaff: USGS Administrative Report), 4, 30. The Durango Herald, October 18, 1994, p. 1, reports the latest big rockslide occurred over the weekend of October 15, 1994, near Grapevine Canyon, exploding down the canyon "like a bomb in a bunkhouse" and causing some severe injuries.

USGS gauge: William Werrell, Richard Inglis, Jr., and Larry Martin, [1992?], "Erosion of Sand Bar 43.1 L along the Colorado River in Grand Canyon in Response to Ground-Water Seepage during Fluctuating Flow Releases from Glen Canyon Dam" in Variable Discharge Regimes, 2, the typical range is three to ten feet although in narrow parts of the canyon it can be as much as thirteen feet.

Beach erosion: According to Brian L. Cluer, [1992?], "Daily Responses of Colorado River Sand Bars to Releases from Glen Canyon Dam, 1990–1991: Instantaneous Erosion and Dependent Deposition," in Variable Discharge Regimes, 5:1, 46, low "weekend" flows cause most of bank failures on sandbars; Werrell, Inglis, and Martin, "Erosion of Sand Bar 43.1 L," 1–3, 18.

Old high-water line: Stevens and Ayers, The Impacts of Glen Canyon Dam, 3/3; Paul S. Martin, 1971, "Trees and Shrubs of the Grand Canyon: Lees Ferry to Diamond Creek" (unpublished manuscript on file at the Library of the Museum of Northern Arizona; 2d ed., 1973), 2, on floods ranging from ten to thirty feet high; Karpiscak, "Vegetational Changes," 1–2, 14–15, in fifty years vegetation at Nankoweap has changed little.

Wood rat middens: John Hutira, 1986, "Analysis of Plants, Pollen, and Coprolites," in A Cross Section of Grand Canyon Archaeology: Excavations at Five Sites along the Colorado River, ed. A. Trinkle Jones (Tucson: Western Archaeological and Conservation Center, NPS, Publications in Anthropology 28), 297; Thomas R. Van Devender, 1987, "Holocene Vegetation and Climate in the Puerto Blanco Mountains, Southwestern Arizona, Quaternary Research 27:51; Guy N. Cameron and Dennis G. Rainey, 1972, "Habitat Utilization by Neotoma lepida in the Mohave Desert," Journal of Mammology 53(2):251–52; Kenneth L. Cole and Larry Mayer, 1982, "Use of Packrat Middens to Determine Rates of Cliff Retreat in Eastern Grand Canyon, Arizona," Geology 10:597–99, using the distance of nests from the mouth of caves, give a retreat rate of the Redwall as 0.18 to 0.72 m/10^3, consistent with other estimates.

4 Springtime Bloom and Buzzing Bees

Carpenter bees: Heinrich, Hot-Blooded Insects, 283–85, 287–88; Linsley, "Temporal Patterns of Flower Visitation," 536, 539.

Pollination: Heinrich, Bumblebee Economics, 198–99; Inouye, "Population Biology of Desert Annual Plants," 31, 39, 41–44; Michael J. Crawley, 1983, Herbivory: The Dynamics of Animal-Plant Interactions (Berkeley: University of California Press), 67, 70, 73; Stephen D. Hendrix, 1988, "Herbivory and Its Impact on Plant Reproduction," in *Plant Reproductive Ecology: Patterns and Strategies*, ed. Jon Lovett Doust and Lesley Lovett Doust (New York: Oxford University Press), 253; the same 1988 volume provides pertinent reading; see Michael Zimmerman, "Nectar Production, Flowering Phenology, and Strategies for Pollination," 92–93, 157, 161, 170, and Robert I. Bertin, "Paternity in Plants," 40; John A. Wallwork, 1982, *Desert Soil Fauna* (New York: Praeger Publishers), 214–15.

Bee flies: Donald J. Borror, Dwight M. DeLong, and Charles A. Triplehorn, 1954, *An Introduction to the Study of Insects* (New York: Holt, Rinehart and Winston), 585–86, one of my favorite basic resources for identification of and information about insects and spiders, used throughout this book, as is Lester A. Swan and Charles S. Papp, 1972, *The Common Insects of North America* (New York: Harper and Row); Harold Oldroyd, 1964, *The Natural History of Flies* (New York: W. W. Norton), 131–33; Url Lanham, 1964, *The Insects* (New York: Columbia University Press), 114–15, 227; Frank R. Cole, 1969, "Bombyliidae," in *The Flies of Western North America*, ed. Robert L. Usinger (Berkeley and Los Angeles: University of California Press), 225–55.

Mushrooms: David Arora, 1986, *Mushrooms Demystified* (Berkeley, Calif.: Ten Speed Press), 46, 719, 722, 724–25; Gary H. Lincoff, 1981, *The Audubon Society Field Guide to North American Mushrooms* (New York: Knopf), 814–15, 840–42.

Riparian vegetation: see note to Chapter 2 on this topic; Clover and Jotter, "Floristic Studies," 620, considered this as close to a "climax vegetation" as the canyon gets; Stevens and Ayers, *The Impacts of Glen Canyon Dam*, 1/1, 2/1; Earle E. Spamer, 1993, "Late Pleistocene(?) Land Snails (Mollusca: Gastropoda) in 'Red Earth' Deposits of the Grand Canyon, Arizona," *Mosasaur* 5:50–51, found shells of snails that need water close along the dry talus pathside on the way up Saddle Canyon, suggesting that there once were more springs here; Saddle Canyon is still rich in snail species.

Hackberry galls/psyllids: Warren T. Johnson and Howard H. Lyon, 1976, *Insects That Feed on Trees and Shrubs* (Ithaca, N.Y.: Cornell University Press), 404; Raymond J. Gagné, 1989, *The Plant-Feeding Gall Midges of North America* (Ithaca, N.Y.: Cornell University Press), 289–90.

The tender of foot might find comfort in carrying a pair of river sandals for walking on the rocky bottoms of these pools.

Crickets: Jerry Dennis, 1992, *It's Raining Frogs and Fishes: Four Seasons of Natural Phenomena and Oddities of the Sky* (New York: HarperCollins), 174–75.

Wolf spiders; Willis J. Gertsch, 1979, *American Spiders* (New York: Van Nostrand Reinhold), 184–85; Rainer F. Foelix, 1982, *Biology of Spiders* (Cambridge, Mass.: Harvard University Press), 7, 9–10, 205–7; at 152–53 Foelix gives a speed of 40–50 centimeters per second (roughly 15–20 inches per second); Gary A. Polis and Tsunemi Yamashita, 1991, "The Ecology and Importance of Predaceous Arthropods in Desert Communities," in *Ecology of Desert Communities*, 182.

Datura: Cynta de Navaez, 1992, "Sacred Datura," *The News* 5(4):18–19; Timothy Johns, 1990, *With Bitter Herbs They Shall Eat It: Chemical Ecology and the Origins of Human Diet and Medicine* (Tucson: University of Arizona Press), 3; Deane M. Bowers, 1990, "Recycling Plant Natural Products for Insect Defense," in *Insect Defenses*, ed. David L. Evans and Justin O. Schmidt (Albany: State University of New York Press), 353–54; Heinrich, *Hot-Blooded Insects*, 388, and Heinrich, 1993, "How Avian Predators Constrain Caterpillar Foraging," in *Caterpillars: Ecological and Evolutionary Constraints on Foraging*, ed. Nancy E. Stamp and Timothy M. Casey (New York: Chapman and Hall), 237; Robert C. Euler, personal communication, October 1992, finds no evidence of Anasazi using datura ceremonially.

Ives quote: Joseph Christmas Ives, 1861, *Report upon the Colorado River of the West, Explored in 1857 and 1858, Part II: Hydrographic Report*, House Executive Document 90, 36th Congress, 1st Session (Washington, D.C.: U.S. Government Printing Office), 110; Van Dyke, *The Grand Canyon*, 212.

Midges: Blinn, Stevens, and Shannon, "The Effects of Glen Canyon Dam," 6; Oldroyd, *Natural History of Flies*, 6–7, 12–14, 58–63; David J. Horn, 1978, *Biology of Insects* (Philadelphia: W. B. Saunders), 130.

Swallows/swifts: Bryan T. Brown, Steven W. Carothers, and R. Roy Johnson, 1983, "Breeding Range Expansion of Bell's Vireo in Grand Canyon, Arizona," *Condor* 85:121, 199; Carothers and Sharber, "Birds of the Colorado River," 117–18; R. R. Askew, 1971, *Parasitic Insects* (London: Heinemann Educational Books), 67–68; Carothers and Brown, *Natural History of the Colorado River*, 152, report cliff swallows were last seen in 1975.

Millipedes: Edwin D. McKee, 1944, "Tracks That Go Uphill," *Plateau* 16(4):70–71; Waller, "Plant Morphology and Reproduction," 39–43, 126, 145–46, 180, 216, 225–26, 237.

Monadnock: Thayer, *Bright Angel Trail*, 21; the best known monadnock in North America is Mount Monadnock in New Hampshire, made famous by Thoreau.

Caddis flies: Robert W. Pennak, 1953, *Fresh-Water Invertebrates of the United States* (New York: Ronald Press), 566–79; Stuart G. Fisher, 1986, "Structure and Dynamics of Desert Streams," in *Pattern and Process in Desert Ecosystems*, ed. Walter G. Whitford (Albuquerque: University of New Mexico Press), 122–23; Lawrence J. Gray, 1980, "Species Composition and Life Histories of Aquatic Insects in a Lowland Sonoran Desert Stream," *American Midland Naturalist* 106:237–40.

Kanab Creek: quote, Kolb, *Through the Grand Canyon*, 249–50; Birdseye and Moore, "A Boat Voyage through the Grand Canyon," 190, complained that they "had hoped to find a good flow of clean, clear water here but found the stream nearly dry, and the little water that was flowing was slightly brackish"; Theodore S. Melis et al., 1993, "Magnitude and Frequency Data for Debris Flows in Grand Canyon National Park and Vicinity, Arizona" (USGS Open-File Report 94), 109; Earle E. Spamer and Arthur E. Bogan, 1993, "Mollusca of the Grand Canyon and Vicinity: New and Revised Data on Diversity and Distributions, with Notes on Pleistocene-Holocene Mollusks of the Grand Canyon," *Proceedings of the Academy of Natural Sciences of Philadelphia* 144:40–41.

Muav/Bright Angel: Turner and Karpiscak, *Recent Vegetation Changes*, 92–93; Potochnik and Reynolds, "Side Canyons," 479–80, 466; Peter W. Huntoon, 1989, "Gravity Tectonics, Grand Canyon, Arizona," in *Geology of Grand Canyon*, 220–21; Elston, "Pre-pleistocene(?) Deposits," 181–83.

End of 1871 trip: H. E. Gregory, 1939, Introduction, "Diary of Almon Harris Thompson," *Utah Historical Society* 7:7, "No scientific purpose would have been served by continuing a route previously explored. The south side of the river had been mapped by Ives in 1861; the north side and the canyon itself could be mapped most advantageously by land parties." Quotes, Don D. Fowler, ed., 1972, *Photographed All the Best Scenery: Jack Hiller's Diary of the Powell Expeditions, 1871–1875* (Salt Lake City: University of Utah Press), 140; Dellenbaugh, *Canyon Voyage*, 243–44.

Speckled dace/anchor worms: Minckley, "Native Fishes," 138, 140, 157–58; Allen S. Miller and Wayne A. Hubert, 1990, *Compendium of Existing Knowledge for Use in Making Habitat Management Recommendations for the Upper Colorado River Basin* (Denver: U.S. Fish and Wildlife Service, Region 6), 58, 195, 429; Richard Valdez, 1992–93, "A Fish with Finesse," *The News* 6(1):12–14 and insert, "Native Fishes of Grand Canyon."

Caddis fly net: Robert L. Usinger, 1956, *Aquatic Insects of California with Keys to North American Genera and California Species* (Berkeley and Los Angeles: University of California Press), 211–12, 237–38; D. G. Denning, 1956, "Trichoptera," in ibid., 247–50.

Bluehead suckers: Haden, "Nonnative Fishes," 19–20; Minckley, "Native Fishes," 137–39, 160–61; Miller and Hubert, *Compendium*, 192, 430.

5 Anasazi Ways and Stanton's Surveys

Cochineal bugs: Jerry A. Powell and Charles L. Hogue, 1979, *California Insects* (Berkeley and Los Angeles: University of California Press), 122–23; Renee S. Lizotte, 1992, "The Cochineal Legacy," *Sonorensis* 12(2):11; Daniel H. Janzen, 1979, "New Horizons in the Biology of Plant Defenses," in *Herbivores:*

Their Interaction with Secondary Plant Metabolites, ed. Gerald A. Rosenthal and Daniel H. Janzen (New York: Academic Press), 347–48; Gary A. Polis, 1991, "Food Webs in Desert Communities: Complexity via Diversity and Omnivory," in *Ecology of Desert Communities*, 395; Charles S. Wisdom, 1991, "Patterns of Heterogeneity in Desert Herbivorous Insect Communities," in *Ecology of Desert Communities*, 169–70; V. B. Wigglesworth, 1974, *Insect Physiology* (London: Chapman and Hall), 65–66.

South Canyon site: Dean J. Saitta, 1991, "Room Use and Community Organization at the Pettit Site, West Central New Mexico," *Kiva* 56(4):392–93; James N. Hill, 1972, "A Prehistoric Community in Eastern Arizona," in *Contemporary Archaeology: A Guide to Theory and Contributions*, ed. Mark P. Leone (Carbondale: Southern Illinois University Press), 323; Donald J. Hughes, 1978, *In the House of Stone and Light: A Human History of the Grand Canyon* (Grand Canyon: Grand Canyon Natural History Association), gives an overview of human occupation/use.

Length of occupation: Linda S. Cordell, 1984, *Prehistory of the Southwest* (Orlando, Fla.: Academic Press), 31–32, 34, 325.

Anasazi: "Anasazi" is the Navajo name that means "enemy ancestors," a term not relished by modern day Hopis, the direct descendants of the Anasazi, some of whom prefer the term "Hi'satsinam."

Kayenta Anasazi/trade/lifestyle: Robert C. Euler, 1988, "Demography and Cultural Dynamics on the Colorado Plateaus," in *The Anasazi in a Changing Environment*, ed. George J. Gumerman (Cambridge: School of American Research and Cambridge University Press), 193–94; Jonathan Haas, 1989, "The Evolution of the Kayenta Regional System," in *The Sociopolitical Structure of Prehistoric Southwestern Societies*, ed. Steadman Upham, Kent G. Lightfoot, and Roberta A. Jewett (Boulder, Colo.: Westview Press), 491, 493–97; George J. Gumerman and Jeffrey S. Dean, 1989, "Prehistoric Cooperation and Competition in the Western Anasazi Area," in *Dynamics of Southwest Prehistory*, ed. Linda S. Cordell and George J. Gumerman (Washington, D.C.: Smithsonian Institution Press), 100–7, 111 ("backwoods"), 117–18, 121, 133–36; this useful 1989 volume contains pertinent chapters: Linda S. Cordell and George J. Gumerman, "Cultural Interaction in the Prehistoric Southwest," and G. A. Johnson, "Dynamics of Southwestern Prehistory: Far Outside—Looking In"; Robert C. Euler, George J. Gumerman, Thor N. V. Karlstrom, Jeffrey S. Dean, and Richard H. Hevly, 1979, "The Colorado Plateaus: Cultural Dynamics and Paleoenvironment," *Science* 205:1090–91.

Stone tools/chert: R. L. Folk and C. E. Weaver, 1952, "A Study of the Texture and Composition of Chert," *American Journal of Science* 250:503.

Number of sites/occupancy: *Draft EIS*, 51; Robert C. Euler, 1969, "The Archaeology of the Canyon Country," in *John Wesley Powell and the Anthropology of* the Canyon Country, ed. Don D. Fowler, Robert C. Euler, and Catherine S. Fowler (Washington, D.C.: USGS Professional Paper 678), 8; Euler, 1967, "Helicopter Archeology," American West Review 1(1); Euler, "Demography and Cultural Dynamics," 193–94; Hereford, Fairley, Thompson, and Balsom, "Surficial Geology, Geomorphology, and Erosion," 12, 14–16; A. Trinkle Jones, ed., 1986, A Cross Section of Grand Canyon Archaeology: Excavations at Five Sites along the Colorado River (Tucson: Western Archaeological and Conservation Center, NPS, Publications in Anthropology 28), found two thousand sites in the whole canyon (see the Introduction, 1, and Chronology, 99); Jan Balsom, (n.d.), Unkar Delta Guide (Flagstaff: Grand Canyon Natural History Association), later added five hundred more.

Hunters-gatherers/sharing: Michael A. Jochim, 1976, Hunter-Gatherer Subsistence and Settlement: A Predictive Model (New York: Academic Press), 7, 11–12, 17, 21–24, 47–49; E. S. Wing and A. B. Brown, 1979, Paleonutrition, Method and Theory in Prehistoric Foodways (New York: Academic Press), 93–94, foraging is an individual activity with found food eaten on the spot, while gathering is a shared activity; Johnson, "Dynamics of Southwestern Prehistory," 372, 379–82, 384–85; Paul Shepard, 1978, Thinking Animals (New York: Viking Press), 141; Fred Plog, George J. Gumerman, Jeffrey S. Dean, Robert C. Euler, Thor N. V. Karlstrom, and Richard Helvy, 1988, "Anasazi Adaptive Strategies: The Model, Predictions, and Results," in The Anasazi in a Changing Environment, ed. George J. Gumerman (Cambridge: School of American Research and Cambridge University Press), 258–59; Jones, Cross Section of Grand Canyon Archaeology, 331–32.

Plant knowledge and use: Hutira, "Analysis of Plants, Pollen, and Coprolites," 295–98, 300–1; Robert E. Gasser, 1982, "Pueblo Plant Foods," Pacific Discovery 35(1):27–28; Cordell, Prehistory of the Southwest, 27–28, 31–32; Wing and Brown, Paleonutrition, 93–94, 161–62, 165; Johns, With Bitter Herbs They Shall Eat It, 2, 7, 9, 220, 227–240, 257–58; John F. Doebley, 1984, "Seeds of Wild Grasses: A Major Food of Southwest Indians," Economic Botany 38(10):62; Katharine Bartlett, 1943, "Edible Wild Plants of Northern Arizona," Plateau 16(1):11–17, presents a detailed listing of plants and their use; Jesse Jennings, 1966, Glen Canyon: A Summary (Salt Lake City: University of Utah, Anthropological Paper 81), 21, found that prehistoric tribes used a substantial percent of the over ninety plant species in the Glen Canyon area for food, medicine, and tools.

Yucca: R. H. Whittaker, 1970, "The Biochemical Ecology of Higher Plants," in Chemical Ecology, ed. Ernest Sondheimer and John B. Simeone (New York: Academic Press), 56.

Hunting: Jochim, Hunter-Gatherer Subsistence and Settlement, 22–24; Douglas W. Schwartz, Richard C. Chapman, and Jane Kepp, 1980, Archaeology of the

Grand Canyon: Unkar Delta (Santa Fe: School of American Research Press), 37–39, 187–88.

Paleonutrition: Wing and Brown, *Paleonutrition*, 2, 17, 21–23, 29, an extra 5 percent of calories are needed to work in temperatures below 55°F or above 99°F; Steven R. James, 1990, "Monitoring Archaeofaunal Changes during the Transition to Agriculture in the American Southwest," *Kiva* 56(1):27–29; Gary F. Fry, 1985, "Analysis of Fecal Material," in *The Analysis of Prehistoric Diets*, ed. Robert I. Gilbert, Jr., and James H. Mielke (New York: Academic Press), 127, coprolite analysis is one of the most reliable ways of establishing prehistoric diet, for it records food actually eaten; Boyd S. Eaton, and Melvin Konner, 1985, "Paleolithic Nutrition: A Consideration of Its Nature and Current Implications," *New England Journal of Medicine* 312:285–88, the vitamin intake of prehistoric people substantially exceeded ours because of the wide variety of food, and they ate not only much less fat but a fat substantially different from that in modern diets, so their diet "may be a reference standard for modern human nutrition and a model for defense against certain 'diseases of civilization.'"

Pottery removal: Arizona Archeological and Historical Society, 1992, "On Personal Collection and Purchase of Prehistoric Artifacts," *Glyphs* 42(7):8, "Whenever an artifact is removed from an archaeological site without careful regard for how it is situated relative to other artifacts, biological materials, and the soil that envelops it, both the artifact and the archaeological site lose some of their potential for providing information about the people who used the artifact and lived at the site"; Balsom, *Unkar Delta Guide*, "Archeological remains are vulnerable and irreplaceable. Our key to unraveling the past is having all artifacts intact and in position relative to one another . . . Not only will disturbing the sites destroy valuable information, *it is illegal*."

Tusayan Corrugated: Cordell, *Prehistory of the Southwest*, 17, 211, 216–18; Schwartz, Chapman, and Kepp, *Unkar Delta*, 124–25, 137–38, 311–313; Stephen Plog, 1980, *Stylistic Variation in Prehistoric Ceramics: Design Analysis in the American Southwest* (Cambridge: Cambridge University Press), 15, 17–18, 27, 83–88, 93–94; Lyndon L. Hargrave, 1974, "Type Determinants in Southwestern Ceramics and Some of Their Implications," *Plateau* 46(3):79–81, "through interpretations made from its [the ceramic's] physical properties, we may draw inferences about peoples; about materials used and manner of use; about time of use and date of manufacture; about similarities and differences in artistic expression; about cultural contacts and areas occupied and abandoned; about trade routes and lanes of migration; about domestic living patterns; about climate, ecology, economy, and many other things."

Brown expedition: Lavender, *River Runners*, 22–23, characterizes Brown as "overweight and impatient" and "given to glimpsing the end of a scheme without worrying unduly about the problems along the way"; Dellenbaugh,

Canyon Voyage, 348–49, "Being a brave, energetic man it was hard for him to believe that this river demanded so much extra prudence and caution, when Powell had successfully descended it twice without, so far as the water was concerned, losing a man"; Lewis R. Freeman, 1924, "Surveying the Grand Canyon of the Colorado: An Account of the 1923 Boating Expedition of the United States Geological Survey," *National Geographic Magazine* 45(5):293–96, who accompanied the Birdseye Expedition in 1923, points out that although boat dimensions were close to those of modern dories, shape and construction were very different (e.g., dories have flat bottoms), and "the inclusion of the open dory in the outfit, and the attempt to raft provisions down the cataracts on the astonishing 'flotilla,' need no comment."

Stanton expedition: Quote, Stanton, *Down the Colorado*, 8, and Stanton, 1892, "The Proposed Railway through the Grand Canyon of the Colorado," *Scientific American* 66:369, a speech read before the American Society of Civil Engineers in which Stanton stated, "The immense width of the canon on top prevents the great mass of rock loosened from above by storms reaching the inner or lower gorge in a way to do any damage," a remarkably naive statement to say the least; Stanton, 1890, "Col. Stanton's Recent Descent of the Colorado River," *American Naturalist* 24:463–66, a speech to the American Society of Civil Engineers; Christmas dinner from p. 246.

Nims: Franklin A. Nims, 1962, *The Photographer and the River, 1889–1890: The Colorado Canyon Diary of Franklin Nims*, ed. Dwight L. Smith (Santa Fe: Stagecoach Press), 63–67, Nims was heroically cared for according to the entry Nims cites from the diary of Leo G. Brown, a member of the party who helped carry Nims out and wrote that they "had great difficulty in carrying him. Impeded by high rocks and overhanging shelves. Had to work over waterfalls, through cracks in the crags, and wade through muddy pools holding him up. Several times had to lift him up rocks with ropes while we held one another from slipping. A fall would have hurled him hundreds of feet below. In less than half a mile climbed nine hundred feet. Carried him in all two and half miles and 1,700 feet up; took eight hours. Nims unconscious all the time."

Photographic record: Freeman, "Surveying the Grand Canyon," 308–10, on loss; Nims, *The Photographer and the River*, 71; Lavender, *River Runners*, 26–30; Stanton *Down the Colorado*, 116–17, 175–76; Melis et al., "Debris Flows," 21, aerial surveys were made from 1935 to 1992.

Mining venture: Lavender, *Colorado River Country*, 159–61, Stanton did find gold in 1898, staked claims upriver, and established the Hoskaninni Company of which Julius Stone was president; Stanton, vice-president, engineer, and superintendent; and Nathaniel Galloway, boatman; the amount actually recovered was less than $100 because most of it was flour gold that would not separate out easily, and the company went bankrupt.

Split-twig figurines: Webb, *Riverman: The Story of Bus Hatch*, 45–46; Robert C. Euler, 1984, "The Archaeology and Geology of Stanton's Cave," in *The Archaeology, Geology, and Paleobiology of Stanton's Cave*, ed. Robert Euler (Grand Canyon National Park: Grand Canyon Natural History Association, Monograph 6) [volume hereafter *Stanton's Cave*], 18–19, 30, all figurines were recovered within ten centimeters of the surface; Euler, 1966, "Willow Figurines from Arizona," *Natural History* 75:62–66; Jones, *Cross Section of Grand Canyon Archaeology*, 7, 133–34, suggests that the figure makers were probably members of the Middle Archaic Pinto culture; Stephen C. Jett, 1968, "Grand Canyon Dams, Split-Twig Figurines, and 'Hit-and-Run' Archaeology," *American Antiquity* 33:343–44, 348–49, of all the figures found in Colorado, Nevada, Utah, and Arizona, more than half are from Grand Canyon.

Stanton's Cave: George C. Simmons and David L. Gaskill, 1969, *River Runners' Guide to the Canyons of the Green and Colorado Rivers: Marble Gorge and Grand Canyon* (Flagstaff: Northland Press and Powell Society), 42, a good geologic guide by mile issued on the centennial of Powell's first trip, shows from the height of Stanton's Cave the clear continuation of the fissure across the river; Arthur L. Lange, 1955, "The Role of Caves in Dating Grand Canyon," *Plateau* 27(3):1–4; P. T. Reilly, 1967, "The Pirated Spring at Stanton Cave," *Caves and Karst* 9(1):5; Otis R. Marston, 1979, "Commentary on Part One: James White's Raft Journey of 1867," in *Colorado River Controversies*, ed. R. B. Stanton (Boulder City, Nev.: Westwater Books, reprint 1982), 247; during these low flows, in August 1963, Marston made the first Sportyak run of the canyon.

Contents of Stanton's Cave: William J. Breed, 1967, "Arizona's Oldest Amphibian," *Plateau* 40(2):69; Jones, *Cross Section of Grand Canyon Archaeology*, 1–4; Euler's *Stanton's Cave* contains a number of estimable papers about one of the most fascinating areas of the Grand Canyon, including Amadeo Rea and Lyndon Hargrave, 1984, "The Bird Bones from Stanton's Cave," 79–88.

Condors: Raymond DeSaussure, 1956, "Remains of the California Condor in Arizona Caves," *Plateau* 29:44–45; Rob Story, 1992, "Wild Things?" *Outside* 17(1):19–20, the Fish and Wildlife Condor Recovery Program has used its $25 million to double the population since 1987 with the object of releasing fifty birds back into the wild.

Otters: Carothers and Brown, *Natural History of the Colorado River*, 105–6, otter sightings 1982–92; E. A. Goldman, 1937, "The Colorado River as a Barrier in Mammalian Distribution," *Journal of Mammalogy* 18:430; quote, Stone, *Canyon Country*, 93–94; Kolb, *Through the Grand Canyon*, 259, noticed "otters disporting themselves near our boats, in one instance unafraid, in another raising a gray-bearded head near our boat with a startled look in his eyes. Then he turned and began to swim on the surface until our laughter caused him to dive."

Harrington's mountain goat: Paul S. Martin, 1984, "Stanton's Cave during and after the Last Ice Age," in *Stanton's Cave*, 134–35, points out that this is the same time that mammoth bones were found in southern Arizona in association with Clovis points, suggesting a possible common cause in the extinction of goats, ground sloths, and mammoths by PaleoIndians; Eleanora I. Robbins, Paul S. Martin, and Austin Long, 1984, "Paleoecology of Stanton's Cave, Grand Canyon, Arizona," in *Stanton's Cave*, 125; this date also coincides with the last record of Shasta ground sloths from Rampart Cave in the lower Grand Canyon; C. R. Harrington, 1984, "Ungulate Remains from Stanton's Cave: An Identification List," in *Stanton's Cave*, 69.

Paleoclimate: R. H. Hevly and T. N. V. Karlstrom, 1974, "Southwest Paleoclimate and Continental Correlations," in *Geology of Northern Arizona with Notes on Archaeology and Paleoclimate*, ed. Thor N. V. Karlstrom, Gordon A. Swann, and Raymond L. Eastwood (Flagstaff: Northern Arizona University, Museum of Northern Arizona, and Geological Society of America, Rocky Mountain Section), 261; according to Robbins, Martin, and Long, "Paleoecology of Stanton's Cave," 117–18, 123–25, the date is plus or minus two hundred years.

Driftwood: Lucchitta, personal communication, April 1994; *Stanton's Cave*, 11; C. W. Ferguson, 1984, "Dendrochronology of Driftwood from Stanton's Cave," in *Stanton's Cave*, 95–96, 98, thinks the river probably carried in the logs twelve thousand years ago; Hereford, "Driftwood, Stanton's Cave: The Case for Temporary Damming of the Colorado River," 101, 104–5; Donald P. Elston, 1984, "Polarity of River-Flood Silt in Stanton's Cave, Marble Canyon, Arizona," in *Stanton's Cave*, 109–10.

Vasey's Paradise: Lange, "The Role of Caves in Dating Grand Canyon," 17; Karpiscak, "Vegetational Changes," 10–11, plant species in a 1924 photograph are almost identical to those shown in 1974, although with the lack of scouring floods, many plants have edged downward, and shoulder-high tamarisk now grow on a sandbar that was bare in the earlier photograph; Czarnecki, Blinn, and Tompkins, *A Periphytic Microflora Analysis*, 7–8, report a temperature variation less than 2°C.

Kanab amber snail: Spamer and Bogan, "Mollusca of the Grand Canyon and Vicinity," 37, 46–47, 55–56, consider Vasey's the most "diverse and productive river corridor molluscan" habitat; the type location of the endangered snail (1992 listing) is near Kanab in two small, now-polluted springs, and Vasey's is now its only known habitat in Arizona; *Final EIS*, 139.

Poison ivy: One botanist calls it "weakly" poisonous, another calls it "virulent," while Martin, "Trees and Shrubs," 9, calls it "potent"; the other patch of ivy is along the path at Deer Creek at Mile 136.2.

Devonian channels: Huntoon, "Gravity Tectonics," 267–68; Hamblin, "Summary of the Stratigraphy of the Western Grand Canyon Region," 31.

Split-twig figurine diagrams: A. Trinkle Jones and Robert C. Euler, 1979, *A Sketch of Grand Canyon Prehistory* (Grand Canyon Natural History Association); Jett, "Grand Canyon Dams, Split-Twig Figurines," 346–47.

6 Redwall Cavern and Dam Sites

Redwall Cavern: The cavern is now off limits for camping; Turner and Karpiscak, *Recent Vegetation Changes*, 60–61; W. Kenneth Hamblin and J. Keith Rigby, 1968, *Guidebook to the Colorado River, Part 1: Lee's Ferry to Phantom Ranch in Grand Canyon National Park* (Provo, Utah: Brigham Young University), 42–43, an excellent geological river guide (the lower river is covered in *Guidebook to the Colorado River, Part 2: Phantom Ranch in Grand Canyon National Park to Lake Mead, Arizona-Nevada*); Potochnik and Reynolds, "Side Canyons," 472–73; Freeman, "Surveying the Grand Canyon," 513–14, thought Powell's estimate of seating fifty thousand too liberal and described the cavern floor as "a succession of terraces of hard, smooth sand, rising like the seats of a stadium until the highest touched the vault of the limestone roof." The terraces no longer exist.

Crinoids: Edwin D. McKee, 1931, "Crinoidal Limestone," *Grand Canyon Nature Notes* 5(12):126–27.

Ant lions: Polis and Yamashita, "The Ecology and Importance of Predaceous Arthropods," 190; Askew, *Parasitic Insects*, 166–67; Heinrich, *Hot-Blooded Insects*, 406; quote, White, *The Bestiary*, 214.

Spiders: Richard Quartaroli, personal communication, May 1994; Lorus Milne and Margery Milne, 1980, *The Audubon Society Field Guide to North American Insects and Spiders* (New York: Knopf), 874–75, confirm these must be desert recluse spiders, *Loxosceles deserta*; the venomous brown recluse does not live in the Southwest.

Nautiloid Canyon: William J. Breed, 1969, "The Discovery of Orthocone Nautiloids in the Redwall Limestone—Marble Canyon, Arizona," in *Geologic and Natural History of the Grand Canyon Region*, ed. D. L. Baars (Durango, Colo.: Four Corners Geological Association), 134; Potochnik and Reynolds, "Side Canyons," 471–73.

Leaf-cutting bees: Linsley, "Temporal Patterns of Flower Visitation," 536–37, 539–42, and Linsley, "The Ecology of Solitary Bees," 5552–59, 5565–66, 5571–73; Clifford S. Crawford, 1991, "The Community Ecology of Macroarthropod Detritivores," in *Ecology of Desert Communities*, 76–77; Andrew J. Beattie, 1985, *The Evolutionary Ecology of Ant-Plant Mutualisms* (Cambridge: Cambridge University Press), 106–8; see also Richard M. Duffield, James W.

Wheeler, and George C. Eickwort, 1984, "Sociochemicals of Bees," in *Chemical Ecology of Insects*, ed. William J. Bell and Ring T. Cardé (Sunderland, Mass.: Sinauer Associates), 388, 399, Quote, J. Henri Fabre, 1991, *The Insect World of J. Henri Fabre*, introduction and notes by Edwin Way Teale (Boston: Beacon Press), 276, also 274–75.

Crab spiders: Polis and Yamashita, "The Ecology and Importance of Predaceous Arthropods in Desert Communities," 184; Robert L. Smith, 1982, *Venomous Animals of Arizona* (Tucson: University of Arizona, College of Agriculture), 17–18.

Dam explorations: The 1952 test adit for the proposed Marble Canyon Dam is at Mile 32.8; at Mile 39.3 are the 1946 test adits made on both sides of the river; Neely H. Bostick, 1937, "The Caves of Marble Gorge, Grand Canyon," *Caves and Karst* 9(1):3–4, to prevent river silts from clogging the Marble Canyon Dam generators, an additional dam was planned at the mouth of the Paria River; U.S. Department of Interior, Bureau of Reclamation, 1946, *The Colorado River: A Comprehensive Report on the Development of the Water Resources of the Colorado River Basin for Irrigation, Power Production, and Other Beneficial Uses in Arizona, California, Colorado, Nevada, New Mexico, Utah, and Wyoming* (Washington, D.C.: U.S. Government Printing Office), is the rationale for damming throughout the Colorado River system; Freeman, "Surveying the Grand Canyon," 493–94.

LaRue: Lavender, *River Runners*, 59, 66, by 1923 LaRue favored a Lees Ferry site over Boulder Canyon; Dawdy, "Hydrology of Glen Canyon," 44–45, LaRue insisted on his ideas so vociferously that he was asked to express them someplace else than in government; LaRue's photographs of the Birdseye trip are in the USGS Library, Denver Federal Center.

Fradkin, *River No More*, 104, "The management of water sometimes is advanced as an end in itself. Flowing from a basic tenet of occidental philosophy that nature, distinct from man, exists to serve him, is a strong and pervasive view of man as a manipulator of nature, and this view places premium on technical proficiency in regulating water volume and quality. Arguments for controlling the flow of the Colorado and for transporting water long distances to make the desert bloom reflect the view than an uncontrolled resource is a wasted resource and that if man has the capacity to control and completely utilize the water of a river he should do so."

Mud daubers: Charles T. Brues, 1946, *Insects, Food, and Ecology* (New York: Dover Publications), 264.

Sand wasps: William O. Romoser, 1973, *The Science of Entomology* (New York: Macmillan), 185; Heinrich, *Hot-Blooded Insects*, 340–41; Fabre, *The Insect World*, 115–20, 116–17: "The spray of dust, kept up evenly for five or ten minutes at a time, is enough to show the dazzling rapidity of the tools employed . . . as it advances and retires first on this side, then on that, without discontinuing its parabolic streams of sand," and quote, 120.

Pheromones: Murray S. Blum, 1974, "Pheromonal Bases of Social Manifestations in Insects," in *Pheromones*, ed. Martin C. Birch (New York: American Elsevier Publishing), 191, and Blum, 1974, "Pheromonal Sociality in the Hymenoptera," in ibid., 222–49; quote, E. O. Wilson, 1992, *The Diversity of Life* (New York: W. W. Norton), 4; E. O. Wilson, 1970, "Chemical Communication within Animal Species," in *Chemical Ecology*, ed. Ernest Sondheimer and John B. Simeone (New York: Academic Press), 133–34, 137–39.

Termites: P. E. Howse, 1984, "Sociochemicals of Termites," in *Chemical Ecology*, 475–76; William MacKay, 1991, "The Role of Ants and Termites in Desert Communities," in *Ecology of Desert Communities*, 114, 122, 132–35; John A. Wallwork, 1982, *Desert Soil Fauna* (New York: Praeger Publishers), 56–58, 99–100, 155, 203, 259; M. V. Brian, 1983, *Social Insects: Ecology and Behavioural Biology*, (London: Chapman and Hall), 158–59, 302–3; Susan Jones, 1985, "New Termite Records for the Grand Canyon," *Southwestern Entomologist* 10(2):137–38; B. Moore, 1974, "Pheromones in the Termite Societies," in *Pheromones*, ed. Martin C. Birch (New York: American Elsevier Publishing), 251, 259–260; M. V. Brian, 1978, Introduction, in *Production Ecology of Ants and Termites*, ed. M. V. Brian (Cambridge: Cambridge University Press), 3; T. G. Wood and W. A. Sands, 1978, "The Role of Termites in Ecosystems," in *Production Ecology*, 245; T. G. Wood, 1978, "Food and Feeding Habits of Termites," in *Production Ecology*, 55, 65; Beattie, *The Evolutionary Ecology*, 16; Douglas W. Whitman, Murray S. Blum, David W. Alsop, 1990, "Allomones: Chemicals for Defense," in *Insect Defenses*, ed. David L. Evans and Justin O. Schmidt (Albany: State University of New York Press), 290.

Termites' cellulose diet: Janzen, "New Horizons in the Biology of Plant Defenses," 347–48; Wigglesworth, *Insect Physiology*, 58, notes the "amazing population of flagellates, ciliates, and spirochaetes" that make digesting cellulose possible; David F. Rhoades, 1979, "Evolution of Plant Chemical Defense against Herbivores," in *Herbivores*, 43; J. P. LaFage and W. L. Nutting, 1978, "Nutrient Dynamics of Termites," in Brian, *Production Ecology*, 166.

Eminence Break Trail/Fault: E. M. Shoemaker, R. L. Squires, and M. J. Abrams, 1974, "The Bright Angel and Mesa Butte Fault Systems of Northern Arizona," in *Geology of Northern Arizona with Notes on Archaeology and Paleoclimate*, ed. Thor N. V. Karlstrom, Gordon A. Swann, and Raymond L. Eastwood (Flagstaff: Northern Arizona University, Museum of Northern Arizona, and Geological Society of America, Rocky Mountain Section), 102–3.

Radio: Freeman, "Surveying the Grand Canyon," 477, 480–82, 497–99, 508, Birdseye's was the first expedition to use a radio, disproving conventional wisdom that radios were useless in a canyon.

Stanton/Hansbrough: Lavender, *River Runners*, 61–62; quote, Stanton, *Down the Colorado*, 132.

Derivation of Grand Canyon flora: Kenneth Cole, 1985, "Past Rates of Change, Species Richness, and a Model of Vegetational Inertia in the Grand Canyon, Arizona," *American Naturalist* 125:289–300; Clover and Jotter, "Floristic Studies in the Canyon," 608–9, 612–15; Phillips, Phillips, and Bernzott, *Annotated Checklist of Vascular Plants*, 4–5, 7, 54; Peter L. Warren, Karen L. Reichhardt, David A. Mouat, Bryan T. Brown, and R. Roy Johnson, 1982, *Vegetation of Grand Canyon National Park* (Tucson: NPS/University of Arizona, Technical Report 9), 1, 10–11, 96–99; Goldman, "The Colorado River as a Barrier," 429–30; Donald A. Jameson, 1969, "Rainfall Patterns on Vegetation Zones in Northern Arizona," *Plateau* 41(3):105–7; O. J. Reichman and George A. Ruffner, 1977, "Life in a Narrow World: Grand Canyon Ecology," *Plateau* 49:21–23; Carothers and Brown, *Natural History of the Colorado River*, 112–16; Bennett, "Some Notes on the Vegetation," 25–27, this terrain has led to "survival of divers plants of unstandardized types and the preservation of species and even genera for very long periods of geological time . . . the Grand Canyon Desert is not uniform in kinds of plants, their heights, their physiognomy or any other single character."

Blackbrush/perennial plant adaptations: Hugh Mozingo, 1984, *Shrubs of the Great Basin* (Las Vegas: University of Nevada Press), 157.

Cryptobiotic crusts: Cynta de Navarez, 1992, "Unappreciated, Misunderstood, and Downtrodden," *The News* 5(2):14–15; quote, 14.

Checkered white butterfly: Richard A. Bailowitz and James P. Brock, 1991, *Butterflies of Southeastern Arizona* (Tucson: Sonoran Arthropod Studies), 142; Frances S. Chew, 1977, "Coevolution of Pierid Butterflies and Their Cruciferous Foodplants, II: The Distribution of Eggs on Potential Foodplants," *Evolution* 31:568, 575–78; P. R. Erlich and P. H. Raven, 1964, "Butterflies and Plants: A Study in Coevolution," *Evolution* 18:599–602; Heinrich, *Hot-Blooded Insects*, 78–79, 515–16.

Rockfall: Julia B. Graf, John C. Schmidt, and Susan W. Kieffer, 1989, "Hydraulic Log of the Colorado River from Lees Ferry to Diamond Creek, Arizona," in *Geology of Grand Canyon*, 42.

7 Toads and Frogs and Unconformities

Amphibians: Bobbi S. Low, 1976, "The Evolution of Amphibian Life Histories in the Desert," in *Evolution of Desert Biota*, ed. David W. Goodall (Austin: University of Texas Press), 174–78; Smith, *Venomous Animals*, 99–101, 174–76; Reichman and Ruffner, "Life in a Narrow World," 22–23.

Great Unconformity/time gap/Vishnu Schist: Seymour L. Fishbein, 1991, *Grand Canyon Country: Its Majesty and Its Lore* (Washington, D.C.: National Geographic Society), 91; Michael Morales, 1990, "Mesozoic and Cenozoic Strata of the Colorado Plateau near the Grand Canyon," in Beus and Morales, *Grand Canyon Geology*, 247; see also Potochnik and Reynolds, "Side Canyons," in the same collection, 461–64; Brad Ilg and Karl Karlstrom, "Metamorphics for the Geologically Impaired—Granite Gorge Schists, Granites and Time," *The News* 15(4):13–16.

Tapeats Sandstone: Quotes, Stanton, *Down the Colorado*, 148; Charles D. Walcott, 1883, "Pre-carboniferous Strata in the Grand Cañon of the Colorado, Arizona," *American Journal of Science* (3d ser.) 26:439; Charles W. Barnes, 1989, "Early Proterozoic Rocks of Grand Canyon, Arizona," in *Geology of Grand Canyon*, 91; Potochnik and Reynolds, "Side Canyons," 477–78, age of Tapeats; Peter W. Huntoon, 1989, "Setting of the Precambrian Basement Complex, Grand Canyon, Arizona," 74–76, and Donald P. Elston, 1989, "Correlations and Facies Changes in Lower and Middle Cambrian Tonto Group, Grand Canyon, Arizona," 132–33, both in *Geology of Grand Canyon*; Larry T. Middleton and David K. Elliott, 1990, "Tonto Group," in Beus and Morales, *Grand Canyon Geology*, 88, 98–101; L. F. Noble, 1914, *The Shinumo Quadrangle, Grand Canyon District, Arizona* (Washington, D.C.: USGS Bulletin 549), 62, "Within the Tapeats sandstone is a record of marine planation that in these vertical sections, which include no soil, is preserved with a clearness that is almost beyond belief . . . No more striking example of a fossil sea cliff can be imagined."

Water tiger: Thomas Eisner, 1970, "Chemical Defense against Predation in Arthropods," in *Chemical Ecology of Insects*, ed. William J. Bell and Ring T. Cardé (Sunderland, Mass.: Sinauer Associates), 193; Wigglesworth, *Insect Physiology*, 53–54; Pennak, *Fresh-Water Invertebrates*, 595–97, 601–2; Spamer and Bogan, "Mollusca of the Grand Canyon and Vicinity," 40, 45–46. Snails are probably Physidae, the most abundant aquatic mollusk in the canyon.

Insect adaptations for water: Ward and Kondratieff, *Mountain Stream Insects of Colorado*, 14; Wigglesworth, *Insect Physiology*, 6–7, 53–54, 140; Pennak, *Fresh-Water Invertebrates*, 488–90, 595–97, 601; even more efficient is to have a thick pile of fine, short, curved-tip hairs to entrap air, sometimes packed more than 2 million per square millimeter of body surface; the hairs resist the pressure of water to compress inheld air space so the volume of air in the film remains constant, and if the water is more than 80 percent saturated with oxygen, pile-bearing insects can remain submerged almost indefinitely.

Bass: William Wallace Bass, ed., 1920, *Adventures in the Canyons of the Colorado by Two of Its Earliest Explorers, James White and W. W. Hawkins* (Grand Canyon: James White and W. W. Hawkins), 8–9, "Up to this time I had never met him [Powell] and when in 1887 he employed me as a guide in some triangulation work on Bill Williams Mountain I was thoroughly convinced as to the doubtful character of certain statements he made to me regarding other work of the same nature he claimed to have done some years previous."

Separation Canyon: Lavender, *River Runners*, 12–13, 16–17; George Y. Bradley, 1947, "Diary," in "Biographical Sketches and Original Documents of the First Powell Expedition of 1869," ed. W. E. Darrah, *Utah Historical Quarterly* 15:70, 72; Frank D. Tikalsky, 1982, "Historical Controversy, Science, and Powell," *Journal of Arizona History* 23:407–21.

Powell's book: Quote, Robert Brewster Stanton, ed., 1932, *Colorado River Controversies* (Boulder City, Nev.: Westwater Books, reprint 1982), 231; Martin J. Anderson, 1979, "Commentary on Part Two: The Affair at Separation Rapids," in ibid., 255–56, that the book was done under pressure from the House Appropriations Committee does not excuse Powell telling Stanton he had written it all in the canyon; Stanton's quote from Sumner's account, ibid., xlii and 104; James M. Chalfant, 1932, Preface, ibid., xvi, "the Major was his own historian, but unfortunately an historian who chose to dress up the facts a bit in his own favor, even at the cost of placing the stigma of cowardice and desertion upon certain of his companions in adventure"; Gregory, Introduction, "Diary of Almon Harris Thompson," 8, criticizes Powell for using notes and maps of other members of the trip without acknowledgment, and for meager scientific results although the 1869 trip "ranks among the most distinguished feats in the history of exploration."

Leamy: Wesley P. Larsen, 1993, "The 'Letter' or Were the Powell Men Really Killed by Indians?" *Canyon Legacy* (Southern Utah Society of Arts and Sciences) 17:12–19. I am indebted to Scott Thybony for Larsen's paper.

Quote: W. E. Darrah, ed., 1947, "Biographical Sketches and Original Documents of the First Powell Expedition of 1869: Newspaper Reports of the Expedition's End . . ." *Utah Historical Quarterly* 15:145.

Lake Mead shore growth: Turner and Karpiscak, *Recent Vegetation Changes*, 1; Arthur M. Phillips III, 1975, "Flora of the Rampart Cave Area, Lower Grand Canyon, Arizona," *Journal of the Arizona Academy of Science* 10:150; Carothers and Brown, *Natural History of the Colorado River*, 24–25.

Wolves: Stone, *Canyon Country*, 103, just below the mouth of Grand Wash, "We see five wolves and several bobcats below the end of the Canyon. I stop and try to get a bobcat, but it disappears among the rocks before I can get a shot." Quote, Henry D. Thoreau, 1852, *The Journals of Henry D. Thoreau* (New York: Dover Publications, 1962 reprint), III:409.

Grand Wash Fault: Quote, Ivo Lucchitta, 1974, "Structural Evolution of Northwest Arizona and Its Relation to Adjacent Basin and Range Province Structures," in *Geology of Northern Arizona with Notes on Archaeology and Paleoclimate*, ed. Thor N. V. Karlstrom, Gordon A. Swann, and Raymond L.

Eastwood (Flagstaff: Northern Arizona University, Museum of Northern Arizona, and Geological Society of America, Rocky Mountain Section), 318, also 341, 344–45; Shoemaker, Squires, and Abrams, "The Bright Angel and Mesa Butte Fault Systems," 383; George H. Billingsley and John D. Hendricks, 1989, "Physiographic Features of Northwestern Arizona," in *Geology of Grand Canyon*, 67.

Quote: Ivo Lucchitta, 1990, "History of the Grand Canyon and of the Colorado River in Arizona," in Beus and Morales, *Grand Canyon Geology*, 318; this and Lucchitta, 1988, "Canyon Maker: Geological History of the Colorado River," *Plateau* 59(2), are the most authoritative and current views; Donald P. Elston and Richard A. Young, 1989, "Development of Cenozoic Landscape of Central and Northern Arizona: Cutting of Grand Canyon," in *Geology of Grand Canyon*, 145; for historical interest, W. M. Davis, 1901, "An Excursion to the Grand Canyon of the Colorado," *Bulletin of the Museum of Comparative Zoology* 38, Geological Series 5(4):158–184; Richard A. Young, 1970, "Geomorphological Implications of Pre-Colorado and Colorado Tributary Drainage in the Western Grand Canyon Region," *Plateau* 42(3):107, 113–15; Eric T. Karlstrom, 1986, "Physiographic Context for Three Archeological Sites," in Jones, *Cross Section of Grand Canyon Archaeology*, 15, potassium-argon dating of lava flows suggests that the river had not established its present course until after about 5.5 million years ago and had cut to within fifty feet of its present position by 1.2 million years ago.

Quotes: Bradley, "Diary," 72; Powell, *Exploration of the Colorado River*, 285; Stanton, *Down the Colorado*, 220; Flavell: Carmony and Brown, *The Log of the Panthon*, 73; Buzz (Haldane) Holmstrom, 1993–94, "Down the Colorado: The Diary of Buzz Holmstrom," *The News* 7(1):34, November 31, 1937; Stone, *Canyon Country*, 103, November 15, 1909.

8 Badger Creek and Running Rapids

Coconino rockfall: Russell Grater and Harold E. Hawkins, "Rock Slide in the Coconino Sandstone," *Grand Canyon Nature Notes* 9(10):368–69.

Badger: John C. Schmidt, [1992?], "Temporal and Spatial Changes in Sediment Storage in Grand Canyon," in *Variable Discharge Regimes*, 12. Quotes: Birdseye and Moore, "A Boat Voyage through the Grand Canyon," 183; Eddy: Webb, *Riverman: The Story of Bus Hatch*, 49; Flavell: Carmony and Brown, *The Log of the Panthon*, 50, Badger "came very near being our last . . . I don't suppose it was more than 20 seconds from the time we entered till we were out, so a person don't have much time to think. But after one is safe and thinks of it, they wonder how it was that the waves gave up when they had the power. It cannot be that water has mercy"; and Holmstrom, "Diary," 30.

Rapids: Graf, Schmidt, and Kieffer, "Hydraulic Log," 37–38; Melis et al., "Debris Flows," 43–44; William L. Graf, 1979, "Rapids in Canyon Rivers," *Journal of Geology* 87:548, 533, defines a rapid as "an accumulation of boulders in a perennial river where the debris particles are numerous enough or large enough to break the water surface at mean annual discharge"; Dolan, Howard, and Gallenson, "Man's Impact on the Colorado River," 393, on the gradient.

Velocity/hydraulics in rapids: Susan Kieffer, 1990, "Hydraulics and Geomorphology of the Colorado River in the Grand Canyon," in Beus and Morales, *Grand Canyon Geology*, 372, gives the following speeds in rapids: 15–25 feet per second on the tongue to values greater than 30 feet per second in constriction and part of the diverging section and 15 feet per second maintained through the tailwaves; at 338–39, she lists and describes the different kinds of waves in a rapid; Lawrence E. Stevens, 1985, "The 67 Elephant Theory or Learning to Boat Big Water Hydraulics," *River Runner* 5(1):25, "Let's put it this way; at 32,000 cfs, 1,000 tons of water are moving through the river channel every second. If an average elephant weighs about 5 tons, this means that the flow of the river is equal to 200 elephants skipping by every second. A hole in the river may take up about a third of the channel, so the hydraulic dynamics in that hole are about the same as 67 elephants jumping up and down on your boat." Stevens's excellent mile-by-mile river guide, *The Colorado River in Grand Canyon* (Flagstaff: Red Lake Books), is full of natural history information.

Boatmen/boatwomen: I use "boatmen" for both men and women in respect of the preference of a majority of boatwomen who addressed this specific question in 1991 in *The News* 4(4):7, such as Jeri Ledbetter, "It's obvious enough that I'm female without drawing additional attention to my gender by insisting on being set apart. I'm proud to be called a boatman," and Edie Crawford, "Definitely unisex! I love the term. 'I'm a Grand Canyon boatman,' I tell people with pride," and Mamcu Rovers, "I don't feel it's sexist! I see it merely as an historical term. Semantics aren't what count on the job—I know what I am (especially at the top of Crystal!)." But in deference to those who decry the sexist word I also use "river guides" on the advice of Brad Dimock: "Boatman implies operating a boat, Guide implies giving guidance. Everyone who runs a boat is a boatman. Not all are guides."

Debris flows: Melis et al., "Debris Flows," 38, a total of 525 tributaries between Lees Ferry and Diamond Creek have the potential to produce debris flows, and 3 of these are capable of transporting boulders up to 330 tons; see also notes to Chapter 9 on Monument Creek debris flow.

Constriction ratio: Susan W. Kieffer, Julia B. Graf, and John C. Schmidt, 1989, "Hydraulics and Sediment Transport of the Colorado River," in *Geology of Grand Canyon*, 55, 63–64; Kieffer, "Hydraulics and Geomorphology of the Colorado River," 385, 405, notes that "the ability of the Colorado River to contour its own channel probably accounts for the remarkable uniformity of constriction that the river exhibits as it passes around each of the major debris fans along its 400 km length in the Grand Canyon."

Flavell/Montéz: Carmony and Brown, *The Log of the Panthon*, 1, 10–13, 9–10, Montéz "must have made up in courage what he lacked in experience," and quote, 1–2; Lavender, *River Runners*, 34–38.

Galloway: Lavender, *River Runners*, 13, 36–37, gives Galloway credit for originating the seated, stern-forward method, although Carmony and Brown, *The Log of the Panthon*, 12–14, opt for Flavell and think Galloway "has often erroneously been credited . . . using this 'face the danger' technique"; Kolb, *Through the Grand Canyon*, 338–39; quote, Stone, *Canyon Country*, 67.

Soap Creek: Kolb, *Through the Grand Canyon*, 175, 183–84; Flavell: Carmony and Brown, *The Log of the Panthon*, 52–53.

Woolley/Hyde trips: Quote, Lavender, *River Runners*, 38–40, 78–84, is one of the best accounts of the honeymoon couple who boated the canyon in 1928 and never came out the other end; the letters of Mr. Hyde, Clyde's father, who was determined to search the river, are in the Emery Kolb Collection, Cline Library, Northern Arizona University, Flagstaff, Special Collections and Archives.

House Rock: Quote, Escalante, "Journals," 95–96; Beaman, "The Cañon of the Colorado," 548, used the name in 1869.

Bighorn sheep: Cordell, *Prehistory of the Southwest*, 32–33; Neal G. Guse, Jr., 1974, "Colorado River Bighorn Sheep Survey," *Plateau* 46(4):135–38; Stone, *Canyon Country*, 96, below Kanab Creek, November 9, 1909, "At 2:15 we see a band of bighorn on a ledge to the left. This is the third lot we have seen to-day. Being short of meat, we stop and go after one, the net result being that we bag two, a young one and a magnificent ram, its horns measuring seventeen inches in circumference at their base. There were five rams in this bunch, and as I went to skin the big one the others walked somewhat leisurely away. A number of others went up a broken-down place in the wall to the next bench above. These animals were so tame that it seems fair to infer that they had not seen human beings before. We might have killed all of them but I am glad no one even suggested shooting any more. This now makes it possible to supply the Ohio State Museum with as fine a pair of *Ovis montana* as I have ever seen."

Dory history: Brad Dimock, 1992, *Dories*, stylishly illustrated by Ellen Tibbetts, is a well-written history of dories.

"The unit": A history of waste provision in the canyon would range from none, which caused unimaginable miasmas on canyon beaches, to various portable arrangements; Mike Yard, 1992," In Memoriam, Polyethylene," *The News*

5(4):22, "Since the late seventies, effluent has been transported out of the canyon by way of plastic bag, the greatest invention since sliced bread. During its infancy we learned a lot about chemical reactions, some of this rivaled military arms development." New regulations mandating a bagless collection system and disposal went into effect for the boating season of 1993; quote, Scott Thybony, 1993, *Canyon Country Parklands, Treasures of the Great Plateau* (Washington, D.C.: National Geographic Society), 10.

Hakatai Shale/Grand Canyon Supergroup: Simmons and Gaskill, *River Runners' Guide*, 65; R. S. Babcock, 1990, "Precambrian Crystalline Core," in Beus and Morales, *Grand Canyon Geology*, 12, 15–16.

Rattlesnakes: Laurence M. Klauber, 1982, *Rattlesnakes: Their Habits, Life Histories, and Influence on Mankind* (Berkeley: University of California Press), 8–10, 38–39, 70, 92–93; Smith, *Venomous Animals*, vii, 110, 111–12; Donald M. Miller, Robert A. Young, Thomas W. Gatlin, and John A. Richardson, 1982, *Amphibians and Reptiles of the Grand Canyon* (Flagstaff: Grand Canyon Natural History Association, Monograph 4), 34, 67, Grand Canyon rattlesnake is a subspecies of the *viridis* complex; Laurie J. Vitt, 1991, "Desert Reptile Communities," in *Ecology of Desert Communities*, 249; Carothers and Brown, *Natural History of the Colorado River*, 155–56, a third, the black-tailed rattler is uncommon and often aggressive, unlike the other two rattlers.

Hance/Hakatai Shale: Simmons and Gaskill, *River Runners' Guide*, 84; J. D. Hendricks and G. M. Stevenson, 1990, "Grand Canyon Supergroup: Unkar Group," in Beus and Morales, *Grand Canyon Geology*, 37.

Lava dam at Hance: Hamblin, "Late Cenozoic Lava Dams," 415–18.

Dike/sill: Hamblin and Rigby, *Guidebook to the Colorado River, Part 1*, 73–74; Elston, "Middle and Late Proterozoic Grand Canyon Supergroup," 99, 101; Potochnik and Reynolds, "Side Canyons," 461–64.

Asbestos mine: J. H. Pratt, 1904, "Grand Canyon Asbestos Deposits," in *Mineral Resources of the United States* (Washington, D.C.: USGS), 1137–40; tailings begin near the base of Bass Limestone.

John Hance: Merrill D. Beal, 1969, "Development and Administration of Grand Canyon National Park," in *Geologic and Natural History of the Grand Canyon Region*, ed. D. L. Baars (Durango, Colo.: Four Corners Geological Association), 19; H. C. Hovey, 1892, "The Grand Canyon of the Colorado," *Scientific American* 66:393, was taken in by Hance and wrote that he "has probably done more actual exploring of the canyons of the Colorado than any other Arizonian; and it is his boast that, in the period of two years, with his own unaided hands, he made the famous Hance Trail, from the highest rim down to the river—certainly one of the greatest engineering feats ever accomplished by one man"; George Wharton James, 1920, Foreword, in *Adventures in the Canyons of the Colorado by Two of Its Earliest Explorers, James White and*

W. W. Hawkins, with introduction and notes by William Wallace Bass (Grand Canyon: James White and W. W. Hawkins), 5, "I knew Hance long before he had dreamed the Canyon would help make him famous; I ate venison stew with him when he was but a cowboy in the employ of the proprietor of the Hull ranch: I wrote the first account of those peculiar and exaggerated yarns of his that gained him his fame as the 'Munchausen of the West.' It was on these yarns alone that his fame reposed. He was never a guide. He knew nothing of the Canyon, east or west, twenty miles from the trail that unfortunately was named after him. He never read a line of its history, and never cared to know who first discovered it. He got lost years after the Canyon was being visited by great numbers of whites, when he attempted to guide a party to the home of the Havasupai Indians, whose ancestors made the trail which he discovered and claimed on his own." Hance died a pauper in Flagstaff in 1919. Quote, G. K. Woods, 1899, *Personal Impressions of the Grand Canyon of the Colorado River near Flagstaff, Arizona, as Seen through Nearly Two Thousand Eyes, and Written in the Private Visitors' Book of the World-Famous Guide Capt. John Hance, Guide, Story-Teller, and Path-Finder* (San Francisco: Whitaker and Ray), 32.

Hance Trail: Spamer and Bogan, "Mollusca of the Grand Canyon and Vicinity," 33; S. B. Jones, 1929, "The Elusive Sceloporus," *Grand Canyon Nature Notes* 4(2):6; only Muir, "The Grand Cañon of the Colorado," 113–14, would think down and back could be made "afoot easily in a day."

Hance Rapid: Graf, Schmidt, and Kieffer, "Hydraulic Log," 43, characterize Hance as one of the rockiest rapids on the river; quotes, Flavell: Carmony and Brown, *The Log of the Panthon,* 57–59, Flavell admitted that he wouldn't have run Hance without an audience; Bradley, "Diary," 63; Kolb, *Through the Grand Canyon,* 209; Freeman, "Surveying the Grand Canyon," 119, 521, boatman on the Birdseye Expedition, thought it was "a fine sporting run."

9 Granite Gorges and Spinning Spiders

Unconformities: see note to Chapter 7 on the Great Unconformity.

Vishnu Schist: Dutton, *Tertiary History of the Grand Canyon District,* 148, "It is a gigantic butte, so admirably designed and so exquisitely decorated . . . and has a surprising resemblance to an Oriental pagoda. We named it Vishnu's Temple." For reactions to this exotic nomenclature, see Van Dyke, *The Grand Canyon,* 13–14, and Stone, *Canyon Country,* 360–61; quote, Powell, *Exploration of the Colorado River,* 247; Babcock, "Precambrian Crystalline Core," 12, 15–17, 28; E. H. Brown, R. S. Babcock, and M. D. Clark, 1974, "A Preliminary Report on the Older Precambrian Rocks in the Upper Granite Gorge of the Grand Canyon," in *Geology of Northern Arizona with Notes on Archaeology and Paleoclimate,* ed. Thor N. V. Karlstrom, Gordon A. Swann, and Raymond L. Eastwood (Flagstaff: Northern Arizona University, Museum of Northern

Arizona, and Geological Society of America, Rocky Mountain Section), 5, 8, 21, 30; Ilg and Karlstrom, "Metamorphics for the Geologically Impaired, 13–16; Charles D. Walcott, 1895, "Algonkian Rocks of the Grand Canyon of the Colorado," *Journal of Geology* 3:312, "The Algonkian rocks of the Grand Canyon are unique among the known unconformable pre-Cambrian rocks both of America and of Europe. Nowhere else has the geologist an equal opportunity to study such a series of ancient sediments nearly as they were laid down on the bed of the Algonkian sea. At no other known locality are there such extended and complete exposures of all the beds forming a great series of pre-Cambrian strata, permitting of such certainty in the determination of stratigraphic position and succession."

Sockdolager: Karlstrom, "Physiographic Context for Three Archeological Sites," 18; Graf, Schmidt, and Kieffer, "Hydraulic Log," 43; Turner and Karpiscak, *Recent Vegetation Changes*, 74–75; Freeman, "Surveying the Grand Canyon," 522; quotes, Flavell: Carmony and Brown, *The Log of the Panthon*, 60; Fowler; Frederick S. Dellenbaugh, 1904, *Romance of the Colorado River* (New York: Putnam's Sons), 328–30; Lavender, *River Runners*, 99–100; quotes: Fowler, *Hiller's Diary*, 137, August 29, 1872, and Sumner, in Stanton, *Controversies*, 195–96.

Peregrine falcons: *Draft EIS*, 39–40; James H. Enderson, 1987, "Survey of Peregrine Falcons at Zion and Canyonlands National Parks and Glen Canyon National Recreation Area, 1985" (NPS Report CX-1200-5-A034), 1–27; E. O. Wilson, "The Little Things That Run the World (The Importance of Conservation of Invertebrates)," *Conservation Biology* 1(4):345, "It needs to be repeatedly stressed that invertebrates as a whole are even more important in the maintenance of ecosystems than are vertebrates." *Final EIS*, 138–39.

Orb-weaver spider: George W. Uetz, 1990, "Prey Selection in Web-building Spiders and Evolution of Prey Defenses," in *Insect Defenses*, ed. David L. Evans and Justin O. Schmidt (Albany: State University of New York Press), 94, 96, 99, 105.

Zoroaster Formation: Ilg and Karlstrom, "Metamorphics for the Geologically Impaired," 13; Glen E. Sturdevant, 1927, "Pegmatite Dikes," *Grand Canyon Nature Notes* 2(4):4–5; several pertinent articles appear in *Geology of Grand Canyon*, among them Barnes, "Early Proterozoic Rocks of Grand Canyon," 90–93; Babcock, "Precambrian Crystalline Core" 19, 28; Brown, Babcock, and Clark, "A Preliminary Report on the Older Precambrian Rocks," 4, 11, 19, 30, 174.

Webs and silk: Eisner, "Chemical Defense against Predation in Arthropods," 173; Natalie Angier, 1994, "Crafty Signs Spun in Web Say to Prey, 'Open Sky,'" *New York Times*, April 19, B5, B8; Warren E. Leary, 1993, "Science Takes a Lesson from Nature, Imitating Abalone and Spider Silk," *New York Times*, August 31, B5–B6, "Spiders produce silk using water as a solvent in the open air, at ambient temperatures and pressure, and it goes through all these stages to become a stable, water-resistant web of great strength. Yet to produce a tough fiber like Kevlar, you have to make it under high pressure using concentrated sulfuric acid. We have a lot to learn."

Monument Creek debris flow: Fisher, "Structure and Dynamics of Desert Streams," 121–22; Robert Webb, 1987, "Occurrence and Geomorphic Effects of Streamflow and Debris Flow Floods in Northern Arizona and Southern Utah," in *Catastrophic Flooding*, ed. L. Mayer and D. Nash (Boston: Allen and Unwin), 247–48, 260; Webb, 1987, "Debris Flows from Tributaries of the Colorado River, Grand Canyon National Park, Arizona: Executive Summary" (USGS Open-File Report 87–117), 1–4; Grater and Hawkins, "Rock Slide in the Coconino Sandstone," 368–69.

Whiptail lizard: Dennis S. Tomko, 1976, "Dietary Characteristics of Some Grand Canyon Amphibians and Reptiles," in *Riparian Zone*, 47; Howard E. Lawler, 1991, "Lizards and Snakes of the Arizona Upland," *Sonorensis* 12(1):12; Carothers, Aitchison, and Johnson, "Natural Resources, White Water Recreation, and River Management Alternatives," 155–56.

Sweat bees: E. O. Wilson, 1971, *The Insect Societies* (Cambridge, Mass.: Harvard University Press), 78–82; David L. Evans and Justin O. Schmidt, eds., 1990, *Insect Defenses* (Albany: State University of New York Press), see especially Schmidt's chapter "Hymenopteran Venoms: Striving toward the Ultimate Defense against Vertebrates," 404–5.

Crystal Rapid: Webb, "Occurrence and Geomorphic Effects," 247, 250, 256–60; 260; Susan W. Kieffer, 1985, "The 1983 Hydraulic Jump in Crystal Rapid: Implications for River Running and Geomorphic Evolution in the Grand Canyon," *Journal of Geology* 93:363, 373–75, 381–82, 388, 392–94, 401, 403–5; Holmstrom, "Diary," 32; one of the most readable explanations is Tom Moody, 1993, "Rocks, Rapids and the Hydraulic Jumps," *The News* 6(3):19–22.

1966 storm: Webb, "Occurrence and Geomorphic Effects," 247, 250, 256–58, from 1974 to 1986, enough marked changes have occurred in enough of the tributary canyons to suggest to geologists that major changes occur on a time scale of decades rather than centuries; Elmer Butler and J. C. Mundorff, 1970, *Floods of December 1966 in Southwestern Utah* (Washington, D.C.: USGS Water-Supply Paper 1870A); M. Cooley, E. B. N. Aldridge, and R. C. Euler, 1977, *Effects of Catastrophic Flood of December, 1966, North Rim Area* (Washington, D.C.: USGS Professional Paper 980); J. O. Rosvedt et al., 1966, *Summary of Floods in the United States during 1966* (Washington, D.C.: USGS Water-Supply Paper 1870D); quote, Muir, "The Grand Cañon of the Colorado," 112; Spamer and Bogan, "Mollusca of the Grand Canyon and Vicinity," 39; Melis et al., "Debris Flows," 90–91, 128; Karlstrom, "Physiographic Context," 15, mean annual precipitation is 12 to 25 centimeters (4.7–9.8 inches) in the Inner Gorge and up to 75 centimeters (29.5 inches) on the Kaibab Plateau.

Crystal Hole: Kieffer, "Hydraulic Jump," 390. The hole was roughly seven feet wide; after one death and several injuries, the park declared it unrunnable for the duration of highest flows.

Crystal studies: Graf, "Rapids in Canyon Rivers," 547–48; Kieffer, "Hydraulic Jump," 363, 370–71, 373–79, 381–82; Melis et al., "Debris Flows," 103–8, note a new rapid that formed in 1993 at Mile 127.6.

Quote: Zane Grey, Museum at the Bright Angel Lodge display; Zane Grey, 1909, "Roping Lions in the Grand Canyon," *Field and Stream* 13:739–49, and ibid., 14:336–42; Stewart Aitchison, 1977, "The Grand Canyon Is a 'World in Itself,'" *Plateau* 49:5, Grey's party "succeeded in roping and transporting on horseback several very wild and very angry mountain lions."

Cicadas: Heinrich, *Hot-Blooded Insects*, 369–71, 374, 380, 514; Maxine S. Heath, 1972, "Temperature Requirements of the Cicada, Okanagana striatipes beameri: A Study for Flagstaff, Arizona," *Plateau* 45(1):31.

10 Travertines and Lavas

Havasu Creek/Canyon: Potochnik and Reynolds, "Side Canyons," 465–66, 469–70, 479–80; Garrett, "Are We Loving It to Death?" 29.

Travertine: Elston, "Pre-pleistocene(?) Deposits," 183, 185; Paul S. Welch, 1952, *Limnology* (New York: McGraw-Hill), 194; Czarnecki, Blinn, and Tompkins, *A Periphytic Microflora Analysis*, 11–12, the algal flora in Havasu Creek is among the richest on the river.

Ripple bugs: Kevina Vulinec, 1990, "Collective Security: Aggregation by Insects as a Defense," in Evans and Schmidt, *Insect Defenses*, 251, 259–74, 276–77.

Mourning cloak butterflies: Johnson and Lyon, *Insects That Feed on Trees and Shrubs*, 126–29; V. G. Dethier, 1983, Introduction, in *Herbivorous Insects: Host-Seeking Behavior and Mechanisms*, ed. Sami Ahmad (New York: Academic Press), xiii; Frank E. Hanson, 1983, "The Behavioral and Neurophysiological Basis of Food-Plant Selection by Lepidopterous Larvae," in *Herbivorous Insects*, 10–11, 16, 20; Maureen L. Stanton, 1983, "Spatial Patterns in the Plant Community and Their Effects upon Insect Search," in *Herbivorous Insects*, 136–38, 145, 151; John C. Reese, 1979, "Interactions of Allelochemicals with Nutrients in Herbivore Food," in *Herbivores: Their Interaction with Secondary Plant Metabolites*, ed. Gerald A. Rosenthal and Daniel H. Janzen (New York: Academic Press), 309–11.

Bumblebees: Smith, *Venomous Animals*, 88–89; Heinrich, *Hot-Blooded Insects*, 253–54, 274–75, 511.

Holmstrom quote: Holmstrom, "Diary," 31.

Bats: Donald F. Hoffmeister, 1955, "Mammals New to Grand Canyon National Park, Arizona," *Plateau* 28(1):5; James H. Fullard, 1990, "The Sensory Ecology of Moths and Bats: Global Lessons in Staying Alive," in Evans and Schmidt, *Insect Defenses*, 203, 216, 220.

Buffalo gnats: Harold Oldroyd, 1964, *The Natural History of Flies* (New York: W. W. Norton), 55–56, 66–69, 71; Smith, *Venomous Animals*, 56–59; Cole, "Bombyliidae," 109, 401–3; K. W. Cummins, 1975, "Macroinvertebrates," in *River Ecology*, ed. B. A. Whitton (Berkeley: University of California Press), 185.

Vulcan's Anvil and related volcanics: W. K. Hamblin, 1970, "Lava Dams in the Toroweap and Prospect Areas of the Grand Canyon," in *Guidebook to the Geology of Utah, Number 23*, ed. W. K. Hamblin and M. G. Best (Salt Lake City: Utah Geological and Mineralogical Survey), 18, 46–51, 128–29; Hamblin, "Late Cenozoic Lava Flows," 41, 43, 54–55; J. Godfrey Fitton, 1989, "Petrology and Geochemistry of Late Cenozoic Basalt Flows, Western Grand Canyon, Arizona," in *Geology of Grand Canyon*, 186, 188–89; Randall Kosaki, personal communication, October 1989—Kosaki, a biologist studying the effects of lava flows on reef fish off the coast of Hawaii, while scuba diving observed lava flows pouring into the ocean and described a horrific scene that must have resembled what occurred in the Grand Canyon.

Lakes behind reservoirs: Hamblin, "Late Cenozoic Lava Dams," 387, 394–95, 399–401, 429–30.

Lava Falls flood: Quotes, Birdseye and Moore, "A Boat Voyage through the Grand Canyon," 52, 192; Lavender, *River Runners*, 63–64, 68; Turner and Karpiscak, *Recent Vegetation Changes*, 6, 98, in 1930 the Freeman party was also caught when the river rose 14 ft. during one night of flooding here.

Sandy terrace: W. K. Hamblin, 1989, "Pleistocene Volcanic Rocks of the Western Grand Canyon," in *Geology of Grand Canyon*, 203–4, suggests the clustering of sand deposits corresponds to the height of lakes behind lava dams.

Toroweap and Prospect Canyons: Prospect Canyon was named by two prospectors working there, one of whom, Franklin French, married Emma Batchelder Lee in 1879; David S. Brumbaugh, 1990, "Earthquakes and Seismicity of the Grand Canyon Region," in *Grand Canyon Geology*, 435; Melis et al., "Debris Flows," 111–14, 126, the last large debris flow in Prospect Canyon was in March 1995—see Bruce Finley, 1995, "The New Canyon," *The Denver Post Magazine*, April 9, 1995, 6–13.

Toroweap: Thybony, *Canyon Country Parklands*, 12–14, 40, describes a miserable trail that drops from 4,000 to 1,200 feet, steep and rough, without water along the way; Philip Ferry, 1951, "Where the Lava Dammed the Colorado,"

Natural History 60(4):172–73, 176, describes the trail dropping down a massive chute at a 35° angle, choked with debris "where one is either slipping, sliding, sitting on one's haunches, leaping from boulder to boulder, dropping down six-foot ledges, or performing other desperate gymnastics. The descent is one of the most trying performances one would wish to undertake in the name of pleasure."

Lava dams: Hamblin, "Late Cenozoic Lava Dams," 387, 394–95, 398, 401–5, 411–15, 423–27, 429–30, by comparison, Niagara Falls migrates headward a little over seven feet per year (eleven miles in the last eight thousand years).

Lava Falls: Robert O. Collins and Roderick Nash, 1978, *The Big Drops: Ten Legendary Rapids* (San Francisco: Sierra Club Books); Kieffer, "Hydraulic Jump," 338–39, 360–61; Hamblin, "Late Cenozoic Lava Dams," 190–92, 201–3, 389, 393, 396.

Whitmore Canyon/Wash: Hamblin, "Late Cenozoic Lava Dams," 422–23; Aitchison, *A Naturalist's Guide*, 157–59, describes the Whitmore Trail, which traverses the lava fill of the old channel, with trailhead elevation at 2,500 feet and a total vertical descent of 920 feet in three-quarters of a mile; although an easy trail, it is difficult to reach the trailhead.

11 Humpback Chub and the Little Colorado

Humpback chub discovery/range/adaptations: WAPA, with U.S. Fish and Wildlife Service, 1989, *Swimming Upstream: The Endangered Fish of the Colorado River* (Washington, D.C.: U.S. Government Printing Office, Series 6), 2; *Colorado River Ecology*, 28–29, 150–51, 135, Minckley, "Native Fishes of the Grand Canyon Region"; Roberta E. Wilson and James Q. Wilson, 1985, *Watching Fishes* (New York: Harper and Row), 33–35, 37–40; Miller and Hubert, *Compendium of Existing Knowledge for Use in Making Habitat Management Recommendations*, 47; Valdez, "Native Fishes of the Grand Canyon," 12, "The humpback chub is the fish species that most strikingly characterizes the graceful beauty of the whitewater canyons of the Colorado River. It is symbolic of how a seemingly harsh and rugged environment can shape such a thing of splendor."

Decline of native fish species: Trevor C. Hughes, 1991, "Reservoir Operations," in *Colorado River Ecology*, 218–20, 224; Miller and Hubert, *Compendium*, 42–43, 398–99, 401–4; Haden, "Nonnative Fishes of the Grand Canyon," 1–11, 20; Minckley, "Native Fishes of the Grand Canyon Region," 124–25, "Demise of the fauna started just after 1900, as the river was progressively harnessed for water supply, flood control, and power production. The fish fauna collapsed from downstream to upstream, in the same sequence as the river was regulated," and 142–45, "the introduction and enhancement of non-native fishes as a result of river alterations forced the native species to extinction . . . I seriously doubt that physiochemical changes wrought by humans in less than 100 years equal those occurring since Miocene, which began 20+ million years ago."

Draft EIS, 12, the Bureau of Reclamation "would make every effort— through funding, facilitating, and technical support—to ensure that a new population of humpback chub is established in one or more of the tributaries within Grand Canyon."

Diet: Miller and Hubert, *Compendium*, 26–28, 47, 398–99, 401–4, 419, 423–24; Minckley, "Native Fishes of the Grand Canyon Region," 124, 127–28, 131, 138–39, 146, 148, 152–53; Harold M. Tyus and W. L. Minckley, 1988, "Migrating Mormon Crickets, *Anabrus simples* (Orthoptera: Tettigoniidae), as Food for Stream Fishes," *Great Basin Naturalist* 48(1):25, 28; Valdez, personal communication, August 1991, stomach pumping relieves the fish's discomfort: when brought to the surface from deep water, its air bladder expands, and when returned to the water, it lurches onto its sides, an indication of distress, whereas stomach-pumped fish swim well immediately.

Richard A. Valdez, William J. Masslich, William Leibfried, and David R. VanHaverbeke, 1991, *Characterization of the Life History and Ecology of the Humpback Chub in the Grand Canyon: Trip Report—1991, Trip 7*, July 9–July 28, 1991 (Logan, Utah: Bio/West, Report PR 250-10), 2; Valdez, "Native Fishes of Grand Canyon," striped bass, stocked in Lake Mead for game fishing, previously came only as far as Diamond Creek at Mile 225.7 but were recently caught upstream at Mile 156.

Time of water transport: Carothers and Brown, *Natural History of the Colorado River*, 25.

Tiger beetle: Horn, *Biology of Insects*, 82–84; Clyde C. Searl, 1932, "Vandals of the Sand," *Grand Canyon Nature Notes* 6(5):41–42; Askew, *Parasitic Insects*, 166–67; Heinrich, *Hot-Blooded Insects*, 201–5, 403–4.

Collared lizard: McKee, "Tracks That Go Uphill," 61–72; L. F. Brady, 1989, "Tracks in the Coconino Sandstone Compared with Those of Small Living Arthropods," *Plateau* 12(2):32–34; C. W. Gilmore, 1926, "Fossil Footprints," *Grand Canyon Nature Notes* 1(1):1–2.

Side-blotched lizard: Donald W. Tinkle, Don McGregor, and Sumner Dana, 1962, "Home Range Ecology of *Uta stansburiana stejnegeri*," *Ecology* 43:223–228; Bayard H. Brattstrom, 1974, "The Evolution of Reptilian Social Behavior," *American Zoologist* 14:35, 37–38, 46; Miller, Young, Gatlin, and Richardson, *Amphibians and Reptiles of the Grand Canyon*, 10, 59, 61, 127–29, "The formidable topography of the Grand Canyon presents considerable difficulty when attempting to survey the reptile and amphibian forms. Indeed, many of these forms exhibit highly secretive habits dictated by the harsh environmental conditions found in the Canyon and vicinity. Consequently, what little work has been done of the herpetology of the area has required an abid-

284

Notes

ing interest in the animals and a concrete physical effort on the part of the investigator."

Desert spiny lizard: Edwin D. McKee, 1928, "The Blue-Bellied Lizard," *Grand Canyon Nature Notes* 3(3):3–4; Miller, Young, Gatlin, and Richardson, *Amphibians and Reptiles of the Grand Canyon*, III, these lizards differ from those on the rim in having a more washed out blue on their chests and under their armpits and backs more lightly speckled; James H. Brown, 1986, "The Roles of Vertebrates in Desert Ecosystems," in *Pattern and Process in Desert Ecosystems*, ed. W. G. Whitford (Albuquerque: University of New Mexico Press), 54; Wallwork, *Desert Soil Fauna*, 70–71; Tomko, "Dietary Characteristics of Some Grand Canyon Amphibians and Reptiles," 7–48, Stewart W. Aitchison, 1975, "Human Impact on the Biota of the Riparian Zone of the Grand Canyon" (Xerox copy on file at the Museum of Northern Arizona Library), 13.

Mites: Polis and Yamashita, "The Ecology and Importance of Predaceous Arthropods in Desert Communities," 189; Daniel E. Sonenshine, 1991, *Biology of Ticks* (New York: Oxford University Press), 15; Wallwork, *Desert Soil Fauna*, 69–70, 143–44; *Ecology of Desert Communities*, 404, "every lizard sustains its own food web, a community of parasites."

Tree lizard: Lawler, "Lizards and Snakes of the Arizona Upland," 12; D. W. Tinkle and A. E. Dunham, 1983, "Demography of the Tree Lizard, *Urosaurus ornatus*, in Central Arizona," *Copeia* 1983:596–97; Larry Michel, 1976, "Reproduction in a Southwest New Mexican Population of *Urosaurus ornatus*," *Southwestern Naturalist* 21(3):281, 298; L. J. Vitt, 1974, "Winter Aggregations, Size Classes, and Relative Tail Breaks in the Tree Lizard, *Urosaurus ornatus* (Sauria: Iguanidae)," *Herpetologica* 30:182–83.

Little Colorado River: Quote, Bradley, "Diary," 61; Sumner: Stanton, *Controversies*, 192–93; Edmund D. Andrews, 1991, "Sediment Transport in the Colorado River Basin," in *Colorado River Ecology*, 62; Kolb, *Through the Grand Canyon*, 203, saw it in flood when "the turquoise-tinted mineral water of the Colorado Chiquito was backed up by the turbid flood waters of the Rio Colorado, forty feet or more above the present level. Now it was a rapid stream, throwing itself with wild abandon over the rocks and into the Colorado."

Fish spawn: *Draft EIS*, 36; Minckley, "Native Fishes of the Grand Canyon Region," 151–52; Miller and Hubert, *Compendium*, 24–26, 132–36, 140–46, 211, 223–24, 253–55, 283, 299–300; Valdez, "Native Fishes of Grand Canyon," 13–14; Kolb, *Through the Grand Canyon*, 127, "On the opposite side of the pool the fins and tails of numerous fish could be seen above the water. The striking of their tails had caused the noise we had heard. The 'bony tail' [humpback] were spawning. We had hooks and lines in our packs, and caught all we cared to use that evening . . . The Colorado is full of them; so are many other muddy streams of the Southwest. They seldom exceed 16 inches in length, and are silvery white in color. With a small flat head somewhat like a pike, the body swells behind it to a large hump."

Blue Springs: Fred B. Eiseman, 1959, "The Hopi Salt Trail," *Plateau* 32(2):25–30, the left river bank of the Little Colorado is closed as far up canyon as Blue Springs, a sacred site for the Hopi; Mischa Titiev, 1937, "A Hopi Salt Expedition," *American Anthropologist* 39(2):244–58, describes an actual journey made in 1912, and quote, 258.

Tapeats Sandstone salt deposits: Edwin D. McKee, 1969, "Paleozoic Rocks of Grand Canyon," in *Geologic and Natural History of the Grand Canyon Region*, ed. D. L. Baars (Durango, Colo.: Four Corners Geological Association), 80; Middleton and Elliott, "Tonto Group," 87–88; Billingsley, *A Synopsis of Stratigraphy*, 3.

Black widow spiders: B. J. Kaston, 1972, *How to Know the Spiders* (Dubuque, Iowa: Wm. C. Brown Company), 99–100; Gertsch, *American Spiders*, 236–40, the odds of being bitten by a black widow are about the same as those for being hit by lightning; Smith, *Venomous Animals*, 11–13.

Radio-tagging: Minckley, "Native Fishes of the Grand Canyon Region," 139–141. Many humpback chubs carry a Passive Integrated Transponder (PIT) tag that is 3 millimeters long and 2 millimeters wide, but it can be picked up only when right on top of the tag; a 9-gram transmitter lasts sixty days, an 11-gram transmitter, for larger fish, lasts up to ninety days; transmitters with external antenna can be heard for greater distances both horizontally and vertically, but the exit hole on the ventral side of the fish toward the tail remains open to irritation and infection; an internal antenna doesn't transmit as far and can be tracked only to 3 vertical feet, while an external one can be tracked to 15 feet; Miller and Hubert, *Compendium*, 180, 187, 208–9, 219–20.

Habitat mapping: Valdez et al., *Life History and Ecology of the Humpback Chub*, 1–2, 5–6, 13, mapping is done on mylar overlays superimposed on detailed infrared photographs made from flyovers, at 1:1,200. This scale permits mapping visual surface differences that accompany changes in river height and flow; collating by computer and plotting these on a chart gives an irregularly shaped area or "polygon" that delineates the perimeter of where a given fish spends its time.

Purkinje effect/night vision: Roger Brown and R. J. Hernstein, 1975, *Psychology* (Boston: Little Brown), 389; Henry Gleitman, 1986, *Psychology* (New York: W. W. Norton), 191–93. Quote: Hovey, "The Grand Canyon," 88.

Cactus mouse: Quote, C. Hart Merriam, 1890, "Results of a Biological Survey of the San Francisco Mountain Region and Desert of the Little Colorado, Arizona," in U.S. Department of Agriculture, *North American Fauna No. 3* (Washington, D.C.: U.S. Government Printing Office), 62; George A.

Ruffner and Dennis S. Tomko, 1976, "Mammals of the Colorado River," in *Riparian Zone*, 64, 86–92, 95–96, 102–4; O. J. Reichman, 1991, "Desert Mammal Communities," in *Ecology of Desert Communities*, 323.

12 Tanner Trail and Mean Mesquite

First Europeans: Katherine Bartlett, 1940, "How Don Pedro de Tovar Discovered the Hopi and Don Garcia López de Cárdenas Saw the Grand Canyon, with Notes upon Their Probable Route," *Plateau* 12(3):39, 41–44; Fishbein, *Grand Canyon Country*, 19; Beus et al., "Preliminary Report on the Unkar Group," 47–50; Stanley S. Beus and Michael Morales, 1990, "Introducing the Grand Canyon," in Beus and Morales, *Grand Canyon Geology*, 5–7; quotes, Bartlett (Castañedas), 39, and Fishbein (Garcés), 19.

Tanner Trail: Thybony, *Canyon Country Parklands*, 12–14; Edwin D. McKee, 1931, "Additional Notes on the Tanner Trail Trip," *Grand Canyon Nature Notes* 5(12):121–22, lists birds seen; Vernon Bailey, 1931, "A Trip down Tanner Trail," in the same issue of *Grand Canyon Nature Notes*, 119, collected bats and rodents; Aitchison, *A Naturalist's Guide*, 90–91, 95.

Grand Canyon rattlesnake: Edwin D. McKee, 1930, "The Grand Canyon Rattlesnake," *Grand Canyon Nature Notes* 4(6):40, its type location is three hundred feet below the South Rim on the Tanner Trail.

Burton Holmes: Garrett, "Are We Loving It to Death?" 28.

Grand Canyon Supergroup: Beus et al., "Preliminary Report on the Unkar Group," 47–50; quote, Van Dyke, *The Grand Canyon*, 69; James W. Sears, 1990, "Geologic Structure of the Grand Canyon Supergroup," in *Grand Canyon Geology*, 76–77.

Stanton's film: Lavender, *River Runners*, 28, 30–31; Stanton, *Down the Colorado*, 146.

Travertine/conglomerate: Elston, "Pre-pleistocene(?) Deposits," 180.

Bert Loper: Quote, Brad Dimock and Lew Steiger, 1993, "Riverwater in His Blood (Interview with Don Harris)," *The News* 6(3):31–32; Lavender, *River Runners*, 55–56.
   Ted Melis, 1993–94, "Speaking of Debris Flows," *The News* 7(1):20–21, an hour-long storm on August 22, 1994, near Comanche Point, instigated a major debris flow down Tanner Canyon that swept into the river and narrowed Tanner Rapid by one hundred feet; Melis et al., "Debris Flows," 71–73.

Mapping: Hereford, Fairley, Thompson, and Balsom, "Surficial Geology, Geomorphology, and Erosion," 6, there is no complete set of 7.5 minute quadrangles available for Grand Canyon; for this study geologists have used computers to generate maps of the Tanner Creek area with a two-meter contour interval, at 1:1,200, or 1 foot to 1,200 feet; a luxuriously explicit map of Palisades-Unkar is now available at a scale of 1:5,000.

Noxious invaders: Phillips, Phillips, and Bernzott, *Annotated Checklist of Vascular Plants*, 6; Johnson, "Historic Changes in Vegetation," 191; Turner and Karpiscak, *Recent Vegetation Changes*, 1–3, 21; David Rindos, 1984, *The Origins of Agriculture: An Evolutionary Perspective* (New York: Academic Press, Inc.), 115–18; Stevens and Ayers, *The Impacts of Glen Canyon Dam*, 8/3; Larry Stevens, 1993, "Controlling the Aliens," *The News* 6(4):28.

Dune habitat: Mary K. Seely, 1991, "Sand Dune Communities," in *Ecology of Desert Communities*, 346, 349–53, 355; Wallwork, *Desert Soil Fauna*, 26–27.

Arrowweed: Martin, "Trees and Shrubs," 15; Johnson, "Historic Changes in Vegetation," 193; Turner and Karpiscak, *Recent Vegetation Changes*, 16.

Sand movement: *Final EIS*, 88–98, 101.

Cogswell: Lavender, *River Runners*, 41.

Galls: Whittaker, "The Biochemical Ecology of Higher Plants," 79, defines galls as "instances of localized abnormal growth in plants, produced by external agents"; M. S. Mani, 1964, *Ecology of Plant Galls* (The Hague: Dr. W. Junk Publishers), 4–5; Gagné, *Plant-Feeding Gall Midges*, 47, 94–96, 274; the 1992 volume *Biology of Insect-Induced Galls*, ed. Joseph D. Shorthouse and Odette Rohfritsch (New York: Oxford University Press), contains current and fascinating papers on gall research, among them F. Dreger-Jauffret and J. D. Shorthouse, "Diversity of Gall-Inducing Insects and Their Galls," 10–11, 19, 23; Koji Hori, "Insect Secretions and Their Effect on Plant Growth, with Special Reference to Hemipterans," 165; J. C. Roskam, "Evolution of the Gall-Inducing Guild," 34–49; H. G. Larew, "Fossil Galls," 56–57; O. Rohfritsch, "Patterns in Gall Development," 63–64, 67–69, 82–83; Robert Bronner, "The Role of Nutritive Cells in the Nutrition of Cynipids and Cecidomyiids," 136.

Water use: For instance, to brush your teeth with the tap on takes two to five gallons, with a wet brush and rinse, only one cup.

Beach restoration: Kim Crumbo, 1993–94, "Site Preservation and Revegetation," *The News* (Winter), 8; Crumbo has also compiled a very good river history, 1981, *A River Runner's Guide to the History of the Grand Canyon* (Boulder, Colo.: Johnson Books); Dolan, Howard, and Gallenson, "Man's Impact on the Colorado River," 401, some beach footpaths have been eroded up to two feet deep.

Visitor numbers: Dolan, Howard, and Gallenson, "Man's Impact," 393, by the early 1950s, 200 people had run the river; twenty years later 100,000 had; Lavender, *River Runners*, 131–32, in 1970, 10,000 people went down the river, and in 1971 the Park Service limited boat trips to around 10,000 people per year; Turner and Karpiscak, *Recent Vegetation Changes*, 21, by 1980, 15,000 passengers a year went down the river and the "user days" concept was developed; Grand Canyon National Park, 1989, "River Use Report" (mimeographed report covering the period May 1, 1989, through September 30, 1989), that year commercial passengers totaled 17,833 and used 99.2 percent of the allotted use of the river during the river season; noncommercial passengers reached 2,983.

Alluvium/colluvium/Anasazi sites/"striped layer": Lucchitta, *Quaternary Geology*, 30; Hereford, Fairley, Thompson, and Balsom, "Surficial Geology, Geomorphology, and Erosion," v, 4, 12, 14–16; a recent survey found 475 prehistoric sites between Glen Canyon Dam and Separation Canyon, of which 238 were on alluvium deposited by the Colorado River; Jennings, *Glen Canyon*, 19, found the same bands of charcoal in Glen Canyon, considered them quite recent, dating probably just before "the recent aggradation postulated as around A.D. 1" and suggesting "fine disseminated charcoal or carbonized vegetative matter," which may have been burning to scare out animals; Sid Davis, May 7, 1991, Report (Xeroxed paper on file with GCES), some of these soils tested as Class I and II under U.S. Department of Agriculture Land Capability Classification, where slopes are less than 2 percent and are considered "prime" farm ground that could support, if irrigated, almost any row crop, including corn, beans, and cotton; however, "if intensively irrigated for several generations in the desert climate of high evapotranspiration rates, salinity problems would show up eventually," and "In summary, the soils I suspected to be 'farmground' do have good agricultural potential—better than any other soils found in this reach of the Canyon."

Edward Goldsmith and Nicholas Hildyard, 1984, *The Social and Environmental Effects of Large Dams* (San Francisco: Sierra Club Books), 134, soil becomes toxic to plant life when concentrations of salts reach a range of 0.5 to 1.0 percent.

Basalt Graben: Donald Elston and C. Sherman Grommé, 1974, "Precambrian Polar Wandering from Unkar Group and Nankoweap Formation, Eastern Grand Canyon, Arizona," in *Geology of Northern Arizona with Notes on Archaeology and Paleoclimate*, ed. Thor N. V. Karlstrom, Gordon A. Swann, and Raymond L. Eastwood (Flagstaff: Northern Arizona University, Museum of Northern Arizona, and Geological Society of America, Rocky Mountain Section), 99–100; Edwin H. McKee and Donald C. Noble, 1974, "RB-SR Age of the Cardenas Lavas, Grand Canyon, Arizona," in ibid., 89, 94; Hendricks and Stevenson, "Grand Canyon Supergroup," 40–41; Beus et al., "Preliminary Report on the Unkar Group," 48–50.

Aphids: L. R. Nault and L. Phelan, 1984, "Alarm Pheromones and Sociality in Pre-social Insects," in *Chemical Ecology of Insects*, ed. William J. Bell and Ring T. Cardé (Sunderland, Mass.: Sinauer Associates), 237–39, 240–42, 245–51; Beattie, *Evolutionary Ecology*, 1, 10–14, 54–58, 64–65, 119–20;

Catherine M. Bristow, 1991," Why Are So Few Aphids Ant-Tended?" in *Ant-Plant Interactions*, ed. Camilla R. Huxley and David F. Cutler (New York: Oxford University Press), 104, 106–8; this 1991 volume contains other articles of interest, such as J. Hall Cushman and John F. Addicott, "Conditional Interactions in Ant-Plant-Herbivore Mutualisms," 93–94; Blum, 1974, "Pheromonal Bases of Social Manifestations," 193; R. J. D. Wensler, 1962, "Mode of Host Selection by an Aphid," *Nature* 195:831; David Janzen, 1968, "Host Plants as Islands in Evolutionary and Contemporary Time," *American Naturalist* 102:592–94; D. J. Stradling, 1978, "Food and Feeding Habits of Ants," in Brian, *Production Ecology*, 85.

Basalt Canyon: Elston, "Pre-pleistocene(?) Deposits," 102–3; Potochnik and Reynolds, "Side Canyons," 465–66; Fitton, "Petrology and Geochemistry of Late Cenozoic Basalt Flows," 186–87; Lucchitta and Hendricks, "Characteristics, Depositional Environment, and Tectonic Interpretations," 179–80.

13 Hilltop Ruin and Beaver Burrows

Quote: Van Dyke, *The Grand Canyon*, 8.

Debris flow: Melis, "Speaking of Debris Flows," 21, estimates there was a debris flow here at the same time as the Tanner Creek flow but much smaller and with no effect on the river channel; Lucchitta, personal communication, August 1992.

Hilltop Ruin: Lavender, *River Runners*, 55–56; Lucchitta, personal communication, August 1992, on the age of deposit including cobbles; Haas, "The Evolution of the Kayenta Regional System," 506–8; Euler and Taylor, "Additional Archaeological Data," 41–44, Hilltop "lies on or near what probably was a cross-canyon trail leading from the villages near Unkar up to the south rim of Grand Canyon. It may well have been a 'lookout' if not a defensive unit."

Sun calendar: William H. Calvin, 1991, *How the Shaman Stole the Moon* (New York: Bantam Books), 7, 69–72, 164–66, 166–72, 174–75; Euler, personal communication, October 1992, does not think that this is a calendar site and knows of none in the canyon; Ray A. Williamson, Howard J. Fisher, and Donnel O'Flynn, 1977, "Anasazi Solar Observatories," in *Native American Astronomy*, ed. Anthony F. Aveni (Austin: University of Texas Press), 203–4, 213–15; Ray A. Williamson, 1984, *Living the Sky: The Cosmos of the American Indian* (Boston: Houghton Mifflin), 38, 40–41, 58–59, 79, 84–85, 315–17, "With their society under climatic stress, the local Anasazi inhabitants undoubtedly needed every available means to assure survival in harsh conditions, and apparently turned to the celestial motions to help them out"; Ruth L. Bunzel, 1932, "Zuni Ritual Poetry," *Annual Report* (Smithsonian Bureau of Ethnology) 47:635; Karl A. Wittfogel and Esther S. Goldfrank,

1943, "Some Aspects of Pueblo Mythology and Society," *Journal of American Folklore* 56:29.

Helicopter flights over Grand Canyon National Park: Mary Tolan, "FAA Assailed on Canyon Flights," *Denver Post*, November 22, 1992, notes criticism of the Federal Aviation Administration for being "capricious" and allowing overflights over the park without consulting the Park Service or inviting public review or comment; in the past dozen years there have been 55 deaths from crashes over the canyon and, despite the fact that Congress passed the National Parks Overflights Act in 1987, flights have nearly doubled; Brad Dimock (one of the most respected river guides), "Wuddyathink?" *The News* (Winter 1992–93), 32, "We, too, exploit and impact the Canyon. We, too, show folks the Canyon from a unique perspective. Our numbers and horsepower (decibels) are limited. Theirs should be too." Jeri Ledbetter, *The News* (Winter 1993–94), 16, gives an update on the situation from her pilot's view; Michael J. Ybarra, 1994, "Scenic Tours in Helicopters Spark Protests," *Wall Street Journal*, B1, B4, helicopters carried 750,000 visitors, at high season flights reach twenty an hour, and "exponential" growth continues.

Harvester ants: Quote, Wilson, "The Little Things That Run the World," 345; J. W. S. Bradshaw and E. Howse, 1984, "Sociochemicals of Ants," in *Chemical Ecology of Insects*, ed. William J. Bell and Ring T. Cardé (Sunderland, Mass.: Sinauer Associates), 443, 446–47; Wallwork, *Desert Soil Fauna*, 6–63, 161–62, 184, 177, 184, 199; MacKay, "The Role of Ants and Termites," 119–120, 125, 128–29, 131, 136; Lawrence E. Stevens, 1976, "An Insect Inventory of Grand Canyon," in *Riparian Zone*, 126–27; Beattie, *Evolutionary Ecology*, 73–74, 77, 87, 93–95, 113–15, 123, 126–27, 145; F. J. Hermann and B. M. Leese, 1956, "A Grass (*Munroa squarrosa*) Apparently Cultivated by Ants," *American Midland Naturalist* 56:506–7, found near the Grand Canyon many ant hills clearly ringed with this grass harvested by ants.

Harvester ant group foraging style: Diane W. Davidson, 1977, "Foraging Ecology and Community Organization in Desert Seed-Eating Ants," *Ecology* 58:716–17, 725, 727–28, 733–35; Deborah M. Gordon, 1991, "Behavioral Flexibility and the Foraging Ecology of Seed-Eating Ants," *American Naturalist* 138:379, 383, 387–92, 407, on "patrollers" and "nest menders"; Walter G. Whitford, 1978, "Foraging by Seed-Harvesting Ants," in Brian, *Production Ecology*, 109; J. Petal, 1978, "The Role of Ants in Ecosystems," in *Production Ecology*, 304; Blum, "Pheromonal Sociality in the Hymenoptera," 233–34; Ruth A. Bernstein, 1975, "Foraging Strategies of Ants in Response to Variable Food Density," *Ecology* 56:213–14, 218–19; Walter G. Whitford, 1978, "Foraging in Seed-Harvester Ants *Pogonomyrmex* spp.," *Ecology* 59(1):187.

Harvester ant nests/storage: Gordon, "Behavioral Flexibility and the Foraging Ecology of Seed-Eating Ants," 408; MacKay, "The Role of Ants and Termites," 129–30, 133–37; Polis and Yamashita, "The Ecology and Importance of

Predaceous Arthropods," 212; Wilson, *The Diversity of Life*, 4–6; Wilson, *The Insect Societies*, 311–12, 443–44; Rindos, *Origins of Agriculture*, 107–8; James F. Reynolds, 1986, "Adaptive Strategies of Desert Shrubs with Special Reference to the Creosote Bush (*Larrea tridentata* [DC] Cov.)," in *Pattern and Process in Desert Ecosystems*, ed. W. G. Whitford (Albuquerque: University of New Mexico Press), 33; Beattie, *Evolutionary Ecology*, 1–4, 14–15, 77, 87, 90–91, 93–95, 98, 108, 144–45; Camilla R. Huxley, 1991, "Ants and Plants: A Diversity of Interactions," in *Ant-Plant Interactions*, ed. Camilla R. Huxley and David F. Cutler (New York: Oxford University Press), 1; D. W. Davidson and S. R. Morton, 1981, "Competition for Dispersal in Ant-Dispersed Plants," *Science* 213:1256, 1261; Crawford, "The Community Ecology of Macroarthropod Detritivores," 78, 105; Brian, *Social Insects*, 59–60, 72–73; Bradshaw and Howse, "Sociochemicals of Ants," 429–34, 450–51; Blum, "Pheromonal Bases," 241–42; S. R. Farkas and H. H. Shorey, 1974, "Mechanisms of Orientation to a Distant Pheromone Source," in *Pheromones*, ed. Martin C. Birch (New York: American Elsevier), 81–84, 88–89; Ronald J. Prokopy, Bernard D. Roitberg, and Anne L. Averill, 1984, "Resource Partitioning," in *Chemical Ecology of Insects*, ed. William J. Bell and Ring T. Cardé (Sunderland, Mass.: Sinauer Associates), 318.

Harvester ant venom: J. O. Schmidt and M. S. Blum, 1977, "A Harvester Ant Venom: Chemistry and Pharmacology," *Science* 200:1064–66; Schmidt, "Hymenopteran Venoms," 387–91, 402, 406, 412; Smith, *Venomous Animals*, 72–73.

Goodding willow: Stevens and Ayers, *The Impacts of Glen Canyon Dam*, 8/1, 8/3, observe that there may be a resurgence of Fremont's cottonwood growing in places less likely to be visited by beavers.

Marshes: Carothers and Brown, *Natural History of the Colorado River*, 104, marshes are most common between the dam and Lees Ferry, Miles 40 and 72, and Miles 166 and 220.

Willow flycatcher: Mark K. Sogge and Timothy Tibbitts, 1992, "Southwestern Willow Flycatcher (*Empidonax traillii extimus*) Surveys along the Colorado River in Grand Canyon National Park and Glen Canyon National Recreation Area," (Summary Report for the NPS Cooperative Park Studies Unit/ Northern Arizona University and U.S. Fish and Wildlife Service), 1, 13–14, 17–18, 25; Mike Yard, 1992, "Willow Flycatcher," *The News* 5(3):3; Bryan T. Brown, 1994, "Rates of Brood Parasitism by Brown-Headed Cowbirds on Riparian Passerines in Arizona, *Journal of Field Ornithology* 65(2):160–68, 25–29, 31; Carothers, Aitchison, and Johnson, "Natural Resources, White Water Recreation, and River Management Alternatives," 254–55; *Draft EIS*, 50.

Beavers: Merriam, "Results of a Biological Survey of the San Francisco Mountain Region," 59, found beaver cuttings at "Tanner's Crossing" and said they still inhabited the lower part of the Little Colorado.

Woodhouse's toad: Low, "The Evolution of Amphibian Life Histories," 149, 160, 181–82; Shepard, *Thinking Animals*, 15, 29; Miller, Young, Gatlin, and Richardson, *Amphibians and Reptiles of the Grand Canyon*, 45; W. Frank Blair, 1976, "Adaptation of Anurans to Equivalent Desert Scrub of North and South America," in *Evolution of Desert Biota*, ed. David W. Goodall (Austin: University of Texas Press), 206, 209–11.

14 River Terraces and Unkar Delta

Saltbush galls: Bradford A. Hawkins and Richard D. Goeden, 1984, "Organization of a Parasitoid Community Associated with a Complex of Galls on *Atriplex* spp., in Southern California," *Ecological Entomology* 9:271–72, 279.

Tapeats/Cardenas contact: Lucchitta and Hendricks, "Characteristics, Depositional Environment, and Tectonic Interpretations," 177–79, examine what they call the "bottle-green member"; John D. Hendricks and Ivo Lucchitta, 1974, "Upper Precambrian Igneous Rocks of the Grand Canyon, Arizona," in *Geology of Northern Arizona with Notes on Archaeology and Paleoclimate*, ed. Thor N. V. Karlstrom, Gordon A. Swann, and Raymond L. Eastwood (Flagstaff: Northern Arizona University, Museum of Northern Arizona, and Geological Society of America, Rocky Mountain Section), 71–73; Beus and Morales's *Grand Canyon Geology* has a group of pertinent pages, among them Billingsley and Elston, "Geologic Log," 15–19; John D. Hendricks, 1990, "Petrology and Chemistry of Igneous Rocks of Middle Proterozoic Unkar Group, Grand Canyon Supergroup, Northern Arizona," 106, 108–9, 113–14; and Hendricks and Stevenson, "Grand Canyon Supergroup," 42–43. Quote, Dutton, *Tertiary History of the Grand Canyon District*, 146.

Pediments and terraces: Hereford, Fairley, Thompson, and Balsom, "Surficial Geology, Geomorphology, and Erosion," 5; Karlstrom, "Physiographic Context for Three Archeological Sites," 16–18, 25–26, 20, the most elaborate sequence of terraces is in Nankoweap Creek valley; Hevly and Karlstrom, "Southwest Paleoclimate," 259–60, 267–68; Dolan, Howard, and Gallenson, "Man's Impact on the Colorado River," 395; Lucchitta, "Canyon Maker," 28, and *Quaternary Geology*, 4, 27–29; Turner and Karpiscak, *Recent Vegetation Changes*, 21, geologists estimate some eighteen glacial cycles during the 4 million years of the Pliocene.

Caliche: Ivo Lucchitta and Sid Davis, personal communication, August 1994, estimate 400,000 years of development on the highest pediments.

Archaeological research: Schwartz, Chapman, and Kepp, *Unkar Delta*, is such a basic reference for this section that further citations are not given; Douglas W. Schwartz, Michael Marshall, and Jane Kepp, 1981, *Archaeology of the Grand Canyon: The Walhalla Plateau* (Santa Fe: School of American Research Press), 8–9; Balsom, *Unkar Delta Guide*, is an excellent pamphlet for walking the sites; Stephanie M. Whittlesey, 1974, "Identification of Imported Ceramics through Functional Analysis of Attributes," *Kiva* 40(1–2):109–10.

Cohonina: Douglas W. Schwartz, 1969, "Grand Canyon Prehistory," in *Geology and Natural History of the Grand Canyon*, ed. D. L. Baars (Durango, Colo.: Four Corners Geological Society), 35–39; Schwartz, Marshall, and Kepp, *Walhalla Plateau*, 129; Euler et al., "The Colorado Plateaus," 1090; Haas, "The Kayenta Regional System," 496–97; Jones, *Cross Section of Grand Canyon Archaeology*, 5–6, 8–9; Robert C. Euler and George J. Gumerman, 1974, "A Resumé of Archaeology of Northern Arizona," in *Geology of Northern Arizona with Notes on Archaeology and Paleoclimate*, ed. Thor N. V. Karlstrom, Gordon A. Swann, and Raymond L. Eastwood (Flagstaff: Northern Arizona University, Museum of Northern Arizona, and Geological Society of America, Rocky Mountain Section), 303, 307–8; Joe Ben Wheat and Pat Wheat, 1954, "A Pueblo I Site of Grand Canyon," *American Antiquity* 19(4):402–3; Jeffrey S. Dean, 1988, "A Model of Anasazi Behavioral Adaptation," in *The Anasazi in a Changing Environment*, ed. George J. Gumerman (Cambridge: School of American Research and Cambridge University Press), 41.

Cohonina ceramics: Douglas W. Schwartz, 1956, "The Havasupai 600 A.D.–1955 A.D.: A Short Cultural History," *Plateau* 28(4):78–79; Robert C. Euler, 1979, "In Search of the Ancient Ones," *National Parks and Conservation Magazine* 53(6):5–7, where the Cohonina went remains a puzzle, and there is no observable continuation of tradition as there is between the Anasazi and the Hopi.

Desert soils: V. A. Kovda et al., 1900, "Soil Processes in Arid Lands," *Arid-Land Ecosystems* 1:445–47.

Population increase: Plog, *Stylistic Variation in Prehistoric Ceramics*, 129–30; Mark N. Cohen, 1977, *The Food Crisis in Prehistory: Overpopulation and the Origins of Agriculture* (New Haven: Yale University Press), 14–15.

Second settlement: Gumerman and Dean, "Prehistoric Cooperation and Competition," 118; Euler et al., "The Colorado Plateaus," 1096–98; Schwartz, Marshall, and Kepp, *The Bright Angel Site*, 85–86; Gasser, "Pueblo Plant Foods," 24–25; Kenneth Lee Petersen, 1989, "AT LAST! Why the Anasazi Left the Four Corners Region," *Canyon Legacy* (Southern Utah Society of Arts and Sciences), 20, 23, dry-farming lands in the Southwest, even today, expand and shrink.

Tusayan ware: Of the thousands of shards cataloged, only some 10 percent were made on site; the rest were brought in from rim-top settlements or as trade items.

Hunter-gatherers/agriculturists: Petersen, "AT LAST," 21; Haas, "The Evolution of the Kayenta Regional System," 500; Plog, *Stylistic Variation in Pre-*

historic Ceramics, 130, 233, 259; Wittfogel and Goldfrank, "Some Aspects of Pueblo Mythology and Society," 19; Cordell and Gumerman, "Cultural Interaction," 7; Cohen, *The Food Crisis in Prehistory*, 15; James M. Hill, 1972, "A Prehistoric Community in Eastern Arizona," in *Contemporary Archaeology: A Guide to Theory and Contributions*, ed. Mark P. Leone (Carbondale: Southern Illinois University Press), 329; Plog, *Stylistic Variation in Prehistoric Ceramics*, 27.

Nutrition: Cordell, *Prehistory of the Southwest*, 172, 179–80, 182–84, and 31, pinyon bears well only every seven to fourteen years; Kenneth W. Decker and Larry L. Tieszen, 1989, "Isotopic Reconstruction of Mesa Verde Diet from Basketmaker III to Pueblo III," *Kiva* 55(1):34–36; Wing and Brown, *Paleonutrition*, 63, 66, 142, 154, one solution for obtaining sufficient protein (corn is an incomplete protein, lacking niacin and some of the essential amino acids) is to combine corn with other vegetables containing the missing amino acids, as does the felicitous combination of corn and beans; beans contain the amino acid lysine, which allows the efficient digestion of the protein available in corn; Schwartz, Marshall, and Kepp, *The Bright Angel Site*, 121–22, the archaeologists' plots of corn failed without watering.

Tree-ring dating: John C. McGregor, 1965, *Southwestern Archaeology* (Urbana: University of Illinois Press), 75–89, since the theory was first developed in 1904 by A. E. Douglas, University of Arizona astronomer, a complete chronology has been constructed and refined for the Southwest so that even individual areas can be dated—this book gives a good overview of Southwestern archaeology; Charles E. Adams, 1983, "The Architectural Analogue to Hopi Social Organization and Room Use, and Implications for Prehistoric Southwestern Culture," *American Antiquity* 48(1):44.

Agriculture: Johnson, "Dynamics of Southwestern Prehistory," 374, Anasazi farmers could achieve a surplus equal to about three-quarters of that of ancient Mesopotamia; Johns, *With Bitter Herbs They Shall Eat It*, 101, 244–45; Reynolds, "Adaptive Strategies," 25; Joseph C. Winter, 1976, "The Processes of Farming Diffusion in the Southwest and Great Basin," *American Antiquity* 41(4):421–25; Gordon V. Childe, 1972, "The Urban Revolution," in *Contemporary Archaeology: A Guide to Theory and Contributions*, ed. Mark P. Leone (Carbondale: Southern Illinois University Press), 44–45; Rindos, *Origins of Agriculture*, 100; Plog, *Stylistic Variation in Prehistoric Ceramics*, 27; Plog et al., "Anasazi Adaptive Strategies," 233; Cohen, *The Food Crisis in Prehistory*, 15, agriculture is *not* easier than hunting and gathering, and the only advantage the former has over the latter is "that of providing more calories per unit of land per unit of time" and so sustaining larger populations; Cordell, *Prehistory of the Southwest*, 187–89, notes that although under much the same environmental conditions in the San Juan Basin, an Anasazi farmer could subsist on half a hectare (1 hectare equals 2.47 acres), a farmer usually cultivated as much as possible; at 360 she adds, "one of the most intriguing is the record it provides of flexible and heterogeneous responses to environmental diversity and extremes. The arid Southwestern climate, with cold winters and hot summers, establishes a difficult baseline for human adaptation. The long prehistoric record indicates that successful adaptation was accomplished, in part, by maintaining a diversity of subsistence and organizational options. At any one time, the people of the Southwest engaged in a mosaic of behavioral strategies ensuring the success of at least some of them."

UN-1/kiva: Saitta, "Room Use and Community Organization at the Pettit Site," 392–93; Williamson, *Living the Sky*, 70–71; Adams, "The Architectural Analogue," 51; quote, Johnson, "Dynamics of Southwestern Prehistory," 377, the number of kivas is roughly in proportion to group size, and the "inward" focus of kivas is atypical, departing from the mass ceremonialism usually found in early societies; at 378–379 Johnson explains that he sees in the kiva a "structure for the organization of consensus among basically egalitarian aggregates of increasing inclusiveness."

Water conservation: Anne I. Woosley, 1980, "Agricultural Diversity in the Prehistoric Southwest," *Kiva* 45(4):317; Cordell, *Prehistory of the Southwest*, 190, the problem is to separate stones probably placed in the cleanup process from those placed for agricultural purposes; R. Gwinn Vivian, 1974, "Conservation and Diversion: Water-Control Systems in the Anasazi Southwest," in *Irrigation's Impact on Society*, ed. Theodore E. Downing and McGuire Gibson (Tucson: University of Arizona Press, Anthropological Papers of the University of Arizona 25), 96–97, 101–3; Dean, "A Model of Anasazi Behavioral Adaptation," 41.

Changes in precipitation: Cordell, *Prehistory of the Southwest*, 188–89, 211, 314–17; Petersen, "AT LAST," 19.

Fourth settlement: Vivian, "Conservation and Diversion," 95, 102, 109; Cordell, *Prehistory of the Southwest*, 25–26, 311–12; Donald A. Jameson, 1969, "Rainfall Patterns on Vegetation Zones in Northern Arizona," *Plateau* 41(3):107–8; Jones, *Cross Section of Grand Canyon Archaeology*, 7–8; Euler and Taylor, "Additional Archaeological Data," 21–22; Woosley, "Agricultural Diversity," 332.

15 Bright Angel Trail: Coda

Bright Angel Trail/Fault: Edwin D. McKee, 1929, "The Bright Angel Fault," *Grand Canyon Nature Notes* 4(3):21–22, and McKee, 1931, "The Origin of Bright Angel Canyon," *Grand Canyon Nature Notes* 6(2):19–20; Shoemaker, Squires, and Abrams, "The Bright Angel and Mesa Butte Fault Systems," 357–58, 363, 374; Joseph Wood Krutch, 1958, *Grand Canyon: Today and All Its Yesterdays* (New York: William Morrow), 70–94, although a classic, it focuses more on rim than river; Lavender, *Colorado River Country*, 48–53; Thayer, *Bright Angel Trail*, is excellent to refer to while walking down the trail.

Footsteps back in time: Thayer, *Bright Angel Trail*, 50, 8.

Mule enhancement: Ray Ring, 1991, ". . . and Not So Fresh," *Outside* 16(4):26, reports that the average mule produces six quarts of urine and forty-four pounds of manure in twenty-four hours, endowing the trail with massive amounts of urine and manure in the course of a year.

Charles Russell: Lavender, *River Runners*, 51–53; quote, Muir, "The Grand Cañon of the Colorado," 113.

Indian Gardens: Garrett, "Are We Loving It to Death?" 29, Kolb planted the cottonwoods around 1908.

Trail/bridge construction: Garrett, "Are We Loving It to Death?" 29; Beal, "Development and Administration of Grand Canyon National Park," 19; F. R. E. Matthes, 1927, "Breaking a Trail through Bright Angel Canyon," *Grand Canyon Nature Notes* 2(6):1–4; Harriet Chalmers Adams, 1921, "The Grand Canyon Bridge," *National Geographic Magazine* 39(6):644–50.

Pipe Creek/migmatites: Hugh H. Waesche, 1933, "How Pipe Creek Received Its Name," *Grand Canyon Nature Notes* 8(3):155–56, Ralph Cameron and a party of miners hiked out of the canyon and Cameron, ahead, found a meerschaum pipe, scratched a fake date of one hundred years previous, and placed it in a tree as a practical joke; Thayer, *Bright Angel Trail*, 44, 57; Babcock, "Precambrian Crystalline Core," 12–13, 20; Ilg and Karlstrom, "Metamorphics for the Geologically Impaired," 16; R. V. Dietrich, 1989, *Stones: Their Collection, Identification and Uses* (Prescott, Ariz.: Geoscience Press), 75.

Bright Angel Creek: W. E. Darrah, footnote to Bradley, 1947, "Diary," 65, Powell did not use this name until giving a lecture in December 1869, when he used it to give "romantic contrast" to the Dirty Devil upstream (Powell, *Exploration of the Colorado River*, 259).

Ouzel: G. E. Sturdevant, 1926, "Water Ouzel *(Cinclus mexicanus)*," *Grand Canyon Nature Notes* 1(2):1, "Perhaps in no part of its range does its voice sound sweeter or carry a greater distance than it does in the deepest cut canyon of its distribution"; Carothers and Sharber, "Birds of the Colorado River," 119.

Bright Angel site: Powell used "Shinumo" as an alternate term for "Pueblo," and other members of the party spoke of this site as "Shinumo ruins"; Euler and Taylor, "Additional Archaeological Data," 22–24; Powell, *Exploration of the Colorado River*, 259; Euler et al., "The Colorado Plateaus," 1097; Schwartz, Marshall, and Kepp, *The Bright Angel Site*, i, 5–6, 7–10, 11–12, 86–87.

Anasazi pathology: Charles F. Merbs and Robert C. Euler, 1985, "Atlanto-Occipital Fusion and Spondylolisthesis in an Anasazi Skeleton from Bright

Angel Ruin, Grand Canyon National Park, Arizona," *American Journal of Physical Anthropology* 67:381–91; both skeletal age and sex can be determined in various ways, see Jerome C. Rose, Keith W. Condon, and Alan H. Goodman, 1985, "Diet and Dentition: Developmental Disturbances," in *The Analysis of Prehistoric Diets*, ed. Robert I. Gilbert, Jr., and James H. Mielke (New York: Academic Press), 281–82; see also in the same volume, Robert I. Gilbert, Jr., 1985 "Stress, Paleonutrition, and Trace Elements," 342.

Yucca poultice: Laura C. Martin, 1993, *The Folklore of Birds* (Old Saybrook, Conn.: Globe Pequot Press), 211–12.

Abandonment: Gumerman and Dean, "Prehistoric Cooperation and Competition in the Western Anasazi Area," 121, 127–31; Euler et al., "The Colorado Plateaus," 1089; Plog et al., "Anasazi Adaptive Strategies," 259; Haas, "The Evolution of the Kayenta Regional System," 501, 506–8; Cordell, *Prehistory of the Southwest*, 311–12; Cohen, *The Food Crisis in Prehistory*, 15; Gasser, "Pueblo Plant Foods," 28–29; Schwartz, Chapman, and Kepp, *Unkar Delta*, xii, "Beyond this sequence of occupation, another picture emerges of pioneers struggling to expand their territory and adapt a way of life to this rugged, agriculturally marginal region. It was a contest they ultimately lost, for in the end their culture could not adjust to critical changes in an unforgiving climate."

Plog et al., "Anasazi Adaptive Strategies," 233, 259; Cordell and Gumerman, "Cultural Interaction," 7; Petersen, "AT LAST," 19–20; Ezra B. W. Zubrow, 1972, "Carrying Capacity and Dynamic Equilibrium in the Prehistoric Southwest," in *Contemporary Archaeology: A Guide to Theory and Contributions*, ed. Mark P. Leone (Carbondale: Southern Illinois University Press), 268–69, 275; Schwartz, Marshall, and Kepp, *The Bright Angel Site*, 132, "If the economic adaptation even during times of above-average precipitation involved farming in as many places as possible, then presumably a decline in rainfall that affected either the plateau or the canyon would have jeopardized the entire system. According to the tree-ring data, such a decline did take place between A.D. 1130 and 1150, during which time the population of the Grand Canyon region almost completely disappeared."

Lucchitta, "Canyon Maker," 31, downcutting was very rapid, perhaps as much as eight meters in a few hundred years, accompanied by a sinking water table that also destabilized the sand in flood plains; Elizabeth Colson, 1979, "In Good Years and Bad: Food Strategies of Self-Reliant Societies," *Journal of Anthropological Research* 35(1): 28, there is "clear evidence that in the past, people have calculated their risks and provided for alternative ways of meeting their needs. Because they were immediately vulnerable to the vagaries of weather, they have had more need than we, in the immediate past, to study how to deal with them. They are rich in resource, even though they may be relatively poor in resources. Those who have a variety of skills are more likely to find a niche or niches in which to survive the hard times, than those who have become highly specialized in a narrow range of skills. And those who know that they can face the bad times because they have done so in the past and come out alive, may have the edge over those who have only known soft living, when the bad times come again."

Lady tourist's comment: John Burroughs, 1911, "The Grand Cañon of the Colorado," *Century Illustrated Monthly Magazine* 59:428.

Acknowledgments

The challenges of this book were considerable and I could never have written it without a munificent grant from Survival Anglia, Ltd., of Norwich, England, and the extraordinary encouragement of Lady Katherine and Lord Aubry Buxton. I cannot thank them enough. I received additional funding through two Jackson Fellowships from the Hulbert Center for Southwestern Studies at Colorado College, timely grants for which I am grateful.

The complexities of this book have made me more dependent than usual on the expertise of experts. The common caveat applies: they have supplied the keen reading, the comments, and the corrections. I thank them for their time and generosity. If errors remain, God forbid, they are mine.

I am especially indebted to the geologists, historians, and archaeologists who tolerated someone with the endless questions of a five-year-old, bountifully shared their research as well as their knowledgeable speculations about the Colorado River, helped with identification and references, and in some cases read portions of the manuscript: Bryan and Susan Jones Brown, Kim Crumbo, Marie and Sid Davis, Robert C. Euler, Achim Gottwald, Richard Hereford, Roy Hugie, Ann Trinkle Jones, Randall Kosaki, David Lavender, William Leibfried, Ken Maxie, Robert Mesta, David Nordstrom, David Sabo, Lawrence Stevens, Stanley Swarts, Scott Thybony, Frank Tikalsky, Richard Valdez, David Wegner, Helen and Mike Yard. I especially thank Ivo Lucchitta, U.S. Geological Survey geologist, boatman, and Renaissance man, for taking time from an incredibly busy professional schedule to review this manuscript in its entirety, a gift beyond measure.

I am in the debt of many fine river guides who blend white-water skills with dedication to and interpretation of the canyon, and shared their insights. They are wonderful people—Owen Baynham, Ann Cassidy, Alida Dierker, Brad and Jeri Dimock, Jock Favour, Chris Geanious, Millet Gray, Peter Gross, Kenton Grua, Roabie and Jerry Johnson, David Lyle, Bill Ott, Richard Quartaroli, Clair and Pam Quist, Kelly Smith, Lou Steiger, Russell Sullivan, Ellen Tibbetts, Whale, Jim Wilson, Teresa Yates. To Ramón Montéz, also known as Lowell Lundeen, my thanks for putting my black manuscript bag where it was safe and available.

To all the people who brought me a new insect or said, "Come look at this spider web!" thank you very much. You gave me extra eyes to see things that, in this huge complexity of place, I would have missed. There simply isn't room to list and thank all the people with whom I shared trips, who were fun to be with, and from whom I learned a great deal, but there are a few who remain in memory, and I would be remiss if I did not tell them so: Mark Applequist, Bonnie and Jay Aronson, Suzanne and Ted Baer, Richard Blaylock, Jack and Georgiana Boyer, Tom and Mimi Brownold, Kris and Hac Brummett, Michelle and Scott Buzan, Kevin Cowperthwaite, Daniel Davidson, Sid and Marie Davis, Achim Gottwald, Nell Hayes, Carol Johnson, Anna Lou Kelso, Dick Kirkpatrick, Jim Koeller, Virginia Korte, Christoph Neander, Irmgard Niemierski, Bill and Miriam Norris, Sara Posegate, Marge Robinson, Charles Silver, George and Jo Yount.

I particularly thank Dorothy House and Barbara Thurber, of the Museum of Northern Arizona Library, the prime repository for Grand Canyon papers. It was a privilege to work there, as it was at the Cline Library Special Collections, Northern Arizona University. I thank also Glen Canyon Environmental Studies librarian Richard Quartaroli, who made available GCES reports and other references. I am always indebted to Tutt Library at Colorado College, especially Julie Jones-Eddy, in the Government Documents Room. For information on Western Area Power Administration, I thank William H. Clagett and Donald P. Hodel and, for calling to my attention the Purjinke effect, John Atkinson. Scott Thybony generously sent information about Separation Canyon and the William Leamy evidence.

Commuting from Colorado Springs to Flagstaff brought its own set of logistical problems. My special thanks to those who eased my weary knees and mind with comfort, good humor, and kindness and raised a glass of wine to the canyon: Fran Joseph, M. L. and Richard Quartaroli, and *most* especially Roabie, Jerry, and Hoover Johnson.

All three of my daughters—Jane, Sara, and Susan—listened patiently to a rumpled, rambling mother. Unbeknownst to them, they helped me focus and sharpen my ideas. There is a lot of them in this book even though they may not be mentioned by name. Jane, who joined me on what I thought was her "last river trip" with me in 1976 and has admirable recall of things I had long forgotten. Susan, with a miserable strep throat, walked up the Kaibab Trail with me in murderous December weather, and dear Sara, in the midst of this book, gave birth to Sally Ann and changed my view of the canyon forever. Given the amount of gear one lugs for river travel, I truly appreciated it when Herman and Icarus International Airlines could deliver me *and* baggage *and* laptop at the same time.

People in Colorado Springs have helped in various ways, and I would like them to know of my gratitude: Herbert Beatty; Richard Dodge; Ava Heinrichsdorf and Pat Musick; and Sally Meadows. The help of Kate Belden, Maria Gonzales, and Katie Warren allowed me precious additional hours of work time. And to Timilou Rixon, who takes a long, cold, experienced look at a manuscript and then nudges me to nitpick it into shape, I can never say how much I appreciate that fine attention to detail, knowledge, and sense of humor. My affectionate thanks to Fran Collin, a patient agent, and to Joanne O'Hare and Elizabeth Hurwit, fine editors, and the rest of the staff at the University of Arizona Press.

Final thanks to Barbara Beatty Williams and Gregory McNamee, then at the University of Arizona Press, who suggested a book on the natural history of the Colorado River in Grand Canyon. I replied that what the world *didn't* need was another book on Grand Canyon and demurred. They persisted. Time will tell who was right. I hope they were.

Index

acacia, cat's-claw (*Acacia greggii*), 190, 207

Adams, Harriet Chalmers, 230–31

agave, Utah (*Agave utahensis*), 41, 78, 94–95

Aiden, R. S., 109

alfalfa (*Medicago sativa*), 205

algae: green, 57, 102, 155, 171, 194; *Cladophera glomerata*, 13, 24; diatoms, 14, 24, 25n; blue-green in cryptobiotic crusts, 95; on stones, 190; stonewort (*Chara* sp.), 151

amaranth (*Amaranthus* sp.), 72, 220

amphipods (*Gammarus lacustris*), 14, 24, 45

Anasazi: abandonment of Grand Canyon, 218, 232, 234–35, 298–99n; agriculture, 71, 189–90, 219–22, 223, 234–35, 294–95n, 295–96n; burial, 233; corn/beans/squash, 220–22, 235; dates of settlement, 70, 190, 218, 219, 223, 233; egalitarian society, 70, 233; erosion control, 41, 219, 222–23, 234–35, 296n; Hi'satsinam, 262n; Kayenta

Branch, 70, 190, 220; kivas, 71, 222, 224, 233, 296n; nutrition, 71, 73, 220, 264n, 295n; pathology, 233; populations/overpopulation, 218, 219–20, 223, 233–34; sites, 70–71, 142, 188, 190, 200–201, 215, 220–24, 232–34, 262–63n (*see also* Bright Angel; Hilltop Ruin; South Canyon; Tanner Creek; Unkar Delta); stone tools, 71, 218; sun calendars, 201, 290n; Virgin Branch, 223, 234; "waffle" gardening," 222. *See also* Cohonina; hunting/gathering; pottery

ants (Formicidae), 39, 202; pheromones, 91; as predator/prey, 91, 169, 171; red, 108, 169, 171; tending aphids, 192–93; velvet (*see* wasps)

ants, harvester, California bearded (*Pogonomyrmex barbatus*), 139, 155, 201–4, 291n; nests, 202–3; venom, 204

ant lions (Myrmeleontidae), 86

Apache plume (*Fallugia paradoxa*), 78

aphids (Aphididae), 91, 192–93

Miller, Robert Rush, 166
millipedes (*Orthoporus* sp.), 60
mining: asbestos, 128; copper/silver,
   184, 230; guano, 110; placer, 123,
   265n; trails, 183
mistletoe (*Phoradendron californicum*),
   151
mites (Acari), 170, 215
Mojave Desert, 93–94; flora, 40, 94,
   154
monadnock, 60, 260n
monkey flowers (*Mimulus* sp.): red
   (*M. cardinalis*), 55, 79; yellow (*M.
   gutattus*), 79
Montéz, Ramón, 7, 122–23, 129, 206,
   276n
Monument Creek, 138–39; debris
   flows in, 139
Mormon tea (*Ephedra* sp.), 41, 71, 78,
   94, 172, 200, 215
mosquitoes (Culicidae), 155
moss, 41, 55, 57, 93, 94, 150
moths, 57, 58, 91, 153–54; sphinx (*Hyles
   lineata*), 58, 106, 173; tiger (Arcti-
   inae), 54; yucca (*Pronubis* sp.),
   175–76
mountain goats, Harrington's
   (*Oreamnos harringtoni*), 77, 78
Mountain Meadows Massacre, 9,
   109–10
mouse/mice, 72, 77, 203; canyon
   (*Peromyscus crinitus*), 86; cactus (*P.
   eremicus*), 86, 176–77; rock pocket
   (*Perognathus intermedius*), 86
Muav Limestone, 23, 38, 96; cave-
   and-channel system, 79; Devonian river channels in, 79–80; at
   Havasu, 150; at Kanab Creek, 61–
   62, 63; at Kwagunt Creek, 41,
   43; at National Canyon, 154; at
   Whitmore Wash, 160
Muir, John, 42, 141, 229
mules, 129, 229–30, 236
mushrooms, 55

muskrat (*Ondatrra zibethica*), 78
mustard family, 95; tansy mustard
   (*Descurainia pinnata*), 221

Nankoweap: Basin, 23; Beach, 21, 37,
   189, 258n; Canyon, 190; Creek, 10,
   16, 23, 24–25, 27, 28, 37, 47, 232;
   name, 21; Rapid, 26; Trail, 184
National Canyon, 152–54
Nautiloid Canyon, 87–88
Navajo: Bridge, 7, 41, 89; guides, 8–9;
   Sandstone, 11
Needles, California, 119, 123
Nellie Powell, 8, 247n
nettle, rock (*Eucnide urens*), 111, 154
Nevills, Norm, 8, 40, 137, 141, 256n
Newberry, John, 17
Nims, Franklin A., 75–76, 265n

oak, scrub (*Quercus turbinella*), 78
ocotillo (*Fouquieria splendens*), 94,
   110, 151
128-Mile Canyon, 60–61
orchids, giant helleborine (*Epipactis
   gigantea*), 53, 56
otters, river (*Lutra canadensis sonora*),
   78, 266n
ouzel (*Cinclus americanus*), 232, 297n
owls: bones in Stanton's Cave, 77;
   western screech (*Otus kennicottii*),
   111

paintbrush, Indian (*Castilleja* sp.), 79,
   167
Paiute names, 21, 61, 217
Palisades, 185, 199, 200, 201, 213;
   Creek, 71
Paria: Riffle, 7; River, 12, 15; silt from,
   13, 15; terraces, 12, 249–50n
Pattie, James Ohio, 206
Pearce Ferry, 8, 108, 112, 183, 247n
pediments, 214–15, 293n
penstemon, firecracker (*Penstemon
   barbatus*), 107

ravens (*Corvus corax*), 25, 26, 29, 31, 32, 77, 96, 140
redbud (*Cercis occidentalis*), 53, 54, 78, 88
Red Canyon, 128
Redwall Limestone, 17, 23, 26, 87, 89, 96, 112, 184; Cavern, 85–87, 89, 268n; caves/channels/solution caverns in, 69, 77, 79, 85; chert in, 71, 85, 218; color, 17, 87; contact with Muav, 80; fossils in, 85–86; in Marble Canyon, 17; in Nautiloid Canyon, 87; joints, 17
Reilly, P. T., 125
Richards, Henry, 75
Rider Canyon, 75, 124
Rio Grande, 234
riparian zone: birds, 22, 206; disappearance of, 21–22; introduced plants, 186, 288n; lizards, 170; new high-water, 93, 205; new low-water, 110; 1983–1984 flood damage, 206; old high-water, 22; plant diversity, 55; rodents, 176–77; vegetation, 21, 55–56, 205, 206, 253n
Roaring Springs, 230
rockcress (*Arabis perennis*), 54
rockfalls/slides, 25, 43–44, 139, 271n, 274n, 257–58n
Rocky Mountains, 13, 42, 63, 214
rodents, 73, 127, 176, 222; burrows and lizards, 169
Ross, Dr. Aaron, 40
rushes (*Juncus* sp.), 38, 113, 149; Torrey's (*J. torreyi*), 205
Russell, Charles Silver, 229

Saddle Canyon, 53–56, 57, 205
sage, purple (*Salvia dorrii*), 53, 108
sagebrush (*Artemisia tridentat*), galls on, 188
saltbush (*Atriplex canescens*), 72; galls on, 188, 213
salts: in basalt, 193–94; deposits, 172;

iron, 193–94; in sand, 110; in soil, 190; in schist, 136; in water, 213
sand, 38, 45–46, 110, 151, 153, 166; eolian, 85–87, 189; grain size, 187, 189; salt in, 110; storage of, 189; water-carried, 189. *See also* bars
sandstones, 12, 17, 44, 126, 193, 214, 215, 231. *See also* Coconino; Tapeats
Sanger, Arthur, 124, 136
San Juan: Mountains, 6; porphyry, 6; River, 40
schist, 60, 103, 104, 135, 231. *See also* Vishnu Schist
School of American Research (Santa Fe), 217–18
sedges (*Carex* sp.), 38, 205
seep willow (*Baccharis* sp.), 106, 111, 167
Separation: Canyon, 108; Rapid, 62, 109, 113
shales, 12, 17, 44, 62, 128, 135, 184, 194, 218. *See also* Dox; Hakatai; Hermit
sheep, desert bighorn (*Ovis canadensis*), 73, 78, 124, 276n
Shinumo: Creek, 57, 64, 107; Quartzite, 128; Wash, 57
Shivwits Indians, 62, 109
Sixty Mile Rapid, 173, 174
skeleton plant (*Stephanomeria pauciflora*), 185
snails, 259n, 272n; Kanab amber (*Oxyloma haydeni kanabensis*), 79, 267n; pulmonate, 105
snakeweed (*Gutierrezia sarothrae*), 169
Soap Creek, 124; Rapid, 75, 123, 124
Sockdolager Rapid, 136–37
soil: agricultural, 189–90; alluvial, 189; caliche, 216; colluvial, 189; cryptobiotic crusts on, 94–95; desert, 95, 186–87, 218–19; erosion, 223, 234–35; salinity in, 110, 190; sandy, 186, 189
Sonoran Desert, 93; plants, 40, 94, 217

About the Author

Ann Zwinger once wrote, "If there was a river in your growing up, you probably always hear it." The sights and sounds of water echo through most of Zwinger's books, especially *Run, River, Run*, which won the John Burroughs Medal for Nature Writing.

Zwinger is known not only for her books of natural history—*Beyond the Aspen Grove, Land above the Trees, A Desert Country Near the Sea, A Conscious Stillness, Wind in the Rock, The Mysterious Lands,* among others —but for the evocative illustrations of plants, animals, and landscape that grace her work. Her essays have appeared in many anthologies and in *Audubon, Orion,* and other magazines.

Trained as an art historian at Wellesley, Zwinger lectures widely and teaches "The Natural History Essay" at Colorado College, where she held the first endowed chair for the Hulbert Center for Southwestern Studies. She lives in Colorado Springs.